The Neighborhood Center
628 Mary Street
Utica, New York 13501

Troubled Families—
Problem Children

Dedication

For all those professionals—nurses, teachers, social workers, psychologists, psychiatrists, physicians, and others—who collaborate with families and support each other in order to alter the future for problem children.

Troubled Families— Problem Children

Working with Parents: A Collaborative Process

Carolyn Webster-Stratton

and

Martin Herbert

JOHN WILEY & SONS

Chichester · New York · Brisbane · Toronto · Singapore

Other Wiley Editorial Offices

John Wiley & Sons, Inc., 605 Third Avenue,
New York, NY 10158–0012, USA

Jacaranda Wiley Ltd, 33 Park Road, Milton,
Queensland 4064, Australia

John Wiley & Sons (Canada) Ltd, 22 Worcester Road,
Rexdale, Ontario M9W 1L1, Canada

John Wiley & Sons (SEA) Pte Ltd, 37 Jalan Pemimpin #05-04,
Block B, Union Industrial Building, Singapore 2057

Library of Congress Cataloging-in-Publication Data:

Webster-Stratton, Carolyn.
    Troubled families—problem children : working with parents : a
collaborative process / Carolyn Webster-Stratton and Martin Herbert.
      p. cm.
    Includes bibliographical references and index.
    ISBN 0-471-94251-0
    1. Problem children—United States.   2. Parenting—United States.
   3. Parent and child—United States.   4. Behavior therapy.
   I. Herbert, Martin.   II. Title.
   HQ773.W38   1994
   362.7′4—dc20   93–47493
                                                CIP

ISBN 0-471-94251-0

Typeset in 10½/12pt Times from author's disks by
Mathematical Composition Setters Ltd, Salisbury, Wiltshire
Printed and bound in Great Britain by
Biddles Ltd, Guildford and King's Lynn

CONTENTS

FOREWORD

THOMAS H. OLLENDICK

TROUBLED FAMILIES—PROBLEM CHILDREN needs little introduction. Carolyn Webster-Stratton and Martin Herbert, sensitive and seasoned clinicians from the United States and Great Britain, speak for themselves. Better yet, they allow parents to tell part of their story for them—the experience of having a "problem" child in the family and the long and frequently circuitous and painful route to recovery. Indirectly, through the eyes of the parents, the authors also tell the story of what it is like to be a "problem" child—such a child is "at times highly tyrannical, destructive, and defiant, and at other times, loving, intelligent, understanding, and sensitive to parents' emotions" (p. 52). The "Jekyll and Hyde" depiction of these children, as reported by the parents, is graphically depicted in several case studies. Of course, the real story from the child's perspective remains to be told.

What sets this book apart from others of its genre is its careful attention to, and elucidation of, the "collaborative process" in working with these oppositional, defiant, and conduct-disordered children and their families. Such a process requires a "working" relationship between the clinician and the family in which the knowledge and expertise of the clinician is brought together with the unique strengths and perspectives of the parents and child. It implies that parents and their child actively participate in the setting of treatment goals, as well as the selection of treatment strategies. This partnership between parents, child, and clinician is proposed by the authors to give dignity, respect, and control back to these troubled families and their problem children.

This collaborative process is illustrated by the following explanation of the treatment program to the parents (p. 112):

> Our job is to work with you, to support you, and to consult with you so that the interactions between you and your child are more positive and so that you can achieve your goals ... we work together as a team and we expect you to be our "co-therapist" in this process ... we each have a contribution ... what we can

offer is more alternatives, information, and resources, and what you can offer is help deciding and implementing the best strategy for your situation.

Essentially, the goal then is to empower the parents and to teach them to cope more effectively with their child. This goal is achieved through use of procedures based in social learning theory, which are nicely and thoroughly illustrated throughout the text.

Consistent with collaborative goal, the authors take issue with the spate of treatment programs that are aimed at simply "training" parents in "parenting" skills. They argue, forcefully and eloquently, that such programs are inadequate in addressing the multiple and complex problems evident in these families and in engaging the families in efficacious treatment. The collaborative process is proposed to be the key to effective and robust treatment outcome. The soundness of their argument notwithstanding, direct comparisions of parent training programs with and without the added collaborative features are obviously called for. This is work for the next generation of clinician–researchers.

There are readers with many different backgrounds who will find this book informative, useful, and pleasurable. The numerous case studies and actual therapy scripts bring the issues "to life", in living color, so to speak. Webster-Stratton and Herbert do not just talk about troubled families and problem children; rather, they bring them to us in rich and graphic detail. Practicing child clinicians and students of child psychopathology will feast on their efforts and will benefit from their creative and synergistic energies. Like the approach they espouse, this book represents a true collaborative effort, and a labor of love. For me, *Troubled Families—Problem Children* is an outstanding and scholarly contribution to the field. It is a book whose time has come.

Blacksburg, Virginia
March 1994

PREFACE

CAROLYN WEBSTER-STRATTON

MANY YEARS ago in the course of interviewing the parent of a child with severe conduct disorders, I asked her whether she had made any prior attempts to get help for her child. The account she gave me was a chilling one, one which I have never forgotten.

She told me she had first gone to see her pediatrician to discuss her frustration over her four-year-old son's problems: he was aggressive, defiant, and noncompliant, and her attempts to toilet train him had been entirely unsuccessful. Her doctor attempted to reassure her, saying that her son would eventually outgrow these problems. He advised her to just "loosen up," "be patient" and wait for the better times that undoubtedly lay ahead.

A year later, her son's behavior problems had escalated. He had repeatedly tried to run away from home. His teachers were threatening to expel him from school for hitting other children and for his generally noncooperative behavior, as well as his habit of soiling in his underpants. This time the mother went to a child psychologist for help. The psychologist told her she was too *"laissez-faire"* in her parenting; she needed to be firmer and more consistent in setting limits with her child. He recommended a book on Time Out techniques. Over the next six months, she said, she disciplined her son constantly, but his aggression only worsened—as did her own frustration.

When her child's teachers finally asked her to find another school for her son because they were unable to manage him in the classroom, she sought the help of a psychiatrist. She told me, "I hoped the psychiatrist would give us some medicine like Ritalin that would help him behave better. But instead she said I needed to work on my own marital problems, and then my son's behavior would improve." However, her husband was against any kind of marital counseling. "So," she said, "what was I to do?"

At the point when this mother came to our Parenting Clinic for help, her now eight-year-old son had no friends and had been rejected from five different schools. She herself was depressed, and her marriage was in considerable turmoil. She felt hopeless about the possibility of getting any real help for her child. She had experienced stigmatization and isolation from parents of "normal" children. She felt blamed for her child's problems—not only by other parents and her son's teachers, but also by the professionals to whom she had turned for help. Moreover, she felt hopelessly confused about which approach to take toward her son's behavior problems.

Over the past 12 years working with the more than 600 families of children with oppositional defiant and conduct disorders who have come through our Parenting Clinic, I have heard countless similar stories during intake interviews. What this mother experienced in her attempts to get professional help is, unfortunately, all too common. These parents' stories suggest that professionals in our field fall into two general categories: on the one hand, those who tend to minimize the child's problems and the family's level of distress and, on the other hand, those who tend to pathologize the family itself, to label its members "antisocial" or "resistant" or "unattached," implicitly or explicitly blaming the parents for the child's problems. Such attitudes on the part of professionals, as reflected through the eyes of these parents of conduct-disordered children, imply a lack of empathy. These parents feel that professionals simply do not understand their situation; we psychologists, nurses, social workers, pediatricians, school personnel, and other professionals are unable or unwilling to grasp the extent to which these parents are experiencing a kind of private hell. Even the research literature concerning conduct disorders tends to contribute to this perception by describing parents of conduct-disordered children as having "parenting skills deficits"; for, in shifting the focus from the child's behavior to the parents' lack of skills, this model implicitly blames the parents for the child's problems.

The "parenting skills deficit" model has had tremendous research, as well as clinical, value for professionals: it has led to greater refinements in intervention, forcing us to identify precisely which behavior management skills to target in treatment programs for parents of conduct-disordered children. Nevertheless, adherence to the deficit model can lead us to consciously or unconsciously attribute blame to the parents, ignoring all the stressful factors in the family's situation which have led to and therefore help explain the breakdown in parenting skills—factors over which parents have little or no control. This is ironic, for the deficit model has spawned our most effective interventions to date. Yet it short-circuits our understanding of these families. It does not help us understand what it is like to be the parents of a conduct-disordered child. And we *need to know* this if we are going to be effective practitioners.

It is this mother's story and the many others like it that lie behind my determination to write about these parents. For very little has been written about the experience of living with a conduct-disordered child from the *parents'* perspectives. What do these parents experience in a typical day with their child? What kinds of feelings come up for them? How do they perceive their child's problem, and what do they think about it? How do they "process" their experience of living with a conduct-disordered child? How is their marital relationship affected? What impact does their child's behavior have on their relationships with other parents and their adult friendships? Are there any effects on their relationships with their own parents (the grandparents) and the extended family? Questions such as these are the focus of Chapter 2. My hope is that a better understanding of these parents' feelings, experiences, and perceptions will help us refine our assessment and treatment approaches. For instance, if we know what these families have experienced in their homes and communities prior to seeking treatment, we may be able to understand better what factors will make it difficult or easy for them to benefit from a particular treatment strategy. Moreover, we may be able to offer help earlier, before they have reached such levels of despair. In any case, an increased understanding should help us avoid those twin professional pitfalls of either minimizing the experience of these parents or pathologizing the family.

In addition to describing what it is like for parents to live with a conduct-disordered child, a second goal for this book was to describe what it is like for families with conduct-disordered children to undergo treatment. How are parent intervention and therapy programs experienced by the parents in them? What is the process like for them? What are their perceptions about their own progress or lack of it? Which aspects of treatment and times during treatment are especially difficult? When treatment is successful, what makes it so? How do they feel about the ways they are treated, and are there ways they would change their treatment, if they could? Again, there has been very little attempt in the literature to describe the therapy process from the parents' perspective. Yet the usefulness of this knowledge seems obvious. By understanding how families perceive and experience therapy during the different phases of parent training, therapists can be better prepared for the resistance and the regressions, can to some extent prepare parents for the difficulties they are likely to encounter while in therapy, and can anticipate and predict the families' eventual acceptance and use of effective coping strategies. Chapter 6 focuses on this aspect of parents' experience.

Parents' experiences of therapy are strongly affected (though not determined) by what we will refer to as the therapy process: therapeutic philosophy, therapeutic aims and methods, the group dynamics (if it is

group therapy), the role the therapist* assumes in relation to them, even
the physical environment in which the therapy takes place. Thus, in
addition to describing in Chapter 6 what we have learned about how
parents experience therapy, it seemed important to provide a qualitative
account of the process of our own intervention with families. (In previous
publications we have given numerous quantitative accounts of our
work—see references.) Surprisingly, in spite of the documented effectiveness of various types of parent-training programs, the literature contains
comparatively little discussion of the actual therapeutic processes utilized
in such intervention programs.

In contrast, there is a rather large body of literature describing the
content of parent-training programs. For example, behavioral principles
such as Time Out, Beta Commands, Praise, Differential Attention,
Response Cost, and the accompanying parenting strategies have been carefully outlined in detail (Forehand & McMahon, 1981; Herbert, 1987;
Kazdin, 1987; Patterson, 1982; Webster-Stratton, 1991a). But descriptions
of the content of parenting programs do not elucidate the mechanisms of
parent training or the ongoing processes of therapy—that is, how exactly
do the therapists go about trying to modify parents' behavior, attitudes,
and practices in parent training? There are many questions to be answered
concerning the "how" of parent training, such as: How do therapists
handle parents' resistance to new concepts and behaviors? How do they
teach new skills without making parents feel inadequate or guilty? How do
they answer parents' questions about such things as the advantages of
spanking or disadvantages of praise and tangible rewards? How do they
ensure that homework is carried out? When and how do they use confrontation? How do they promote parents' feelings of self-confidence and
effectiveness? How do they teach new skills to parents with low self-esteem
without exacerbating their feelings of incompetence? How do they make
their training program culturally sensitive? And, more generally, which
teaching/training methods and strategies are best with this population?
Perhaps some approaches used productively by therapists in other situations are counterproductive with these families. Perhaps some methods
actually perpetuate the distress, guilt, and incompetence typically felt by
these families. For example, we postulated that if families appeared to be
"difficult" or "resistant" in treatment, perhaps it was due to the nature of
the therapy process. We felt it was therefore important to describe our
therapeutic philosophy and processes of intervention. Chapter 4 focuses
on this topic, while Chapter 7 presents parents' typical questions

---

*The word "therapist" is used in this book to refer generically to any professional involved
in therapeutic work with families—such as nurse clinicians or practitioners, physicians,
psychologists, social workers, psychiatrists, and others.

concerning the content of our interventions, discussing the therapists' possible responses.

While some of the ideas expressed above have appeared previously in shorter articles, the impetus for writing a book on this subject occurred while I was on sabbatical at Oxford University, England. At that time I met Dr. Martin Herbert, who for many years had worked with a similar population of families of fairly young children with oppositional defiant and conduct disorders. In the course of our conversations, we discovered that we shared a similar perspective on the therapy process. It was the excitement generated by this sharing that provided the "fuel" necessary for writing this book. In doing so, we hope to stimulate further dialogue with other therapists and researchers so that all of us can begin to expand our empirical base for parent intervention programs.

The parent population that served as the data base for the qualitative studies described in this book came from more than 600 families who have attended the Parenting Clinic at the University of Washington, School of Nursing. The University of Washington Parenting Clinic, funded by the National Center for Nursing Research and the National Institute of Mental Health, was founded in 1981 to develop and evaluate treatment programs for young children, ages three to eight years, with oppositional defiant and conduct disorders. The families we have treated in our clinic are representative in socioeconomic terms of most families of young conduct-problem children: one-third are on welfare, one-third are middle-class, and one-third are upper-class families. Their family structure is also representative: one-third are single-parent families and two-thirds are married, with half of the married couples experiencing significant marital turmoil. Study children included four boys for every girl treated, with an average of 21.3 behavior problems per child before treatment according to the Eyberg Child Behavior Inventory (ECBI), indicating that the children were clearly in the clinic range according to Eyberg and Ross (1978) (for nonclinic range, mean = 6.8, standard deviation = 3.9).

Quantitative accounts of the Parenting Clinic's intervention programs in previous publications have shown that our programs are effective in promoting more positive parent–child interactional behaviors and in reducing child conduct disorders, as well as promoting more positive parental attitudes, in comparison to untreated control families and families who received only the parent group discussion treatment (Webster-Stratton, 1984; Webster-Stratton, Hollinsworth, & Kolpacoff, 1989). In deciding to present some qualitative accounts of our programs, we had an enormous amount of data to draw from, since our clinic had videotaped all intake and group therapy sessions as well as individual consultation and feedback sessions. These data provide a window into the experience of parents both prior to and during therapy. Working with

Dr. Ada Spitzer, we were able to use these data to conduct qualitative analyses of how parents experienced life with a conduct-disordered child, how they perceived and reacted to the videotape parenting program, what their questions and unique needs were while participating in the program, and what they felt was missing from the program (Spitzer, Webster-Stratton & Hollinsworth, 1991). We also analyzed the therapists' interactions with parents, looking specifically at how they tailored the videotape program to fit the needs of these families better. These analyses provide the basis for the discussions in Chapters 2, 4, and 7.

REFERENCES

Eyberg, S.M. & Ross, A.W. (1978). Assessment of child behavior problems: The validation of a new inventory. *Journal of Child Psychology*, **16**, 113–116.

Forehand, R. & McMahon, R. (1981). *Helping the noncompliant child: A clinician's guide to parent training.* New York: Guilford.

Herbert, M. (1987). *Conduct disorders of childhood and adolescence: A social learning perspective* (2nd edn.). Chichester, UK: Wiley.

Kazdin, A. (1987). Treatment of antisocial behavior in children: Current status and future directions. *Psychological Bulletin*, **102**, 187–203.

Patterson, G. (1982). *Coercive family process.* Eugene, OR: Castalia.

Spitzer, A., Webster-Stratton, C. & Hollinsworth, T. (1991). Coping with conduct-problem children: Parents gaining knowledge and control. *Journal of Child Clinical Psychology*, **20**(4), 413–427.

Webster-Stratton, C. (1984). Randomized trial of two parent-training programs for families with conduct-disordered children. *Journal of Consulting and Clinical Psychology*, **52**, 666–678.

Webster-Stratton, C. (1988). *Parents and Children Videotape Series. Basic and Advanced Programs 1 to 7.* 1411 8th Avenue West, Seattle, WA 98119.

Webster-Stratton, C. (1991a). Annotation: Strategies for working with families of conduct-disordered children. *British Journal of Child Psychiatry and Psychology*, **32**, 1047–1062.

Webster-Stratton, C. (1991b). *A cognitive social skills training manual for preschool children.* The Dinosaur Curriculum. Unpublished manuscript.

Webster-Stratton, C. (1992). *The Incredible Years: A Trouble-Shooting Guide for Parents of Children Aged 3 to 8 Years.* Toronto, Canada: Umbrella Press.

Webster-Stratton, C., Hollinsworth, T. & Kolpacoff, M. (1989). The long-term effectiveness and clinical significance of three cost-effective training programs for families with conduct-problem children. *Journal of Consulting and Clinical Psychology*, **57**, 550–553.

PREFACE

MARTIN HERBERT

I WELL remember the growing dismay I experienced when I accepted an invitation to act as an Honorary Consultant Clinical Psychologist at a paediatric assessment centre in Leicester (England). This was in the early 1970s; it seems an age ago. Indeed, such it was, in terms of the availability (more often unavailability) in Britain at that time of validated treatments for children with a conduct disorder. My dismay deepened as I was confronted by despairing parents—usually mothers—asking for *practical* advice on how to cope (indeed survive) with children who were not only difficult to rear but often hard to love. Their children presented, from a tender age, what I came to think of as "high demand characteristics". These were sometimes associated with physical problems or intellectual impairments; they might also be the behavioural outcroppings of the adverse temperamental attributes described by Thomas, Chess and Birch (1968). I was seeing the precursors, in some of them, of potentially serious conduct disorders.

Like the hapless parents, I found myself wilting before the intensity of their offsprings' tantrums, the intractability of their refusals and the implacable wilfulness of their commands. And, sadly, I had little or nothing in my therapeutic armamentarium—skills based upon psychotherapy (notably play therapy) with emotionally disturbed children—to offer them. It was a salutary, if chastening, experience, to share their sense of being deskilled, to be able to empathise with their feelings of helplessness.

Coming from a psychodynamic background, my turning to behavioural theory and therapy was—to say the least—reluctant. But a drowning person clutches, as they say, at straws. Fortunately, owing to the seminal work of psychologists (operating a triadic model of therapy) in the United States, the straws were fairly substantial. But not substantial enough! There was a high degree of resistance by patients referred to me to some of the early manuals and programmes. Like the unfortunate term "programme", they tended to come across as linear, prescriptive and (in more than one sense of the word) "instrumental". Some vital ingredients seemed to be missing. I, personally, found the "expert" role adopted by many behaviour therapists unappealing. There had to be a better way.

Thus began my own faltering journey down the highways (not many of those) and byways of the Conduct Disorders, while exploring the possibilities of a behavioural approach with a more "human" face—one in which dynamic, developmental and systemic considerations could play their part (Herbert, 1974; 1978). I was truly fortunate, in the following years, in having within the Child Treatment Research Unit, which we founded at the University of Leicester, the company of dedicated social work and clinical psychology trainees, Ph.D. students and colleagues. We worked mainly in home and school settings, providing treatment, evaluative research and training. The results of our efforts were published in textbooks, journals, manuals and guides for parents and professionals (see Herbert, 1991; 1992). Our commitment to training, and the broadening of our theoretical rationale, bore fruit in our development of the first University-accredited multidisciplinary Course in Applied Social Learning Theory in the United Kingdom (Hollin, Wilkie & Herbert, 1987).

It was inevitable, given the home settings in which we worked and our growing awareness of the importance of coercive concepts in family relationships and interactions, that we should be forced to think *systemically* in our clinical formulations and multilevel interventions. The name of our unit was changed to the Centre for Behavioural Work with Families to reflect our enlarged role and perspective as "behavioural family therapists". However, the move toward a systemic approach was decidedly not at the expense of work (where necessary) with the individual child.

What dawned on us, increasingly, in the course of our efforts to help more effectively with those notoriously intractable behaviour problems, was the need to respect the parents' expertise, to elicit their ideas and theories about childhood and parenthood, and to acknowledge their feelings of anger, frustration and helplessness. Such considerations reinforced our desire to make use of a partnership or collaborative model, the better to "tease out" and define the ineptly named "non-specific" process variables which, in our growing conviction, could make or break a behavioural intervention.

I am attracted to the metaphor of therapy as a craft—an amalgam of applied science and art. Just as the potter who works from a scientific base of empirical knowledge about the nature of clay creates a work of art by the use of imagination, the therapist applies facts and findings (the content component analysis of successful programmes) to individuals and their circumstances in a manner that is creative and socially sensitive. This can be realized by means of a collaborative process which takes account of the *whole* client and his or her family—as proactive, thoughtful human beings with minds of their own.

Dr. Webster-Stratton and I have arrived, by different routes, at similar conclusions about these process variables—so significant but so frustratingly elusive when it comes to defining and operationalizing them. Our own collaboration, sharing ideas and insights, has proved a stimulating one. I hope something of this excitement and enthusiasm is conveyed to our readers.

REFERENCES

Herbert, M. (1974). *Emotional problems of development in children*. London: Academic Press.

Herbert, M. (1978). *Conduct disorders of childhood and adolescence*. Chichester, UK: Wiley.

Herbert, M. (1991). *Clinical child psychology: Social learning, development and behaviour*. Chichester, UK: Wiley.

Herbert, M. (1992). *Working with children and the Children Act*. Leicester, UK: BPS Books.

Hollin, C.R., Wilkie, J. & Herbert, M. (1987). Behavioural social work: Training and application. *Practice*, **1**, 297–304.

Thomas, A., Chess, S. & Birch, H.G. (1968). *Temperament and behaviour disorders in children*. London: University of London Press.

ACKNOWLEDGMENTS

I OWE a great deal to the 600 or more families from the Parenting Clinic at the University of Washington who permitted us to videotape intake appointments and therapy sessions in order to make these qualitative analyses possible. These families have taught us so much and will continue to do so if we listen carefully.

I am particularly indebted to two people in regard to this book. The first is Ada Spitzer, who was a doctoral student at the time when she worked with me on the qualitative analyses of the data which provided the bases for Chapters 2 and 5. She taught me most of what I know about qualitative analysis and gave me a new lens from which to view and understand these families. Second, I am indebted to Deborah Woolley Lindsay who was not just the editor for this book—but even more importantly the person with whom I debated and discussed ideas and who provided the motivation and enthusiasm for me to write the book in the first place!

The cartoons were drawn by David Mostyn.

C.W.-S.

I am indebted to Viv Doughty for her patience, good humour, and deciphering and typing skills in transforming my messy scripts into a readable manuscript.

M.H.

OVERVIEW

PART I focuses on understanding the problem of child conduct disorders. Chapter 1 (Webster-Stratton) begins with a general discussion of child conduct disorders, looking at behavioral characteristics, causal factors, the course of the disorders, and a brief overview of the research regarding family behavioral approaches for treating this disorder. In Chapter 2, (Webster-Stratton and Spitzer) the conduct-disordered child is described from the parent's perspective. This chapter includes a description of the child's characteristics from the parent's viewpoint and a discussion of the impact of the child's problems on the family, extended family members, and community. A series of cognitive/emotional phases, which appear to describe the typical experience of parents living with a conduct-disordered child, is presented in Chapter 3 (Herbert) where the process of assessing children with conduct disorders and their families is discussed.

Part II focuses on treatment of child conduct disorders. Chapter 4 (Webster-Stratton) describes the therapy process and methods of helping families as practiced in Webster-Stratton's Parenting Clinic at the University of Washington. It is argued that parents learn to manage their children's behavior problems when therapy is based on a collaborative model. This model involves six different roles for the therapist: typically in collaborative therapy, therapists move freely among these six roles. In Chapter 5 (Herbert) the cognitive-behavioral theories behind the development of conduct disorders and how therapists can help parents understand these behavioral principles are discussed. In Chapter 6 (Webster-Stratton, Spitzer & Hollinsworth) parents' experiences in therapy are described, specifically in her clinic's videotape modeling parent training program, and the process by which parents learn to cope more effectively with stresses related to their children's behavior is analyzed. Parents go through a definable sequence of phases; knowing what these phases are can help therapists guide and support these parents through therapy. The meaning of the different phases is discussed in light of the psychological theory of stress. Chapter 7, (Webster-Stratton) presents a wide range of questions and objections that parents typically raise during the course of parent training, and highlights the key themes and processes that contribute to the therapist's responses. Chapter 8, (Herbert and Webster-Stratton) summarizes the authors' thoughts in an "epilogue" and discusses future directions for working with children with conduct disorders.

A NOTE OF CAUTION

This book does not attempt to provide a comprehensive review of all the assessment procedures, theories, therapeutic approaches, or treatment research regarding conduct disorders. These areas have been well described in other books and articles (e.g,. Forehand & McMahon, 1981; Herbert, 1987; Kazdin, 1987; Patterson, 1982; Webster-Stratton, 1988; 1991a; 1992). Rather, this book represents an in-depth qualitative analysis of the experience of parents with conduct-disordered children—their lives outside and their lives once they are in therapy—and a qualitative analysis of the therapist's role, using one particular type of intervention program as a model (The Parents and Children Videotape Curriculum at the Parenting Clinic). Undoubtedly, other therapists doing family behavioral therapy— whether with individuals or groups—may be using similar processes. However, the authors believe it is important to detail these processes in order to illustrate that there is much more to a successful parent behavioral program than merely conveying behavioral techniques or skills. Moreover, greater discussion among therapists of the precise therapeutic processes utilized in different parent intervention programs could bring to light differences and similarities among programs, suggesting new avenues for research regarding intervention strategies and family change processes.

It should be noted that the family behavioral processes and examples described in this book are based primarily on families with young children aged three to eight years. Issues related to adolescents with conduct disorders are not discussed. The focus on this young age group is due to the authors' strong belief that one strategic point in the child's development for intervention is the major transition period between preschool and the early grades when children are aged four to eight years. The decision to focus interventions at this age period is based on the evidence that oppositional defiant disorder (ODD) and conduct disorder (CD) children are clearly identifiable at this age. Studies by Webster-Stratton and others have revealed that even children as young as four have already been expelled from two or more preschools and have experienced considerable peer and teacher rejection. The authors believe that if very young ODD and CD children can be taught positive, rather than antisocial interactions —interactions that are supported through positive interactions with parents (and teachers)—then it may be possible to change the developmental trajectory from antisocial behavior to well-established negative reputations, peer rejection, low self-esteem, and spiraling academic failure.

A final cautionary note is that this book addresses only the parent's point of view and interventions for parents—it does not focus on the child's perspective or child training approaches, nor on school interventions. This perspective is not meant to imply that the role that child factors or school factors play in the development of conduct disorders is not acknowledged or valued. Indeed, Webster-Stratton is currently researching and evaluating a cognitive-behavioral training program in social and problem-solving skills—the Dinosaur Program—designed specifically for preschool and early school-age children, which she hopes can be used by teachers in schools (Webster-Stratton, 1991b). The authors believe that the most effective interventions will ultimately be those that involve parents, teachers, and children as agents of change, as well as those that promote positive bonds and continuity in efforts between the home and school environments. However, space limitations require that the qualitative descriptions of these approaches are left to another book.

REFERENCES

Eyberg, S.M. & Ross, A.W. (1978). Assessment of child behavior problems: The validation of a new inventory. *Journal of Child Psychology*, **16**, 113–116.

Forehand, R. & McMahon, R. (1981). *Helping the noncompliant child: A clinician's guide to parent training*. New York: Guilford.

Herbert, M. (1987). *Conduct disorders of childhood and adolescence: A social learning perspective* (2nd edn). Chichester, UK: Wiley.

Kazdin, A. (1987). Treatment of antisocial behavior in children: Current status and future directions. *Psychological Bulletin*, **102**, 187–203.

Patterson, G. (1982). *Coercive family process*. Eugene, OR: Castalia.

Spitzer, A., Webster-Stratton, C. & Hollinsworth, T. (1991). Coping with conduct-problem children: Parents gaining knowledge and control. *Journal of Child Clinical Psychology*, **20**(4), 413–427.

Webster-Stratton, C. (1984). Randomized trial of two parent-training programs for families with conduct-disordered children. *Journal of Consulting and Clinical Psychology*, **52**, 666–678.

Webster-Stratton, C. (1988). *Parents and Children Videotape Series. Basic and Advanced Programs 1 to 7*. 1411 8th Avenue West, Seattle, WA 98119.

Webster-Stratton, C. (1991a). Annotation: Strategies for working with families of conduct-disordered children. *British Journal of Child Psychiatry and Psychology*, **32**, 1047–1062.

Webster-Stratton, C. (1991b). *A cognitive social skills training manual for preschool children*. The Dinosaur Curriculum. Unpublished manuscript.

Webster-Stratton, C. (1992). *The Incredible Years: A Trouble-Shooting Guide for Parents of Children Aged 3 to 8 Years*. Toronto, Canada: Umbrella Press.

Webster-Stratton, C. & Herbert, M. (1993). What really happens in parent training? *Behavior Modification*, **17**, 407–456.

Webster-Stratton, C., Hollinsworth, T. & Kolpacoff, M. (1989). The long-term effectiveness and clinical significance of three cost-effective training programs for families with conduct-problem children. *Journal of Consulting and Clinical Psychology*, **57**, 550–553.

PART ONE

Understanding the Problem
of Child Conduct Disorders

1 INTRODUCTION TO CHILD CONDUCT DISORDERS AND OVERVIEW OF TREATMENT APPROACHES*

CLINICIANS WORKING with families typically encounter children who exhibit persistent patterns of antisocial behavior—significant impairment in everyday functioning at home or school, or conduct considered unmanageable by parents or teachers. The term "externalizing" has generally been used to summarize a set of negativistic behaviors which commonly co-occur during childhood. In the preschool years, typical "externalizing" behaviors include noncompliance, aggression, tantrums, and oppositional-defiant behaviors; in the school years, violations of classroom and adult authority such as lying and cheating; in adolescence, violations of the law or of community authority such as shoplifting. These problems are widespread: the referral of children to clinicians for treatment of externalizing and aggressive behaviors comprises one-third to one-half of all child and adolescent clinic referrals. These children and their families utilize multiple social and educational services, sometimes on a daily basis. Moreover, the prevalence of these behavioral disorders is increasing, creating a need for service that far exceeds available resources and personnel. Recent projections suggest that fewer than 10% of children who need mental health services actually receive them (Hobbs, 1982).

These behaviors are by no means abnormal. At one time or another, most children lie, cheat, take things that belong to others, hit when they are angry, tantrum, and refuse to do what their parents ask them to do. Rather, the distinction between difficult behaviors and "behavioral disorders" is one of severity and extent: it is the degree of the destruction and disruption, the occurrence of the behaviors in more than one setting (e.g., at home and at school), and the persistence of these behaviors over time, beginning at an early age, that cause concern for families and clinicians alike.

This chapter deals with features that characterize children to whom the labels of "oppositional defiant disorder" and/or "conduct disorder" are frequently applied. These children typically exhibit a "complex" or pattern of behaviors (i.e., lying, cheating, stealing, hitting, and noncompliance to

---

*This chapter is derived from an earlier paper by the author (Webster-Stratton, 1993).

parental requests) and, to a lesser extent, violations of social rules. In addition to diagnostic issues, we discuss the prevalence, course and prognosis for the disorder, as well as some theories regarding the etiology of the problem. Finally, we provide a brief review of the research regarding treatment approaches for reducing child conduct problems.

The following case descriptions will help to illustrate the type and severity of problems represented by the conduct-problem child. Eric is an eight-year-old boy living at home with his father, mother, younger brother, and infant sister. He was referred to the clinic because of excessive aggressive behavior. Eric made a recent attempt to stab his younger brother and makes frequent threats of violence towards both younger siblings. Eric's history reveals an escalation in aggressive activity, including the initiation of physical fights with peers, destruction of household property, and refusal to do what his parents request. Eric's parents express exasperation and exhaustion in dealing with Eric, and talk about placing him in a boarding school. They have experienced difficulties managing his behavior since he was a toddler. Although initially they were told by professionals that he would "outgrow" these problems, they found he became increasingly aggressive and defiant. He was expelled from four preschools before he started grade school. The parents report that they have tried every discipline strategy they could think of—such as Time Out, yelling, hitting and spanking, taking away privileges, and grounding him. They feel that none of these approaches has worked with him. The parents report feeling isolated and stigmatized by other parents with more "normal" children; they also feel that his teachers have blamed them for his misbehaviors.

An evaluation of his behavior in grade 3 reveals inattentiveness and distractability in the classroom, aggression towards his peers—particularly during recess—and frequent reports of teacher calls to his mother to take him home from school because of misbehavior. His intellectual performance is within the normal range (WISC-R full scale IQ = 105), yet his academic performance is barely passable. His school absences and physical fights have resulted in frequent contact between school officials and his parents, including threats of expulsion.

Eric's home life includes a mother with moderate depression and a father who drinks heavily. The father becomes abusive when he drinks; often the children as well as the mother are targets of the abuse. Less than a year ago, the mother had another child; this has increased the stress in the family in that the mother is unable to take responsibility for the care and supervision of the older children.

Melinda is a six-year-old girl who screams and tantrums when she fails to get her own way at kindergarten. She also behaves impulsively and can be hyperactive in the classroom. Her teachers have threatened to expel her from kindergarten for these behaviors. Her mother reports that at home Melinda throws chairs and threatens her with knives. She whines incessantly to get what she wants and refuses to brush her teeth, to get dressed, or to go to bed. Her mother feels unable to go out in public with Melinda because of her emotional outbursts. She reports that every request involves a series of intensive negotiations and cajoling. The mother says Melinda has been difficult since she was eight months old. She reports feeling exhausted and trapped, isolated from other adults by her situation and unable to invite friends over socially. She feels that her daughter "blackmails" both her parents and her teachers to get what she wants by means of her aggressive outbursts, which sometimes last for over an hour.

Melinda's mother says she feels her own temperament is similar to Melinda's in that as a child she had similar emotional outbursts until she was in grade 5 or 6. She separated from Melinda's father a year ago after seven years of marriage. She feels her husband is manic depressive and at times psychotic, but reports that he will not seek help. He is also an alcoholic and a drug user. She left her husband because she could not handle his erratic behavior, although she states she still loves him. They have joint custody and Melinda goes to stay with her father every other weekend as well as one night a week.

Melinda's mother obtained her Master's degree in nursing and is currently working full time and managing to support herself and her daughter on this income. Melinda's father came from a wealthy family, but his mother (Melinda's paternal grandmother) was seriously depressed when he was a child and spent much of her time in hospital. Currently unemployed, he is unable to pay child custody support.

The family background reveals that Melinda's mother had a close relationship with her own mother, who was a social worker. At the time Melinda was born, Melinda's maternal grandmother died. Melinda's mother described her own father as cold, nonsupportive, paranoid, and prone to emotional outbursts.

DIAGNOSTIC ISSUES

DSM-IV Draft Criteria

According to the DSM-IV Draft Criteria American Psychiatric Association [APA], (1993), externalizing behavior problems are referred to collectively as "Disruptive Behavior and Attention-deficit Disorders." There are three subgroups related to this larger category: Oppositional Defiant Disorder

(ODD), Attention Deficit/Hyperactivity Disorder (ADHD) and Conduct Disorder (CD). As Conduct Disorder is rarely diagnosed before the age of six, most young children with externalizing symptoms fit the criteria for ODD, ADHD, or a combination of the two disorders. The primary features of conduct disorder are conduct disturbance lasting at least six months, conduct problems, and violation of the rights of others. A diagnosis of conduct disorder requires a disturbance lasting for at least six months during which three of the following symptoms are present: often bullies, threatens, or intimidates others; often initiates physical fights; has used a weapon that can cause serious physical harm; has stolen with confrontation of a victim; has been physically cruel to people; has been physically cruel to animals; has forced someone into sexual activity; often lies or breaks promises; often stays out at night despite parental prohibitions; beginning before age 13: has stolen items of nontrivial value; has deliberately engaged in fire setting; has deliberately destroyed other people's property; has run away from home overnight at least twice while living in parental home; often plays truant from school; beginning before the age of 13 has broken into someone else's house, building or car (APA, 1993).

The DSM-IV Draft Criteria (APA, 1993) mention two subtypes of Conduct Disorder. The Childhood onset type which consists of at least one conduct problem occurring before the age of 10 and the adolescent onset type where there are no conduct problems prior to the age of 10. Also severity is rated from mild through moderate to severe.

The diagnoses of ODD requires a pattern of negativistic, hostile, and defiant behavior lasting six months during which four of the following are present: often loses temper; often argues with adults; often actively defies or refuses to comply with adults' rules; often deliberately does things that annoy other people; often blames others for his or her mistakes; is often touchy or easily annoyed; is often angry and resentful and is often vindictive.

Other Classifications

Another method for classifying conduct disorder is through empirically derived syndromes. Two distinct syndromes that consistently emerge from the literature are "undersocialized-aggressive" and "socialized-aggressive" (Quay, 1986). The undersocialized-aggressive syndrome includes such behaviors as fighting, disobedience, temper tantrums, destructiveness, lack of cooperation, and impertinence. The socialized-aggressive syndrome includes truancy from school, absence from home, stealing with peers, loyalty to delinquent friends, and gang involvement (Quay, 1986). It is important to remember that conduct disorder, although relatively stable, is manifested by different patterns of behavior in children of different age or gender.

Another method of categorization is known as the "salient symptom" approach. This method suggests subcategorizing conduct disorder based on the specific behaviors displayed by the child. The dimensions of the subcategorization are the "overt" dimension (e.g., physical aggression, disobedience, destruction of property) and the "covert" dimension (e.g., lying, stealing, truancy). The overt–covert distinction is supported by evidence that certain behaviors tend to cluster together, and that the two dimensions differ in their response to treatment (Wicks-Nelson & Israel, 1991).

Co-morbidity

There seems to be considerable diagnostic ambiguity regarding CD, ODD and ADHD in the young preschool age group as well as true comorbidity (i.e., hyperactive, impulsive, inattentive children have externalizing problems). Current reports suggest that as many as 75% of children who are diagnosed as having attention deficit disorder with hyperactivity (ADHD) can also be identified as conduct-disordered (Safer & Allen, 1976). It has been proposed that hyperactivity may influence the emergence of conduct disorder; Loeber (1985) has even suggested that hyperactivity is inherent in conduct-disordered children. However, careful assessment of the child may reveal that the child actually meets the criteria for one but not the other, for the criteria for ADHD and conduct disorder, while similar, are not identical. It is important that ODD and ADHD be differentiated if possible, for both clinical and empirical reasons. Furthermore, those children who display concurrent ODD and ADHD appear to be at heightened risk of development of severe antisocial behavior when compared to children with either disorder (i.e., ODD *or* ADHD, but not both) (Walker et al., 1988).

Developmental Progression from ODD to CD

A number of theorists have shown high continuity between disruptive and externalizing problems in the preschool years and externalizing problems in adolescence (Loeber, 1990; Rutter, 1985). Recently, developmental theorists have suggested that there may be two developmental pathways related to conduct disorders: the "early starter" versus "late starter" model (Patterson, DeBaryshe & Ramsey, 1989). The hypothesized early onset pathway begins formally with the emergence of oppositional disorders (ODD) in early preschool years and progresses to aggressive and non-aggressive (e.g., lying, stealing) symptoms of conduct disorder in middle childhood, and then to the most serious symptoms by adolescence (Lahey et al., 1992). In contrast, the "late starter" pathway first begins with symptoms of CD during adolescence after a normal history of social and behavioral development during the preschool and early school years. The prognosis for "late starter" adolescents appears to be more favorable than for adolescents who have a chronic history of conduct disorders stemming from their preschool years. Adolescents who are most likely to be chronically antisocial are those who first evidenced symptoms of ODD in the preschool years (White et al., 1990). These early-onset CD children also account for a disproportionate share of the delinquent acts in adolescents. Thus ODD is a sensitive predictor of subsequent CD; indeed, the primary developmental pathway for serious conduct disorders in adolescence and adulthood appears to be established in the preschool period.

Course of the disorder

Research has indicated that a high rate of childhood aggression, even in children as young as three years, is fairly stable over time (Robins, 1981). Richman, Stevenson, and Graham (1982) found that 67% of children with externalizing problems at age three continued to be aggressive at age eight. Other studies have reported stability correlations between 0.5 and 0.7 for externalizing scores (Rose, Rose & Feldman, 1989). Loeber (1991) contends that the stability may actually be higher than these estimates, because manifestations of the problems are episodic, situational, and changeable in nature (i.e., from tantrums to stealing). Early onset of ODD appears to be related to later aggressive and antisocial behavior, as well as to the development of severe problems later in life (e.g., school drop out, alcoholism, drug abuse, juvenile delinquency, adult crime, marital disruption, interpersonal problems, and poor physical health) (Kazdin, 1987). However, it is important to note that not all conduct-disordered children incur a poor prognosis as adults. Data suggest that fewer than 50% of the most severe conduct-disordered children become antisocial as adults. The fact that fewer than one-half of conduct-disordered children continue into adulthood with significant problems, whereas almost all adolescents diagnosed with conduct disorders had antisocial problems earlier in childhood, means that early onset of conduct problems is a necessary but not a sufficient condition for the development of antisocial conduct in adulthood.

Although not all ODD children become CD and not all children become antisocial adults, certain risk factors contribute to the continuation of the disorder:

■ Early age of onset (preschool years) of ODD and CD. Those children with conduct symptoms prior to age six are at greater risk for developing antisocial behavior as adults than those whose problems start during adolescence.

■ Breadth of deviance (across multiple settings, such as home and school). The children most at risk of continuing antisocial behavior as adults had conduct problems which occurred not only in the home but also at school and in other settings.

■ Frequency and intensity of antisocial behavior. The likelihood of becoming an antisocial adult increases in direct proportion to the number of different behavior problems evidenced as a child. Whereas 18% of adolescents with a minimum of three conduct problems were later diagnosed as antisocial, 46% of those youngsters exhibiting at least six conduct behavioral indices were so diagnosed as adults (Robins, Tipp & Przybeck, 1991).

■ Diversity of antisocial behavior (several versus few) and covert behaviors at early ages (stealing, lying, firesetting). The greater the variety of both covert and overt behavior problems, the greater is the likelihood of becoming an antisocial adult, although aggressive behavior is probably the most stable behavior over time.

■ Family and parent characteristics (Kazdin, 1987). Children whose biological parent has an antisocial personality are at greater risk.

However, a delineation of contributing risk factors does not convey a complete understanding of the complex nature of variables involved, nor the relationship of the variables with one another. It is probably the combined interactive effects of these risk factors, as well as the number of risk factors, that contributes most to the child's risk of developing CD.

CAUSES OF THE DISORDER

It is widely accepted that multiple factors contribute to the development and maintenance of child conduct disorders. It is important to review these factors briefly because of their implications for designing interventions. These include: child, parent, family and school-related factors.

Child Factors

Child factors: temperament

The "child deficit" hypothesis argues that some abnormal aspect of the child's internal organization at the physiological, neurological, and/or neuropsychological level (which may be genetically transmitted) is at least partially responsible for the development of externalizing behavior problems. Temperament has perhaps been the most researched factor with regard to conduct problems. Temperament refers to aspects of the personality that show consistency over time and across situations, and are identified as constitutional in nature: the child's activity level, emotional responsiveness, quality of mood, and social adaptability (Thomas & Chess, 1977). Research has indicated that there are links between specific temperament scales and specific behavior problem scales. For example, there is a strong correlation between a lack of adaptability and later aggressive problems (Bates, 1990). Frequent and intensive negative child affect also consistently predicts behavior problems (Bates, 1990). In one longitudinal study, maternal reports of infant difficultness (at six months) and infant resistance to control (at one year) proved to be significant predictors of externalizing problems at ages six and eight years (Bates et al., 1991).

Although studies have shown that early assessments of temperament predict later behavior problems, the amount of variance in terms of behavior problems accounted for by temperament is relatively small. Factors such as degree of family conflict, level of support, and quality of parent management strategies appear to interact with temperament to influence outcome. Several recent studies have shown that in the context of favorable family conditions, extreme (difficult) infant temperament is not likely to increase the risk of disruptive behavior disorders at age four (Maziade et al., 1989). In general, the findings on temperament clearly support the notion of Thomas and Chess (1977), that "no temperamental pattern confers an immunity to behavior disorders, nor is it fated to create psychopathology" (p. 4).

Child factors: other neurological difficulties

Neurological abnormalities are inconsistently correlated with conduct disorders. An association exists more generally with childhood dysfunction, rather than with conduct disorders in particular (Kazdin, 1987). There is much speculation, and some evidence, that deficits in verbal functioning, language comprehension, impulsivity, and emotional regulation in aggressive children may be based in the left frontal lobe and its relation to the limbic system (Gorensten & Newman, 1980). However, it is important also to note that conduct-disordered children have an increased likelihood of history of physical abuse, including head and facial injuries, which may contribute to some of their neurological abnormalities (e.g., soft signs, EEG aberrations, seizure disorders).

Other psychophysiological variables have been implicated in child conduct disorders. There is some evidence of a low resting heart rate (lower vagal tone) among antisocial youth (Raine & Venables, 1984). Skin conductance responses have been found to differentiate between conduct-disordered youth and nonconduct-disordered controls in both adolescents and younger children (Schmidt, Solanto & Bridger, 1985). While one cannot determine cause and effect from correlation data, these data do suggest a possible autonomic arousal system deficit in some of these children.

Child factors: cognitive and social skills deficits

In addition to temperament, other organic factors have been implicated in child conduct disorders and antisocial behavior. It has been suggested that children with conduct disorders distort social cues during peer interactions (Milich & Dodge, 1984), including attributing hostile intent to neutral situations. Aggressive children search for fewer cues or facts when determining another's intentions (Dodge & Newman, 1981) and focus more on aggressive cues (Goutz, 1981); the child's perception of hostile intentions from others may, in turn, encourage the child to react aggressively. There are also data indicating that deficits in social problem-solving skills contribute to poor peer interactions (Asarnow & Callan, 1985). These children may define problems in hostile ways, seek less information, generate fewer alternative solutions to social problems, and anticipate fewer consequences for aggression (Richard & Dodge, 1982; Slaby & Guerra, 1988). Research examining the relationship between empathy and aggression also reveals some interesting information about children's development. Aggressive behavior in children is correlated with low empathy across a wide age range (Feshbach, 1989). In other words, aggressive children have difficulty perceiving or understanding another person's point of view or feelings, which may explain their lack of interpersonal competencies and their antisocial behavior. It is unclear whether aggressive children's processing of social information is a result of negative experiences with parents, teachers or peers, or is defective a priori.

Child factors: academic deficits

Academic performance has been implicated in child conduct disorders. Low academic achievement often manifests itself in children with conduct disorders early on, during the elementary grades, and continues through high school (Kazdin, 1987). Reading disabilities in particular are associated with conduct disorders (Sturge, 1982). One study indicated that conduct-disordered children exhibited reading deficits defined as a 28-month lag in reading ability behind that of normal children (Rutter et al., 1976). Complicating this association is the fact that the relationship between academic performance and conduct disorders is not merely unidirectional, but is considered bidirectional; that is, it is unclear whether disruptive behavior problems precede or follow the academic difficulties, language delay, or neuropsychological deficits. However, there is some evidence that cognitive and linguistic problems may precede disruptive behavior problems (Schonfeld et al., 1988).

Heredity versus environment

Longitudinal studies suggest that conduct disorders are stable across generations. This suggests the role of genetic factors, as discussed above. There is some direct evidence regarding genetic contributions to child conduct disorders. For example, twin studies have shown greater concordance of antisocial behavior among monozygotic than among dizygotic twins (Kazdin, 1987). Adoption studies, where the child is separated from the biological parent, indicate that offspring of antisocial parents show a greater risk of antisocial behavior (Kazdin, 1987). The increased risk owing to antisocial behavior in the biological parent establishes some credence for the inclusion of genetics in accounting for a portion of the variance in conduct disorders. However, it has also been established that genetic factors alone do not account for the emergence of the disorder. Rather, these studies affirm the effect of genetic influences in conjunction with environmental factors such as adverse conditions in the home (e.g., marital discord, psychiatric dysfunction), ineffective family problem-solving and limited coping techniques (Cadoret & Cain, 1981).

Family and Ecological Factors

Parent factors: parent skills deficits

Parenting interactions are clearly the best-researched and most important proximal cause of conduct problems. Research has indicated that some parents of conduct-disordered children lack certain fundamental parenting skills. For example, parents of such children have been reported to exhibit fewer positive behaviors, to be more violent and critical in their use of discipline, to be more permissive, erratic, and inconsistent, to be more likely to fail to monitor their children's behaviors, and to be more likely to reinforce inappropriate behaviors and to ignore or punish prosocial behaviors (Patterson & Stouthamer-Loeber, 1984; Webster-Stratton, 1985, 1992a). The most influential developmental model for describing the family dynamics that underlie early antisocial behavior is Patterson's theory of the "coercive process" (Patterson, 1982), a process whereby children learn to escape or avoid parental criticism by escalating their negative behaviors, which in turn leads to increasingly aversive parent interactions. These negative responses, in turn, directly reinforce the child's deviant behaviors.

In addition, it is important to note the affective nature of the parent–child relationship. There is considerable evidence that a warm, positive bond between parent and child leads to more positive communication and parenting strategies and a more socially competent child (Baumrind, 1971). Of course, the parenting difficulties of parents with conduct-disordered children could also stem from having to cope with a more difficult and unresponsive child. Children with conduct disorders engage in higher rates of deviant behaviors and noncompliance with parental commands than do other children. When interacting with their mothers, CD children exhibit fewer positive verbal and nonverbal behaviors (smiles, laughs, enthusiasm, praise) than do other children. In addition, children with conduct disorders exhibit more negative nonverbal gestures, expressions, and tones of voice in their interactions with both mothers and fathers. These children have less positive affect, seem depressed, and are less reinforcing to their parents, thus setting in motion the cycle of aversive parent/child interactions.

Parent factors: interpersonal

Parent psychopathology places the child at considerable risk for conduct disorders. Specifically, depression in the mother has been shown to increase the child's risk for conduct disorders. For example, in a recent community study, maternal depression when the child was five was related to parent and teacher reports of behavior problems at age seven (Williams et al., 1990). This correlation is complicated by the fact that maternal depression is associated with misperception of a child's behavior, e.g., mothers who are depressed are more likely to perceive their child's behavior as maladjusted or inappropriate.

Depression also influences the parenting behavior directed toward a child's misbehavior. For example, depressed mothers often increase the number of commands they give their children. The child, in response to the increase in parent commands, displays an increase in noncompliance or deviant child behavior (McMahon & Forehand, 1988; Webster-Stratton & Hammond, 1988). Depressed mothers also give an increased number of criticisms, a form of negative attention. It is hypothesized that maternal depression and irritability indirectly lead to behavior problems as a result of negative attention, reinforcement of inappropriate child behaviors, inconsistent limit-setting, and emotional unavailability.

Maternal insularity is another parental factor implicated in child conduct disorders. Insularity is defined as "a specific pattern of social contacts within the community that are characterized by a high level of negatively perceived social interchanges with relatives and/or helping agency representatives and by a low level of positively perceived supportive interchanges with friends" (Wahler & Dumas, 1984, p. 387). This definition is important because it appears that, rather than the number or extent of social contacts, it is the individual's perception of the social contact as supportive or positive that makes the social contact advantageous. Mothers characterized as "insular" are more aversive and use more aversive consequences with their children than "noninsular" mothers (Wahler & Dumas, 1985). Insularity and lack of support have also been reported to be significant predictors of a family's relapse or failure to maintain treatment effects (Webster-Stratton, 1985).

As might be expected, the presence of antisocial behavior in either parent places the child at greater risk for conduct disorders. In particular, criminal behavior and alcoholism in the father are consistently demonstrated as parental factors increasing the child's risk (Frick et al., 1991). Grandparents of conduct-disordered children are also more likely to-show antisocial behavior than grandparents of children who are not antisocial. How much are the child's conduct disorders due to the inappropriate modeling of antisocial behaviors by the parent? How much are they due to a genetically transmitted predisposition? This question is as yet difficult to unravel.

Parent factors: interparental

Specific family characteristics have been found to contribute to the development and maintenance of child conduct disorders. Interparental conflict leading to and surrounding divorce is associated with, but is not a strong predictor of, child conduct disorders (Kazdin, 1987). In particular, boys appear more apt to show a significant increase in anti-social behaviors following divorce. However, there is considerable variation: after a separation or divorce, some single parents and their children appear to do relatively well over time, whereas others are chronically depressed and report increased stress levels.

One explanation for the poor child outcomes in some single-parent families might be that, for some single parents, the stress of divorce sets in motion a series of stages of increased depression and increased irritability; this increased irritability leads to a loss of friendships and social support, placing the mothers at increased risk for more irritable behaviors, ineffective discipline, and poor problem-solving outcomes; the poor problem-solving of these parents in turn results in increased depression and stress levels, completing the spiraling negative cycle. This irritability simultaneously sets in motion a process whereby the child also becomes increasingly antisocial (Forgatch, 1989).

Once researchers began to differentiate between parental divorce, separation, and discord, they began to understand that it was not the divorce per se that was the critical factor in shaping the child's behavior, but rather the amount and intensity of parental conflict and violence (O'Leary & Emery, 1982). For example, children whose parents divorce but whose homes are subsequently conflict-free are less likely to have problems than children whose parents stay together but experience a great deal of conflict; children whose parents continue to have conflict during and after divorce have more conduct problems than children whose parents experience conflict-free divorce. In our own studies of families with conduct-problem children, half of the married couples reported experiences with spouse abuse and violence. Taken together, these findings highlight the importance of parents' marital conflict and violence, rather than family structure, as a key factor influencing children's externalizing problems.

Marital conflict is associated with more negative perceptions of the child's adjustment, inconsistent parenting, the use of increased punitiveness and decreased reasoning, and fewer rewards for children (Stonemen, Brody & Burke, 1988). Conflictual, unhappy marriages where aggressive behavior is displayed contribute to the formation of conduct disorders. It is consistently demonstrated that if aggressive behavior is present in the marital relationship, the likelihood of conduct disorders is greater than if marital conflict alone is present without overt aggression (Jouriles, Murphy & O'Leary, 1989). This provides another explanation for the increased incidence of conduct disorders in maritally distressed families: namely, the child models the aggressive behaviors observed in the marital interactions.

Frick et al. (1989) have proposed two models to help explain the correlation between marital distress and child conduct disorders. One model proposes a direct *and* an indirect path from marital satisfaction to child conduct disorders; that is, marital satisfaction or dissatisfaction directly influences the development of conduct disorders (i.e., negative parental affect and conflict disrupt the child's emotional regulation). Their second model proposes that the significant correlations between marital dissatisfaction and child conduct problems are more an artifact of the common effects of maternal antisocial personality and social class. They found the relationship between marital dissatisfaction and child conduct problems was based primarily on the common association with maternal antisocial personality, but that social class did not play an important role as a third variable. These findings seem to argue for the importance of parents' psychological adjustment (e.g., marital distress, depression) as a primary determinant of the effects of stress on parent–child interactions, rather than environmental factors such as poverty or low social status.

Family factors: environmental stress

Research suggests that life stressors such as poverty, unemployment, crowded living conditions, and illness have deleterious effects on parenting and are related to a variety of forms of child psychopathology, including conduct disorders (Rutter & Giller, 1983; Kazdin, 1986). Families with conduct-disordered children report major stressors at an incidence two to four times greater than for nonclinic families (Webster-Stratton, 1990b). Parents of conduct-disordered children indicate that they experience more day-to-day hassles as well as major crises than nonclinic families. An accumulation of minor day-to-day chronic life hassles is related to more aversive maternal interactions—for example, higher rates of coercive behavior and irritability in the mother's interactions with her children. Recent reports have also shown maternal stress to be associated with inept discipline practices, such as explosive discipline and "nattering" with children (Forgatch, Patterson & Skinner, 1988; Webster-Stratton, 1990b).

There is probably no link between social class and child conduct disorders. Often social class includes multiple confounding variables such as overcrowding, poor supervision, and other potential risk factors (Kazdin,

1987). When control is obtained for these risk factors, social status shows little relation to conduct disorders. Social class as a summary label that includes multiple risk factors can influence child conduct disorders (Kazdin, 1987).

School Factors

School-related factors: peer and teacher–child interactions

Once they enter school—be it preschool or grade school—negative school and social experiences further exacerbate the adjustment difficulties of children with conduct problems. Children who are aggressive and disruptive with peers quickly become rejected by them (Ladd, 1990), and this rejection can extend across the school years. Over time, peers become mistrustful of such children and respond to them in ways that increase the likelihood of reactive aggression (Dodge & Somberg, 1987). Because of their noncompliant, disruptive behavior, aggressive children also develop poor relations with teachers and receive less support and nurturing in the school setting (Campbell & Ewing, 1990). There is some evidence to suggest that teachers retaliate in a manner similar to parents and peers. One study reported that antisocial children were much less likely to get encouragement from teachers for appropriate behavior and more likely to get punished for negative behavior than well-behaved children (Walker & Buckley, 1973). Frequently, these children are "expelled" from preschools and classrooms. In our studies with conduct problem children, ages three to seven years, we found that over 50% of the children had been asked to leave two or more schools.

The school setting has been studied as a risk factor contributing to conduct disorders. Rutter and his colleagues (1976) found that characteristics such as degree of emphasis on academic work, amount of teacher time spent on lessons, extent of teacher use of praise, degree of emphasis on individual responsibility, extent of teacher availability, school working conditions (e.g., physical condition, size), and teacher–student ratio were related to oppositional behaviors, delinquency, and academic performance.

School and home connections as factors

Bronfenbrenner (1979) has elucidated the importance not only of interactions that children have within their growing fields such as family, peers, and school (microsystems), but also of the connections between these

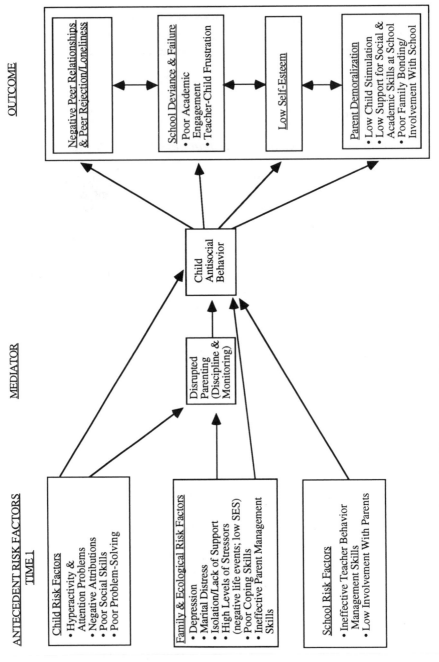

Figure 1.1 Causal model. (Reproduced by permission from Webster-Stratton, 1992b)

social fields (exosystems). The child's "bonding" to social institutions (both family and school) as well as the family's bonding to the child and school are believed to be critical features in prevention of deviant behavior. For example, many parents of children with ODD and CD have had negative encounters with teachers concerning their children's behavior problems. Such encounters only add to parents' feelings of incompetence, their sense of helplessness regarding strategies to solve the problems, and their alienation from the school. A spiraling pattern of child negative behavior, parent demoralization and withdrawal, and teacher reactivity can ultimately lead to a lack of coordination and support between the socialization activities of the school and home—a weak exosystem, to use Bronfenbrenner's term. In a recent study, teachers reported that parents of behavior problem children were less interested in knowing the teacher, seemed to hold different goals for their children and seemed to value education less than did parents of socially competent children (Coie et al., in press). These differences suggest that an intervention model requires not only the development of appropriate social, cognitive, and behavioral skills in the child and parent, but in addition healthy bonds between parents and school, child and school, and parents and teachers. With a strong family–school bond, the child benefits because of the parents' increased expectations, interest in, and support for the child's social and academic performance (Hawkins & Weiss, 1985).

CURRENT TREATMENTS: A BRIEF REVIEW OF FAMILY-BASED BEHAVIORAL INTERVENTIONS

Parent Intervention

One of the major treatment strategies for reducing child conduct disorders, as well as child conduct problems in general, involves parent training interventions. The central assumption for this approach is the model suggesting that the parents' skills deficits are the major factor in the development and maintenance of conduct disorders. Intervention approaches based on this model have been aimed directly at the parents of the aggressive child rather than at the child him/herself; the aim is to change the child's behavior by changing the parents' behavior—to teach parents to use more effective parenting techniques. In these programs, parents learn to change the interpersonal antecedents and consequences that are eliciting and maintaining the child's negative behaviors. They are taught how to identify and reward their children's prosocial behaviors through praise and attention and how to decrease inappropriate behaviors through Time Out and response–cost procedures (Forehand & McMahon 1981; Patterson 1975; Patterson & Stouthamer-Loeber 1984; Webster-Stratton, 1981a,b).

Reviews of these parent training programs are highly promising (Kazdin, 1986). The short-term treatment outcome success has been documented in quantitative terms by significant changes in parents' and children's behavior and in parental perceptions of child adjustment (McMahon & Forehand, 1984; Patterson, 1975; Webster-Stratton, 1981a,b; 1984; Webster-Stratton, Kolpacoff & Hollinsworth, 1989). Home observations have indicated that parents can reduce children's levels of aggression by 20–60% (Patterson, 1982; Webster-Stratton, 1984). Generalization of behavior improvements from the clinic setting to the home (Patterson, 1982; Peed, Roberts & Forehand, 1977) over reasonable follow-up periods (one to four years) and to untreated children in the family has also been demonstrated (Arnold, Levine & Patterson, 1975; Forehand et al. 1986; Webster-Stratton, 1982a; 1990b; Webster-Stratton, Kolpacoff & Hollinsworth, 1989). However, the same does not seem to be true in the case of children's behavior at school: improved child behavior at home does not necessarily generalize to the school setting. Studies have indicated, in many cases, that although a child's behavior improves at home, his or her teacher does not report improvements in conduct problems and peer relationships (Breiner & Forehand, 1982; Forehand et al., 1979). Most parent-training programs have received high ratings from parents in terms of acceptability and consumer satisfaction (Cross Calvert & McMahon, 1987; McMahon & Forehand, 1984; Webster-Stratton, 1989b).

An example of a comprehensive and extensively evaluated parent–training program for young conduct-disordered children was developed by Webster-Stratton (1981a,b; 1982a,b; 1984) at the University of Washington Parenting Clinic. The content of the BASIC parenting program, which was designed for parents with children aged three to eight years, includes components of the training model of Hanf and Kling (1973) and of the "child-directed play" approach of Forehand and McMahon (1981), as well as the strategic use of differential attention and effective use of commands. The BASIC content incorporates Patterson's (1982) discipline components concerning Time Out, Logical and Natural Consequences, and Monitoring. The program also includes parental problem-solving and communication strategies with their children (D'Zurilla & Nezu, 1982; Spivak, Platt & Shure, 1976).

What is unique about these programs is the concern with developing the most effective *methods* of working with parents—that is, methods that are cost-effective, widely applicable and sustaining. Based on Bandura's

(1977) modeling theory, the program utilizes videotape modeling methods. Efforts are made to promote the modeling effects for parents by creating positive feelings about the models shown on the videotapes. For example, the videotapes show models of differing sexes, ages, cultures, socio-economic backgrounds, and temperaments, so that parents will perceive the models as similar to themselves and their children. There are 10 video-tape programs of modeled parent skills in the BASIC series (250 vignettes, each of which lasts one to two minutes) which are shown by a therapist to groups of parents (8–12 parents per group). After each vignette, the therapist leads a group discussion on the relevant interactions.

The use of videotape modeling training methods for parents of young conduct-problem children has been shown to be not only more effective in improving parent–child interactions (in comparison to group discussion approaches and one-to-one therapy with an individual therapist), but also highly cost-effective as prevention. Furthermore, videotape modeling has the potential advantage of being accessible to illiterate parents or those who simply have difficulties with reading assignments and verbal approaches in general. Videotape modeling has potential for mass dissemi-nation and low individual training cost when used in groups or in self-administered programs (Webster-Stratton, 1981b; 1982a,b; 1984; 1992a; Webster-Stratton & Hammond, 1988). In addition, videotapes provide a more feasible, flexible method of treatment because they can portray a wide variety of models in different settings and situations, which may help parents generalize the concepts.

Nonetheless, despite the general overall success of a variety of compre-hensive parent-training programs in producing statistically significant changes in parent and child behaviors, there is also evidence that some families do not respond to treatment and continue to have children with clinically significant behavior problems after treatment. If one defines the criterion for treatment response as the extent to which parents and teachers report children's adjustment within the normal or the nonclinical range of functioning, then the results of these interventions look less robust. Long-term follow-up studies suggest that 30–50% of treated parents and 25–50% of teachers report children to continue to have behavior problems in the deviant or clinical range (Schmaling & Jacobson, 1987; Forehand, Furey & McMahon, 1984; Webster-Stratton, 1990a,b; Webster-Stratton & Hammond, 1990).

A broad-based family training model

Researchers have convincingly demonstrated that parental personal factors such as depression, marital discord, lack of social support, and environmental stressors disrupt parenting behavior and contribute to parent-training treatment-relapses (Dumas, 1984; Dadds, Schwartz & Sanders, 1987; Webster-Stratton, 1990b; Rickard et al., 1981). As a result, broader-based expansions of family training have been developed to focus on adjunctive strategies to address these family interpersonal issues (e.g., marital communication, stress management). In this model, broader-based interventions are hypothesized to help mediate the negative influences of these family stressors on parenting skills and to promote increased maintenance and generalizability of treatment gains. Unfortunately, few studies have specifically assessed the relative contribution of adjuncts; however, those which have been completed have suggested promising results (Dadds & McHugh, 1992; Webster-Stratton, in press). In a recent study at the Parenting Clinic, we found that families who attended both the basic videotape parent-training program as well as an expanded video-tape training program which focused on parental personal issues such as effective communication skills, anger management, coping with depression, and problem-solving strategies resulted in significantly enhanced improvements in comparison with families who received only the basic parent skills training approach (Webster-Stratton, in press).

Another possible reason for the nonresponse to parent-training inter-vention for some families, suggested by studies with older conduct-disordered children and adolescents, is that the intervention has come too late, after children's negative behavior patterns and negative reputations with peers and teachers have been established. Once established, these are difficult to reverse. Our own studies with younger conduct-problem children show more positive results. Early intervention—in the critical transitional period from preschool to school, when the parents are still the primary socialization influences in the child's development (as opposed to peers and teachers)—offers promise for preventing the trajectory from ODD to CD.

Child Intervention

Another possible reason for the lack of long-term effectiveness of the traditional parent-training approaches, for some families, may be due to the exclusive focus on parent skills as the locus of change and the failure to acknowledge the role played by child, peer, and school factors in the development of conduct disorders. For those who subscribe to the theory that children's deficits in cognitive, social, and behavioral skills lead to the development of conduct disorders, interventions have been aimed directly at the children. The following discussion briefly highlights a few of the promising child-training programs.

A variety of innovative child-training programs have been developed in recent years (for review, see Beck & Forehand, 1984; Bierman, 1989). There have been two basic types of child skills training approaches. The first approach attempts to train the child in target social behaviors based on the hypothesized social skills deficit. Such programs coach children in positive social skills such as play, friendship, and conversational skills (e.g., Gresham & Nagle, 1980; Ladd & Asher, 1985; LaGreca & Santogrossi, 1980; Minken et al., 1976; Mize & Ladd, 1990; Spence, 1983), academic and social interaction training (Coie & Krehbiel, 1984), and behavioral control strategies (Bierman, Miller & Stabb, 1987). Some of these programs have targeted a few specific skills such as conversational skills (Bierman & Furman, 1984; Ladd, 1981) or game skills (Oden & Asher, 1977), while other programs have focused on a wider variety of skills, such as LaGreca and Santogrossi's program (1980) which targets nine behaviors (including smiling, greeting, joining, inviting, conversing, sharing, cooperating, complimenting, and grooming).

The second type of child-training approach relies on cognitive-behavioral methods and focuses on training children in the cognitive processes (e.g., problem-solving, self-control, self-statements) or the affective domain (e.g., empathy training and perspective taking) (Camp & Bash, 1985; Kazdin, 1987; Kazdin et al., 1987; Kendall & Braswell, 1985; Lochman et al., 1984; Spivack & Shure, 1974). The methods used in both of these approaches usually include verbal instructions and discussions, opportunities to practice the skill with peers, role-playing, games, stories, and therapist feedback and reinforcement. Most of these programs are school-based, time-limited (4–12 weeks) and, rather surprisingly, have not involved the parents in the training. Moreover, the majority of programs (e.g., Kendall & Braswell, 1985; Spivack, Platt & Shure, 1976) have not specifically targeted children with conduct disorders. Those that did specify this population have tended to intervene with preadolescents (aged eight and above) and adolescent delinquents rather than young aggressive children and did not include direct behavioral observations in the home (Kazdin, 1987; Kazdin et al., 1987; Lochman et al., 1987; Lochman, Nelson & Sims, 1981).

A review of this social skill and cognitive intervention research with children is only mildly encouraging (Asher & Coie, 1990; Kendall & Braswell, 1985; Rubin & Krasnor, 1983). While few programs were actually conducted with clinical samples referred because of conduct disorders, there does seem to be evidence that the younger or less mature children and the more aggressive children are relatively unaffected by the existing child social skills training (Asher & Renshaw, 1981; Coie, 1990b; Kendall & Braswell, 1985). Moreover, because few studies have employed direct observational measures of aggression or noncompliance, it is unknown whether those children who do show improvements in cognitive processes, social skills, and sociometric ratings will also show reductions in conduct problems. There has been a failure to show convincingly that improvements in social or cognitive skills in the laboratory, inpatient setting, or in analog situations generalize to the home or that the long-term effects of child treatments are maintained (Bierman, 1989).

The cognitive-behavioral programs with preadolescents look somewhat more promising. In one study Lochman et al. (1984) reported that their cognitive-behavioral program was more effective than either goal-setting alone or no treatment in reducing disruptive aggressive off-task behavior in the classroom. The addition of goal-setting to the cognitive intervention resulted in greater reduction in aggressive behavior than did the cognitive intervention alone. The long-term effects of this program remain unknown, however. In regard to the Kazdin et al. (1987) Problem-Solving and Social Skills Training (PSST) program for older children and adolescents, studies have suggested that PSST is superior to relationship therapy and attention placebo control conditions on both parent and teacher ratings of behavior problems at post-treatment and at one-year follow-up. A second investigation showed similar results when PSST was combined with parent training and compared with placebo control (Kazdin et al., 1987). However, since there were no observational assessments of behavior in the laboratory, schools, or homes, it is unclear what behavior changes occurred and whether they generalized across settings. Finally, few studies have elaborated on the predictors that contribute to social skills treatment successes or failures except, as noted above, to suggest that the greater the level of child aggression, the less effective the treatment.

School and Community Interventions

Several preventive interventions relevant to conduct disorder have focused on the school and the community. The High/Scope Perry Preschool Program was designed to aid children who are considered at risk for school failure. The parents of these children had low incomes, lived in stressful environments, and had low levels of education—all risk factors for child conduct disorders. The children began the program at age three and participated for a two-year period (Schweinhart & Weikart, 1988). The program addressed intellectual, social, and physical needs involved in the development of decision-making and cognitive processes.

Another strategy aimed at preventing conduct disorder emphasizes the development of conventional values and behaviors as a way of protecting the child against deviance. Social bonding refers to the integration of commitment, attachment, and adherence to the values of the family, school, and peers (Hawkins & Lam, 1987; Hawkins & Weis, 1985). The intervention included several components. The classroom component uses interactive teaching and cooperative (peer-involved) learning techniques. The family component consists of parent management training and conflict resolution for family members. Peer social-skills training and community-focused career education and counseling are also included. The multiple contexts of family, school, and peers may increase the bonding necessary to reduce the onset of antisocial behavior (Kazdin, 1990).

The School Transitional Environmental Program (STEP) (Felner & Adan, 1988) was developed to help children through the normal process of entering a new school (e.g., middle to high school). Transitions are associated with decreased academic performance and psychological problems, including antisocial behavior. STEP attempts to reduce the effect of school transitions and increase the child's coping responses.

In addition to prevention programs, school and community efforts have also focused on populations where conduct disorder is evident. One school-based program was designed to prevent further adjustment problems among children who evinced signs of low academic motivation, family problems, and a record of disciplinary referrals (Bry & George, 1980). The program includes meetings with students where rewards are given for appropriate classroom behavior, punctuality, and a reduction in the amount of disciplinary action. Meetings are also scheduled with teachers and parents to focus on specific problems with individual children.

Another school-based approach targeted anger control in an "Anger Coping Program" (Lochman et al., 1987). The content includes teaching interpersonal problem-solving skills, strategies for increasing physiological awareness, and learning to use self-talk and self-control during problem situations. Another example for older school-aged children with conduct disorders is the Problem-Solving Skills Training (PSST) program (Kazdin et al., 1987), which is based on the programs developed by Kendall and Braswell (1985) and focuses on the child's cognitive processes (perceptions, self-statements, attributions, expectations, and problem-solving skills) which presumably underlie maladaptive behavior. The primary focus of treatment is on the thought processes rather than on the behavioral acts that result, and teaches children a step-by-step approach to solving problems. Shure and Spivack (1982) also developed an interpersonal problem-solving training program that has been used with a variety of populations to train children to be socially competent. Finally, Webster-Stratton (1991) has developed a videotape-based curriculum for young children aged three to eight years which focuses on understanding feelings, problem-solving, anger management, friendship behavior, and success in school. This program uses life-size puppets, real (nonacted) videotape examples of children at home and in school situations, cartoons, and homework assignments for parents and teachers.

Community-based interventions include prevention (for those young people at risk for antisocial behavior) and treatment (those young people identified with signs of antisocial behavior). One extensive program targeted a housing project with over 400 children (ages 5–15) from poverty-stricken families considered to be at risk for antisocial behavior (Offord & Jones, 1983). Youths were involved in activity programs and trained in specific skill areas (e.g., swimming, hockey, dancing, and playing musical instruments). Children were evaluated on their progress in the programs, and rewards were provided for attendance and participation.

Another program was designed for youths identified as delinquent. The intervention assigned the youth to a college student volunteer who worked with the young person for six to eight hours per week in the community (Davidson & Basta, 1988). Weekly supervision for the volunteers was provided by a juvenile court staff member, and supervision took place in the court worker's office (Wicks-Nelson & Israel, 1991).

Community-based interventions have also addressed both prevention and treatment. One program utilized existing community facilities in order to intervene with delinquent youths, as well as with youths who had no history of prior arrests (Fo & O'Donnell, 1975; O'Donnell, Lygate & Fo, 1979). Adults were recruited from the community and trained to conduct behavior modification programs with the youth. They also involved the young people in various activities (e.g., arts and crafts, fishing, and camping). Individualized reward programs focused on such behaviors as homework completion and school attendance (Kazdin, 1990).

The programs reviewed have provided some evidence to indicate that early preventive interventions can reduce the factors that place children at risk for conduct disorders (e.g., abusive child-rearing practices).

LIMITATIONS OF PROGRAMS

We have provided examples of a number of promising cognitive-social-learning-based treatment programs for helping families of children with conduct disorders. We have reviewed three broad types of programs, one which is family-focused and aimed at treating the parents, one which is child-focused and aimed directly at the child, and a third which is community-focused. In this review, it appears that parent-training programs not only comprise the largest body of literature in this area, but also have presented the most effective and promising results, particularly if offered to parents of young children with ODD or CD. Nonetheless, while a parent-training approach holds much promise for effectively treating conduct-disordered children, there are several important limitations to this approach. The first of these is the failure of child improvements brought about by parent-training programs to generalize beyond the home to school and peer relationships. Consequently, while the majority of children improve their social behavior at home, 30–50% of the children continue to have significant school problems, such as social acceptance, conduct problems, and academic underachievement. Intervening with children's teachers as well as their parents would seem to offer far better possibilities of generalizing improved social skills across the home and school settings. A second limitation is that, despite the documented links between underachievement, language delays, reading disabilities, and conduct disorders, parent-training programs have rarely, if ever, included an academic skills enhancement program for parents. Parents need to know not only how to help their children with their antisocial problems, but also how to teach and support them regarding their academic difficulties. They need to know how to work with teachers and schools in order to foster a supportive relationship between the home and school settings. Such a coordinated effort between the home and school regarding social and academic goals would also offer the possibility for better generalization of child improvements across settings. A third limitation of a parent intervention approach is the possibility that parents will refuse to participate in such programs. Some parents may not participate either because of their own dysfunction or because they have given up and are not motivated to change their behaviors.

In contrast, child-training programs have the practical advantage of being available through school programs to children whose parents are reluctant or unwilling to participate in parent-training programs. However, studies to date have presented comparatively less convincing and less potent results. There are several possible reasons for this. The first is that many of the child-training studies in recent years have been carried out with older middle-grade school children or adolescents who have already had a five- to ten-year history of negative relationships with peer groups and teachers (Coie & Kupersmidt, 1983; Dodge, 1983). It is highly likely that by the middle grades the aggressive child's negative reputation and social rejection by his or her peer group may be well established (Coie, 1990a). This chronic pattern may make it difficult for such children, even if they learn more appropriate social skills during the middle grades, to utilize these skills and change their image (Bierman & Furman, 1984). Intervention at a younger age may be more strategic in terms of helping children develop social competence before these negative behaviors and reputations develop into permanent patterns (Dodge et al., 1986).

A second possible reason for the lack of effectiveness of the child skills training programs, particularly with younger, aggressive, peer-rejected children, is the fact that the content of most traditional programs (with some exceptions such as the programs of Lochman and Kazdin) did not focus specifically on the conduct-disordered child's problems of aggression and noncompliance; nor did they address these children's specific academic problems such as reading delays. In fact, direct behavioral prohibitions or specific consequences for negative behaviors such as Time Out are rarely included in most social skills training programs (Coie & Krehbiel, 1984; Ladd, 1981). Social skills intervention programs must be tailored to the specific needs, problems, and age of conduct-disordered children.

A third possible reason for the lack of success in social skills programs with very young children may be that the programs were too cognitively sophisticated and not developmentally appropriate for this age group. Indeed, there has been a lack of specific attention to the most effective methods of training young children. Nonetheless, research evaluating the effects of television on children's behaviors suggests that younger children may benefit from a concrete, performance-based model, such as verbally mediated videotape modeling, rather than a cognitive or predominantly verbal model (Singer, 1982; Singer & Singer, 1983). When designing the content and methods of intervention programs for young children, ages four to eight years, compared to those for preadolescent children, greater attention needs to be paid to developmental differences. For example, imaginary play is highly important in children of three to eight years old, but less critical at other ages (Connolly & Doyle, 1984). Currently the University of Washington Parenting Clinic is investigating the effectiveness of a child-training program designed specifically for conduct-disordered children aged four to eight. The Dinosaur Social Skills and Problem-Solving Curriculum is based heavily on videotape modeling methods as well as role play, rehearsal, fantasy play, and activities. The content of this program includes empathy training, problem-solving, anger management, friendship skills, communication skills, and academic training (Webster-Stratton, 1991).

A final reason for the failure of social skills training programs to generalize from the child treatment setting to the home, school, or peer settings may be the exclusive focus on the child as the locus of change, rather than including a parent- or family-training component. Focusing only on the child—like the aforementiond problem regarding an exclusive focus on the parents—would seem to limit the likelihood of any effects generalizing across settings. Indeed, in Kazdin's study it was reported that the combination of parent training plus child problem-solving training was more effective in treating adolescent antisocial boys than parent training alone (Kazdin, 1987; Kazdin et al., 1987).

SUMMARY

The need to help families of conduct-disordered children is particularly urgent, for in the absence of treatment, the long-term outlook for conduct-problem children is poor. We have seen that multiple influences, including child genetic or biological factors as well as environmental factors such as parent, school, and family-related factors, contribute to the development and maintenance of child conduct disorders. Effective interventions must address and integrate as many of these individual and social factors as possible. This review of the research indicates that many creative interventions have been developed, offering much hope for effective treatment of families with conduct-disordered children. Such programs also hold promise as prevention programs which could be offered early with high-risk populations, before the disorder develops in the first place.

We have also noted that the preschool age is a particularly favorable time to first intervene with the family to facilitate children's social competence and to improve parenting skills. If the problems persist, it will be useful to involve schools, teachers, and peer group and to include help with personal issues. For example, in the case examples outlined at the beginning of this chapter, it will be necessary for the parents of Eric to have help with their depression and alcoholism as well as with their parenting skills. Clearly the teachers who are about to expel this child also need to be part of the team, joining the parent and therapist in designing an appropriate intervention. Melinda's mother will need help adjusting to her divorce and some strategy for alleviating financial difficulties as well as reducing her social isolation from other families. She too will need a coordinated plan of action involving the school. Thus, effective intervention programs need to encompass various levels of the microsystems and ecosystems—family, community, school, peer, and child.

Moreover, the importance of developing programs designed to identify oppositional and conduct-problem children in their early preschool years cannot be overemphasized. Eric's and Melinda's problems began in infancy, and these families should have been offered support long before

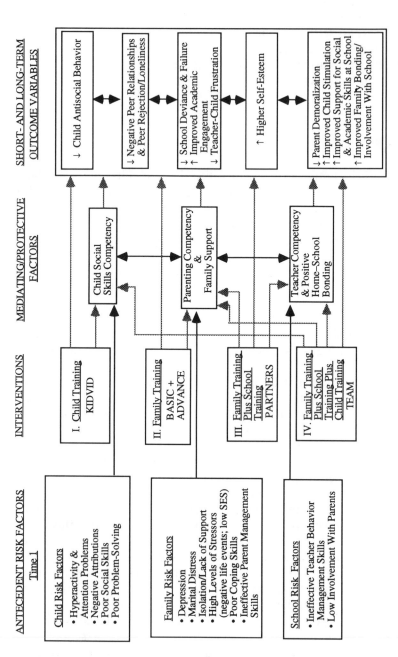

Figure 1.2 Theoretical model embedded in interventions. Dotted lines represent hypothesized intervention effects. Interventions I–IV indicate additive levels of interventions increasing the number of risk factors targeted. Level I is child training designed to promote child social competence; level II is family training designed to enhance family support as well as effective parent management strategies; level III adds a school component for teachers and parents to family training; level IV adds child social skills to family training and the school component. (Reproduced with permission from Webster-Stratton, 1992b)

their child was faced with expulsion from school. Finally, program design must also consider that conduct disorder is a chronic problem transmitted across generations. Therefore, successful intervention necessitates periodic training and support offered at critical stages throughout the child's and family's development, and within a variety of contexts.

REFERENCES

American Psychiatric Association (1993). *Diagnostic and statistical manual of mental disorders* (4th edn. Draft Criteria). Washington, DC: American Psychiatric Association.

Arnold, J.E., Levine, A.G. & Patterson, G.R. (1975). Changes in sibling behavior following family intervention. *Journal of Consulting and Clinical Psychology*, **43**, 683–688.

Asarnow, J. & Callan, J. (1985). Boys with peer adjustment problems: Social cognitive processes. *Journal of Consulting and Clinical Psychology*, **53**, 80–87.

Asher, S.R. & Coie, J.D. (1990). *Peer rejection in childhood*. Cambridge: Cambridge University Press.

Asher, S.R. & Renshaw, P.D. (1981). Children without friends: Social knowledge and social skill training. In S.R. Asher & J.M. Gottman (Eds.), *The development of children's friendships* (pp. 273–296). New York: Cambridge University Press.

Bandura, A. (1977). *Social learning theory*. Englewood Cliffs, NJ: Prentice-Hall.

Bates, J. (1990). Conceptual and empirical linkages between temperament and behavior problems: A commentary on the Sanson, Prior, and Kyrios study. *Merrill-Palmer Quarterly*, **36**(2), 193–199.

Bates, J.E., Bayles, K., Bennett, D.S., Ridge, B. & Brown, M.M. (1991). Origins of externalyzing behavior problems at eight years of age. In D.J. Pepler & K.H. Rubin (Eds.), *The development and treatment of childhood aggression* (pp. 93–120). Hillsdale, NJ: Erlbaum.

Baumrind, D. (1971). Current patterns of adult authority. *Developmental Psychology Monograph*, **4**, (1, Pt.2).

Beck, S.J. & Forehand, R. (1984). Social skills for children: A methodical and clinical review of behavior modification studies. *Behavioral Psychotherapy*, **12**, 17–45.

Bierman, K.L. (1989). Improving the peer relationships of rejected children. In B.B. Lahey & A.E. Kazdin (Eds.), *Advances in clinical child psychology*, **12**. New York: Plenum.

Bierman, K.L. & Furman, W. (1984). The effect of social skills training and peer involvement on the social adjustment of preadolescents. *Child Development*, **55**, 151–162.

Bierman, K.L., Miller, C.M. & Stabb, S. (1987). Improving the social behavior and peer acceptance of rejected boys: Effects of social skill training with instructions and prohibitions. *Journal of Consulting and Clinical Psychology*, **55**, 194–200.

Breiner, J. & Forehand, R. (1982). Mother–child interactions: A comparison of a clinic-referred developmentally delayed group and two non-delayed groups. *Applied Research in Mental Retardation*, **3**, 175–183.

Bronfenbrenner, U. (1979). *The Ecology of Human Development*. Cambridge, MA: Harvard University Press.

Bry, B. & George, F. (1980). The preventive effects of early intervention on the attendance and grades of urban adolescents. *Professional Psychology*, **11**, 252–260.

Cadoret, R. & Cain, C. (1981). Environmental and genetic factors in predicting adolescent antisocial behavior. *The Journal of the University of Ottawa*, **6**, 220–225.

Camp, B.W. & Bash, M.A.S. (1985). *Think aloud: Increasing social and cognitive skills – A problem-solving program for children in the classroom.* Champaign, IL: Research Press.

Campbell, S.B. & Ewing, L.J. (1990). Follow-up of hard-to-manage preschoolers: adjustment at age 9 and predictors of continuing symptoms. *Journal of Child Psychology and Psychiatry*, **31**, 871–889.

Coie, J. D. (1990a). Adapting interention to the problems of aggressive and disruptive rejected children. In S.R. Asher & J.D. Coie (Eds.), *Peer rejection in childhood* (pp. 309–337). Cambridge: Cambridge University Press.

Coie, J.D. (1990b). Toward a theory of peer rejection. In S.R. Asher & J.D. Coie (Eds.), *Peer rejection in childhood* (pp. 365–398). Cambridge: Cambridge University Press.

Coie, J.D. & Krehbiel, G. (1984). Effects of academic tutoring on the social status of low-achieving, socially rejected children. *Child Development*, **55**, 1465–1478.

Coie, J.D. & Kupersmidt, J.B. (1983). A behavioral analysis of emerging social status in boys' groups. *Child Development*, **54**, 1400–1416.

Coie, J.D., Lochman, J.E., Terry, R. & Hyman, C. (in press). Predicting early adolescent disorder from childhood agression and peer rejection. *Journal of Consulting and Clinical Psychology*.

Connolly, J.A. & Doyle, A.B. (1984). Relation of social fantasy play to social competence in preschoolers. *Developmental Psychology*, **20**, 797–806.

Cross Calvert, S. & McMahon, R.J. (1987). The treatment acceptability of a behavioral parent training program and its components. *Behavior Therapy*, **18**, 165–179.

Dadds, M.R. & McHugh, T.A. (1992). Social support and treatment outcome in behavioral family therapy for child conduct problems. *Journal of Consulting and Clinical Psychology*, **60**, 252–259.

Dadds, M.R. Schwartz, S. & Sanders, M.R. (1987). Marital discord and child behavior problems; a description of family interactions during treatment. *Journal of Clinical Child Psychology*, 16, 192–203.

Davidson, W. & Basta, J. (1988). Diversion from the juvenile justice system: Research evidence and a discussion of issues. In B. B. Lahey & A. E. Kazdin (Eds.), *Advances in clinical child psychology*, **12**. New York: Plenum.

Dodge, K.A. (1983). Behavioral antecedants of peer social status. *Child Development*, **54**, 1386–1389.

Dodge, K.A. & Newman, J.P. (1981). Biased decision-making processes in aggressive boys. *Journal of Abnormal Psychology*, **90**, 375–379.

Dodge, K.A. & Somberg, D.R. (1987). Hostile attributional biases are exacerbated under conditions of threat to the self. *Child Development*, **58**, 213–244.

Dodge, K.A., Pettit, G.S., McClaskey, C.L. & Brown, M.M. (1986). Social competence in children. *Monographs of the Society for Research in Child Development*, **51** (2, Serial No. 213).

Dumas, J. E. (1984). Interactional correlates of treatment outcome in behavioral parent training. *Journal of Consulting and Clinical Psychology*, **52**, 946–954.

D'Zurilla, T. & Nezu, A. (1982). Social problem-solving in adults. In P.C. Kendall (Ed.), *Advances in cognitive behavioral research and therapy*, **1**. New York: Academic Press.

Felner, R. & Adan, A. (1988). The school transitional environmental project: An ecological intervention and evaluation. In R.H. Price, E.L. Cowen, R.P. Lorion & J. Ramos-McKay (Eds.), *14 ounces of prevention: A casebook for practitioners* (pp. 111–122). Washington, DC: American Psychological Association.

Feshbach, N. (1989). The construct of empathy and the phenomenon of physical maltreatment of children. In D. Cicchetti & V. Carlson (Eds.), *Child maltreatment: Theory and research on the causes and consequences of child abuse and neglect*, (pp. 349–373). Cambridge, MA: Cambridge University Press.

Fo, W. & O'Donnell, C. (1975). The buddy system: Effect of community intervention on delinquent offenses. *Behavior Therapy*, **6**, 522–524.

Forehand, R.L., Furey, W.M. & McMahon, R.J. (1984). The role of maternal distress in a parent training program to modify child noncompliance. *Behavioral Psychotherapy*, **12**, 93–108.

Forehand, R., Lautenschlager, G.J., Faust, J. & Graziano, W.G. (1986). Parent perceptions and parent–child interactions in clinic-referred children: A preliminary investigation of the effects of maternal depressive moods. *Behavior Research and Therapy*, **24**, 73–75.

Forehand, R. & McMahon, R. (1981). *Helping the noncompliant child: A clinicians' guide to parent training.* New York: Guilford.

Forehand, R., Sturgis, E.T., McMahon, R.J., Aguar, D., Green, K., Wells, K. & Breiner, J. (1979). Parent behavioral training to modify child noncompliance: Treatment generalization across time and from home to school. *Behavior Modification*, **3**, 3–25.

Forgatch, M. (1989). Patterns and outcome in family problem-solving: The disrupting effect of negative emotions. *Journal of Marriage and the Family*, **51**, 115–124.

Forgatch, M., Patterson, G. & Skinner, M. (1988). A mediational model for the effect of divorce in antisocial behavior in boys. In E.M. Hetherington & J.D. Arasteh (Eds.), *Impact of divorce, single parenting, and step-parenting on children*, (pp. 135–154). Hillsdale, NJ: Lawrence Erlbaum.

Frick, P., Lahey, B., Hartdagen S. & Hynd, G. (1989). Conduct problem in boys: Relations to maternal personality, marital satisfaction, and socioeconomic status. *Journal of Clinical Child Psychology*, **18**, 114–120.

Frick, P.J., Lahey, B.B. Kamphaus, R.W., Loeber, R., Christ, M.G., Hart, E.L. & Tannenbaum, L.E. (1991). Academic underachievement and the disruptive behavior disorders. *Journal of Consulting and Clinical Psychology*, **59**, 259–294.

Gorensten, E.E. & Newman, J.P. (1980). Disinhibitory psychopathology: A new perspective and model for research. *Psychological Review*, **87**, 301–315.

Goutz, K. (1981). Children's initial aggression level and the effectiveness of intervention strategies in moderating television effects on aggression. Cited in Goutz, K.R. (1987). Attention and social problem-solving as correlates of aggression in preschool males. *Journal of Abnormal Psychology*, **15**, 181–197.

Gresham, F.M. & Nagle, R.J. (1980). Social skill training with children: Responsiveness to modeling and coaching as a function of peer orientation. *Journal of Consulting and Clinical Psychology*, **84**, 718–729.

Hanf, E. & Kling, J. (1973). *Facilitating parent–child interactions: A two-stage training model.* Unpublished manuscript, University of Oregon Medical School Eugene OR.

Hawkins, J. & Lam T. (1987). Teacher practices, social development and delinquency. In J.D. Burchard & S.N. Burchard (Eds.), *Prevention of delinquent behavior*, (pp. 241–274). Newbury Park, CA: Sage.

Hawkins, J. & Weiss, J. (1985). The social development model: An integrated approach to delinquency prevention. *Journal of Primary Prevention*, **6**, 73–97.

Hobbs, N. (1982). *The troubled and the troubling child*. San Francisco, CA: Jossey-Bass.

Jouriles, E., Murphy, C. & O'Leary, K. (1989). Interspousal aggression, marital discord, and child problems. *Journal of Consulting and Clinical Psychology*, **57**, 453–455.

Kazdin, A. (1986). *Treatment of antisocial behavior in children and adolescents*. Homewood, IL: Dorsey.

Kazdin, A. (1987). Treatment of antisocial behavior in children: Current status and future directions. *Psychological Bulletin*, **102**, 187–203.

Kazdin, A. (1990). *Prevention of conduct disorder*. Paper presented at the National Conference on Prevention Research, NIMH, Bethesda, MD, June 1990.

Kazdin, A., Esveldt-Dawson, K., French, N. & Unis, A. (1987). Effects of parent management training and problem-solving skills training combined in the treatment of antisocial child behavior. *Journal of the American Academy of Child and Adolescent Psychiatry*, **25**, 416–424.

Kendall, P. & Braswell, L. (1985). *Cognitive-behavioral therapy for impulsive children*. New York: Guilford.

Ladd, G.W. (1981). Effectiveness of a social learning method for enhancing children's social interaction and peer acceptance. *Child Development*, **52**, 171–178.

Ladd, G.W. (1990). Having friends, keeping friends, making friends, and being liked by peers in the classroom: predictors of children's early school adjustment. *Child Development*, **61**, 1081–1100.

Ladd, G.W. & Asher, S. R. (1985). Social skill training and children's peer relations: Current issues in research and practice. In L. L'Abate & M. Milan (Eds.), *Handbook of social skill training* (pp. 219–244). New York: Wiley.

LaGreca, A. & Santogrossi, D. (1980). Social skills training with elementary school students: A behavioral group approach. *Journal of Consulting and Clinical Psychology*, **48**, 220–227.

Lahey, B.B., Loeber, R., Quay, H.C., Frick, P.J. & Grimm, J. (1992). Oppositional defiant and conduct disorders: Issues to be resolved for DSM-IV. *Journal of Academy of Child Psychiatry*, **31**(3), 539–546

Lochman, J.E., Burch, P.R., Curry, J.F. & Lampron, L.B. (1984). Treatment and generalization effects of cognitive-behavioral and goal-setting interventions with aggressive boys. *Journal of Consulting and Clinical Psychology*, **52**, 915–916.

Lochman, J.E., Nelson, W.M. & Sims, J.P. (1981). A cognitive behavioral program for use with aggressive children. *Journal of Clinical Child Psychology*, **10**, 146–148.

Lochman, J., Lampron, L., Gemmer, T. & Harris, S. (1987). Anger coping intervention with aggressive children: A guide to implementation in school settings. In P.A. Keller & S.R. Heyman, (Eds.), *Innovations in clinical practice: A source book*, **6**, (pp. 339–356). Sarasota, FL: Professional Resource Exchange.

Loeber, R. (1985). Patterns and development of antisocial and delinquent child behavior: A review. *Child Development*, **53**, 1431–1446.

Loeber, R. (1990). Development and risk factors of juvenile antisocial behavior and delinquency. *Clinical Psychology Review*, **10**, 1–41.

Loeber, R. (1991). Antisocial behavior: More enduring than changeable? *Journal of the American Academy of Child and Adolescent Psychiatry*, **30**, 393–397.

Maziade, M., Cote, R., Bernier, H., Boutin, P. & Thivierge, J. (1989). Significance of extreme temperament in infancy for clinical status in pre-school years I. *British Journal of Psychiatry*, **14**, 535–543.

McMahon, R. & Forehand, R. (1984). Parent training for the noncompliant child: Treatment outcome, generalization, and adjunctive therapy procedures. In R.F.

Dangel & R.A. Polster (Eds.), *Parent training: Foundations of research and practice*, (pp. 298–328). New York: Guilford.

McMahon, R. & Forehand, R. (1988). Conduct disorders. In E.J. Mash & L.G. Terdal (Eds.), *Behavioral assessment of childhood disorders*. New York: Guilford.

Milich, R. & Dodge, K. (1984). Social information processing in child psychiatric populations. *Journal of Abnormal Child Psychology*, **9**, 127–140.

Minken, N., Braukmann, C.J., Minken, B.L., Timbers, G.D., Fixsen, D.L., Phillips, E.L. & Wolf, M.M. (1976). The social validation and training of conversation skills. *Journal of Applied Behavior Analysis*, **9**, 127–140.

Mize, J. & Ladd, G.W. (1990). Toward the development of successful social skills training for preschool children. In S.R. Asher & J.D. Coie (Eds.), *Peer rejection in childhood* (pp. 338–361). Cambridge: Cambridge University Press.

Oden, S. & Asher, S.R. (1977). Coaching children in social skills for friendship making. *Child Development*, **48**, 495–506.

O'Donnell, C., Lygate, T. & Fo, W. (1979). The buddy system: Review and follow-up. *Child Behavior Therapy*, **1**, 161–169.

Offord, D. & Jones, M. (1983). Skill development: A community intervention program for the prevention of antisocial behavior. In S. B. Guze, F. J. Earls & J.E. Barrett (Eds.), *Childhood psychopathology and development*, (pp. 165–188). New York: Raven.

O'Leary, K.D. & Emery, R.E. (1982). Marital discord and child behavior problems. In M.D. Levine & P. Satz (Eds.), *Middle childhood: Developmental variation and dysfunction* (pp. 345–364). New York: Academic Press.

Patterson, G. (1975). *Families: Applications of social learning to family life*. Champaign, IL: Research Press.

Patterson, G. (1982). *Coercive family process*. Eugene, OR: Castalia.

Patterson, G. R., Chamberlain, P. & Reid, J.B. (1982). A comparative evaluation of a parent training program. *Behavior Therapy*, **13**, 638–650.

Patterson, G.R., DeBaryshe, B.D. & Ramsey, E. (1989). A developmental perspective on antisocial behavior. *American Psychologist*, **44**, 329–335.

Patterson, G.R. & Stouthamer-Loeber, M. (1984). The correlation of family management practices and delinquency. *Child Development*, **55**, 129–307.

Peed, S., Roberts, M. & Forehand, R. (1977). Evaluations of the effectiveness of a standardized parent training program in altering the interaction of mothers and their noncompliant children. *Behavior Modification*, **1**, 323–350.

Quay, H. (1986). Classification. In H.C. Quay & J.S. Werry (Eds.), *Psychopathological disorders of childhood*, 3rd edn. New York: Wiley.

Raine, A. & Venables, P. (1984). Tonic heart rate level, social class and antisocial class and antisocial behavior in adolescents. *Biological Psychology*, **18**, 123–132.

Richard, B.A. & Dodge, K.A. (1982). Social maladjustment and problem solving in school-aged children. *Journal of Consulting and Clinical Psychology*, **50**, 226–233.

Richman, N., Stevenson, L. & Graham, P.J. (1982). *Pre-school to school: A behavioural study*. London: Academic Press.

Rickard, K.M., Forehand, R., Wells, K.C., Griest, D.L. & McMahon, R.J. (1981). Factors in the referral of children for behavioral treatment: a comparison of mothers of clinic-referred deviant, clinic-referred non-deviant and non-clinic children. *Behavior Research and Therapy*, **19**, 201–205.

Robins, L. (1981). Epidemiological approaches to natural history research: Antisocial disorders in children. *Journal of Consulting and Clinical Psychology*, **50**, 226–233.

Robins, L.N., Tipp, J. & Przybeck, T. (1991) Antisocial personality. In L.N. Robins & D.A. Reegier (Eds), *Psychiatric disorders in America* (pp. 258–290). New York: The Free Press.

Rose, S.L., Rose, S.A. & Feldman, J. (1989). Stability of behavior problems in very young children. *Development and Psychopathology*, **1**, 5–20.

Rubin, K.H. & Krasnor, L.R. (1983). Social-cognitive and social behavioral perspectives on problem-solving. In M. Perlmuller (Ed.), *Minnesota symposia on child psychology* (Vol. 18). Hillsdale, NJ: Lawrence Erlbaum.

Rutter, M. (1985). Resilience in the face of adversity: Protective factors and resistance to psychiatric disorder. *British Journal of Psychiatry*, **147**, 598–611.

Rutter, M. & Giller, H. (1983). *Juvenile delinquency: Trends and perspectives.* Harmondsworth, Penguin.

Rutter, M., Tizard, J., Yule, W., Graham, P. & Whitmore, K. (1976). Research report: Isle of Wight studies. *Psychological Medicine*, **6**, 313–332.

Safer, D. & Allen R., (1976). *Hyperactive children: Diagnosis and management.* Baltimore, MD: University Park Press.

Schmaling, K.B. & Jacobson, N.S. (1987). *The clinical significance of treatment gains resulting from parent training interventions for children with conduct problems: An analysis of outcome data.* Paper presented at the meeting of the Association for the Advancement of Behavior Therapy. Boston, MA, 1987 (November).

Schmidt, K., Solanto, M. & Bridger, W. (1985). Electrodermal activity of under-socialized aggressive children: A pilot study. *Journal of Child Psychology and Psychiatry*, **26**, 653–660.

Schonfeld, I.S., Shaffer, D., O'Connor, P. & Portnoy, S. (1988). Conduct disorder and cognitive functioning: Testing three causal hypotheses. *Child Development*, **59**, 993–1007.

Schweinhart, L. & Weikart, D. (1988). The High/Scope Perry Preschool Program. In R.H. Price, E.L. Cowen, R.P. Lorion & J. Ramos-McKay (Eds.), *14 ounces of prevention: A casebook for practitioners*, (pp. 53–66). Washington, DC: American Psychological Association.

Shure, M.B. & Spivack, G. (1982). Interpersonal problem-solving in young children: a cognitive approach to prevention. *American Journal of Community Psychology*, **10**, 341–356.

Singer, D.G. (1982). Television and the developing imagination of the child. In D. Pearl, L. Bauthelet & J. Lazar (Eds.), *Television and behavior: Ten years of scientific progress and implications for the eighty's.* Washington, DC: US Government Printing Office.

Singer, J.L. & Singer, D. G. (1983). Implications of childhood television viewing for cognition, imagination, and emotion. In J. Bryant & D. R. Anderson (Eds.), *Children's understanding of television* (pp. 265–298). New York: Academic Press.

Slaby, R. & Guerra, N. (1988). Cognitive mediators of aggression in adolescent offenders: 1. Assessment. *Development Psychology*, **24**, 580–588.

Spence, S.H. (1983). Teaching social skills to children. *Journal of Child Psychology and Psychiatry*, **24**(4), 621–627.

Spivack, G., Platt, J. & Shure, M. (1976). *The problem-solving approach to adjustment.* San Francisco, CA: Jossey-Bass.

Spivack, G. & Shure, M.B. (1974). *Social adjustment of young children: A cognitive approach to solving real-life problems.* San Francisco, CA: Jossey-Bass.

Stonemen, Z., Brody, G. & Burke, M. (1988). Marital quality, depression, and inconsistent parenting: Relationship with observed mother–child conflict. *American Journal of Orthopsychiatry*, **59**, 105–117.

Sturge, C. (1982). Reading retardation and antisocial behavior. *Journal of Child Psychology and Psychiatry*, **23**, 21–31.

Thomas, A. & Chess, S. (1977). *Temperament and development*. New York: Brunner/Mazel.

Wahler, R. & Dumas, J. (1984). Changing the observational coding styles of insular and noninsular mothers: A step toward maintenance of parent training effects. In R.F. Dangel & R.A. Polster (Eds.), *Parent training: Foundations of research and practice*, (pp. 379–416). New York: Guilford Press.

Wahler, R. & Dumas, J. (1985). Maintenance factors in coercive mother–child interactions: The compliance and predictability hypothesis. *Journal of Applied Behavioral Analyses*, **19**(1), 13–22.

Walker, H.M. & Buckley, N.K. (1973). Teacher attention to appropriate and inappropriate classroom behavior: an individual case study. *Focus on Exceptional Children*, **5**, 5–11.

Walker, J.L., Lahey, B.B., Hynd, G.W. & Frame, C.L. (1988). Comparison of specific patterns of antisocial behavior in children with conduct disorder with or without hyperactivity. *Journal of Consulting and Clinical Psychology*, **55**, 910–1013.

Webster-Stratton, C. (1981a). Modification of mothers' behaviors and attitudes through a videotape modeling group discussion program. *Behavior Therapy*, **12**, 634–642.

Webster-Stratton, C. (1981b). Videotape modeling: A method of parent education. *Journal of Clinical Psychology*, **10**(2), 93–98.

Webster-Stratton, C. (1982a). The long term effects of a videotape modeling parent training program: Comparison of immediate and 1-year followup results. *Behavior Therapy*, **13**, 702–714.

Webster-Stratton, C. (1982b). Teaching mothers through videotape modeling to change their children's behaviors. *Journal of Pediatric Psychology*, **7**(3), 279–294.

Webster-Stratton, C. (1984). Randomized trial of two parent-training programs for families with conduct disordered children. *Journal of Consulting and Clinical Psychology*, **52**(4), 666–678.

Webster-Stratton, C. (1985). Comparisons of behavior transactions between conduct disordered children and their mothers in the clinic and at home. *Journal of Abnormal Child Psychology*, **13**(2), 169–184.

Webster-Stratton, C. (1989a). *The Advanced Videotape Parent Training Programs*. Therapist manual and videotapes. Seattle, WA: Seth Enterprises.

Webster-Stratton, C. (1989b). Systematic comparison of consumer satisfaction of three cost-effective parent training programs for conduct problem children. *Behavior Therapy*, **20**, 103–115.

Webster-Stratton, C. (1990a). Long-term follow-up of families with young conduct problem children: From preschool to grade school. *Journal of Clinical Child Psychology*, **19**, 144–149.

Webster-Stratton, C. (1990b). Stress: A potential disrupter of parent perceptions and family interactions. *Journal of Clinical Child Psychology*, **19**(4), 302–312.

Webster-Stratton, C. (1991). *The Dinosaur Videotape Curriculum for Young Children*. Therapist manual and videotapes. Seattle, WA: Seth Enterprises.

Webster-Stratton, C. (1992a). Individually administered videotape parent training: 'Who benefits?' *Cognitive Therapy and Research*, **16**, 31–35.

Webster-Stratton, C. (1992b) Preventing conduct disorder in young children. Unpublished. Grant submitted to NIH.

Webster-Stratton, C. (1993). Strategies for helping early school-aged children with oppositional defiant and conduct disorders: The importance of home–school partnerships. *School Psychology Review*, **22**, 437–457.

Webster-Stratton, C. (in press). Advancing videotape parent training: A comparison study. *Journal of Consulting and Clinical Psychology*.

Webster-Stratton, C. & Hammond, M. (1988). Maternal depression and its relationship to life stress, perceptions of child behavior problems, parenting behaviors, and child conduct problems. Journal of *Abnormal Child Psychology*, **16**(3), 299–315.

Webster-Stratton, C. & Hammond, M. (1990). Predictors of treatment outcome in parent training for families with conduct problem children. *Behavior Therapy*, **21**, 319–337.

Webster-Stratton, C., Kolpacoff, M. & Hollinsworth, T. (1989). The long-term effectiveness and clinical significance of three cost-effective training programs for families with conduct problem children. *Journal of Consulting and Clinical Psychology*, **57**, 550–553.

White, J., Moffit, T., Earls, F. & Robins, L. (1990). Preschool predictors of persistent conduct disorder and delinquency. *Criminology*, **28**, 443–454.

Wicks-Nelson, R. & Israel, A.C. (1991). *Behavior disorders of childhood*. Englewood Cliffs, NJ: Prentice-Hall.

Williams, S., Anderson, J., McGee, R. & Silva, P.A. (1990). Risk factors for behavioral and emotional disorder in preadolescent children. *Journal of the American Academy of Child and Adolescent Psychiatry*, **29**, 413–419.

2

PARENTING A CHILD WITH CONDUCT DISORDERS: "FAMILIES UNDER SIEGE"*

IN RESPONSE to the increasingly large numbers of children with conduct disorders, there has been growing emphasis on understanding the factors which contribute to the development of this problem. Parenting style in particular has received much attention. Yet in spite of the documented association between the more coercive styles of parental discipline and child conduct disorders, the literature contains comparatively little discussion of the impact of the conduct-disordered child on the parents and family system—that is, how the child's problems affect relationships within the family (e.g., relationship between parents, or relationships of parents with other siblings)—and on relationships between the family system and outside systems or agencies (e.g., relationships with grandparents, or relationships with teachers). While there is research to indicate that families of conduct-disordered children experience high rates of major and minor life stressors (e.g., Forgatch, Patterson, & Skinner, 1988; Patterson, 1982; Wahler & Dumas, 1984; Webster-Stratton, 1988,1991), marital stress (e.g., Furey & Forehand, 1985; Schaughency & Lahey, 1985; Webster-Stratton, 1989; Webster-Stratton & Hammond, 1988), and social isolation or lack of social support (Dumas & Wahler, 1985; Wahler & Dumas, 1984; Webster-Stratton, 1985a,b), it is unclear exactly how child conduct disorders contribute to these stresses. We know very little from the parents' point of view of the difficulties they encounter as they try to cope with the child's conduct disorders, as they try to manage the stresses within the family system as well as the accompanying stresses in their relationships with outside individuals and agencies.

This chapter will examine the meaning for parents of the experience of having a child with conduct disorders. We will discuss four major domains of this experience, namely, the child's profile, the impact on the family system, the impact on the family's relationships within the community, and the dynamics of living with a conduct-problem child—the experience

* This paper is derived from an unpublished paper co-authored by Dr. Webster-Stratton and Dr. Ada Spitzer, Dean, A. Yelin School of Nursing, Haifa, Israel. The follow-up qualitative interviews were conducted by Diana Brehm, M.N. at the University of Washington.

of learned helplessness. These dynamics and themes were derived by Webster-Stratton working with Spitzer after analyzing the transcripts and videotapes of over 70 intake interviews with mothers and fathers who participated in the Parenting Clinic programs.

THE CHILD'S PROFILE

In order to understand the meaning of living with a conduct-disordered child, it is crucial to understand first how these children are perceived by their parents. This perspective is critical, for it is parents' understanding of their child and the meaning they ascribe to his/her behavior that shape their reactions to the child in general and to his/her conduct problems in particular.

Child as Tyrant

When asked to name the dominant characteristic of their child's mis-behavior, these parents specified aggression. While the child's aggression would take various forms and be directed toward various targets, the overall impression conveyed by parents was one of the child being a tyrant in the family.

Aggression against parents

Parents reported that often when their child was angry, s/he would act aggressively towards them, sometimes to the extent of physical abuse. They reported feeling victimized and tyrannized. They often spoke to us about feeling deeply insecure when around their children as a consequence of this abuse. They described having to be "on guard" in case the child should unexpectedly hit them. It is worth noting that such feelings were more commonly expressed by mothers than fathers.

MOTHER: I don't know if you have suffered the physical abuses—I have. Just a few weeks ago, he threw his booster seat in my face and hit my jaw. And he thought it was funny! ... He was acting up, and I think he had already had one Time Out for yelling and screaming and interrupting us at the table. And I said, "Fine, you are going upstairs now. You are not having dessert." And he just flew into a rage. He picked up a metal fork and threw it with all his force, and hit me—barely missed my eyes. There was blood on my forehead. I was screaming, I was hysterical. And I was terrified, I mean, to see that type of behavior, that type of rage.

In addition to the physical aggression, parents typically described being the targets of frequent verbal and emotional aggression from their children.

MOTHER: She tells me she is going to run away from home and that she wants to leave. She told her father she wished he was dead so that way he won't wake up.
. . .

FATHER: One of the things that really bothers me is that she says, "I hate you. Why don't you move out?"

Aggression against siblings

Children with conduct disorders were described by their parents as both verbally and physically aggressive toward siblings and other family members (e.g., cousins). Parents reported being afraid of the possible results of this aggression; they felt that they had to be always on guard to ensure the other children's emotional and physical safety.

MOTHER: He is so violent with his sister. He split her lip a couple of times. And he almost knocked her out once when he hit her over the head with a five-pound brass pitcher. He's put plastic bags over her head. Even things that you wouldn't think could be dangerous, you have to make sure and keep out of his reach.

They were also concerned that younger children would develop similar aggressive problems by watching their older sibling's inappropriate behaviors. Furthermore, parents reported that other children in the family would refuse to play with the aggressive child or would retaliate by "setting the child up" for punishment and disapproval from parents.

Aggression against animals

Parents reported that their children abused their pets and intentionally harmed them, with no evidence of remorse or regret.

MOTHER: He is just real violent with animals. And I have repetitively taught him how to stroke animals nicely. He can't help himself. I caught him holding the cat in the toilet with the lid shut.

Aggression against other children

Parents reported that their children's aggression extended to other children in daycare settings, home activities with friends, and strangers in public places.

MOTHER: He is aggressive around other children. We can't really trust him not to walk up and wallop the smaller ones. He pokes them in the eyes or pushes them down ... I understand a lot of children go through this thing with aggression—but again, it seems so exaggerated, it's almost like he seeks out other children to hurt them. If you take him to the zoo, here we are in a situation where we could be having fun, talking about animals, walking, ... and he's seeking out little children in strollers and picking up handfuls of sand and throwing it in their faces.

Sometimes this aggression towards other children was of an aggressively sexual nature: pulling down other children's underwear, touching children in their genital areas, using sexually provocative language, and so on.

Such repeated episodes of verbal and physical aggression towards other children led to their children being disliked, rejected, and ridiculed by other children. Moreover, other parents did not want their children to associate with the aggressive child. Consequently, these misbehaving children were rarely invited to birthday parties or for after-school play times with other children. Frequently parents reported that their child had no friends. This feedback from teachers and other parents was an important indicator for parents that their children were not like other children. It was also a key element in the tension between parents of conduct-disordered children and parents of other "normal" children, contributing to their own feelings of rejection and isolation.

Dismantling the house

Frequently parents recounted incidents in which their children had been destructive to the house or household objects.

MOTHER: I have really tried to value the children more than I value the house, but it's been incredibly painful to watch our brand new house—brand spanking new—be destroyed. And we've told ourselves, it's all fixable, but he has caused an incredible amount of destruction which has been painful to watch. When you work and personally invest yourself in your home, when other people don't respect it or take care of it, it's painful.

In summary, parents uniformly portrayed their conduct-disordered child's behavior in terms of verbal and physical aggression towards parents, siblings, animals, and other children. This dominant quality of their children's behavior has a major impact on their children's relationships, not only with family members but also with other children in the community.

Child's Noncompliance and Defiance

Another dominant characteristic of children with conduct disorders, as described by their parents, was their noncompliance and defiance. Parents reported that their children's refusal to comply to parental requests controlled not only the parents but the entire family by virtue of the power they commanded through their resistance.

FATHER: He's the most stubborn child or person I have ever met, because he won't stop. His power is that he won't stop. He usually ends up crying and he gets like a mule—he kind of digs his heels in, and doesn't want to do it.

MOTHER: He just digs his heels in, "That's it, I am not wearing these socks! Forget it, I'm not going!" And he is right. He's gone to school in his pajamas, without lunch, in the pouring rain without any coat. "I've made up my mind, Mom, that's it!" and he'll say to me, "Mom, we are done." He will explain to me, "Mom, we are done with this discussion" . . . He doesn't have an easy-going bone in his body. He is not ever going to say, "Okay, I'll put that turtleneck on." It's going to be, "I will do something but only on my terms . . . I will do nothing that you want me to do and furthermore I'll throw such a tantrum and throw this cereal bowl all over the wall, so you will be late, and mad at me when you clean it up . . ." He enjoys that power.

Parents described vividly the arguments that they would get into with their children, which usually ended up in screaming fights. Faced with these continually defiant reactions, the parents had to expend an immense amount of energy to get the child to comply. As a result, it was typical for parents to feel progressively more tired.

Developmental Problems

Aside from the unique characteristics ascribed by parents to children with conduct disorders, these children were also reported to have various developmental problems that are common among children between three and eight years of age. The intensity of these problems, coupled with the predominant conduct disorder characteristics, made it more difficult for parents to handle these normal developmental problems.

MOTHER: I notice he's going through the potty language stage. And I'm hoping it's just a stage—and believe me, every negative stage that a child may or may not go through, he's gone through.

The developmental problems most often described by these parents were related to sleeping, eating, transitions, fears, and hyperactivity.

Sleep problems

Parents often reported that their children did not need a lot of sleep and that getting them into bed at night was therefore a major battle.

MOTHER: One day we tried just to wait him out. At 6:00 I said, "We've got to go to bed." Six a.m.! We waited all night and he never did go to sleep.

In addition to a limited need for sleep at night, parents described how their children would become noncompliant and defiant when the parent tried to get them to bed at a certain time.

FATHER: You have to follow them every step of the way to get them to go to bed. And then, once they are in bed, they're either turning on the light and getting up and playing with their toys, or else sneaking around the house. They won't stay put. I found the only thing that I can do to really control that is: I take a chair down at the end of the hall, park it in front of their door, and sit and read a book. Then they'll settle down and go to sleep.

Eating problems

Eating problems were mainly the result of an inability to sit in the same place for a long period of time due to the conduct-disordered child's high activity level. Parents described their children's lack of concentration and lack of interest in eating.

FATHER: A meal at our house is like a circus. It's like two rats out of a sack. One goes one way and one goes the other. He'll run around the table. He'll take a bite of food, he'll sit down half on the chair, take another bite of food and then run off and chew it and run around.

They also described resorting to various extreme measures in order to achieve some semblance of family mealtimes.

MOTHER: He is so hyperactive at meals that even at age four we keep him in a high chair to get him to eat. We joke about how we have to break his legs to get him in the high chair. We are just so determined to have a family meal where he is not running around and causing havoc.

Transition difficulties and poor adaptability

Although transitions are difficult for many children between the ages of three to eight years, for these conduct-disordered children almost any change in routine was reported by the parents to result in defiant behavior. At the root of this is the child's inability to adapt. Most often parents would say that if their child were offered any new activity, the child would respond by saying, "No, I don't want to."

MOTHER: Transitions are really hard for him. We try to give him warning like, bedtime is in ten minutes. And then sometimes you get a temper tantrum getting his teeth brushed. Because even though he's had warnings, it hasn't assimilated that we mean, you are going to bed, we're going to turn the light off. He thinks he can still play.

Fears and suicide talk

In contrast to a commonly accepted belief that externalizing, rather than internalizing, behaviors typify the population of conduct-disordered children, interviews with parents indicated that these children also exhibited many internalizing problems such as fears and suicidal thoughts.

FATHER: He has night fears. It's been awful. It started about a year ago but it got really bad about four months ago. The toys started moving their heads, and the stuffed animals . . . and then I had this long conversation with him in the bathtub the other day and he is scared of thunder and lightning and it comes every night. He thinks that the thunder and lightning can throw bowling balls down from the roof and they can come and get him . . . it took about 20 minutes to get through that conversation. He has anxiety in his room—he lies awake for hours. We give him flashlights—sometimes he'll be awake at 2 or 3 in the morning from anxieties.

FATHER: He often talks about wanting to die and how he wants to kill himself. Like the other day he was angry because he got pulled out of swim lessons for not keeping his hands to himself and he said, "It's so terrible, I should just die."

Hyperactivity, distractability, high intensity

Many of the parents talked about their children's high-intensity temperaments. They described their children as highly active, easily "wound up,"
overexcited, loud, and wild and out-of-control since birth. Moreover, they
felt their children had trouble listening and concentrating even for brief
periods of time. When they make requests of their children, they say their
children often "tune them out" or get so distracted by their surroundings
that they forget what the parents requested. They typically complained
that their children could not sit still to play with Lego or puzzles and
constantly demanded attention—so that the parent never got a break or
quiet moment during the day. For these parents, their children's activity
level is so high as to make their safety and survival a major parenting issue.

MOTHER: From 15 months he started running and destroying everything in sight
and has not stopped since then. Keeping him alive became paramount. Once he
crawled out of his car seat and over the seat when I was doing 50 miles an hour
and he hit the door and it flew open. He was so reckless that I could not shower
unless he was in his crib asleep. I could not have him out of my sight for a minute.
Life with him was a nightmare. One time I put him in his room for a nap, and
turned on the shower. And I heard this frantic banging on my door, and it was
my neighbor telling me that his second floor window was open—he had thrown
a book on the roof and was going to get it. And so from 15 months to three, it
was this incredible desire to keep him alive. We couldn't afford one mistake.

FATHER: He's mentally fine, but his emotions are twisted in some ways—he doesn't
seem to have the normalities that a lot of kids have. I look at my nieces and
nephews and, while they have their moments, most of the time they can listen and
talk. But with Keith he goes off into outer space and won't come back—he's not
even on this planet! He's crazy, running around the house screaming, jumping on
the bed, and goes into a fit of hyperactivity trying to accumulate as many things
wrong as possible in that time. To get him under control we have to restrain him
until he's so worn out, he's exhausted.

Difficulty learning from experience and/or parental instructions

Many parents expressed concern about their child's inability to learn
from experience. Too often they had seen their child suffer the negative
consequences of a particular action, yet repeat the same self-defeating
behaviors on other occasions. Similarly, they would describe their efforts
to explain and help the child understand a problem, only to be met with

either a blank expression or a deliberately defiant continuation of the troublesome behavior. This led parents to worry about their child's future.

FATHER: I am concerned because he is so experimental. If you tell him (or explain to him) not to do something, that guarantees he will try it at least one more time. He's so impulsive he doesn't think out the consequences of what he does. He has a kind of destructive curiosity which will get him into big trouble if he is still doing that as a teenager.

MOTHER: I'm concerned because he makes a mistake and we talk about it, but there is no carryover to the next situation. He still makes the same mistake. Then when I try to talk about it with him, he has this blank face with rolling eyes and I get scared that a kid this young is tuning me out.

Child's Positive Qualities

Along with reporting the negative aspects of their children's behaviors, most parents made a conscious effort to talk about the positive aspects of their children's personalities. Parents often portrayed their children as particularly sensitive and reactive to others' moods. Many also described their children as having unique cognitive abilities and being more developmentally advanced than other children in their age group.

FATHER: She amazes me—the intelligence she has. The things she says, and thinks, and the rationale that she uses are junior high. She has an incredible memory.

While the children's sensitivity and intelligence were seen as positive characteristics by the parents, they also represented another challenge in terms of parenting. For example, parents were reluctant to talk openly in the family about problems or about sensitive issues for fear of the children's emotional response.

MOTHER: He doesn't like to see anybody upset. It really bothers him. He just becomes very emotional. Say if I'm upset, he really catches on to it. Or if my husband and I are having a disagreement, he'll immediately start hollering at my husband to side with me, to get him to stop screaming.

As a result, many parents had become acutely conscious of how they presented ideas or concerns, in order to minimize any adverse reactions.

Child as "Jekyll and Hyde"

The personality profile of the conduct-disordered child that emerged from parents' perceptions was a mixture of negative and positive characteristics, with the negative predominating. The child was experienced by his/her parents as a "Jekyll and Hyde"—at times highly tyrannical, destructive, and defiant, and at other times loving, intelligent, understanding, and sensitive to parents' emotions.

FATHER: He has three personalities—I'd give the hyper episodes a couple of times a week, the disobedience about 60–70% of the time and the part where you can actually talk to him about 20% of the time, and I don't know about the rest.

MOTHER: He is like a "Jekyll and Hyde." Sometimes he can be sweet, charming, loving, easy to get along with, he's a very good-natured child. But then there's the other side of him which emerges—an angry, hostile, aggressive, hurting child, who will do violent things to try to get his way. He is rough with animals and mean with little children, and he is very noncompliant. By the time he is ready to be loving again, you are fed up.

FATHER: We have these stressful times where he is very defiant and argumentative, we all lose our temper and perhaps he finally gets a swat. Then there is this emotional breakdown followed by big make-up sessions where he tells us he loves us. It is an emotional roller coaster.

As mentioned earlier, it was somewhat surprising to find that children with conduct disorders demonstrated not only externalizing problems, but also internalizing problems. Almost without exception, parents reported their children had frequent internalizing problems such as nighttime fears, somatic complaints (e.g., headaches and stomachaches), depression, anxieties, low self-esteem, shyness, and withdrawal or avoidance behaviors. At this young age, according to parents, it did not appear that children were "pure" externalizers but rather exhibited high rates of both types of problems.

It was the unpredictability of these negative behaviors—"the Jekyll and Hyde" phenomenon—and their escalating nature, that seemed to cause parents so much stress. They always had to be on their guard. Behavior problems might arise any time, any place.

IMPACT ON THE FAMILY SYSTEM: "THE RIPPLE EFFECT"

In summary, it is evident from these descriptions that conduct-disordered children are not only nonreinforcing to their parents' efforts but actually physically and emotionally punishing. Parents' feelings of victimization were coupled with feelings of unpredictability and lack of control over what kind of response they might get from their children at any time. As described by these parents, a child's conduct disorder creates a ripple effect, impacting the family in ever-widening circles; first the parents, then the marital relationship, then other siblings, then the extended family, and then the family's relationships with the community are affected.

Impact on Marital or Couple Relationships

The relationship between the parents is stressed by the need continually to monitor and discipline the child. Very little time and energy are left for parents to devote to themselves or to each other.

MOTHER: One of the things that is so frustrating is that he has consumed our lives. Since he's been born, 99% of our conversation is about Matthew and what we are going to do to deal with his behavior problems. We don't have a life— everything revolves around Matthew.

Except in the unusual situations where the father was the primary caretaker, the mother was the one who was the most "under siege" with the child. The father, on the other hand, typically spent less time with the child and therefore had a less intense, somewhat easier relationship with the child. This difference between the mother–child and father–child relationships typically resulted in different perceptions of the child's problems, often creating conflict in the parents' own relationship.

Parents described several dynamics in their relationships. First, many fathers talked about feeling left out, unsure how to contribute when mother and child were locked in battles around dressing or going to bed, and so forth. At the end of a long day with a conduct-disordered child, mothers typically felt tense and frustrated, sometimes even blaming themselves for the day's problems. They needed to share these feelings with their partners. But fathers often reported experiencing guilt, confusion, and even anger, which discouraged rather than encouraged communication. Fathers said they felt guilty about their reactions, but frequently their distress was so great that they withdrew from the situation or avoided discussions with their partners about the children.

FATHER: On a micro level, if my son gets my wife upset, she doesn't distinguish between him and me. If it's a weekday and I've had a hard day at work I have limited resources when I get home at night. I may try to smooth the waters a little but I'm often not successful and sometimes I get concerned about the way he is treated. I feel real angry about it but I haven't done anything.

For their part, many mothers reported feeling angry because they interpreted their partners' withdrawal as insensitivity to the situation or a lack of caring. On the other hand, if their partner overreacted with anger towards the child, they became angry with him. They also felt jealous and resentful if the father had an easier time with their children.

Unsure of how to react to their wives' tension and frustration, many fathers reported taking their anger or criticism out on the child.

FATHER: I'll come home and she [my wife] will tell me what the children did to her today. And I'll get mad, and then the first time they do something I'm set for it. I'm primed to discipline them for her, or whatever. And so the first thing they do, that sets me right off.

Observing their wives engaged in long episodes of cajoling and yelling at the child, fathers often questioned these approaches and were critical both of the approach and of any inconsistency. We commonly heard fathers express the belief that their wives were "too easy" and "not tough enough." These criticisms were bolstered by the fathers' awareness that they did not have the same kinds of problems with their children that their wives experienced. Of course, these kinds of responses from fathers contributed to the mothers' anger and frustration, and only exacerbated the fathers' isolation from the problem, thereby undermining the support system potential in the relationship between husband and wife.

Furthermore, mothers often took on a disproportionate sense of responsibility for the child. Typically this imbalance created a situation where mothers were exhausted and beleaguered, desperate for some time alone, and with little energy to spare for husbands.

MOTHER: I always feel that if you [looking at husband] took a bigger role in parenting we could do it together and share the role. I feel it is you against "us" (Mom and the children). I want it to be "us" and "them."

Both mothers and fathers reported this, with fathers often feeling resentful and complaining that their partners were too preoccupied with the child.

FATHER: Since our son was born, you [looking at his wife] have become really obsessed with parenting. Even during the pregnancy you were always reading really big books about how to parent and trying to be supermom. I am not willing to put my mind, body, and soul into parenting all day and night. I'm going to have walls and boundaries. You are constantly attached—even when we go out for time alone, what do you talk about? Nothing but the kids! I finally made it a rule when we are out with friends not to talk about the children. The separation in our relationship began when he was born.

Both parents' anger and resentment only intensified the situation. Consequently there was a loss of intimacy due not only to the practical aspects of the situation—too little time and too little privacy for a sex life—but also due to the intense feelings surrounding their respective issues.

MOTHER: He (child) comes into our room every night. He would never tolerate our door being locked or he would go to pieces and tantrum. Consequently we have a nonexistent sex life.

MOTHER: She (child) doesn't allow us to talk together—with the kids we don't get enough time together. As far as a romantic sexual type relationship, for the past four years, it's been shot to hell! We don't have time to talk, we don't have time to pull in together and, you know, just have a relationship.

Some mothers reported feeling guilty not only for their failure to manage the children well and their preoccupation with parenting—guilt that was often reinforced by their husbands' criticisms—but also for the failure in the marriage. Their sense of incompetence seemed to spill over from the parenting role to other aspects of their marital relationship, resulting in paralyzing depression and a sense of hopelessness.

MOTHER: Once we had kids I put the focus there. Then our son took so much of my attention. You see, I'm the emotional one and I get bothered by things that bother the children and my intensity goes into the children. Well, we started taking one night out a week because we were getting lost in caring for the children. I know I get so emotionally involved with the kids that I haven't given as much to the marriage as I should have.

Impact on Siblings

According to parents, living with a conduct-disordered child has both a direct and an indirect impact on siblings. The direct impact on the siblings is experienced mainly through the conduct-disordered child's aggressive behavior, which is often directed toward them. (For further details see the section on Child as Tyrant, p. 44 above.) The indirect impact on siblings is felt in siblings' relationships with their parents and the expectations that their parents developed for them. Typically, parents described the siblings as competing with the conduct-disordered child for their attention. Most parents felt the excessive attention constantly required to manage the child's behavior problems left them with very little time and energy to attend to the sibling who was behaving well. In addition, parents typically developed unrealistic expectations of siblings, because they felt unable to tolerate misbehavior from more than one child.

MOTHER: Our life is such a nightmare when both children are there that almost every weekend his older brother goes away for the weekend to a friend's house. I feel so guilty, but I can't take them both at home.

Siblings, therefore, were often expected to be model children, or were placed in a shared parenting role—always expected to be responsible, always in control, always helping their parents care for the conduct-disordered child. Not only does this attitude place an unfair burden on the sibling in terms of age-inappropriate responsibilities, it also is likely to create a sense of resentment on the part of the sibling towards the misbehaving child because of the comparative lack of attention and interest s/he receives from his/her parent.

MOTHER: What happens in our family dynamic is that our nonproblem child always has to be responsible. Wrongly, but you know, because life with his brother is so incredibly complicated, he is expected to act like a 40-year-old and think like a 40-year-old. The consequences for him are great. I expect too much of him, I expect him to act, to use his head every minute of every day about dangers for his brother—that's more than an eight-year-old should have to contend with. Because life with his brother is so dangerous for everybody and because we try to control his brother's behavior, we are constantly on to him to control his. And that is hard . . . he never gets to have a bad day, he never gets to throw a tantrum, he never gets to do anything because we are so maxed out on his brother, there's nothing left for him. He has to shut up, behave, and not talk to us about any of his concerns and problems.

In addition, for many parents the "good sibling" was becoming as difficult as their problem child by mimicking the problematic behaviors—a predictable result of the excessive parental attention given to the problem child.

MOTHER: He definitely requires a lot of attention. And basically what we are feeling now is a backlash from giving him so much attention, that my older one, who used to be my "great kid," is now acting up and being sneaky and starting to get that way.

Impact on Extended Family Reactions

The parents reported that their children's conduct disorders had become a source of tension between themselves and their parents and/or siblings—that is, between the parents and grandparents or between the parents and aunts and uncles. Often the parents reported that grandparents attributed the child's misbehaviors to a lack of good parenting. Many parents reported that their parents (the child's grandparents) were always giving advice about how they "should" handle the problems, and typically advocated a stricter approach to negative behavior.

MOTHER: When Grandma comes to visit about once a month, he (child) just goes ape. He starts terrorizing the cats, he starts throwing his toys, he starts going ape. And he has a real hard time when Grandpa is there and Grandpa likes him. But Grandma thinks we should "nail the little sucker a good plant a couple of times on the rear end."

On the other hand, sometimes the children did not behave as badly with grandparents as they did at home with their parents. If this occurred, parents interpreted the fact that grandparents could manage the child when they could not as evidence of their own inadequacy. This interpretation further exacerbated their feelings of guilt.

IMPACT ON RELATIONSHIPS WITH COMMUNITY: "MORE RIPPLES"

Parents' descriptions of the ways in which having a child with conduct disorders impacts their lives conjures up an image of ripples in a pond that widen until eventually the entire pond is affected. Eventually the child's problems affect the parents' and family's relationships with professionals, teachers, and other parents in their community. In general, these relationships become characterized by negative feedback to the parents: stigmatization, social isolation, and rejection.

Professionals' Reactions

Parents were confused, frustrated, and even angry at professionals' reactions to their child's problems. They had sought help from a variety of professionals, such as pediatricians, psychologists, counselors, and psychiatrists. Many times they had received conflicting opinions regarding the seriousness of their child's problems and conflicting advice about how to deal with them. Many parents reported being told that their child was "normal," that s/he would soon "outgrow" the problems, and that they should just "loosen up" and "be patient." Being told that their child was normal then caused parents to blame themselves for their overreactions to the problem behaviors. On the other hand, other professionals would tell them to "be more consistent and get stricter control" of their children's problems. The net result, regardless of the type of advice given, was to make the parents feel at fault and confused about how to cope with the situation.

MOTHER: I've talked to our pediatrician about it. I went and saw a counselor, and I've talked to him about it. And everyone basically told me, "Oh, he's just a normal kid." Well, I mean our life at home is not normal . . . and they say, "he is just like a normal four-year-old . . . nothing is wrong with your child." And he goes, "I wouldn't worry about it." And he kept telling me, "I wouldn't worry about your kid, I would worry about the ones that are quiet and compliant and do everything they're told." So you know I was just pulling my hair out—while they are trying to make you happy and realize that you don't have a weird child— but that's not what I wanted to hear. I wanted to hear step one, two, three, four . . . and I really don't know what to do.

Parents also felt rejected and isolated by teachers' and daycare providers' reactions to their children's misbehaviors. The children's aggressive, defiant behaviors created problems with their peer group at school and in their relationships with teachers. Their children caused other children to cry or misbehave and generally increased the aggression in the classroom. Moreover, as the child's antisocial identity was established, s/he frequently became the target of other children's ridicule, teasing, and rejection. Teachers, too, became more disapproving and punishing toward these children. Parents frequently reported they had been asked by teachers to find another daycare or school for their child because their child was unmanageable and consumed too much of the teacher's time.

MOTHER: It started when he was 18 months old. He was always the most aggressive, the most outgoing, the loudest child in every group he's ever been in. And I remember after his first day at daycare—I picked him up and I got a phone call. It was on my answering machine—I mean the teacher never confronted me in person and she just said she didn't think it was going to work—he was terrorizing other children and really being a disruptive force to her preschool. And I had to drop that daycare. So you know, no notice—and it's just been like that from that point. I remember getting a phone call on my answering machine, and with it one of the teachers asking me to call back—I was just holding my breath, wondering if she was going to tell me to take him out. ... I would come back after three hours and just the expression on her face—it was this horrified, painful expression.

A further "ripple effect" was that the disproportionate amount of teacher time devoted to the child's problems resulted in parents of other children in the school or daycare being resentful and/or complaining to other parents and teachers. This intense negative feedback compounded the parents' feelings of isolation and lack of support.

MOTHER: The principal came up to me and said, "Your boy is a very sick boy and is going to need many years of psychoanalytic counseling,"—I feel all the teachers knew this and set us up in the school so we couldn't win. I felt everyone else in this kindergarten was on this raft while we were swimming around trying to clutch to get on. We said we'd pay for books and I'm helping out twice a week in class and I'm offering to be a personal aid and we'll pay for a social skills teacher—and everywhere we'd go around the raft and try to get on someone would step on our fingers.
Yes, and we even sent away for literature to provide ADD handbooks for the teachers which were never read. By the end of the school year we started realizing that the kindergartern raft was sailing away, and when they told us not to come back, we felt we were left drowning in the water.

Community relationships

As the ripples spread, these parents experienced increasing isolation.

MOTHER: Basically I feel I am really in a minority. Because of all the other mothers I've talked to ... they've never been hit. I mean, to me it's unimaginable not to be slapped and kicked. And I have a friend. I was telling her about it and she says, "What? Your son hits you? My daughters never hit me." I mean other parents look at me like I just walked off another planet. So I feel very isolated. I feel like no one is like me! No one has my situation.

This lack of empathy was often perceived as rejection or condemnation. The tremendous amount of negative feedback these parents received from other parents in their neighborhoods and in their schools bred feelings of stigmatization. When they invited other children to come over to their house to play with their child, they were turned down. Their children seldom received invitations to another child's house.

Parents even felt this rejection from strangers in grocery stores, parks, and restaurants.

MOTHER: There have been times when he has been aggressive enough that I've seen a look in other people's eyes that just makes me feel horrible to the core. One day I took him to the Children's Museum by myself, and by the time we left, maybe 45 minutes later, I was really an emotional wreck because I'd seen a look and posture in the other parents there that showed repulsion on their part. And I felt that as a couple, we were really being rejected. And I literally saw other people come into a play area and, seeing we were there, just turn their own child away.

This feeling of social isolation and rejection by the community even extended to an inability to find babysitters. Typically a babysitter, after spending several hours with their child, would not want to come back.

MOTHER: She has run off three babysitters. No one wants to babysit her. I mean, one day she was jumping on the bed, pulled down the curtains, threw pillows all over the place, wouldn't mind the babysitter. We came home, everything was trashed. And the babysitter said, "Look what this child did."

This perceived blame and rejection from extended family members and from the community led parents to feel more and more isolated.

MOTHER: There is huge isolation. My mother doesn't understand, my stepfather is hypercritical and other parents think it's awful—rarely do we get support. Other parents walk in our house and look at the holes and think, "My God, what kind of children live here, obviously these parents are letting things run amok." Isolation has been a huge issue for me, I don't think anyone else understands. Nobody has a child like him.

Parents reported becoming more and more insular. Frequently they reported having stopped taking their children to grocery stores and restaurants in order to avoid having to deal with possible tantrums and negative behavior in these public places.

MOTHER: I won't take him shopping with me because he throws temper tantrums, and with child abuse laws the way they are now you can't discipline him in public any more. So I won't take him. I won't even take him to a restaurant.

LIVING WITH A CONDUCT-DISORDERED CHILD: AN EXPERIENCE OF LEARNED HELPLESSNESS

Parents of conduct-disordered children are often blamed for their child's misbehaviors, by lay people and professionals alike. Typically, parents are given the message that they could have solved their child's problems if only they had been more dedicated or had used certain discipline strategies. However, individuals outside the family often have only a superficial view of the lives of these parents and do not understand the complexities of the ripple effect—they see the situation only within the context of their own generally positive experiences with childrearing. Such an approach is insensitive to the disrupting process that parents go through while raising a child with conduct disorders.

Findings from this study indicate that the experience of parenting a child with conduct disorders is a process of learned helplessness. This process contains three phases which are influenced by the chronicity of the child's problems, the futility of the search to understand the cause of the problems, and experiences with attempting to discipline the child—experiences that tend to convince the parent that the situation is inalterable.

Phase I: "Treading Water"

Most parents in this study told us that they felt their child's problems started at birth. Many describe infants who were not cuddly and who reacted to physical affection by withdrawing, becoming rigid, or escalating anger.

FATHER: Since he was born, he has never liked to be touched or to be held—he didn't want to be constricted in any way even as a baby. It was so frustrating because you know how you want to be close to a baby—well, not with him. It made bonding difficult. He just wanted to be left alone. It's a privilege now to get a sincere hug or for him to sit still with physical contact—that's a major thing.

Clearly, these infants did not reinforce their parents' efforts to comfort them in time of distress. As toddlers, they had more than their share of tantrums and defiance. The initial reaction of these parents was to wait for the toddlers' irritability, defiance, noncompliance, and tantrums to disappear with maturity. Typically, parents had anticipated that by age three the child would have grown out of such problems. This belief led them to focus less on the child's problems and more on the hope that soon they would not have to deal with the problems.

The combination of the child's young age and the parents' hope that the problem would disappear was reflected in the fact that these parents attempted to ensure the child's physical safety but made no consistent effort to alter the child's misbehaviors through parenting skills.

MOTHER: Even though my personal life was a shambles, from 15 months till three, I got through it because it was like, this is part of having a busy toddler. Keeping him alive became paramount. But we went through it all because that's what you do when you have little kids ... My expectation was that we would get through this—every other family does. Our older child stopped at three. He could walk in a room and stop making messes. So my expectation was that at three, no matter how bad it is, it would calm down. But at three nothing happened. In fact, it got worse, because he got bigger and it was harder to contain him. And as he got bigger and more things were available to him, his destruction level went up.

The belief that the child's problems would decrease with age was also supported by professionals such as pediatricians and nurses, who reassured the parents that nothing was wrong and that soon their child would "outgrow" the problems.

Phase II: Problem Recognition

It is not easy for parents to admit that they have a child with serious behavior problems, a child who is different from other children. Yet after three years of disruptive behaviors with no relief as the child matured, most parents realized that their child might be different from other children. Three categories of problem recognition were identified: grasping the problem, searching for reasons, and mounting self-blame.

Grasping the problem

As the children grew older and their behavior problems escalated, parents began to realize that these problems were not going to disappear. This awareness came gradually, as parents made comparisons between their problem child and other children of the same age, or other siblings in the same family.

MOTHER: I took him to parent–toddler classes. And he was always the one that wouldn't sit for the story time, he never did the art projects, he was always racing around.

Searching for reasons: Why? Why? Why?

As parents started realizing their child's behavior was different from other children's, they began to search for reasons for these behavior problems.

This search for reasons can be seen as a coping process; it contains elements of problem-solving and of emotional regulation.

The problem-solving was characterized by parents' attempts to identify factors influencing the child's misbehaviors in the hope that these factors could be eliminated, thereby alleviating the behavior problems. Typical external factors included nutrition and sleep. Many parents reported trying different fad diets. Many reported eliminating sugary foods, food additives, milk, or other elements from the child's diet in order to bring about an improvement in the child's behaviors. Many reported being continually concerned that their child get enough sleep at night so as to be sure the child was not misbehaving due to fatigue. Mothers searched their memories for things they might have done wrong during their pregnancy and for birth and postnatal difficulties which could possibly have contributed to the child's problems.

MOTHER: He was premature and came home after five and a half weeks. So initially I remembered feeling there was not that bonding you are supposed to have within hours of birth.

Parents also searched for external factors in the children's schools or the approaches of a particular teacher that might be contributing to the child's difficulties. Frequently, they sought out new schools, hoping to find one that was more sensitive to their child's specific learning style, intelligence, and temperament.

MOTHER: He was in daycare where he was the youngest, and it didn't seem he was watched out for. It could have been he was overlooked, and there were some occasions perhaps when he was picked on. And when I realized what was going on, then I changed situations.

They searched for clues in their own family histories and in their own lives and marriages that could be contributing to the child's problems.

FATHER: A lot of the problem is when we moved into my mother's house. There were too many authoritarian figures over him and he didn't know exactly who to listen to. He was only three and a half, and there were all these authority figures, my brother, my mother, my sister, me and my wife, and sometimes my sister's husband.

The search for reasons also served the function of emotional regulation —that is, trying to modulate and deescalate angry and/or depressive feelings. Typical emotional regulation strategies of coping involved parents analyzing their own childhoods. Often fathers told stories of having similar problems with aggression when they were children. They spoke of being hit and otherwise abused by their parents, as well as rejected by their peer group at school.

FATHER: Perhaps some of it is genetic. I mean, I had some problems when I was a kid. I was very aggressive. I almost got kicked out of preschool. I bit kids and hit kids and I was somewhat of a terror as well. I would want toys and if someone tried to get the toys from me, I'd throw a block at them.

While these painful memories allowed them to identify with their children's difficulties and therefore feel less alienated from them, there was a negative aspect as well: they became more discouraged because they felt the family pattern was repeating itself.

FATHER: Well, I was always in trouble as a child—always in the principal's office—and my Dad, he whipped me constantly. Now my son has the same problems I did and as a parent I want to respond differently, but I see myself doing the same things.

Adoptive parents were inclined to search for the roots of the child's problems in the genetic backgrounds of the biological parents, but they also questioned their own motivation, attachment, and readiness for adoption—feeling that perhaps these factors contributed to the child's insecurities and misbehaviors.

FATHER: He was adopted and we got him at four weeks. He came suddenly and I don't think we were prepared to deal with it. It has been a series of stressful changes.

Self-blame

For most parents, the process of looking for reasons for the child's problems involved looking internally as well as externally. This acknowledgment of their own limitations promoted feelings of self-blame and guilt. Parents' hypotheses regarding their own contributions to their children's problems included such things as moves to new neighborhoods, ineffective parenting approaches, lack of time to attend to their children's needs, unemployment, too much time devoted to their jobs, medical problems, use of drugs during pregnancy, divorce or death in the family, poor housing accommodation, and their own personal inadequacies or health problems.

MOTHER: The reason we're having so much trouble disciplining him is because I don't like conflict. It's almost like sometimes I'm trying not to start any conflict—but that's not helping him.

FATHER: I think a lot of his playing rough could be partially due to me, because when I play with him I like to play rough. We tumble around, and roll around and punch each other—so a lot of it could be my fault.

FATHER: We moved and my wife was on bedrest for five months with our second child—she couldn't pick him up. It's kind of like he got hit with a lot in a short period of time. We put him in daycare. All of a sudden there is competition for affection ... so he's learned that by being uncooperative and bad he definitely gets attention. Let's assume my wife never was on bed rest and he never ended up in daycare, and we did all this when he was five instead of two—it would have been totally different.

MOTHER: He screams really violently if he doesn't get his way. I know why he does that—because when I was having a lot of bad headaches a few months ago, whenever he'd scream, I'd usually give in to him. So now it's become a habit.

FATHER: I feel like I lack the skills to help him become a mature person primarily because the environment I grew up in there was no training—I don't really know how to do it. I worry about my responses to his behavior—whether I provide a model or a way to do things positively. My father died when I was young, so I'm not sure about myself as a father or a parent in general. I know that I love him and want the best, but I'm not sure I'm helping him. You know, I feel that I express love, but when things get tough I feel that I have a tendency to withdraw from everybody.

Sometimes these feelings of self-blame for the child's problems were reinforced by professionals' theories regarding the causes of misbehavior in children. However, as most of these parents consulted a variety of professional sources, they had encountered conflicting explanations, which contributed to a sense of bewilderment.

MOTHER: Well, I went to the pediatrician who told me to "loosen up" and said he was normal. I tried that for a while but things just got worse. Then I went to a psychologist who said I wasn't strict enough with him—well, clamping down didn't seem to work either. Finally I went to a psychiatrist who said if I'd only get my marriage together my son would be okay. But my husband didn't want marriage counseling, so what was I to do?

Phase III: Learned Helplessness

This phase was characterized by a transition from self-blame to trying desperately to understand and to cope with the problems into a mode of giving up. Three categories were identified as elements of learned helplessness: "nothing works," "mounting anger and loss of control," and the "paradoxical investment."

"Nothing works"

As parents realized that their child's behavior problems were not going to disappear, they coped with their feelings of self-blame by launching into a variety of discipline approaches with their child. Parents reported seeking help from books, from courses, and from various professionals. They reported trying a range of discipline strategies such as teaching, yelling, criticism, spanking, Time Out, taking away privileges, and positive reinforcement. Although their use of a broad range of strategies may seem positive, in fact it indicates how desperate these parents were, since they were inconsistent in the choice of any particular strategy and lacked confidence about when to use a particular strategy with a specific type of problem.

After several years of struggling to control the child's behavior problems with only limited, if any, success they began to believe they were doomed to be ineffective in changing their children's behaviors. In fact, typically the children's misbehaviors were gradually escalating under what parents perceived as their own best efforts. Parents reported reaching a point at which they believed "nothing works."

FATHER: I get agitated easily, I mean, this has been four years of this. And I am 42 years old, and I've just about had it. So now I'm kind of at my wit's end, like what to do. Because nothing is working. Time Outs don't work. If I put her in her room, she'll go and start kicking the door, or throwing toys—so then I'll lose it, I'll go in and I'll spank her.

MOTHER: We've done a lot of parenting. Both of us are professionals and we work with people a lot and we've had a lot of resources. We've been in counseling since he was three years old and seen several psychologists and psychiatrists and we've worked very hard, but haven't gotten very far. He's still got the same traits and that's scary.

They felt helpless and inadequate in their parenting roles, and more generally, as human beings. Moreover, their extended family members, teachers, professionals, and other parents seemed to confirm these feelings of ineptness.

Mounting anger and loss of control

The basic premise of the learned helplessness theory (Seligman, 1975) is that, during contact with an uncontrollable situation, an organism learns that outcomes and responses are noncontingent (Abramson, Seligman & Teasdale, 1978; Maier & Seligman, 1976; Seligman, 1975). The transition from intense feelings of inadequacy to learned helplessness was evident in parents' reports of intense feelings of being overwhelmed and paralyzed by their children's problems. This helplessness was often expressed in terms of parents feeling victimized by their children, "held hostage." Parents talked at times as if they believed their children were "out to get them." As the embattled parents felt increasingly helpless, they began seeing their children as the powerful ones. In an inversion of the usual power structure, the children were controlling their parents' lives. Thus, the parents became victims and the children oppressors. In response to their sense of victimization, the parents' anger increased, as if in an effort to regain control and power in the relationship. Parents talked about expressing their escalating anger by yelling and hitting the child. However, these powerful feelings of anger were coupled with fears of losing control both of their own behaviors with their children and of their own sanity. Furthermore, many parents talked about their fantasies of getting rid of the child or of running away themselves.

MOTHER: I was ready to just walk away from everybody. It was just too much—his screaming, the temper tantrums all day. And I thought I was completely loony bins. I felt like a real failure as a human being. . . . There are times when he just drives me to distraction. . . .

Sometimes parents reported they did lose control of themselves and used excessive physical punishment. Such out-of-control reactions further inflamed parents' feelings of self-blame, setting in motion a "vicious circle" of guilt, fear, and ineffective parenting. These reactions and feelings, in turn, further aggravated the child's aggressive responses. Eventually, the fear of their own angry responses led parents to withdraw, to become depressed, and eventually to give up trying to discipline their child.

MOTHER: It's like he pushes, and pushes, and pushes me . . . I feel real helpless . . . and what I do is, rather than react appropriately, I shut down. I mean it's like

I'm in shock. That's when I feel really incompetent. ... I have truly never questioned my own sanity, as I have with the kind of episodes I told you. It really overwhelms me—it scares me.

MOTHER: Every time I've gotten to the point where I've just felt like I'm losing control, because nothing is working, and I'm spanking, I tried in the past to get on the phone and call a crisis clinic, a parenting group, somebody to provide help. And there really isn't any help out there. You try calling somebody in a crisis situation and what you get is an answering service or a disconnected number. Or you get a recording, you know, leave your name and number. "I'm hurting my child now, call me back when I am sane." People beat their children. I understand their frustration.

Paradoxical investment

Another characteristic of the learned helplessness—one that was very difficult for parents to accept—was a sense of having continuously invested in their conduct-disordered child with little or no "return" for their investment—that is, little or no joy and pleasure in their relationship with their child. This situation, where parents felt few rewards for the difficult work of parenting, created a sense of incompetency or paradox for parents: The discrepancy between what they were "putting in" and what they were "getting out" was just too great.

MOTHER: I've noticed other mothers and families, and they really enjoy their little girls and their little boys, because it's a real different situation for them. And it's not like that for me. I don't have that real enjoyment.

In sum, they felt stuck with a child who was unresponsive and aggressive, with no support or understanding from others.

DISCUSSION

Qualitative analyses of these parents' interviews indicated that the process of parenting a child with conduct disorders involved three phases: "treading water," problem recognition, and eventual learned helplessness. As mentioned earlier, the cornerstone of the learned helplessness hypothesis is that people who undergo experiences in which they have no control over what happens to them often develop certain motivational, cognitive, and emotional deficits. The motivational deficit which occurs is characterized by retarded initiation of voluntary responses. The cognitive deficit is a belief or expectation that outcomes are uncontrollable. The emotional deficit is characterized by depressed affect (Abramson, Seligman & Teasdale, 1978; Maier & Seligman, 1976, Seligman, 1975).

Parents of conduct-disordered children learn through repeated experiences that no matter what parenting strategy they use—Time Out, spanking, explanation, positive reinforcement, etc.—the child's aversive behavior remains constant. In other words, the outcome is rarely influenced by their actions. Moreover, on those occasions when they were able to influence their child's behavior, these parents came to feel that there was no predicting which parenting strategy would produce a particular outcome. For example, Time Out might be effective at one time, but not so at a different time—even in response to the exact same problem behavior.

According to the learned helplessness hypothesis, the attribution a person makes about an event is crucial (Folkman & Lazarus, 1988). Abramson, Seligman and Teasdale (1978) distinguish between universal and personal helplessness. In universal helplessness, the person believes that neither s/he nor anyone can solve the problem, whereas in personal helplessness the person believes that while the problem is solvable, s/he lacks the skills to solve it (i.e., low self-efficacy expectations). Analysis of the attributions of the parents of conduct-disordered children in our study revealed that these parents developed a sense of personal helplessness. Parents constantly compared their childrearing skills with those of other parents and came to believe that they were incapable of controlling their child's behavior. These internal comparisons were reinforced by feedback from family members, teachers, and other professionals, who also attributed the child's misbehaviors to their lack of parenting skills—thereby increasing their sense of personal helplessness.

Our findings also indicated that these parents reported very low self-esteem and/or high depression. This finding is supported by the learned helplessness theory, which claims that individuals who feel personally helpless show lower self-esteem than individuals who experience their helplessness as universal (Abramson, Seligman & Teasdale, 1978).

Bandura (1982, 1985, 1989) has developed a related hypothesis. He proposes that self-efficacy beliefs are central to an individual's transactions with environment. For example, in his view a parent may understand how to do Time Out with an aggressive child, but be unable to do it because of self-doubts. In addition, Bandura (1989) has suggested that the relationship between self-efficacy and performance is bidirectional. Self-efficacy beliefs are enhanced or decreased, respectively, by success or failure experiences. The parents in our study reported feeling ineffective owing to their repeated failure experiences trying to parent their difficult conduct-disordered children. Thus, they stopped trying.

Learned helplessness varies in terms of generality, chronicity, and intensity of the problem (Abramson, Seligman & Teasdale, 1978; Kofta & Sedek, 1989; Mikulincer & Casopy, 1986; Miller & Norman, 1979). With regard to generality, these parents of conduct-disordered children felt inadequate in multiple areas of their lives—not just childrearing, but also marital relations and relationships with teachers, other parents, and professionals in the community. Many felt isolated, stigmatized, and even rejected. Thus, their sense of helplessness became somewhat globalized, rather than remaining specific to the child. With regard to chronicity, these parents reported waiting endlessly for their child's problems to disappear before they even began to try to control them—and when they did try to handle them, they were unsuccessful. Most had therefore experienced chronic helplessness for several years. With regard to intensity, the high intensity felt by these parents evolves from the importance our society places on childrearing and the family. Abramson and colleagues (1978) have suggested that intensity of helplessness will be higher to the extent that the event about which the person feels himself helpless is highly preferred or valued. It is not difficult to understand the intense feelings of helplessness that can occur when parents develop the conviction that they lack the skills for rearing behaviorally normal children.

This formulation of the perceptions of parents with conduct-problem children has important implications for treatment, because learned helplessness and low self-efficacy beliefs can be reversed by experiences of success. Teaching effective parenting skills undoubtedly starts with a reversal process and begins to give parents some expectation that they will eventually be able to control outcomes—that is, their children's behaviors. However, because of the global nature of the helplessness, it is also important to modify any unrealistic expectations, substituting realistic plans and promoting revised parent self-efficacy—both in the context of dealing with their child's misconduct and also more generally in relation to their relationships, problem-solving and coping skills. This also argues for the importance of enhancing social support, especially for single and maritally distressed parents. Indeed, group-based approaches combined with individual interventions may prove particularly effective.

REFERENCES

Abramson, L.Y., Seligman, M.E.P. & Teasdale, J.D. (1978). Learned helplessness in humans: Critique and reformulation. *Journal of Abnormal Psychology*, **87**, 49–74.
Bandura, A. (1982). Self-efficacy mechanism in human agency. *American Psychologist*, **37**, 122–147.

Bandura, A. (1985). *Social foundations of thought and action: A social cognitive theory*. Englewood Cliffs, NJ: Prentice-Hall.

Bandura, A. (1989). Human agency in social cognitive theory. *American Psychologist*, **44**, 1175–1184.

Baumrind, D. (1971). Current patterns of parental authority. *Developmental Psychology Monographs*, **1**, 1–102.

Dumas, J.E. & Wahler, R.G. (1985). Indiscriminate mothering and contextual factors in aggressive-oppositional child behavior: "Damned if you do and damned if you don't." *Journal of Abnormal Child Psychology*, **13**, 1–17.

Folkman, S. & Lazarus, R.S. (1988). Coping as a mediator of emotion. *Journal of Personality and Social Psychology*, **54**(3), 466–475.

Forgatch, M.S., Patterson, G.R. & Skinner, M. (1988). A mediational model for the effect of divorce on antisocial behavior in boys. In E.M. Hetherington & J.D. Aresteh (Eds.), *Impact of divorce, single parenting, and step-parenting on children* (pp. 135–154). Hillsdale, NJ: Erlbaum.

Furey, W.H. & Forehand, R. (1985). *What factors are associated with mothers being more subjective and less objective in evaluating their clinic-referred child's behavior?* Unpublished manuscript. University of Georgia.

Kofta, M. & Sedek, G. (1989). Repeated failure: A source of helplessness or a factor irrelevant to its emergence? *Journal of Experimental Psychology: General*, **118**, 3–12.

Maier, S.F. & Seligman, M.E.P. (1976). Learned helplessness: Theory and evidence. *Journal of Experimental Psychology*, **105**, 3–46.

Mikulincer, M. & Casopy, T. (1986). The conceptualization of helplessness: A phenomenological structural analysis. *Motivation and Emotion*, **10**, 263–277.

Miller, I. & Norman, W. (1979). Learned helplessness in humans: A review and attribution-theory model. *Psychological Bulletin*, **86**, 93–118.

Patterson, G.R. (1982). *Coercive family process*. Eugene, OR: Castalia Press.

Schaughency, E.A. & Lahey, B.B. (1985). Mothers' and fathers' perceptions of child deviance: Roles of child behavior, parental depression, and marital satisfaction. *Journal of Consulting and Clinical Psychology*, **53**, 718–723.

Seligman, M.E.P. (1975). *Helplessness: On depression, development, and death*. San Francisco, CA: Freeman.

Strauss, A.L. (1987). *Qualitative analysis for social scientists*. Cambridge: Cambridge University Press.

Wahler, R.G. & Dumas, J.E. (1984). Changing the observational coding styles of insular and noninsular mothers: A step toward maintenance of parent training effects. In R.F. Dangel & R.A. Polster (Eds.), *Parent training: Foundations of research and practice* (pp. 379–416). New York: Guilford.

Webster-Stratton, C. (1985a). Comparison of abusive and nonabusive families with conduct-disordered children. *American Journal of Orthopsychiatry*, **55**(1), 59–69.

Webster-Stratton, C. (1985b). Predictors of treatment outcome in parent training for conduct disordered children. *Behavior Therapy*, **16**, 223–243.

Webster-Stratton, C. (1988). Mothers' and fathers' perceptions of child deviance: Roles of parent and child behaviors and parent adjustment. *Journal of Consulting and Clinical Psychology*, **56**(6), 909–915.

Webster-Stratton, C. (1989). The relationship of marital support, conflict and divorce to parent perceptions, behaviors, and childhood conduct problems. *Journal of Marriage and the Family*, **51**, 417–430.

Webster-Stratton, C. (1991). Stress: A potential disruptor of parent perceptions and family interactions. *Journal of Clinical Child Psychology*, **19**, 302–312.

Webster-Stratton, C. & Hammond, M. (1988). Maternal depression and its relation-ship to life stress, perceptions of child behavior problems, parenting behaviors, and child conduct problems. *Journal of Abnormal Child Psychology*, **16**(3), 299–315.

3

THE PROCESS OF ASSESSING FAMILIES OF CHILDREN WITH CONDUCT DISORDERS

A COMPREHENSIVE, reliable assessment is the *sine qua non* of effective intervention. Nevertheless, this chapter provides only a brief account of the *content* of the assessment phase of our parenting programs. Information about the specific "nuts and bolts" of our—and others'—assessment methods is dealt with comprehensively in several texts (Barkley, 1987; Herbert, 1987a,b; Patterson, 1982; Webster-Stratton, 1992). Here, we have chosen to describe ideas about the *collaborative process* that underpin our approach to assessing children and their families.

We have seen in Chapter 2 the variety and intensity of problems that beset parents of children with a conduct disorder, and their impact on family life. The content and style of the early assessment interviews with families are of vital importance if parents are to become engaged in the assessment and, later, fully committed to the treatment—to the extent that they will not be tempted to opt out when the going gets tough. The very nature of conduct disorders (including the way in which they undermine parental self-esteem and confidence) makes these tasks delicate ones indeed.

A mother made the following comments soon after the beginning of assessment:

> First of all, there was a feeling of relief. Something was at last being done. Something concrete. I was going to be helped. For a short while I felt euphoric . . . but I was defensive as well because I felt that I must accept a certain responsibility for the way Emma was. I did not want to do that. I'd had enough of failure. But I recognized I would have to face up to the truth if I went ahead with treatment. It was quite a struggle at times and my pride took quite a battering.

The Joining Phase

Therapists use their skills to "join" with, and, in a sense, to become "absorbed" into, the family. The collaborative process comes into play from the very beginning of the assessment. The initial interviews are designed to engage families in the therapeutic endeavor by forging a good working relationship and, where necessary, by reassuring parents who are seeking help at a time of particular vulnerability. The therapist tries to enter into the parents' experience and feelings by listening carefully to the meaning of the child's problem for the family. Throughout the interview the therapist tries to follow the parents' agenda, beginning where the parents want to begin and covering their points of concern.

This process of accommodation creates a new system—family and therapist. It may take several sessions to create this new system. Because it is essentially a transitory one, the therapist carefully monitors any signs that family members are going to drop out of therapy and thereby disrupt the new system. This could occur early on because parents may be angry and confused; it may have to do with misapprehensions about the nature of the program, doubts about "who's who" among the personnel, and sometimes resentments or uncertainties about why they have been referred for help. It is vital to explain the function of the clinic and its staff, and to anticipate, answer, or clarify the why, who, what, and how questions which are generally in parents' minds. They tend to be as follows:

- "Why am I here?" or "Why do you need me to be so involved, when it's my child's problem?"

- "Who will I be seeing?"

- "What is going to happen … what does the treatment involve?"

- "How will you be able to help us?"

- "What are the chances of success?"

Making a Start

At the point of first contact, or perhaps even before, it is useful to provide a brochure or handout explaining the work of the clinic. It is also helpful to go through the referral letter (if there is one) with the parents, to clarify points of ambiguity, check on the accuracy of information and establish the beginnings of mutual respect. Working out a preliminary genogram is a helpful way of obtaining factual information about the family and their perception of what are significant relationships. Because parents and children are on familiar terrain—after all, they know their family members —and are providing the therapist with helpful information, it is a good "warm-up" method for engaging the family in a working relationship. It is important to draw the children into the process of naming the immediate family members plus significant others. For example:

THERAPIST: You will be mentioning several names that will be new to me when you begin to discuss the reasons for coming to see us at the Clinic. It would help me if we could draw a family tree on this flip chart. Where shall we begin?

It is often difficult for the professional (and, indeed, parents) to know where to begin. Parents are sometimes bursting with worries which they wish to share but feel embarrassed to express – out of a sense of failure, shyness, fear, or shame (the last two particularly where there is a history of child physical abuse or, indeed, "parent abuse"). Parents have their own agenda and although the clinician may wish to shift that agenda by introducing his/her own terms of reference, it is crucial to give parents plenty of opportunities to express *their* concerns—their thoughts, feelings, and theories about the problems.

A further exploration concerns what life is like at home with the child. Parents are asked to explain the approaches they have tried—those which have or have not worked—as well as their theories regarding the possible causes of the child's problems. It is vital for the therapist to remember that low morale, guilt, and depression are likely to be among the burdens which parents (notably mothers) commonly bring to the clinic when they have been struggling to cope, to little avail, with an oppositional child.

As Emma's mother said:

I was desperately unhappy and depressed with no clear understanding of how I came to be so. Each day I moved through a suffocating fog of failure, frustration, and guilt. I saw myself as an unattractive and undesirable individual. I felt that my intellect had atrophied. My daily round of housework and the endless confrontations with the children held no rewards, but left me bored and exhausted. Against this background a natural shyness had developed into a real fear of going out and talking to people. The fear of rejection was greater than the fear of loneliness. My home had become a prison.

Process vs. Content

After discussing the parents' general experiences and preliminary perceptions of their child's problems, their explanatory model, and their hopes for therapy, we then share with them a detailed assessment—the what, why, and how questions—of the child's difficulties, and the part other members of the family play in relation to them. The temptation for professionals to be judgmental is very powerful, for the misleading axiom,

"There are no problem children, only problem parents," still lingers on in the public mind, affecting professionals and our clients. This stigmatizing stereotype makes the issue of the *process* (as opposed to the content) of the assessment interview/s a particularly crucial one! Engaging parents in a genuine partnership does much to counter their sense of failure. This involves:

- Listening to the parents' views of their difficulties

- Explaining what lies ahead, what is involved

- Establishing a relationship based on respect

- Reducing stress by adopting a calm, nonjudgmental manner

- Sharing your thinking and knowledge

This is not always as straightforward in practice as it sounds in theory! Understandably, parents are in a hurry to receive answers, preferably a formula or prescription for immediate use! For this reason, the therapist may be either tempted or pressured to adopt the "expert" role. However, there is a need to slow things down so as to explain the rationale of the collaborative approach.

It has to be acknowledged that although the collaborative model puts demands upon parents which bring about long-term, as opposed to short-term, benefits, to engage in an *active* partnership requires more work and commitment from them, not less. Parents may have mixed feelings about their involvement in the process of therapeutic change. As one mother put it:

> I remember feeling disappointed, surprised, and somewhat put out when I left the clinic, not with some immediate useful advice about how to put Darren straight, but with some recording forms and ideas about how to observe his good behavior as well as his bad behavior. There wasn't much of the former to talk about, to tell the truth. Not only that, but also my own thoughts and feelings and actions were to be recorded in a sort of diary. Funnily enough, after getting used to it, I began to enjoy keeping a note of things. I felt I was playing an important part in the treatment. It also gave me a chance to calm down when I got angry with him, having to write things down.

There is another conceptual difficulty for some parents, those whose attributions reflect an axiom different from the one quoted earlier, one that assumes (at least in their own case) that "there are no problem parents, only problem children." For these parents, problematic behaviors are reified into entities which reside within the child. The parents do not share, in any way, in the "ownership" of the problem. Such a disengagement from any role in the child's negative behaviors is very difficult to deal with clinically, as we shall see in a later chapter. With these parents, both the *process* of assessment (the partnering role) and the *content* can modify their attributions—by encouraging parents to make connections ("Do you see anything of yourself in your child's behavior?" "Were you like Jan at her age?"), and to think about behavior sequentially and contingently (the ABC functional analysis—matters we shall return to shortly). Problems are not unidirectional; there is two-way traffic—powerful reciprocal influences—in the interactions between parents and children. Post mortems of the chicken–egg type (which came first: adverse parental influences or difficult child behavior) are not helpful when carrying out assessments with parents who are suspicious, even cynical, about the possibility of being helped. It requires sensitivity and nonjudgmental clinical explanations (formulations) on the part of the therapist if they are to be helped to gain, or regain, confidence in the management of their children and to reverse the hostile, rejecting attitudes they have toward them.

Using Theory and Systemic Thinking to Guide your Assessment

A consistent theoretical framework is of vital importance to the professional trying to make sense of, and predictions about, the interactions of families that tend to be dysfunctional in their organization and relationships. Social learning theory, with its emphasis on the active nature of learning, the social context in which learning takes place, and the role of cognition and meaning, is well suited to such a remit (see Bandura, 1977). The view put forward here is that much abnormal behavior in children (and their caregivers) is learned or results from a failure of learning. It does not differ, by and large, from *normal* behavior in its development, its persistence, and the way it can be modified. Learning occurs within a social nexus; rewards, punishments, and other events are mediated by human agents and within attachment and social systems, and are not simply the impersonal consequences of behavior. Children do not simply respond to stimuli; they interpret them. They are relating to, interacting with, and learning from, people who have meaning and value for them. They feel antipathetic to some, attached by respect and/or affection to others; thus they may perceive, for example, an encouraging word from the latter as "rewarding" (i.e., positively reinforcing), but from the former as valueless, perhaps even aversive.

Any individual in a family system is affected by the activities of other members of the family, activities which his/her actions or decisions, in turn, influence. Systemic behavior therapists in contemporary practice concentrate not only on the individual but on the system of relationships in which s/he acts out his/her life. The focus of help is not prejudged as the child who was referred to the clinic; the unit of attention is defined as the whole family (or one of its subsystems—e.g., parent–child interactions). This is something that parents cannot—or will not—always accept.

The assessment process must take into account the behavior, attitudes, and relationships within four interlocking systems, three of which are dealt with here:

- The child

- The parents

- The family

- The school

ASSESSING THE CHILD'S BEHAVIOR

The preliminary information about the child's behavior needs to be as precise as possible. This information usually comes from the parents, who often tend to report their children's problems in terms of rather vague and global labels such as "tantrums," "disobedience," "rebelliousness", or "aggressiveness." These terms may refer to very different kinds of behavior as used by different parents and, indeed, by the same parent on various occasions. Therefore it is important to encourage the parent to give descriptive examples of the problem, in other words to define what s/he means in specific and observable terms when s/he uses a particular label. A verbatim account of several examples of the problem behavior provides not only an operational definition of what the problem is, but also gives the context of antecedent and consequent events which will be useful during the next phase of the analysis. The problem (e.g., aggressive behavior) is specified in terms of observable responses which are accessible to other people (parents, teachers, the therapist) as well as to the child. This includes what the child has to say (self-report).

When parents have had an opportunity to describe *their* views of the child's misbehaviors, it is important to gradually broaden the therapist's agenda to include others besides the child who is being complained about. For example:

THERAPIST: Before you can change your child's behavior you have to look at that behavior very closely; also your own and other members of the family. ... The undesirable behaviors you wish to change (you have said) are Peter's frequent temper tantrums; but *your* feelings and ideas, and those of your family, are also important.

In home- and clinic-based behavioral family therapy it is regarded as essential to elicit the views of all the family members as to what is, and what is not, problematic in family relationships. The referred child is not the only object of the assessment. With this in mind, the therapist tries to elicit the parents' and others' hopes and goals for therapy. S/he asks questions such as, "What is your greatest hope for what will happen as a result of coming to therapy?" Defining the family members' goals at the outset helps the therapist to correct any unrealistic expectations of therapy. In addition, it helps the family to focus on a more positive future at a time when they may be feeling depressed and hopeless.

Assuming that parents and other members of the family have been invited to express their concerns in their own words and have been given enough time to do so, one technique for assessing what they require by way of help is to find out what *positive changes* they desire to make in order to make parenting and family relationships easier. The problems within the family are likely to reflect complaints about the child (disobedience, demandingness, tantrums, antisocial activities), difficulties involving relationships among various members (for example, sibling rivalry and parental ineffectiveness, marital discord), lack of knowledge (for example, ignorance of what to expect of children at different ages), disagreements over the sharing of finite resources (such as money, time, attention), and conflict (over policies such as rules, discipline, routines).

The clinician's brief will be (*inter alia*) to pinpoint problematic behaviors, attitudes, beliefs, and interactions in terms of examples of what people *do* and *say*; to examine contingencies (the ABC of behavior/beliefs); to put these into a *developmental* framework which takes account of *family dynamics*; to teach parents/child to observe (and possibly record) interactions; and then to discuss the data fully with them (i.e., to arrive at a shared "clinical formulation").

To be more precise, the questions to be asked include: "*What* is the child doing that is problematic? Under *what* conditions are these behaviors produced? *What* are the effects of these acts? *What* changes result from these behaviors? *What* other alternative behaviors did the child have? *What* situations are being avoided? *What* behaviors may be encouraged and shaped up?" Each "what" in these questions directs the parent to define for us the specifics of the problem and its effects (the pay-off) for the child. These questions also elucidate situational factors: the circumstances under which the problematic behavior occurs and those under which it does not. Behavioral recordings (described below) will give precision to the parents' answers.

Recording the Observations: Context

The first step is to encourage parents to sit down in a quiet moment and think about what happens in the distressing interactions with their child that are giving cause for concern. They should then list these behaviors in detail.

THERAPIST: I would like you to keep a record of what your child does and says in particular trying situations, and what *you* do and say to deal with the child.

PARENT: Why do you put so much emphasis on what my child does and says? I want to know why my child is so awful to me and his sisters. It's as if he has the devil in him.

THERAPIST: It is often tempting to speculate about children's motives and about the reasons why they behave in the way they do, but all this is guesswork. They are simply not visible to us. We have to rely upon what children tell us about them, and young children are not always able to put these things into words. In any event, they may be unaware of what their motives are, or may need to mislead us about them. In contrast, observable behavior can be described in objective terms, terms which any group of reliable witnesses would agree upon.

This list should be composed of descriptions of each of the child's "provocative" actions. Alongside each of these, the parent should note his/her characteristic manner of dealing with it. This list can be checked by keeping a record of what actually happens. The object is to identify how persistent a particular problem actually is, and to provide baseline data against which can be charted any improvement after a treatment program.

Having drawn up the first list, the next task is to make a second one which records examples of the child's prosocial behaviors and the parent's responses to them. When it comes to recording these behaviors, the parent will often find that on those rare occasions when the child does as s/he is told, the parent provides little or nothing in the way of a response. In other words, the child receives no attention and, therefore, no reinforcement for prosocial behavior. It is small wonder that these positive behaviors tend to be underrepresented in the child's repertoire.

With antisocial behavior, the picture is very different. All too often it becomes apparent that the parent is "taking the bait" which the child is offering. The child is "winding up" the parent or siblings because it gets him/her noticed by the parents and attended to in one way or another (i.e., increased verbal or physical interaction, closer proximity). Looking at the two lists, the parents gain insight on their own; they can see that, without realizing it, they have been responding to—rewarding—the unacceptable behavior and failing to reward the acceptable.

Children, and indeed adults, vary their actions to some extent according to the situations—and their perceptions of the situations—in which they find themselves. The term "situation specificity" refers to the fact that behavior is not usually manifested on a random basis. The probability of a specific action occurring varies according to contingencies (circumstances) in the surrounding environment. Thus, for example, a child may display his/her unacceptable behavior in the home but not in the classroom, in the classroom but not on the playground, etc.

One technique used to tease out the specificity (and context) of family interactions is the record of a "typical day" in the life of the child and family (Herbert, 1987a). The "typical day" is recorded in minute behavioral detail, pinpointing the precise events in those areas which cause confrontations and concern. It includes the times of day, the places at which they occur, and the persons with whom they occur. The typical day (or days) makes for a reasonable sampling of the child's antisocial *and* prosocial behaviors and the family members' *reactions* to them. We ask for a "blow-by-blow account" of what happens in a particular problematic situation. Who does what? And then what ensues?

A useful question to ask is whether there are particular persons (grandmother, sibling, parent, uncle, friend) who get the best out of the child, in the sense that s/he does not display his/her problem behavior with them. If so, the interactions of those persons with the child are worth studying. Here we are looking at *proactive behavior* on the part of significant others in the life of the child. Below are abbreviated illustrations of the conversational process between the therapist and clients as they "problem-solve" together through the various assessment steps.

Step 1: Identify and pinpoint the problems

THERAPIST: Would you like to tell me in your own words about what is worrying you—the concerns you would like us to help you with? Don't feel you have to hurry; take your time.

[*Pause at suitable intervals to summarize what the client has said.*]

THERAPIST: I would like to pause for a moment to see whether I've understood properly the points you have made.

[*Later*]

THERAPIST: Are there any other matters you'd like to go into? Thank you for that helpful account. I can see that you are worried. I would like to clarify some of the points you have made by asking you for some other examples of your child's behavior.
(A behavior checklist may prove useful.)

Illustration No. 1

PARENT: Darren is forever arguing with me about doing what I ask him to do or ignoring me when I ask him to stop doing something or other. He *never* listens!

THERAPIST: Would you give me an example of his arguing, preferably a recent one? What does he do and say that makes you call it "arguing"?

PARENT: I'll ask him to put away his toys and get ready for bed. He argues by saying it isn't time, or he's in the middle of a TV program, or some other excuse.

THERAPIST: Perhaps you could show me, using your actual words, what happens. Imagine I'm Darren and you are wishing to get me to stop whatever I'm doing. How would things go?

PARENT: Right ... Darren, it's time for bed, isn't it? Will you put the TV off and go upstairs?

THERAPIST: What happens next?

PARENT: Darren is likely to say "No."

THERAPIST: What is your next move?

PARENT: I try to keep calm and give him reasons for going to bed ... like he'll be tired for school next day. He takes no notice ... then I begin to shout at him and he shouts back. I find it so exhausting!

THERAPIST: What other ways have you used to get him to obey you? [*Later*] Tell me how you feel during these exchanges. [*Also*] Do you ever really believe that he will obey you?

Illustration No. 2

PARENT: Paula is so aggressive; she has such an awful temper and I don't seem to be able to control her.

THERAPIST: What does she do and say that makes you think of her as being an aggressive child?

PARENT: Well, if she doesn't get her own way she has a tantrum.

THERAPIST: What does that involve?

PARENT: She shouts and screams, stamps her feet and bangs the furniture with her fists, and carries on alarmingly.

THERAPIST: It sounds as if she hurts herself rather than anyone else.

PARENT: Yes, I suppose so, but it *is* frightening.

THERAPIST: Let us look at the various situations in which she loses her temper. We'll take some other examples and look at the way you manage them; also what other members of the family do on these occasions. Would you take one of the most common situations where this happens?

PARENT: I feel so embarrassed at my failure to cope. I feel such a fool.

THERAPIST: You'd be surprised how many parents experience the same kind of difficulties and have similar feelings. A three-year-old in the middle of a temper tantrum can be very formidable. Let us see together whether we can make some sense of them. They may be her way of trying to solve a problem; after all, she's still a learner. What do you think about that notion? Let's see what she "achieves" by tantruming. How do these episodes end? Are there pay-offs, favorable outcomes for her?

Illustration: Pinpointing

PARENT: Sally is always disobedient.

THERAPIST: It will be difficult to plan our program if we are vague about her behavior. Let us try to be more precise about the word disobedient. Let us look at recent episodes of what you call disobedience. Give me an example of precisely what happens.

[*Later*]

PARENT: Sally has a temper tantrum when I insist that she obeys me, for example when I tell her to eat breakfast. This happens every morning. With me, not her father.

Step 2: Identify the child's assets

THERAPIST: You have pointed out some of your problems with Yusef. If we look at this form you will see that it has a credit and debit column. I've listed on the debit side all of his behaviors that you find unacceptable; now let us list his good points on the credit side.

PARENT: It's difficult to think of any ...

THERAPIST: Well, let's try. In any event, I want you to take this form home and look out for pleasant, helpful, and other positive things that Yusef does and note them down. I will also ask you to observe his negative behaviors on another form so that we can study them together and work out a plan of action.

Step 3: Identify desired outcomes (goals)

THERAPIST: If I had a magic wand and could wave it and give you three wishes so that Anne's behavior was different, what would you wish her to change? OR If you were to wake up one morning to find that Anne had changed for the better, how would you know? What would be different about her behavior or attitude?

[*Later*]

THERAPIST: You have three extra wishes. Would you want anything in the family to be different so as to make life easier or more contented? (Other members of the family are given an opportunity in a similar manner.)

At a later (second or third) session:

Step 4: Work out and observe the ABC of behavior/beliefs/interactions

THERAPIST: Before you can change your child's behavior you have to look at that behavior very closely; also your own and that of other members of the family. What sets the stage for the undesirable behaviors you wish to change? These, you have said, are Jessica's frequent bouts of defiance. What, at the time, are your feelings (you mentioned helplessness)? How do you react? What consequences flow from these confrontations?

At this stage the ABC model is explained—verbally and/or with a handout. For example:

THERAPIST: When experience leads to a relatively permanent change of behavior, attitude, or knowledge, we say that learning has occurred. Memorizing a formula, recognizing a face, reading music, becoming fearful of doing maths or going to parties, are all examples of learning. We have to distinguish between *learning* an action or behavior and actually *performing* it. A child may learn something but not do it. Reward is anything that makes a child's actions worthwhile! A behavior will be strengthened (made more likely) if it has favorable consequences; it will be weakened (that is, it will be less likely to occur again) if it is not followed by a reward—what, technically, we call "positive reinforcement." Also if it is penalized. If your child does something you do not like, such as losing her temper too easily, you may increase her ability to think first and hold her temper by either *rewarding* her (with words of praise) for maintaining self-control and/or by avoiding the sanctions (penalties) you consistently apply for her failing to do so. In the latter you are providing what is called "negative reinforcement" for her efforts to "keep her cool." You may not have to apply the penalty if she believes your threat because of your record of keeping your word. For instance, if you say, 'Donna, if you do not think first, but lash out at your sister, I will not allow you to watch the television,' then her resolve to think first and desist from hitting out will be strengthened.

In the more technical terms of social learning theory, aggressive anti-social behavior and interactions are regarded as a function of somatic factors, previous learning experiences, and contemporary events in combination. The assessment of these events is a matter of identifying precisely the antecedent, outcome, and symbolic conditions which control the problem behavior. First, problem behavior may be a response to certain antecedent conditions which are eliciting or reinforcing that behavior. Second, there may be certain outcome conditions which either reinforce problem behavior or punish or extinguish prosocial behavior. Finally, any of these inappropriate forms of antecedent or outcome control may be operating in the child's symbolic processes rather than in his/her external environment or physiological changes. For example, there may be an impairment of his/her problem-solving capacity. The assessment process might continue as follows:

Step 1: Specify the target behaviors

THERAPIST: The behaviors you wish to change are sometimes called "target behaviors." Remember the ABC of behavior which we have discussed. The B term stands for *behavior* (Wayne's temper tantrums in this instance), and it also stands for *beliefs* (your feelings and attitudes about what is happening in this instance).

THERAPIST: Let us be clear about what you are going to observe at home and elsewhere. So what is it that he *does* and *says* that makes you call his actions and words a "temper tantrum"?

PARENT: Wayne stamps his foot, clenches his fists, kicks the chairs, etc. He also screams and swears.

THERAPIST: So stamping, fist-clenching, kicking, screaming and swearing are—more precisely—our target behaviors?

Step 2: Observe the frequency of the target behaviors

THERAPIST: I want you to count the number of tantrums (defined by those actions you described) that Wayne has per day, i.e., the number of episodes. (You could also time how long each episode lasts.) Do this for three or four days.

Step 3: Look at the ABC of behavior

THERAPIST: I want you to keep a diary record of some of the episodes, with particular emphasis on the ABC sequence:

A: What led up to the
B: TANTRUM? and
C: What happened immediately afterwards?

Here are two sample excerpts from the parent's diary of ABC sequences. The first is vague and therefore uninformative. The second provides a firm foundation for further assessment.

(1) Wayne was playing with his cars when I asked him to get ready for school. He took no notice. I snatched away his toys and there was a scene. As a result he had one of his tantrums and gave me a lot of abuse.

(2) Wayne was playing with his cars. I told him it was already 7:30 and time to get washed, dressed, and ready to leave for school. He didn't answer or make a move. I told him the time again and repeated my instructions. Wayne asked for a few minutes' play. I said he was already late and told him to put the cars away. He now said, "No!" just like that. I snatched his cars away. He lay down, screamed, and kicked his legs on the floor for a few minutes until I smacked him. He then went to change, muttering that he hated me and would leave home. I took no notice. His father took no interest in what went on; he

ignored the entire thing. I was left feeling guilty for hitting Wayne and angry with his father for opting out.

The second example is informative because it not only tells us, in useful sequential detail, something about the kind of situation in which Wayne confronts his mother, but it provides us with a clue to one of the sources of the mother's discontent with her marital relationship and her sense of being unsupported in her struggles with an oppositional child.

Here is an example of the same mother's formulation of an ABC sequence:

A: I was waiting my turn at the checkout counter at the supermarket. Wayne kept putting chocolates in the basket. I kept taking them out. He said, "I want a sweet!" I said, "No, love, you can have a biscuit when we get home." He said loudly, "Give me a bloody sweet!" I asked him please not to make a fuss.
B: He began to scream and kick the counter; then he lay down on the floor, blocking the counter so other people couldn't get to it.
C: Everyone was looking at me and I felt so embarrassed I gave him a chocolate and said, "Just wait 'til we get home. . . .!" He quieted down immediately and began to eat it. I felt very angry, resentful, and humiliated.

THERAPIST: And then?

PARENT: I said no more at home, to keep the peace.

Step 4: Analyze your information: antecedents

THERAPIST: When you look at your diary after a few days, and your tally of tantrums, are they part of a more general pattern? (Are the As, the antecedents, rather similar?)

PARENT: Yes, they seem to form a pattern of defiance. They follow two lines. Either Wayne commands me to do something; if I don't, he insists, and eventually has a tantrum. Or I ask Wayne to do something; he ignores me or says "I won't!", and if I insist, he has a tantrum.

Step 5: Be specific about the problem behaviors

THERAPIST: When you look at your tally, do the tantrums seem more frequent:

■   at certain times?

■   in certain places?

■   with certain people?

■   in particular situations?

PARENT: The answer in this case is yes to all those questions. They are most frequent in the morning and at night; in the bedroom and at the dinner table; with me; when I try to dress him, get him to eat up his meal, or put away his toys.

Step 6: Analyze the consequences

THERAPIST: Looking at your diary again, can you see any kind of pattern in the Cs, the consequences or outcomes, to these upsetting confrontations? [*Parent is given an opportunity to think about it.*]

[*Later*]

THERAPIST: Do you think you may have slipped into the habit of simply repeating your commands like a broken record—over and over again—without really expecting any results? Do you always give way, perhaps because it's the easiest thing to do? (Anything for a quiet life!)

PARENT: Yes, Wayne usually gets his own way . . . not always, but nearly always. He also gets me going. I sometimes end up in tears. He always gets me into an argument and I have to devote a lot of time to the dispute.

THERAPIST: You might ask yourself, "Who was I really observing?" The answer inevitably will be not only your child. You are observing, as part of your analysis of As and Cs—in the ABC sequence—your child in relation to yourself *and* others. It is not possible to understand a child's behavior without looking at the influence of other people on him, and his influence on them.

Step 7: Identify the reinforcers

THERAPIST: In this instance, you (and others) have unwittingly reinforced (strengthened) the very behaviors (tantrums) that you wished to reduce in frequency. For example, one reinforcer is that he gets his own way; the second is that he riles you and enjoys winding you up; the third reinforcer is that he monopolizes your attention—even if it is scolding it is rewarding. You can tell that it is rewarding and not punishing because of the fact that the behavior is as persistent as ever.

It has to be made clear to parents that it is not simply a matter of A leading to B leading to C (linear causation), but that Cs become As in a pattern of recursive causation; also that the intervention of other members of the family complicates matters, and thus our analysis.

Step 8: Identify goals

THERAPIST: Be quite clear in your mind how Wayne must change in order for the situation to improve. Also be specific. For example, "I expect him to obey me when I make a reasonable request or command, so that if (say) I ask him to put his toys away he does so without endless arguments or fits of temper." [*These issues are discussed and debated thoroughly.*]

THERAPIST: There are two general principles involved in putting right the unsatisfactory situation we have gradually disentangled and thus clarified. In retraining Wayne you will need to *reduce* the undesirable actions and at the same time, *strengthen* a desirable action that is incompatible (i.e., competes) with the undesirable one. Your child tantrums too easily, so you will attempt to weaken tantruming while (at the same time) you strengthen a competing behavior such as "cooperating with mother." He can't aggravate *and* cooperate at one and the same time. All of this means that you will also need to change some of your actions and ideas. Would you be prepared to try?

ASSESSING PARENTAL BEHAVIOR

There are several features to look out for in the parents, and indeed, the families of conduct-disordered children.

Coercive Interactions

The concept of coercive power has led to an awareness of the crucial role of coercive interactions in the lives of families of conduct-disordered children. It is important to observe and note these in the assessment. These coercive interactions are so typical of these families as to be recognized in theories of conduct disorder. For example, Patterson (1982) has emphasized the role of negative reinforcement in the escalation and maintenance of coercive behavior. He proposed an S–R–C paradigm as follows:

Aversive stimulus   → child's response   → removal of aversive stimulus
(parental command)   (child's noncompliance)   (withdrawal of parental command)

Faced with noncompliance, the parent may either withdraw the command, thus negatively reinforcing the noncompliance and other behaviors, or respond with coercive behaviors of his/her own (for example, yelling). If the child complies to the latter response, the parent's coercive behavior is reinforced. Here is a typical coercive sequence of the kind frequently observed during an assessment home visit:

(1) Mother "annoys" Sophie by demanding that she goes to bed.
(2) Sophie reacts by having a violent temper tantrum.
(3) Mother cannot stand the noise, so stops "annoying" Sophie by letting her stay up.

Sophie has coerced her mother into terminating her annoying behavior, and Sophie's aggression has been positively reinforced by getting her own way. Given many repetitions of such sequences, her aggression could become habitual.

Coercive parent–child interactions tend, over time, to persist and, indeed, escalate into what has been called "coercive spirals." Wahler and Dumas (1986), addressing the question of why this occurs, put forward the "compliance hypothesis" as a partial explanation of how some parents and children "ratchet up" their aversive exchanges into progressively more painful coercive—sometimes dangerous—interactions. The compliance hypothesis proposes that the mother's or father's caving in to her/his child's demands and aversive behavior acts as a *positive (intermittent) reinforcer* for the child's aggression, and is thus a major factor in the maintenance of this kind of behavior. The parent complies—gives in, gives way—to "turn off" the child's temper tantrum, hitting, screaming, or whatever. The pay-off of relief from painful stimuli, with its escape and avoidance implications, makes further parental compliance more and more likely (negative reinforcement). This process of reciprocal reinforcement by the removal of aversive stimuli has been described as the "negative reinforcer trap" (Wahler, 1976).

A parent who spends time reasoning with the child after an act of noncompliance could also be reinforcing the behavior with unwittingly gratifying verbal attention. In this example, Sophie's mother has fallen into the so-called "positive reinforcement trap." The identification of these traps is an important aspect of assessment, helping to determine goals for the treatment program.

Observations suggest that mothers and siblings in coercive families are the ones most caught up in these coercive interactions, because their own rates of aversive behavior are significantly higher than those manifested by their counterparts in nonproblem families (Patterson, 1982). Patterson makes the point that, as coercive sequences lengthen in duration, there is an increased likelihood of physical aggression by the parents and among the siblings (Patterson, 1982). Although parents caught in this coercive spiral escalate their threats and nagging in response to the child's coercive behavior, they are inconsistent in their follow-up to their threats. However, at unpredictable intervals their anger and frustration explode and they resort to extreme forms of physical punishment (Reid, Taplin & Loeber, 1981). In fact, these authors reported that one-third of the boys with conduct problems in their study were known to have been physically abused by their parents. The siblings of aggressive children are very likely to initiate and sustain aggressive interactions within the brother/sister relationship, the most pronounced effects of such exchanges being observed in middle childhood and early adolescence (see Patterson, 1982).

Ineffectual Discipline and Communication

The communication, cues and unspoken messages in the homes of conduct-disordered children are frequently negative ones, with the "sound and fury" of incessant criticism, nagging, crying, and shouting. Patterson (1982) refers to much of it as ineffectual *nattering* on the part of the parents. His position—and he qualifies it carefully—is that the control of antisocial behavior requires the contingent use of some kind of punishment. But why does aggressive behavior that is punished by the parents of conduct-disordered children not diminish or disappear, as would be predicted from learning theory?

Berkowitz & Graziano (1972) argues that it is not punishment *per se*, but the *kind* of punishment used by parents of aggressive children that may be ineffective. He makes a case for the necessity of punishing aggressive child behaviors, but in the context of a warm, loving relationship where reasoning and explanations are used in conjunction with *nonviolent punishment*. (Parents need to be reminded that reasoning with a child in an agitated, angry state is not only ineffective; it is actually counterproductive.)

Patterson agrees with Berkowitz's position, based upon his research conclusions arising from two decades of intervention studies with families of aggressive children (Patterson, 1982). Time Out and logical consequences (such as work details or loss of privileges) are definitely aversive; however, they are *not* violent. Patterson vouches for their relative effectiveness (Patterson, 1975; 1982). Certainly there is overwhelming evidence that extremes of physical punishment, particularly when perpetrated against a background of uncaring indifference or outright rejection, constitute the slippery slope for the creation of a violent youngster (Herbert, 1974; 1987b).

Poor Limit-Setting

Among the critical antecedents to examine in the assessment of noncompliant, aggressive behavior are the *rules* (implicit and explicit) enforced at home and school. These include the conventional rules of good manners and of correct behavior toward particular persons or situations, rules that involve sympathy and respect for others, keeping faith, helping, and honesty (Herbert, 1978). Some of these are about good manners; others are moral rules which are essential (many people would insist) to the maintenance of social order and a civilized life. The induction of the child into the social system (socialization) involves the transmission to the child of social *and* moral codes by the family and other agents of society.

An important issue in assessment—given the defiance of rules by conduct-disordered children—is thus the nature of the boundaries and limits established by parents for their children. In this sense, boundaries are defined by "rules" which specify an individual's role within the family, the subsystem s/he belongs to, and the appropriate behaviors which such membership entails. Boundaries can be clear (because the rules are easily recognized and accepted), diffuse (ambiguous and chaotic because rules are unstable or absent), or rigid (where rules are inflexible, unadaptable). Behavioral family therapists are especially concerned to assess those areas where families manifest weak boundaries or reversed territories between generations, a condition in which conduct problems flourish (Herbert, 1987a,b). For example, parents may be "obedient" to unreasonable demands from their offspring; in such cases, the child usurps the role of the parent by taking control in the home to a significant extent—the boundaries between parent and child are not clear.

The literature on moral and social development is important as a knowledge-base for the conduct disorders because of their flouting of moral and social conventions (Wright, 1971). We have seen that amongst children referred to mental health clinics, noncompliance is the most frequent presenting problem (Patterson & Reid, 1973); the youngster refuses to obey commands, prevaricates, or even does the opposite of what is asked (negativism). It is impossible to describe in anything but superficial detail the reasons why certain children find it easier than others to conform to parental and societal rules. To summarize a few important points, however:

- There is a fairly high correlation between overall *parental* negativism and childhood deviance. In an investigation of some of the processes involved, Johnson and Lobitz (1974) were able to create conditions (by instruction) in which parents in 12 families could manipulate the deviancy level in their children (aged four to six years) according to prediction. They did this by increasing their rate of ignoring or commanding their offspring, and of being negative, restrictive, disapproving, and noncompliant.

■ The best discriminating factor between "normal" children and children referred for psychological treatment was a parental negativeness score (Lobitz & Johnson, 1975).

■ Parents of referred children give more commands (Lobitz & Johnson, 1975). Interestingly, there is a great deal of overlap in the distributions of deviancy rates in referred and nonreferred children, although the former show significantly higher rates. Parents of "antisocial" children issue more negative and vague commands than their "normal" control counterparts (Patterson, 1982). More recently, Patterson and Bank (1986) confirmed this view by showing that the most common failure of these parents in parenting skills was inept discipline: scolding, threatening, and nagging (toward the child), and the use of frequent and intense physical punishment.

■ When comparing problem and nonproblem preschool children, relationships that subvert or negate socialization differ markedly, not only with regard to the aversive interactions they have with their mothers, but also to the positive ones, as indicated by the amount of time spent in positive activities and warmth during joint play (Gardner, 1987). Conduct-disordered children are disadvantaged here too.

Other Factors in Assessment

It is clear that early learning and development are important factors in the evolution of hostile and antisocial styles of behavior. The therapist's knowledge of such factors may well influence the direction taken in planning an assessment and intervention with a family. Not surprisingly, there is considerable variability in children's (and, for that matter, parents') responses to stress. Some individuals are completely overcome by circumstances which leave others relatively unscathed (Werner & Smith, 1982). An assessment that does not take into account developmental factors could well miss the impact of early experiences on the child's development which determine his/her vulnerability or, conversely, resistance to stressful life events. Some of these factors constitute risks that accumulate (and interact in a complex manner) to affect a child adversely, but others constitute opportunities and protective influences that ameliorate outcomes. These can be built upon in the intervention. For example, the child who experiences one parent as alcohol-dependent or abusive may have another parent or family relation who is supportive and can provide a buffer against some of this adversity. Similarly the child who is temperamentally difficult with problems of hyperactivity, impulsivity, and language delays may live in a warm, supportive family who maximize his/her potential for learning academic and social skills.

Other considerations for assessment are organismic variables such as state variables (e.g., age, fatigue, hunger, anxiety level); intellectual level; health and developmental status (e.g., stage of development, developmental delay). The issue of organismic influences is pertinent to the child's use of coercive strategies to modify parental behavior. Patterson (1975) suggests that applications of pain control techniques (e.g., crying and screaming) by infants may be innate. Their yelling when in distress has obvious survival value. The use of these methods is maintained and, indeed, extended by many toddlers and in some cases refined later into coercive "weapons" of great effectiveness for countering or shaping parental behavior. Again we see the recursive or spiraling nature of negativistic behavior in parent-to-child/child-to-parent interactions so central to conduct problems.

Why do some children fail to substitute more adaptive, more mature behavior for their infantile and primitive coercive repertoire? Patterson (1982) offers a list of possibilities:

- The parents might neglect to condition prosocial skills (e.g., they seldom reinforce the use of language or other self-help skills);

- They might provide rich schedules of positive reinforcement for coercive behaviors;

- They might allow siblings to increase the frequency of aversive stimuli which are terminated when the target child uses coercive behavior;

- They may use punishment inconsistently for coercive behavior; and/or

- They may use weak-conditioned punishers as consequences for coercive activities.

The research literature suggests that many of these conditions apply in the families of conduct-disordered children (Herbert, 1987b).

What is Normal Disobedience?

The perennial problem for the professional assessing the seriousness of noncompliance is the ubiquity of disobedience in childhood. This "problem" is, in a sense, a "normal" response to the rigors of socialization; indeed, up to a point disobedience—representing (as it does) the striving for independence—is undoubtedly adaptive, and its complete absence would be a matter of concern. Noncompliance occurs normally throughout the general population (Forehand, Gardner & Roberts, 1978), and more frequently, and with greater intensity, at certain stages of the life-cycle (Haswell, Koch & Wenar, 1981). Toddlers show a great deal of oppositional behavior in their struggle for autonomy, as do adolescents in their quest for independence as they near adulthood.

For the therapist carrying out an assessment of such noncompliant or oppositional children, the task is to determine whether the level or generality—indeed, the nature of the defiance—has serious ramifications for the child's ongoing development, putting him/her at risk of more serious psychological problems (see Forehand & McMahon, 1981). What is that "point" at which noncompliance is thought to be excessive, counter-productive and thus maladaptive? This question raises the issue of the generality of noncompliance as a personality trait.

Johansson, Johnson, Wahl, and Martin (undated) made a study of the social and behavioral correlates of compliance and noncompliance in 33 "normal" children of four to six years of age and their families. The children and their families were observed in their homes on five separate occasions for 45 minutes on each occasion. The behavior of the target child and that of any family members who interacted with him/her was recorded with the use of a behavioral coding system designed for rapid sequential recording. It was found that there was significant consistency in children's compliance and noncompliance to their mothers and fathers. The authors found consistent evidence of a negative relationship between children's compliance ratio and the display of all other deviant behaviors; this suggests that noncompliance may be a more general tendency towards deviant activities.

Forehand's (1977) review of the scanty normative data that are available indicates that compliance to parental commands for normal preschool samples ranges from approximately 60 to 80%. Conduct-disordered children, by way of contrast, are noncompliant some two-thirds of the time. The *frequency*, *intensity*, and *duration* of the noncompliance—and its appropriateness—become the watchwords of an assessment.

ASSESSING THE FAMILY

In a sense, the family is a system, with a life and a developmental history of its own. Behavioral family therapy (also referred to as systemic behavioral work) is an intensive casework approach to individual families. Much of the work is likely to take place in the home or is geared by means of homework tasks to the home. It contains many of the elements found in behavioral parent training, but it encompasses the analysis and modification of complex interpersonal dynamics (interactions and relationships) which are part of family life. A systemic perspective means dealing with parents and their children in their own right as individuals, analyzing their relationships to each other (as dyadic attachment subsystems), and viewing their communications, interactions, boundaries, and perceptions of one another within a holistic and dynamic family system (Herbert, 1992). Day-to-day nuances and patterns of relationship—communication and interaction—between family members are inferred from highly charged or repetitive sequences observed and analyzed.

The behavioral family therapist's first step (as we saw earlier) is to form a collaborative partnership with the family, to participate in its transactions and observe members' roles, their communications, and the boundaries both within the family and between the family system and other systems. The family "organism," like the individual person, moves between two poles: one pole representing the security of the known, the other being the exploration of the unknown (the "different") necessary for adaptation to changing conditions. When the family comes to treatment it is in crisis because it is stuck trying to maintain old ways which no longer meet the demands of changed and changing circumstances and the needs of the family under those new circumstances. The crisis, usually formulated by parents in terms of the child—i.e., the problem is the child's "impossible" behavior—is more often than not also about other issues: marital problems, personal difficulties (e.g., depression), and a variety of stress-inducing life situations. Thus the child's behavior serves as a scapegoat for these other, often unacknowledged, issues.

In behavioral family work, explanations in terms of a functional analysis can operate at two levels (Herbert, 1994). At a somewhat interpretive level the child's behavior may have the function of solving (or attempting to solve) a developmental or life problem. To make sense of it one might ask (*inter alia*): "What immediate 'solutions' (even if self-defeating in the longer term) do the child's actions provide for him/herself?" and "What purpose does the child's behavior serve in terms of his/her family life and its psychological and social dynamics?" The child's behavior is seen in terms of its function in the family system. At another level of analysis, dysfunctional behavior is seen as a function of certain contingent stimuli in the person's internal and/or external environment. Here the questions discussed earlier, "What triggers (elicits) the aggression?" and "What reinforcement does the child get for behaving this way?" are important. Both levels of functional analysis are helpful in understanding the dysfunctional behaviors that are a feature of conduct-disordered children, notably aggression and defiance (e.g., Patterson, 1982), in that they emphasize what the child gains from behavior that, on the surface, would appear to be unproductive and self-defeating.

In behavioral family therapy, as compared with individual treatment, there is somewhat less emphasis on the contingency management of specific target behaviors, and more emphasis on broad principles of child management, the setting of limits (boundaries), the interpersonal interactions of members of the family, the marital relationships (which are often poor in the parents of problematic children), and the perceived self-efficacy of caregivers. This therapeutic approach lends itself particularly to cases of child abuse where there are disciplinary, child management, communication, and attachment (bonding) difficulties.

In working with families, there is unfortunately an all-too-common tendency for professionals to patronize their clients and to overlook parents' capacity to think and theorize. Parke (1978) comments scathingly that some professionals' work with parents would seem to imply that mothers' cognitive complexity is scarcely more sophisticated than that of their infants. Contemporary behavior therapists are more willing to acknowledge that parents have expertise, theories (attributions) about behavior, and ideologies about child-rearing. For example, the assessment of the nature, sources, and consequences of parents' ideas about development (see Goodnow & Collins, 1990) is vitally important in the child therapist's work with children and their conduct problems (Herbert, 1991). Furthermore, parents commonly make plans for their children that influence their behavior by placing them in particular niches (e.g., schools) within society (Rutter et al. 1979; Whiting, 1963). These are matters which are important in assessment, and issues which behavioral family therapists are likely to discuss in their therapeutic work with parents.

As can be seen from Chapter 2, assessment needs also to include the meaning of having a conduct-disordered child from the parents' perspective—that is, parents' psychological status (e.g., depression, anger, stress level), as well as the extrafamilial stressors impinging on the family (e.g., income level, isolation, or support). The therapist needs to inquire about the actual ramifications of transition and change in family life.

There is another aspect to the issue of cognitive processes: what are called "mutual cognitions." Maccoby and Martin (1983) observe that, if we are to study the effect of ideas on parenting and on parent–child interactions, we shall need to ask about the causes and consequences of a lack of match in the parents' and children's ideas and expectations which arise from differences in conceptual level. Smooth interactions require that both parent and child must act from the same "script" (Maccoby, 1984). Mismatches are thought to promote conflict (e.g., Damon, 1989).

A particular difficulty for therapy arises when parents are unable or reluctant to see any connection between their own actions and those of their child or between their own personality and that of their child. To try to probe this conceptual gap, we make use of what we call "connecting" questions and statements as part of our therapy. They include the following:

- Do you see anything of yourself (your partner) in your child (his/her behavior/ attitudes/personality)?

- Have your parents ever commented that you were similar to your child at his/her age?

- Do you remember being anything like your child at his/her age (in behavior/attitudes/ personality)?

- How have your child's actions (behavior/attitudes/personality) influenced your own actions—perhaps against your better judgment?

- In what ways do you believe that your influence has made its mark on your child (positive influences; negative influences)?

- If you make out a balance sheet (proforma) of "credits" (positives) and "debits" (negatives) in your personality/behavior, which items do you share with your child (partner) in either column?

- To what extent do you and your child share a common outlook (values/philosophy/ attitudes)?

- What are the most significant things children learn from parents?

- What are the most significant things parents learn from children?

- When should parents begin to discipline their children? Why?

- At what age should parents stop disciplining their children? Why?

- What do you think your child is trying to "say" to you when s/he behaves in that way (alternative: what problem is s/he trying to solve)?

Cognitive mismatches between the parents must also be addressed. A substantial component of behavioral work with families is the discussion of rules, expectations, and values as a strategic background to the particular tactics (methods) that are adopted in order to bring about change. As part of the assessment of goals, both parents need to think out their attitudes to discipline and discuss them fully. Only they can decide on the values (and the rules, routines, and standards that underlie them) that are important in their families, and therefore worth insisting on. As it will be important for them to support each other in their decisions regarding rules and family values, this prior discussion of values and expectations is crucial, and the therapist can assist with this discussion as part of assessment.

MONITORING CHANGE

Learning, for parents and children, is all about change, as is growth and development. Without an objective assessment and record-keeping system it is not possible to evaluate accurately and reliably the progress made by the child and parents in the therapeutic situation. It is clear that many children's problems are transient, and change can occur often as a function of time and nonspecific placebo effects. For these reasons a controlled evaluation of the therapeutic process is essential. Objective data make possible two important goals: determining whether a child (and, indeed, parent) in treatment is changing, and the direction and extent of change.

A great variety of resources exist for developing assessment programs for children who are conduct-disordered (e.g., Ollendick & Hersen, 1984). A "multiple-gating approach" has been suggested as a means of identifying children at risk for delinquency (Loeber & Dishion, 1983). This approach involves using less costly assessment procedures, such as behavioral rating scales, as screening instruments and then using the more involved home observations for the families who seem to warrant them. The goal for these assessment procedures is to be able to select the most appropriate treatment model for the family. No matter what specific measure is chosen, a proper assessment should include multiple methods (e.g., behavioral rating scales, direct observations, interviews) completed by multiple informants (mothers, fathers, teachers, children) concerning the child in different settings and situations.

In Appendix I we provide a brief description of a few of the assessment procedures used at the University of Washington Parenting Clinic. This list is not intended to be a comprehensive review of all the assessment measures, but rather a prototype for the kinds of assessments a therapist might want to consider.

REFERENCES

Bandura, A. (1977). *Social learning theory*. Englewood Cliffs, NJ: Prentice-Hall.

Barkley, R.A. (1987). *Defiant children: A clinician's manual for parent training*. London: The Guilford Press.

Berkowitz, I.H. (1987). Aggression, adolescence, and schools. *Adolescent Psychiatry*, **14**(483), 483–499.

Berkowitz, B.P. & Graziano, A.M. (1972). Training parents as behavior therapists: a review. *Behavior Research and Therapy*, **10**, 297–318.

Damon, W. (1989). *The social world of the child*. San Francisco, CA: Jossey-Bass.

Forehand, R. (1977). Child non-compliance to parental requests: Behavioral analysis and treatment. *Progress in Behavior Modification*, **5**, 111–147.

Forehand, R., Gardner, H. & Roberts, M. (1978). Maternal response to child compliance and noncompliance: Some normative data. *Journal of Clinical Child Psychology*, **7**, 121–123.

Forehand, R.L. & McMahon, R.J. (1981). *Helping the noncompliant child: A clinician's guide to parent training*. New York: Guilford.

Gardner, F. (1987). *Observation study of preschool children with behaviour problems*. Unpublished Ph.D. thesis, University of Oxford.

Goodnow, J.J. & Collins, W.A. (1990). *Development according to parents: The nature, sources and consequences of parents' ideas*. Hillsdale, NJ: Lawrence Erlbaum.

Haswell, K., Koch, E. & Wenar, C. (1981). Oppositional behavior of pre-school children: Theory and intervention. *Family Relations*, **30**, 440–446.

Herbert, M. (1974). *Emotional problems of development in children*. London and New York: Academic Press.

Herbert, M. (1978). *Conduct disorders of childhood and adolescence: A behavioural approach to assessment and treatment* (1st ed.). Chichester, UK: Wiley.

Herbert, M. (1987a). *Behavioural treatment of children with problems: A practice manual*. London: Academic Press.

Herbert, M. (1987b). *Conduct disorders of childhood and adolescence: A social learning perspective* (revised ed.). Chichester, UK: Wiley.

Herbert, M. (1991). *Clinical child psychology: Social learning, development and behaviour*. Chichester, UK: Wiley.

Herbert, M. (1992). *Working with children and the Children Act*. Leicester, UK: BPS Books.

Herbert, M. (1994). Behavioural methods. In M. Rutter et al. (Eds.), *Child and adolescent psychiatry*. Oxford: Blackwell.

Johansson, S., Johnson, S.M., Wahl, G. & Martin, S. (undated manuscript). Compliance and noncompliance in young children: A behavioral analysis. University of Oregon, Eugene, OR.

Johnson, S. & Lobitz, G. (1974). Parental manipulation of child behavior in home observations. *Journal of Applied Behavior Analysis*, **7**, 23–31.

Lobitz, H.C. & Johnson, S.M. (1975). Parental manipulation of the behavior of normal and deviant children. *Child Development*, **46**, 719–726.

Loeber, R. & Dishion, T.J. (1983). Early predictors of male adolescent delinquency: a review. *Psychological Bulletin*, **94**, 68–99.

Maccoby, E.E. (1984). Socialization and developmental change. *Child Development*, **55**, 317–328.

Maccoby, E.E. & Martin, J.P. (1983). Socialization in the context of the family: Parent–child interaction. In P. Mussen (Ed.), *Handbook of child psychology*, Vol. 4. New York: Wiley.

Ollendick, T.H. & Hersen, M. (1984). *Child behavior assessment: Principles and procedures*. New York: Pergamon Press.

Parke, R.D. (1978). Parent–infant interaction: Progress, paradigms and problems. In G.P. Sackett (Ed.), *Observing behavior Vol. I: Theory and applications in mental retardation*. Baltimore, MD: University Park Press.

Patterson, G.R. (1975). *A social learning approach to family intervention. Vol. I. Families with aggressive children*. Eugene, OR: Castalia.

Patterson, G. (1982). *Coercive family process*. Eugene, OR: Castalia.

Patterson, G.R. & Bank, L. (1986). Boot strapping your way on the normological ticket. *Behavioral Assessment*, **8**, 49–73.

Patterson, G.R. & Reid, J.B. (1973). Interventions for families of aggressive boys: replication studies. *Behavior Research and Therapy*, **11**, 383–394.

Reid, J., Taplin, P. & Loeber, R. (1981). A social interactional approach to the treatment of abusive families. In R. Stewart (Ed.), *Violent behavior: Social learning approaches to prediction, management and treatment*. New York: Brunner/Mazel.

Rutter, M., Maugham, B., Mortimore, P. & Auston, J. (1979). *Fifteen thousand hours: Secondary schools and their effects on children*. London: Open Books.

Wahler, R.G. (1976). Deviant child behavior within the family. Developmental speculations and behavior change strategies. In H. Leitenberg (Ed.), *Handbook of behavior modification and behavior therapy*. Englewood Cliffs, NJ: Prentice-Hall.

Wahler, R.G. & Dumas, J.E. (1986). Maintenance factors in coercive mother–child interactions: The compliance and practicality hypothesis. *Journal of Applied Behavior Analysis*, **19**, 3–22.

Webster-Stratton, C. (1992). Annotation: Strategies for helping families with conduct disordered children. *Journal of Child Psychology and Psychiatry*, **32**, 1047–1062.

Werner, E. & Smith, R.S. (1982). *Vulnerable, but invincible: A longitudinal study of resilient children and youth*. New York: McGraw-Hill.

Whiting, B. (1963). *Six cultures: Studies of child rearing*. New York: Wiley.

Wright, D. (1971). *The psychology of moral behaviour*. Harmondsworth, UK: Penguin.

4

WORKING WITH PARENTS WHO HAVE CHILDREN WITH CONDUCT DISORDERS: A COLLABORATIVE PROCESS*

THERE IS a rather large body of literature describing the content of parent training programs. For example, strategies such as Time Out, Beta Commands, Praise, Differential Attention, Response Cost, and so on, along with the behavioral principles that underlie them, have been carefully described in detail. But descriptions of the content of parent training do not elucidate the mechanisms or ongoing processes of parent training—that is, the processes and strategies which therapists can use to try to change or modify parents' behaviors, attitudes, and practices—and the literature contains comparatively little discussion of the actual therapeutic processes utilized by therapists in such intervention programs.

Considering the documented effectiveness of various types of parent-training programs, this is puzzling, for there are many questions to be answered concerning the therapist's role in parent training. How can therapists handle parents' resistance to new concepts? How can they ensure that homework is carried out? What are the preferred teaching methods and strategies? How do they ensure that the training is culturally sensitive? When should confrontation be used? How can therapists promote self-confidence and self-efficacy in parents?

Patterson (1985) has argued that we need to move "beyond the technology" in developing an empirical base for parent training. In that vein, Patterson and Forgatch (1985) reported on one of the most comprehensive microsocial analyses of therapist-client interchanges in the parent-training literature. They showed that directive therapist behaviors such as "teach" and "confront" increased the likelihood of parental resistance and lack of cooperation, while nondirective therapist behaviors such as "facilitate" and "support" led to reliable decreases in client noncompliance. Patterson and Chamberlain (1988) have proposed a therapy model which postulates that therapist behaviors play a secondary role to extrafamilial, interpersonal, and child factors in predicting parent response during the early stages of treatment, but play a primary role in predicting client noncompliance in the later stages of therapy. In another

---

*This chapter is derived by permission, from Webster-Stratton & Herbert (1993).

study, Alexander et al. (1976) examined the role of therapist characteristics in predicting outcome (as defined by completion of treatment and recidivism rate) for families that participated in functional family therapy (FFT). They found that "relationship" characteristics (affect, warmth, humor) accounted for 45% of the variance in outcome, whereas "structuring" characteristics (directiveness and self-confidence) accounted for only 15%.

These studies are important; however, they do not place the therapist's characteristics and behaviors within the larger context of the ongoing therapeutic process. The purpose of this chapter, therefore, is to provide a qualitative description of the process of working with parents who have conduct-disordered children as practiced at the University of Washington Parenting Clinic.

THERAPY MODELS

There are many competing therapeutic models, each with different sets of assumptions about the therapist's role with clients, the cause of family problems, and the level of responsibility the client or therapist assumes for resolving problems. For purposes of discussion, let us pose four hypothetical therapeutic models, each an extreme—Models A, B, C. and D. In Model A, the therapist does not hold parents responsible for their problems; the responsibility lies with past experiences or the demands of society. Neither does the therapist hold parents responsible for arriving at their own solutions to the problems which brought them into therapy or which emerge during therapy. In such a model, the therapist, who is the expert in the relationship, has the responsibility for gradually uncovering the problems hidden in the client's subconscious, in past experiences, and/or in the family dynamics, and interpreting them to the individual client—or to the entire family. In such a model the client is seen as a relatively passive recipient of the therapist's analysis, interpretations, advice, and prescriptions. The advantage of Model A therapy is that it allows parents to seek and accept help for their own or their child's problems without feeling that they are to blame for them. However, this model brings with it the disadvantages of dependency on the therapist, usually over a long period of time, and in some cases isolates parents from the child's therapy process. For example, the child may be in play therapy with a therapist to work through some prior traumatic experience, while the parent is left out of the process and unaware of how s/he can help the child.

Model B therapies appear both to blame parents for their problems and to imply they are unable to control certain aspects of their lives. For example, how often are cases of child abuse explained in terms of the parent's attachment to the child—either absence of attachment or distorted attachment? Emotional and physical abuse have been linked causally with a failure on the part of the mother to become "bonded" to her child (Lynch & Roberts, 1977; Valman, 1980). Such assumptions may well lead to a therapeutic process that creates or reinforces a negative self-image in clients and a mistrust of self.

In hypothetical Model C, the therapist is not primarily concerned with the client's past, but rather focuses on the problem at hand. The therapist's job, according to this model, is to teach specific skills so that clients can assume the responsibility for solving their own or their family's problems. This theoretical assumption leads to relatively time-limited programs. Many parent-training programs fall within this model because in them parents learn to alter their maladaptive thoughts or learn new behavior management strategies to use with their children. After treatment, families are expected to be self-sufficient. Working from an assumption that behavior is intrinsically rather than extrinsically determined, such therapies allow parents to direct their energies toward solving their own problems and learning new skills. These newly acquired skills lead to an increase in parents' perceived self-efficacy (Bandura, 1977). Parents are given credit for their improvements; as a result, they come to feel more competent. Yet this therapeutic model has several possible disadvantages. First, it may suggest there are "quick fixes" for children's problems. Second, Model C may create feelings of failure or self-blame because of the raised expectations brought about by high levels of initial success—and the dashed expectations brought about by subsequent reversals of gains. Third, this type of therapy may be delivered in a directive or prescriptive fashion, which, like Model A, will foster parents' dependency and lack of self-reliance, and may also leave parents feeling blamed for their childrens' problems.

In contrast to Models A, B, and C, each of which assumes a deficit motivation, therapies based on hypothetical Model D assume the client has it within him/herself to find solutions and change. For example, Rogerian theory, which epitomizes the humanistic approach, is client-centered, nondirective, nonintrusive, and supportive (Rogers, 1951). The Rogerian therapist's "unconditional positive regard" for clients helps them to help themselves by searching for their own answers, moving towards self-actualization and maturity. The advantage of this therapeutic approach is that it promotes the client's positive self-esteem and self-direction; on the other hand, this type of therapy can be a lengthy process and may not be appropriate for clients who do not have solid communication and problem-solving skills.

At the Parenting Clinic, our theoretical approach for working with parents of conduct-disordered children falls within Model C, while integrating some of the core elements of Model D. We have chosen not to call our approach "parent training" because this term implies (as in Model C) a hierarchical relationship between the therapist and parent wherein the expert therapist is fixing some "deficit" within the parent. A term such as "parent coaching" is preferable. Terminology aside, the underlying helping process we advocate for working with parents of conduct-disordered children is a collaborative model. Webster's New Collegiate Dictionary defines collaboration as simply "to labor together." Collaboration implies a reciprocal relationship based on utilizing equally the therapist's knowledge and the parents' unique strengths and perspectives. Collaboration implies respect for each person's contribution, a non-blaming relationship built on trust and open communication. Collaboration implies that parents actively participate in the setting of goals and the therapy agenda. Collaboration implies that parents provide ongoing evaluation of each therapy session so that the therapist can refine and adapt the intervention to make it responsive to the family's needs.

In a collaborative relationship, the therapist works with parents by actively soliciting their ideas and feelings, understanding their cultural context, and involving them in the therapeutic process by inviting them to share their experiences, discuss their ideas, and engage in problem-solving. The therapist does not set him/herself up as the "expert" dispensing advice or lectures to parents about how they should parent more effectively; rather, s/he invites parents to help write the "script" for the intervention program. The therapist's role as collaborator, then, is to understand the parents' perspectives, to clarify issues, to summarize important ideas and themes raised by the parents, to teach and interpret in a way which is culturally sensitive, and finally, to teach and suggest possible alternative approaches or choices when parents request assistance and when misunderstandings occur.

This partnership between clients and therapist has the effect of giving back dignity, respect, and self-control to parents who are often seeking help for their children's problems at a vulnerable time of low self-confidence and intense feelings of guilt and self-blame (Spitzer, Webster-Stratton & Hollinsworth, 1991). It is our hypothesis that a collaborative model, which gives parents responsibility for developing solutions (alongside the therapist), is more likely to increase parents' confidence and perceived self-efficacy in treatment than are models which do not hold them responsible for solutions. Support for the value of this approach comes from the literature on self-efficacy, attribution, helplessness, and locus of control. For example, Bandura (1982, 1989) has suggested that self-efficacy is the mediating variable between knowledge and behavior. Therefore, parents who are self-efficacious will tend to persist at tasks until success is achieved. The literature also indicates that people who have determined their own priorities and goals are more likely to persist in the face of difficulties and less likely to show debilitating effects of stress (e.g., Dweck, 1975; Seligman, 1975). Moreover, research (Backeland & Lundwall, 1975; Janis & Mann, 1977; Meichenbaum & Turk, 1987) suggests that this collaborative process has the multiple advantages of reducing attrition rates, increasing motivation and commitment, reducing resistance, increasing temporal and situational generalization, and giving both parents and the therapist a stake in the outcome of the intervention efforts. On the other hand, controlling or hierarchical modes of therapy, in which the therapist makes decisions for parents without incorporating their input, may result in a low level of commitment, dependency, resentment, low self-efficacy, and increased resistance (Janis & Mann, 1977; Patterson & Forgatch, 1985). In fact, if parents are not given appropriate ways to participate, they may see no alternative but to drop out or resist therapy as a method of asserting their independence and their control over the process.

SETTING THE STAGE FOR COLLABORATION

The Setting

There are four main settings in which behavioral work with families of behavior-problem children takes place: the child's home, the school, the clinic, and the community center. Behavior therapy, based on the one-to-one (dyadic) or behavioral family therapy (systemic) model, tends to take place in the clinic consulting room/suite or home setting. Behavioral training based on the triadic or behavioral consultation model (using significant caregivers or teachers as mediators of change) may be located in the school. When behavioral training involves group work, the clinic or a community-based center is usually the preferred setting.

It is debatable whether there are clearly differentiated criteria for choosing the home as opposed to the clinic as the setting for training/ treatment of conduct-disordered children and their families, or the related issue of choosing a group, as opposed to an individual (family) modality, for the detailed work. The issue of group work being more economical and, indeed, as or more effective than individual casework, has been thoroughly investigated. Webster-Stratton has demonstrated clear advantages for the kind of group-based work that utilizes video modeling and the collaborative process of discussion and debate (Webster-Stratton, Kolpacoff & Hollinsworth, 1989; Webster-Stratton, 1990a,b). Are there occasions, however, when there is a case for choosing an individual family approach to treatment? Are there particular clients who require something other than, or in addition to, the clearly effective group-based method?

There is a category of parents who may respond more favorably to, and welcome, interventions in their own homes (Herbert, 1978). They and/or their children find clinic and group settings somewhat daunting—for a variety of reasons. For example:

- They tend not to be very articulate and to suffer from very low self-esteem; they find the social/verbal ethos of the group difficult to cope with.

- They do not share consensus values about life and child rearing, and sense themselves as "outsiders."

- Family life is disorganized, if not chaotic. To come out to regular appointments (the organization required, and the mobility demanded) may be beyond them.

- They are particularly *private* about their personal/familial disadvantages, tragedies, and "failings" and cannot envisage public discussion of personal issues, whatever the preliminary briefing and reassurance given.

- Child/spouse abuse in the family makes them wary of a public commitment to therapy.

- They (and this often means the child) feel safer/more comfortable working from home.

- They believe the therapist cannot really understand *their* reality unless s/he sees what actually happens in the home.

- They withhold trust, and belief, in the therapist unless they see him/her "getting stuck in" where the actions (the problematic interactions) are taking place—i.e., the "front line."

- There is a potentially subversive partner (this usually is the father) who refuses to attend a clinic; the only way to access him may be to work with *all* the family in his home.

- Both parents are poorly motivated for therapy. The only way to "engage" them in a change process is a relatively long process of "joining" the family over many home visits (or by means of intensive *day* programs).

These observations are based upon statements gathered from parents at intake evaluation sessions. None of these factors necessarily excludes a group approach, but when several converge on one family, they may make it difficult to engage the person in a commitment to clinic-based group meetings to which they have to make a regular self-directed journey. It has to be added that group and individual interventions are not necessarily an either/or choice. They may take place in parallel or sequentially if *both* modalities are thought to be required.

If the therapy is to take place in the clinic or a room in a community setting (e.g., church or school) it is important to try to find a setting for services that is informal and accessible. Our offices at the Parenting Clinic include a large comfortable group room with a lending library and a place to make coffee and tea. Many parents come to our group sessions early just to have coffee and cookies and chat informally with other parents before the group session starts. Initially, our therapists provide snacks for the mid-group break, but very soon we find other parents offering to bring in food for the group such as pizza, cakes, and so forth. This informality helps to decrease the distance not only from the therapist but also from the other parents and promotes a comfortable environment.

The Intake Interview

A collaborative approach begins at the very first encounter with the parents—-the initial intake interview. During this interview, the therapist tries to enter into the parents' experience and feelings; a typical question is, "Tell me what life is like at home with your child." Parents are asked to explain the disciplinary approaches and coping strategies they have tried—those that have worked and those that have not—as well as their theories regarding possible causes of the child's problems. Through questioning, the therapist elicits the parents' explanatory model and attributions for the child's problems. Parents are asked to list the problems they are concerned about and to prioritize them from their own perspective. Ideally, they come to feel that the therapist is making a genuine effort to understand their internal reality.

Next the therapist tries to elicit the parents' hopes and goals for therapy. S/he asks questions such as, "What is your greatest hope for what will happen as a result of coming to therapy?" Hearing the parents define their goals at the outset enables the therapist to correct any unrealistic expectations on their part. A secondary effect of goal definition is that, at a time when parents may be feeling depressed and vulnerable, it helps them focus on a more positive future. During the intake, the therapist listens carefully to the text and to the subtext of what the parents are saying; s/he listens with a "third ear" to discover not only what the child's problem are, but what those problems have meant to the family. Throughout the interview, the therapist tries to follow the parents' agenda, beginning where the parents want to begin and covering their points of concern. Thus, during the first interview the therapist has already begun to demonstrate empathic understanding and to involve parents immediately in therapy as a collaborative enterprise.

After discussing the parents' perceptions of their child's problems, their experiences attempting to deal with those problems, their explanatory model, and their hopes for therapy, we then share with them our philosophy regarding the causes of child conduct disorders. We explain our program, emphasizing its collaborative nature. For example:

THERAPIST: Our job now is to work with you, to support you, and to consult with you so that the interactions between you and your child are more positive and so that you can achieve your goals. The way our program works is we meet each week with a group of parents (whose children are similar to yours) in order to study and discuss together some videotapes of parent–child interactions about child behavior management. We work together as a team and we expect you to be our "cotherapist" in this process. This means that as we analyze the videotapes and decide together on some strategies for you to try out at home with your child, you become the experts on what works or doesn't work with your child. When things don't work, you bring this information back to us and we put our heads together to come up with a better strategy for the problem. You see, we each have a contribution: What we can offer is more alternatives, information, and resources, and what you can offer is help deciding and implementing the best strategy for your situation. How does that sound to you?

This collaboration is also discussed in our clinic brochure.

We sometimes find that parents have a preexisting cognitive "set" regarding therapy which may be quite different from our approach. For example, they may expect us to "fix" the child through child therapy, or to alter the child's temperament with medication. Or, because we place such a strong emphasis on parental involvement, they may incorrectly assume that we blame parents for the problems they are experiencing with their child. While self-blame and guilt are recurring themes throughout the process of therapy, it is important for parents to hear from the outset that we take a nonblaming, nonjudgmental stance towards the causes of the child's behavior problems and to see this attitude reflected consistently in our interactions with them. We want them to realize that we are interested in supporting parents and helping work to improve their situation rather than determining who is at fault, and that our orientation is toward the malleable present and future, not the unalterable past. The therapist might say:

THERAPIST: We appreciate hearing your own theories regarding the reasons for your child's problems. Our own approach when we see children misbehaving is not to assume either that the child is at fault (a "bad egg") or that the parent is inept. Rather we feel that—for whatever reason—the interaction between the parent and child has gone askew and is "out of synch." This may have occurred because the child has a more difficult temperament and is more resistant to discipline than other children, or because stresses on the family make it particularly hard to keep up the difficult work of parenting, or some combination of these factors.

The concepts of partnership, cotherapy, group discussion and support, education, and problem-solving are brought up repeatedly throughout the initial therapy sessions to emphasize the collaborative nature of the intervention program and to educate parents concerning its elements.

Initial Group Meeting

The initial group meeting is critical in terms of establishing not only the structure and ground rules for all future meetings but also in setting a tone for therapy. First, the therapist explains the group rules in terms of starting and ending meetings on time, the value of active participation in discussions, the importance of one person talking at a time, and the therapist's strategies for handling digressions or disagreements. The therapist again presents the collaborative philosophy, objectives, and rationale for the program to the whole group so that parents can raise any questions that may have come up since the intake interview. Next, group members are asked to share a little of their personal experiences with their children as well as their goals and hopes for participating in the program. This discussion results in the group members building rapport; they quickly realize that they are all experiencing similar difficulties and that they are not alone in their problems. It becomes evident that the therapist and parents are all working collaboratively towards similar goals.

The collaborative model of interacting with parent groups is demonstrated by the therapist's open communication patterns and accepting attitudes toward all the families in the program. By building a relationship based not on authority but on rapport with every member of the group, the therapist attempts to create a climate of trust, making the group a safe place for everyone to reveal their problems and frustrations. The therapist needs to be empathic and listen carefully to indicate that s/he appreciates and wants to understand everyone's point of view. During this initial session (as well as later on), it is important to use open-ended questions when exploring issues, for open-ended questions are more likely to generate lively discussion and collaboration, whereas questions that can be answered with a "yes" or "no" tend to produce very little exchange of ideas. Open-ended questions include questions designed to elucidate factual information (cognitive questions) as well as feeling information (affect questions) and ideas. For example, useful open-ended questions might include: "Why do you think your son gets so frustrated?' or "How might you feel if this were happening to you?" or "What kinds of things might a parent do in this situation?" Debate and alternative viewpoints are encouraged so that the therapist and parent groups can begin to engage in problem-solving. All viewpoints are respected; when possible, parents are encouraged to draw their own connections and develop their own insights. The therapist's empathic understanding will be conveyed by the extent to which s/he actively reaches out to the parents, attempts to understand (rather than analyze) their perspectives, and elicits their ideas.

While the collaborative relationship is the underlying structure for our process of intervention, within this relationship the therapist assumes a

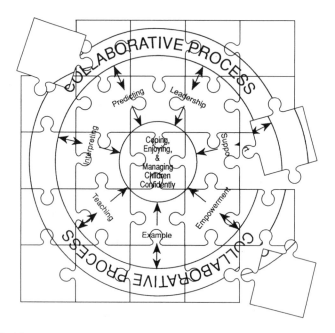

Figure 4.1   The collaborative process of working with parents

number of different roles. These include: building a supportive relationship; empowering parents; teaching; interpreting; leading; and what we call "prophesizing." Each of these roles is one specific expression of the collaborative relationship. In Figure 4.1 we have depicted the collaborative process as a jigsaw. The therapist's job is to sort out where and when to use each of the pieces of the puzzle; only when all the pieces are integrated will the collaborative process be complete.

THERAPIST ROLE No. 1: BUILDING A SUPPORTIVE RELATIONSHIP

As mentioned above, a collaborative approach requires that the therapist be empathic and use effective communication skills. This paper will not review these counseling skills, as there is an extensive literature describing the therapeutic skills needed for effective relationship enhancement (for reviews see Truax & Carkhuff, 1967; Brammer, 1988). Suffice it to say that empathy involves recognizing the feelings and perceptions (conscious and unconscious) that the parent has communicated. Empathy is conveyed unambiguously through the use of summaries of the parents' statements as well as supportive and reflective statements. In our therapy, we emphasize several relationship-building strategies in particular.

Use of Self-disclosure

As discussed earlier, the collaborative therapist does not present her/himself as an "expert" who has worked out all the answers to the parents' problems, an expert who stands apart from the families' problems. Instead, the therapist is not only empathic and caring, respectful and kind, but "genuine." These core conditions (as described by Carl Rogers, 1951) are necessary underpinnings for the cognitive-behavioral methodology. One way to be "genuine" is for the therapist to be willing to be known—to share personal experiences, feelings, and problems of his/her own. Therapists always have a rich array of stories, either from their own families or from work with other families, which they can draw upon at will. The author (Webster-Stratton) once shared with a parent group her intense anger and frustration when her four-year-old child would not go to bed during the months following the birth of her second child. Afterwards, a father who had been very quiet throughout the first sessions came up to her and said with an incredulous expression, "You mean you have problems too?" This led to an important discussion between the two of them and much more active participation on his part in subsequent sessions, which in turn laid the basis for a stronger therapeutic relationship.

This use of self-disclosure concerning one's personal issues should, however, be planned strategically. It cannot be overemphasized that the purpose of this strategy is not for families to learn about the therapist's feelings and problems; rather, the purpose of such examples is to help parents learn about themselves. By sharing some personal experiences, the therapist can help families understand that the process of parenting for everyone involves learning to cope and profit from mistakes; it is not a process of achieving "perfection." Thus the therapist's personal example in this case was intended to demystify the therapist and to discredit the notion that there are perfect parents. It served to normalize the parents' reactions and to give them permission to make mistakes. The intended message was something like this: "Even the therapist, in her 15 years of studying children, doesn't know what to do at times. She makes mistakes and gets angry too. I guess I'm not such a bad parent after all." A coping model, in which the therapist puts herself on the same level as the parents, is more effective than a mastery model, which would simply demoralize parents further because of the perceived discrepancy between their skills and those of the therapist. Moreover, this genuineness on the part of the therapist serves to enhance the therapist's relationship with the group members, introducing intimacy, affection, and closeness. Such a relationship, combined with the respect parents feel for the therapist, fuels the collaborative process.

Use of Humor

Our therapists make deliberate use of humor to help parents relax and to reduce anger, anxiety, and cynicism. Parents need to be able to laugh at their mistakes; this is part of the process of self-acceptance. Humor helps them gain some perspective on their stressful situation, which otherwise can become debilitating. Some of the videotape scenes in our program were actually chosen more for their humor value than for their content value. Our therapists use humorous personal examples to interject a comic note to the discussion. Humerous cartoons of parents and children, which are found in abundance in newspapers and magazines, are also helpful; parents can take them home to put on their refrigerator and laugh about later. Another strategy is to rehearse or role-play a situation doing everything wrong—i.e., with lots of criticisms, anger, and negative self-talk. This exaggeration inevitably evokes lots of laughter and helps build group spirit. Furthermore, when the parents find themselves engaging in some of this behavior at a future date, they may be able to stand back and laugh at themselves.

Optimism

Another form of support is for the therapist to establish positive expectations for change. Parents are often skeptical about their ability to change, especially if they see in their behavior a family pattern, for patterns often seem fixed and irreversible. For example, one parent said, "My mother beat me, now I beat my children." In such a case, the therapist must express his/her confidence in the parent's ability to break the family cycle. The therapist can point out each small step toward change—even the step of coming to therapy in the first place—as evidence that the problem is not fixed or irreversible. These parents need to be reinforced through positive feedback for each success, however small, and for each change in their behavior, whether or not it results in improvement in their child's behavior. It can be helpful to cite examples of other parents in similar situations who have been successful in teaching their children to behave more appropriately.

THERAPIST: It is good that you are working with your child now while he is still young. You are helping him stop his negative behaviors before they become permanent patterns.

Advocating for Parents

Each of the therapist approaches discussed above—self-disclosure, humor, and optimism—serves the overall purpose of building a supportive relationship. The therapist can also actively support parents by acting as an advocate for them in situations where communication with other professionals may have become difficult. In the role of advocate, the therapist can bring relevant persons, programs, and resources to the family, or bring the family to them. For example, the therapist can organize and attend meetings between parents and teachers so as to help the parents clarify the child's problems, agree upon goals, and set up behavior management programs which are consistent from the clinic to home to school.

It must be emphasized that the ultimate goal of this advocacy role is to strengthen the parents' ability to advocate for themselves and for their children. The danger of advocacy is that, if it is handled in a non-collaborative way, it can result in the parents feeling dependent or even uncommitted. An example of this might be the therapist who makes recommendations to a teacher, without the parent being present or being involved in formulating the recommendations. On the other hand, our collaborative advocacy approach goes as follows. In preparing to go on a school visit with a parent, we might say to the parent, "We want you to share with the teacher the strategies which are working for you at home in order to see whether the teachers might consider setting up a similar program at school." In some cases we help arrange the meeting with the school and talk with the teacher on the telephone. But we always suggest that the parent as "cotherapist" attend the meeting and take the initiative in working out the plan. By giving parents responsibility for their own advocacy, sharing their own solutions and advocating with (rather than for) parents, we again emphasize the collaborative process.

THERAPIST ROLE No. 2: EMPOWERING PARENTS

The essential goal of our collaborative therapy is to "empower" parents by building on their strengths and experience so that they feel confident about their parenting skills and about their ability to respond to new situations that may arise when the therapist is not there to help them. Bandura (1977) has called this strategy strengthening the client's "efficacy expectations"—that is, parents' conviction that they can successfully change their behaviors. There are several strategies that can help to empower parents.

Reinforcing and Validating Parents' Insights

Through the use of open-ended questions, parents are asked to problem-solve, drawing upon their ideas and prior experiences. Parents are encouraged to explore different solutions to a problem situation, rather than settling for "quick fixes" or the first solution that comes to mind. The therapists studiously avoid giving any pat answers, keeping the focus of the discussion on the parents' insights.

When therapists notice and comment upon a parent's problem-solving skills, parents feel validated. This affirming process helps parents to have confidence in their own insights, in their ability to sort out problems and to learn from their mistakes (Brown & Harris, 1978). For instance:

FATHER: I was just so frustrated with him! He wouldn't get dressed and was dawdling—I was going to be late for work. I got angrier and angrier. Finally, I went into his bedroom and shook him by the shoulders and yelled, "You want negative attention, you're going to get negative attention!" Then suddenly I thought, "What am I doing? Where is this getting me?" and I walked out of the room.

THERAPIST: So you were able to stop yourself in the middle of an angry tantrum. Good for you! That's remarkable. It sounds like your ability to stand back from the situation, to be objective and think about your goals, really helped you stop what you were doing. Is that true? What do you usually find helps you keep control of your anger? How would you replay the situation if it happens again?

In this example, the therapist's role is to reinforce the father's insight and to draw attention to his coping skills during the conflict situation. The therapist also helps the father to learn from the experience by rehearsing how he might respond in the future.

Because in most groups there are varying levels of educational background and communication skills, it is important that the therapist reinforce every parent for sharing his/her ideas so that every member gradually feels comfortable participating in the discussions. As part of this process, the therapist has to clarify for the group any unfocused or confusing statements made by parents so that they are not ridiculed, ignored, or criticized because of something they have said. We call this "finding the kernel of truth" in what a parent has said: underscoring its value by showing how it contributes to the understanding of the topic under discussion. One approach is for the therapist to keep a flip chart on which parents' useful ideas are recorded such as, "Sally's mealtime principle" or "John's rule when..." The developmental literature suggests that mothers who have confidence in their child-rearing, and who feel they have broad community support for what they do, actually do better at parenting (Behrens, 1954; Herbert, 1980).

Modifying Powerless Thoughts

When parents seek professional help for their problems, they usually have experienced or are experiencing feelings of powerlessness and mounting frustration with their children due to a history of unsuccessful attempts to discipline them. This powerlessness is often expressed in terms of feeling victimized by their children—"Why me?" The feeling of helplessness typically is accompanied by intense anger and a fear of losing control of themselves when trying to discipline their children.

FATHER: My wife's been at work and comes home and asks, "How did things go tonight?" I say, "Do the words 'living hell' mean anything to you?" That's our

MODIFYING PARENTS' POWERLESS THOUGHTS

sort of little joke. I'm labeling the kids in my mind as never doing what I say and I'm very angry at them.

Because none of us feel good about ourselves when we become angry at our children, parents' anger towards their children is likely to cause them to blame themselves and to then feel depressed in reaction to their guilt. Furthermore, they feel depressed about their interactions with their children, seeing themselves as a causal factor in their child's problems.

Therefore, a powerful and necessary aspect of empowering parents is to help them learn to stop the spiraling negative self-talk and, more generally, to modify their negative thoughts. For example, a parent may say, "It's all my fault, I'm a terrible parent. This is more than I can cope with, everything's out of control." The therapist then helps the parent learn how to stop this kind of powerless, self-defeating train of thought and to challenge it by substituting calmer, coping self-statements such as, "Stop worrying. These thoughts are not helping me. I'm doing the best I can. He's just testing my limits. All parents get discouraged at times, I'm going to be able to cope with this. I can manage." We ask parents to keep records of their thoughts in response to extremely stressful situations with their children at home. We then invite them to share some of this record with the group. As the group discusses these thoughts, unrealistic expectations and irrational beliefs are challenged and become modified through discussion. This strategy is in accordance with the cognitive restructuring strategies described by Beck and his colleagues (1979). The process of recognizing angry, helpless, self-critical, blaming, catastrophizing thoughts, and learning to substitute more adaptive and positive thoughts empowers parents by showing them they can cope with their thought patterns as well as their behaviors.

MOTHER: I just can't get the hang of it—I know I should be less critical and yell less and be more positive, but I just blew it when he wouldn't get dressed this morning.

THERAPIST: Hey, but that's the first step in behavior change—you are now aware of what you are doing. Recognizing something after you've done it is a good place to start. Analyzing that situation and thinking about what you want to do differently will help you the next time it occurs. Then you might catch yourself in the middle or even before you start to yell.

It is often necessary to counter the myths and attributions that get in the way of therapeutic change. Below are some typical examples of some myths and unhelpful attributions.

Sole ownership

■ It's my child's problem; s/he's the one who has to change.

■ It's me who's to blame.

If it doesn't hurt it doesn't work

■ A good belting is all he needs.

■ Kindness doesn't work with her/him! All s/he understands is a good hiding.

Narrow limit-setting

■ Give her/him an inch and s/he takes a mile.

Broad limits

- S/he won't love me if I insist.

- I feel so guilty if I say no.

Gender issues

- Only fathers can set firm limits.

- It's a mother's job—the discipline side of things.

Scapegoating

- It's the father's bad blood coming out in her/him.

Attributions

- There's a demon in her/him.

- I don't trust her/him; s/he has her/his father in her/him.

Catastrophizing

- I'm a complete failure as a parent.

- I can't forgive myself for the mistakes I've made.

Intergenerational ideas

- The hidings I had from my father did me no harm, so they won't do her/him any harm.

Unrealistic assumptions

- Other parents all seem to cope.

■ Children should change overnight.

■ Why should s/he be praised for doing what s/he should be doing anyway?

Discussing distressing thoughts in a parent group is also very reassuring for parents because it helps to "normalize" thoughts which they may previously have considered abnormal or crazy. As parents discover that other parents have the same kinds of "crazy" thoughts and reactions, they stop blaming themselves. It also helps if the therapist can share some examples from his or her experience in which negative cognitions led him/her to respond inappropriately. In addition to worrying that their own reactions are abnormal, parents often see their child's behavior as abnormal or pathological. The therapist normalizes this behavior by saying, "Indeed, things don't sound happy, but all children have behavior problems from time to time and all parents 'lose it' with their kids—no one is perfect." Thus the therapist helps the parents reexamine their expectations for themselves and their child, with the result of reducing their self-blame and anger. As these perceptions are altered, the parent feels less abnormal and more empowered.

Promoting Self-empowerment

Another element in empowering parents is self-empowerment. We try to help them learn how to give themselves a psychological "pat on the back." Parents are encouraged to look at their strengths and think about how effectively they handled a difficult situation. We ask them to express their positive feelings about their relationship with their child and to remember good times before this stressful period. We teach parents actively to formulate positive statements about themselves such as, "I had a good day today with Billy, I handled that situation well," or "I was able to stay in control, that was good." Parents, too, need tangible rewards for their efforts, such as dinner out with a spouse or a friend, a long hot bath, or a good book; and therapists can help them learn to set up these rewards for themselves.

Building the Family and Group Support Systems

Parents of conduct-disordered children experience a sense of being stigmatized and socially isolated from other parents—those with "normal" children. They also fear that if they are honest with their friends about their difficulties with their children, they will be met with misunder-standing, indifference, or outright rejection. The therapist's role, then, is to facilitate the parent group so that it serves as a powerful source of support, an empowering environment.

During group discussions, the therapist can help parents collaborate in problem-solving, express their appreciation for each other, and learn to cheer each other's successes in tackling difficult problems. The other side of the coin is that the therapist can encourage parents to share their feelings of guilt, anger, and depression as well as their experiences that involve mistakes on their part or relapses on the part of their child. (However, swapping "horror stories" must not go on too long or they will engender a mood of pessimism.) These discussions serve as a powerful source of support. They decrease feelings of isolation, empowering parents through the knowledge that they are not alone in their problems. For instance, the following comments were made in one of our groups:

FATHER: You know, when this program is finished, I will always think about this group in spirit.

MOTHER: This group is all sharing—it's people that aren't judging me, that are also taking risks and saying, "Have you tried this? or have you considered you are off track?"

In addition to building the support system within the group, the therapist can also build support within the family. The parents in our program report frequent arguments and fights with partners, grand-parents, and teachers over how to handle the child's problems, resulting in stressed marital relationships as well as stressed individuals. Frequently, the energy required to care for the children leaves parents feeling exhausted, too tired to make plans to spend time with adult friends, let alone interact with them. Yet, time away from the child with spouses and friends can help parents feel supported and energized. It helps them gain perspective so they are better able to cope with the child's parenting needs. Sometimes parents almost seem to have forgotten their identity as individuals rather than as parents; time away reminds parents of this important aspect of their identity. The therapist needs strongly to advocate evenings out and other breaks away from the children, and parents should be encouraged to take "caring days" on which they do something nice for themselves (Stuart, 1980).

We encourage every parent to have a spouse, partner, close friend, or family member (such as grandparent) in the program with them to provide mutual support. Our follow-up studies have indicated that the greatest likelihood of treatment relapses occurs in families in which only one person is involved in the treatment program (Herbert, 1978; Webster-Stratton, 1985). Wahler's (1980) research has indicated that single mothers who had contact with other people outside the home fare much better in their parenting than mothers without such contacts, while maternal insularity or social isolation results in the probability of treatment failure (Dumas & Wahler, 1983). During therapy sessions, the therapist helps the parents (or the parent and partner) define ways they can support each other when feeling discouraged, tired, or unable to cope with a problem. This feeling of support and understanding from another family member or friend contributes to a sense of empowerment.

THERAPIST ROLE No. 3: TEACHING

What about the therapist's role as teacher? Since a knowledgeable teacher might also be called an "expert" in his/her field, there may be some question about whether our approach allows the therapist to function in this capacity. Is this role compatible with a collaborative relationship, or is there a contradiction between "collaborator" and "expert"? Does the therapist have to renounce her expertise?

It is our contention that a therapist's expertise is not only compatible with but essential to a collaborative therapeutic relationship. Just as the parents function as experts concerning their child and have the ultimate responsibility for judging what will be workable in their particular family and community, the therapist functions as expert concerning children's developmental needs, behavior management principles, and communication skills. (The specific content of parent programs will not be discussed here, as it can be found in Webster-Stratton's training manual and videotapes, and is alluded to in Chapter 7.)

However, teaching can be collaborative or noncollaborative. A noncollaborative teaching approach is didactic and nonparticipative—the teacher lectures, the parents listen. The noncollaborative teacher presents principles and skills to parents in terms of absolutes and "prescriptions" for successful ways of dealing with their children. Homework assignments are rigid, given without regard for the particular circumstances of an individual family. We reject this approach because, for one thing, it is unsuccessful: it is likely to lead to higher attrition rates and poor long-term maintenance. Furthermore, it is ethically dubious to impose goals on parents which may not be congruent with their goals, values, and lifestyle and which are not adapted to the unique temperament of the child. In contrast, a collaborative teaching model implies that, as far as possible, the therapist stimulates the parents to generate ideas and insights based on their experiences, and to generate appropriate solutions based on their family's particular set of circumstances. When parents come up with appropriate solutions, the therapist can then reinforce and expand on these ideas. Homework assignments are adapted so that they are perceived as useful by parents. This approach increases the chance that the content of the parent program is relevant, clearly understood, and utilized by the parents.

The net result of collaborative teaching is to strengthen the parents' knowledge base and their self-confidence, instead of perpetuating a sense of inadequacy and creating dependence on the teacher. Since we want parents to adopt a participative, collaborative, empowering approach when teaching their own children, it is important to use this approach with them in therapy—to model with them the teaching approach we wish them to use with their children. This "inductive" form of teaching leads to greater internalization of learning in children (and very likely adults) (Herbert, 1980). There are several strategies a therapist can use in his/her role as teacher.

Persuading, Explaining, Suggesting and Adapting

Therapeutic change depends on persuasion, which means giving parents the rationale for each component of the program. The treatment principles, objectives, and methods should not be shrouded in mystery. It is important for the therapist to voice clear explanations based upon valid information and knowledge of the developmental literature as well as hard-earned practical wisdom and experience. Research has indicated that parents' understanding of the social learning principles underlying the parent-training program leads to enhanced generalization or maintenance of treatment effects (McMahon & Forehand, 1984).

However, it is also important that these rationales and theories be presented in such a way that the parent can see the connection with his/her stated goals. Rationales should be given not as absolutes or commands, but rather in the context of thoughtful discussion. When we introduce a new principle or component of the program, we try to relate it to topics previously discussed; whenever possible, connections are made with issues previously raised by the parents. For example, when providing the rationale for the child-directed play interactions, the therapist explains how this approach fosters the child's self-esteem and social competence, while at the same time decreasing his/her need to obtain control over parents by negative behaviors. In this example, supplying the rationale is important not only because parents may not immediately see the connection between playing with their children more and helping their child be less aggressive, but also because of the connection made between this new aspect of the program and the parents' original reason for seeking help (their child's aggressiveness). If they do not understand the rationale for the play sessions, they may not be motivated to do them at home. To take another example, when explaining the Ignore and Time Out procedures, the therapist not only explains the conceptual basis for withdrawing parental attention from child negative behaviors (namely, to avoid reinforcing the child's misbehavior with parental attention), but also makes a connection with a previously expressed concern of this parent:

FATHER: He hit her and hurt her. I have talked to him over and over about how he's making other children feel bad. I get so frustrated with him. He doesn't seem to have any guilt.

THERAPIST: It *is* frustrating. But it looks like you're doing a nice of job of beginning to help him understand the perspective of others in a situation. You know, the development of empathy in children—that is, the ability of a child to understand another person's point of view—takes years. Not until adulthood is this aspect of development fully matured. Young children are at the very beginning steps of gaining this ability. The paradox of this is that one of the best ways you can help your son learn to be sensitive to the feelings of others is for you to model your understanding of him. Children need to feel understood and valued by their parents before they can value others.

In this example, the therapist identifies the parent's frustration with his son, empathizes with it, reinforces his efforts to promote empathy in his child, and then explains some child development principles concerning moral development. In doing so, the therapist is collaborating with the parent's goal of promoting empathy in his son and helping him gain a new perspective on how to pursue this goal.

Adapting

In addition to persuading and explaining, the process of collaborative teaching involves the therapist working with parents to adapt concepts and skills to the particular circumstances of the parents and to the particular temperamental nature of the child. For example, a parent who lives in a one-room trailer is unlikely to have an empty room for Time Out and will even have difficulty finding a suitable spot to put a Time Out chair. A parent living in an apartment, where walls are not sound-proofed, will be acutely sensitive to the possible reactions of neighbors when s/he tries to ignore the screaming child; that parent may resist using that approach. Collaborative teaching means that the therapist attempts to understand the living circumstances of each family and involves the families in problem-solving to adapt the concepts to their particular situation. To take another example, a highly active, impulsive child will not be able to sit quietly and play attentively with his parents for long periods of time. Such children will also have more difficulty sitting in Time Out than less active children. Some children are not particularly responsive to Tangible Reward programs. The therapist needs to be sensitive to these individual differences in child temperament so that s/he can begin the collaborative process of defining with parents which approach will be best for a particular child.

Giving Assignments

The teacher role involves giving an assignment for every session. This usually involves asking parents to do some observing and recording of behaviors or thoughts at home and/or experimenting with a particular strategy. Assignments are critical because there is an important message value that goes with them: namely, that participation in group therapy is not "magic moondust"; parents must collaborate with the therapist by working at home to make changes. The assignments and experiments help transfer what is talked about in therapy sessions to real life at home. They also serve as a powerful stimulus for discussion at the subsequent session. For example, one assignment we use for parents is to play one-on-one with their child each day for 15 minutes; another assignment is to record how often they praise between 5 and 6 p.m. for two days, and then to double their base rate for the remainder of the week. A third example of an assignment is for parents to keep track of their thoughts in response to a conflict situation with their child on three occasions.

Parents need to understand the purpose of the assignments in general, as well as particular assignments. "Homework" should be presented as an integral part of the learning process.

THERAPIST: You can't learn to drive a car or play the piano without practicing, and this is also the case with the parenting skills you are learning here. The more effort you put into the assignments, the more success you will have with the program.

Parents are more likely to take the assignments seriously if they know the therapist is going to begin each session by reviewing the assignment from the previous week, before presenting new material.

When a parent questions the usefulness or feasibility of an assignment this should receive immediate attention, though not the kind of attention it might receive from a "hierarchical" teacher. Rather, the problem should be explored in a collaborative fashion. For example, a single parent with four young children says she is unable to do 15 minutes of play time each day with an individual child. The therapist responds:

THERAPIST: I imagine you barely have two minutes to yourself all day—let alone 15 minutes with an individual child. Let's talk about ways to practice the play skills with several children at the same time. Or, would it be possible to play in brief bursts of two to three minutes throughout the day? Or, are there any times when you have only one or two children at home?

When a parent fails to complete an assignment from the previous session, the reasons for this should be explored in a collaborative fashion. For example, the therapist can ask, "What made it hard for you to do the assignment?" "How have you overcome this problem in the past?" "What advice would you give to someone else who has this problem?" "Do you think it is just as hard for your child to learn to change as it is for you to change?" "What can you do to make it easier for you to complete the assignment this week?" "Do you think there is another assignment that might be more useful for you?" These questions could be explored as a group discussion topic. It is important to explore reasons why some parents might be having difficulty doing their home assignments; otherwise, parents may conclude that the therapist is not really committed to the assignments, or does not really want to understand their particular situation. It can be helpful to ask parents to set their own goals for assignments for the following week—these goals should be manageable and realistic, optimizing the chance of success. We often give parent personal mottos to use when trying to accomplish a goal:

- *Challenge but don't overwhelm yourself.* In the same way as if you were learning to drive: you wouldn't immediately venture out into the motorway.

- *Get better before you feel better.* Engaging in difficult homework tasks may make you feel worse, but you are learning to cope better. This is true of recovery from various conditions such as a broken limb or an operation.

Reviewing and Summarizing

Another aspect of the teacher role is reviewing and summarizing for the benefit of all. The therapist can end each session with a summary of the major points of discussion from that session and a review of the handouts and assignments for the next week. Our parents like to be given notebooks into which they can put handouts that review each session's content, as well as take notes and record their weekly assignments. Along with ensuring that everyone understands the assignment for the next week, the therapist needs to express confidence in the parents' ability to carry it out. We also try to provide parents with current articles that either reinforce concepts or stimulate group discussion. These, of course, will only be useful for parents with reading skills. For illiterate parents, we use "cues" such as cartoons and stickers to help remind them of essential concepts at home. For example, we use red sticker dots to remind parents to decrease their negative self-talk, and green dots to increase positive self-talk. We suggest that parents put these cartoons and stickers on the refrigerator or a place where they will see them often and be reminded of the concept.

Ensuring Generalization

Generalization means teaching parents how to apply the specific skills being taught in the program to their own situation. It also means teaching them how to apply the same skills in other settings or to new types of misbehavior that may occur in the future. For instance, some parents learn how to manage their children effectively at home, but have great difficulty knowing how to handle misbehavior when it occurs in public. They have difficulty seeing how principles such as Ignore, Time Out, and Logical Consequences can be applied at the grocery store, cinema, park, or school. Other parents have difficulty knowing how to use the approaches with siblings who are exhibiting somewhat different behaviors. To counter this inability to generalize, the therapist can periodically interject a few different types of problems and situations (not raised by the group) and ask the group to problem-solve strategies to deal with them. After working on a problem area the therapist should regularly ask, "For what other child problems could you apply this strategy?" or "Are there situations where this strategy wouldn't work?" Videotapes are another powerful means of enhancing generalization, since they can depict a variety of problems in different situations and settings. (The use of videos is discussed below.) Finally, the group discussion format itself is another means of promoting generalization, in that it exposes group members to a variety of different family situations; it provides opportunities to hear other parents applying the principles to a variety of behavior problems involving children of different ages and temperamental styles.

Using Videotape Modeling Examples

There are also a number of props that can be helpful in the therapist's teaching role. The Webster-Stratton's program relies heavily on videotape modeling as a therapeutic method. We developed a series of 16 videotape programs (over 300 vignettes) showing parents and children of different sexes, ages, cultures, socioeconomic backgrounds, and temperamental styles. Parents are shown in natural situations interacting with their children: during mealtimes, getting children dressed in the morning, toilet training, handling child disobedience, playing together, and so forth. Scenes depict parents "doing it right" and "doing it wrong." The intent in showing negative as well as positive examples is to demystify the notion that there is "perfect parenting" and to illustrate how parents can learn from their mistakes. Our research has indicated that therapist-led group discussion based on videotape modeling is superior to therapist-led group discussion without videotapes, as well as to videotape alone (Webster-Stratton, 1984; Webster-Stratton, Kolpacoff, & Hollinsworth, 1988; 1989).

However, it is important to emphasize that the videotapes are used in a collaborative way—as a catalyst to stimulate group discussion and

USE VIDEOTAPES IN A COLLABORATIVE WAY
TO ENHANCE TEACHING

problem-solving, not as a device which renders the parents passive observers. When we show a videotape vignette, we pause the tape to give parents a chance to discuss and react to what they have observed. Sometimes after watching a vignette, group members are uncertain about whether the kinds of responses shown in the scenes are appropriate. If this is the case, the therapist may then ask open-ended questions such as, "Do you think that was the best way to handle that situation?" or "How would you feel if your child did that?" (Suggested questions and discussion topics are included in the therapist's manual.) The vignettes have been designed to illustrate specific concepts, it is up to the therapist to make sure the ensuing discussion addresses the intended topic and is understood by the parents. If participants are unclear about specific aspects of the parent/child interaction, or if they have missed a critical feature of the vignette, the therapist rewinds the tape and has the group watch the scene again. The goal is to have parents become actively involved in problem-solving and sharing ideas about the vignette. It would be inappropriate (and noncollaborative) to show the tapes without pausing or inviting extensive discussion and debate. The therapist can also facilitate learning by asking the parents how the concepts illustrated in the vignettes do or do not apply to their own situations. For example, a mother may make the following comment after watching a few of the play vignettes:

MOTHER: I don't have any toys at home. I can't afford toys like those shown on the tapes—I'm living on a welfare check.

THERAPIST: You know, even if you had the money it is not important to have fancy toys. In fact, some of the best toys for children are things like pots and pans, empty cereal boxes, dry macaroni, and string. Why don't we brainstorm some ideas for inexpensive things you could use to play with your child at home?

This interaction between the therapist and mother illustrates the importance of collaborating with parents in order to be sure the concepts shown on the videotapes are relevant to their particular cultural and socioeconomic situation.

Role-play and Rehearsal

Role-playing—modeling and rehearsing newly acquired behaviors—is one of the most common components of parent training programs; it has been shown to be quite effective in producing behavioral changes (Eisler, Hersen & Agras, 1973; Twentyman & McFall, 1975). Role-play helps to tease out sequences in behavior, enabling parents to anticipate situations more clearly.

USE ROLE PLAY TO ENHANCE TEACHING

It is helpful to do at least one role-play for each content area, but because many parents feel inadequate regarding their parenting behavior, they may feel reluctant to undertake role-playing. Besides presenting a clear rationale for conducting the role-play, we have found that it is often best for the therapist to do the first role-play in order to reduce parents' self-consciousness and anxiety. If the therapist can make the role-play humorous by exaggerating roles, so much the better. For example, the therapist who is role-playing the parent may go out of the room and shout from a distance (e.g., kitchen) for the child (role-played by parent) to put away the toys. This usually raises chuckles of recognition, for there is no way for the parent to know whether the child registers the command, takes any notice of it, complies, or not. This role-play is an effective introduction to the session and the videotape concerning commands.

After the therapist has done the first role-plays, we then break the parent group into pairs to practice particular skills. Later on, as groups become comfortable with each other, parents role-play a situation in front of the whole group—for example, role-playing the use of Time Out with a "difficult child." In this case, one parent plays the child and another parent the child's parent. The rest of the parent group act as coaches for the parent who is in the parent role. Sometimes it is helpful to "freeze frame" the role play and then ask the group to brainstorm, "Now what should she do?" or "What is the child trying to communicate or achieve by behaving like that?"

Evaluating

Part of the teacher role is to ensure that each session is evaluated by the parents. This gives the therapist immediate feedback about how each parent is responding to the therapist's style, the quality of the group discussions, and the information presented in the session. The evaluations bring problems to light—the parent who is dissatisfied with the group, the parent who is resisting a concept, the parent who fails to see the relevance of a particular concept to his/her own situation, the parent who wants more group discussion. The therapist may want to meet with parents individually to resolve these issues. If several participants are having difficulty understanding a particular concept, the therapist will want to bring it up in a subsequent session with the whole group. This ongoing process, where the therapist responds to parents' evaluations by taking action, emphasizes the collaborative nature of the therapy process. At the end of the program, the entire treatment program should be evaluated. This information is useful not only in planning future parent groups, but also in identifying parents who may need further help.

THERAPIST ROLE No. 4: INTERPRETING

The therapist role of teacher is closely allied to another role, that of interpreter. As an interpreter, the therapist "translates" the language of cognitive, behavioral, and developmental concepts into words and behaviors that the parents can apply. But the interpreter role is more than this: the therapist must also interpret the language and culture of the family in order to help that family. The latter can occur only if there is collaboration. It is here that therapy shows itself as a craft—an amalgam of applied science and art. No matter how good the science (the theoretical framework and empirical findings), without the creative element of translating abstract and complex ideas into concrete, interesting applications which are relevant to the family's circumstances, the science is not likely to achieve much.

Use of Analogies and Metaphors

The therapist can be a more effective interpreter by using images and analogies to explain theories and concepts. S/he needs to be creative in thinking up vivid mental pictures to convey important concepts. Ideally, these analogies should be developed out of themes which are unique to a particular community or cultural group. Here are a few that we have either invented or borrowed from discussions with other therapists.

■ *Hard wax/seal analogy*: Socrates used to send out letters to his friends and seal the letters with wax and his seal. His friends would complain when they received the letter that they couldn't make out the imprint of the seal and would ask him, "Why don't you get a new seal?" Socrates commented, "No one ever asked me if the problem was that the wax was too hard to receive the seal."

■ *Therapist's interpretation*: We can't change the nature of our children's "wax," but we can work hard to get the best imprint possible.

This analogy depicts the concept that socialization takes longer with some children; conduct-disordered children do not "take the imprint" easily. By pointing to the wax rather than the seal—or the person who tries to use it—as the source of the difficulty, this analogy shifts the blame away from the parents. Further, it helps them to make allowances for the child's temperament.

■ *Diamond analogy*: These children are like diamonds—parents need to chip away carefully at the hard edges of the diamonds to see their beauty. Of course, hard diamonds are very valuable.

This analogy is used to reframe the parents' negative perceptions of their child's temperament. Thinking of these difficult children as hard diamonds waiting to be made beautiful emphasizes not only their innate value, but also the parent's socialization role.

■ *Flossing analogy*: Teaching children is like flossing your teeth: You have to keep doing it over and over to get long-term results.

With this analogy we hope to convey the notion that daily repetition and constant monitoring can achieve long-term results, even though it seems that not much is accomplished day by day.

■ *Bank account analogy*: Think of praising and playing with children as building up your bank account. You have to keep putting something in all the time—only then will you have something to draw on when you need it. Time Out and other forms of discipline will not work unless there is a "bank account" of positive resources to draw from. In fact, Time Out from an aversive relationship may actually be reinforcing.

With this analogy we are emphasizing the need for positive interaction with the child as a foundation for discipline.

- *Priming the pump analogy*: You know the old farm pumps that had to be pumped a dozen times before water would come out? Parents have to "prime the pump" with lots of supportive input to build children's self-esteem. You also have to "prime your own pumps" so that you can keep on functioning as an effective parent—that is, you need to fill yourself with positive thoughts and take time to refuel your own energy.

With this analogy we are explaining the idea that parents need to keep "pumping in" positive messages before they will receive positive behavior in return.

- *Gas on the flames analogy*: Arguing and reasoning with a child when he is noncompliant and angry is like throwing gas on the flame.

This analogy is used when trying to help parents learn to ignore children's misbehavior rather than yell and scold. It is important they understand that such an approach actually fuels the problem rather than dampening it.

- *Megaphone analogy*: Think about yourself using a megaphone when you praise your child—that is, do it more strongly and enthusiastically than you might otherwise be likely to do. Sometimes these children seem deaf, as if hidden in a suit of armor and a helmet—there is so much armor that it takes quite a lot of repetition to penetrate. Sometimes these children even deflect the praise because they have a hard time accepting a new—a positive—image of themselves and are more comfortable with the old image.

This analogy is used to encourage parents to praise their children more frequently and more often than they otherwise would. It also helps prepare them for the occasions where children reject praise and suggests why this may happen.

- *Vending machine analogy*: Remember, when you first ignore a child's misbehavior, it will escalate before the behavior improves. For the child, the experience of being ignored is a little like the experience that sometimes happens with vending machines. Let's say you put in a dollar but no Coke comes out. You press the lever a few times—still no Coke. Then you start banging the machine because the machine is ignoring you. But what would happen if a Coke happened to come out as you were banging? Next time you lost a dollar and needed a drink you would start out banging!

This analogy is helpful to parents in preparing them not only for the tantrums and misbehavior that will be the child's response to Ignore and Time Out procedures, but also as a warning to parents of what will happen if they give in to this misbehavior.

- *Choose your battles analogy*: Your military resources, to use an image, are not unlimited. Think about choosing those battles that are really important to you and save your energy for those. For example, wearing seatbelts, not hitting, and getting to bed on time may be more important than clean plates, wearing a different shirt, or picking up toys. In that case, it's not worth expending your resources in battle for those causes.

This analogy helps parents prioritize which household rules they are prepared to enforce and which ones they can let slide for the time being.

- *Radar antennae analogy*: Monitoring kids means keeping your radar antennae up at all times, so that you know where your child is and what he or she is doing. That way, you can spot potential problems before they develop. Antennae are important not only so that you can assure yourself that your child is not in trouble, but also so that you can spot positive behaviors that need to be reinforced.

Parents sometimes have false expectations that children can be left unattended. This analogy helps parents understand that constant monitoring on their part is required at all times. This analogy also encourages parents' understanding that effective parents anticipate problems and nip them in the bud (based on an early signal on their "radar") by distracting their child or by stopping the behavior early on.

- *Tug-of-war analogy*: Arguing with children is like parents and children playing "tug of war," both pulling the rope at opposite ends. When you find yourself in such a struggle, say to yourself that you're going to drop the rope.

This analogy helps parents understand that constant arguing only perpetuates the struggle, whereas withdrawing from the tug-of-war ends it.

- *Children are wearing L plates*: In England, when one is learning to drive, an L plate—for "Learner"—is put on the car. Imagine that your child also has an L plate on his or her back. This will remind you to be patient and tolerant when your child makes a mistake. Children are, after all, learners in life.

This analogy helps remind parents of children's developmental processes. They are still learning and, like the person who is learning to drive, will behave unpredictably and make mistakes.

Reframing

Therapeutic change depends on providing explanatory stories, alternative explanations which help clients to reshape their perceptions of and their beliefs about the nature of their problems. Reframing by the therapist (cognitive restructuring) is a powerful interpretive tool for helping clients understand their experiences, thereby promoting change in their behaviors. It involves altering the emotional and/or conceptual viewpoint of the client in relation to an experience, by placing the experience in another "frame" which fits the facts of the situation well, thereby altering its meaning.

In our program, one common strategy is for the therapist to take a problem a parent is having with a child and reframe it from the child's point of view rather than the parent's perspective. For example:

FATHER: He's so defiant! He should be able to be toilet trained by now—he's three and a half years old! He's doing it on purpose! He even tells us right after he has had a poop in his pants. I get so angry with him!

THERAPIST: Hey, but you know what? That's a great sign—the fact he's telling you after he poops means he's getting ready to be trained. Remember how we said we recognize something after we've done it and change it the next time, whereas children tell us afterwards? But with your support he will soon learn to recognize the sensations before he goes. You know, the fact he is telling you he has done it in his pants is also a very good sign—it's much harder when children fear their parents' anger and learn to hide their underpants in closets.

FATHER: But it feels so deliberate to me—he's so advanced in other areas of his development, such as his manipulation skills with my tools and so forth. He should be toilet trained by now.

THERAPIST: Ah, this is often the case with development: As one area is maturing and developing, another area may lag behind. Think about babies. When they are learning to walk, they often slow down in their language. And for others it is the reverse—while their language is developing, they are not walking. All these areas of development—verbal, intellectual, social, moral, physical, language—develop at different rates, as does control of bowel movements.

OR

MOTHER: She yells and screams at bedtime and needs water, a cookie, a hug, and on and on.

THERAPIST: Yes, those bedtime rituals get to be a drag. But you know, they are so important, because if they are predictable they will give the child a sense of security. And going to sleep is a time when children really need this predictability and routine, because going to sleep represents a separation from you—a loss.

OR

PARENT: Now he just stands at the window screaming at other kids to come and play with him—he is so needy for friends. I don't understand why he has to do that.

THERAPIST: Well, you know, these aggressive kids have frequently been rejected by other kids, so they are pretty insecure about friendships. It will take time to teach him the positive social skills so that he learns how to approach other children more appropriately. But, you know, the fact he is so interested in making friends is really a good sign—he hasn't gotten to the point of rejecting other kids himself.

OR

PARENT: My son has these incredibly long, angry outbursts when he is in Time Out. He's really out to make it difficult for me.

THERAPIST: Do you suppose he might be really testing the strength of your limit setting to see if he can get you to "lose it" or back down?

OR

PARENT: My child has gotten incredibly worse this week—she is impossible to handle and I've had to use Time Out a lot. She's wearing me down.

THERAPIST: You know, I think kids always regress to test the security of the limits in their environment before they take a major new step forward in their development.

OR

THERAPIST: Rather than thinking of your child as having a problem or being a problem, it may help to think of her/him as trying to solve a problem. That behavior you don't like may be her/his way of trying to deal (not very successfully; but after all he/she's a learner) with one of life's difficulties. Let us try to see what s/he is trying to achieve; what are the developmental tasks s/he has to solve at this stage of life?

In all of the examples above, the parent saw the child as defiant, angry, uncooperative, immature, and was exhausted by the effort of trying to cope with the behavior. The therapists reframed the situations to help the parents see the developmental stage the behavior represents or to understand the child's emotions in the situation. Helping parents perceive the behavior as testing the security of limits, or reacting to the loss of the important parent, or moving towards independence helps the parents see the behavior as appropriate or normal—in some cases even positive. Seen in this light, the situations are part of the normal developmental process. With this view of the situations, parents can feel that they are participating in a process of growth for the child, rather than becoming angry or feeling helpless. This attitude enables them to cope. In essence, reframing involves changing a negative label for a behavior into a positive one; as we mentioned earlier, it can be a tool of empowerment for the parent.

Making Connections

Another way to interpret the language and culture of the family is to help the parents see the connections between their own childhood experiences and those of their child. This is a powerful way of promoting empathy and bonding between the parent and his/her child.

THERAPIST: As you talk about your child's impatience, high energy level, and difficulty conforming in the classroom, do you see any similarities to yourself or your experiences as a child

How do these similarities between you both affect your reactions to your child? Having been a high energy and independent child yourself, what do you think helped you the most? or the least?

In the case where the parent does acknowledge similarities between his/her personality and his/her child's, the therapist's role is to help the parent see how similar personalities may create possible conflict in their reactions as a parent and to move the parent on to seeing how this similarity makes him/her uniquely suited to judging what parenting strategies might be most useful with his/her child.

The therapist can also help parents see how their reactions and responses as parents are based on their own parents' parenting skills (either in imitation or in reaction) and how these experiences may be causing them to resist learning alternative approaches.

FATHER: When my son gets angry and defiant like that—I think to myself—my father would never have put up with any of this shit! He would have smacked me hard.

THERAPIST: How do those thoughts about your father influence your ability to stay calm? What do you tell yourself when you hear your father's voice in your head? How do you counter them?

Here the therapist's role is to help the parent see the connection between what the father learned from his own father regarding parenting, how this influences him (e.g., escalates his anger level toward his son) and what he would like to do differently or the same with his son.

A third way to help parents reframe their conflicts between their own childhoods (and parents) and their current experiences is to talk about "laying ghosts to rest."

THERAPIST: You may be finding it difficult to put all your thought and energy into the present difficulty. Perhaps there are some "ghosts" from the past (things you blame yourself for needlessly in your child rearing) that still haunt you. Let us try to put them to rest by talking about them; then you may feel more confident about facing the future.

It is one of the strengths of behavioral work that treatment and the choice of methods do not depend necessarily upon the discovery and understanding of the historical causes of behavior problems. The identification of the current problem and its contemporary antecedents and consequences is the main agenda in treatment. Very rarely can current problems be traced to specific past experiences with any degree of confidence. Nevertheless, many of the therapeutic methods in traditional psychotherapy are formulated as a response to an historical analysis of the parent's life. Such a retrospective look at past events is often of interest (and potentially of use), but essentially an exclusive or predominant preoccupation in assessment with the past history has the effect of "distancing" the problem, keeping it vague because it remains at arm's length. It certainly tends to alienate parents who are struggling with *current* problems in the child. Nevertheless, there *is* a place in the collaborative model of treatment for a brief consideration of the child's and parents' past. The stories people tell themselves about themselves and their offspring (schema) are important because they influence their actions. These stories, particularly of a mother or father who struggled to rear a difficult infant, are often negative, self-deprecatory ones. Thus it may be necessary for the therapist to help parents "lay the ghosts" of the past that still haunt them before s/he can apply him or herself wholeheartedly (i.e., without debilitating regret and guilt) to problems in the here-and-now.

THERAPIST ROLE No. 5: LEADING AND CHALLENGING

Are there times when the therapist must take control of the group, even confront parents? If so, how does this role fit into the collaborative model?

The most obvious reason for the therapist to lead the group is that otherwise the group will lack focus and organization. Our evaluations have indicated that parents become frustrated if the discussion is permitted to wander or if one person is allowed to monopolize the session. Parents appreciate having enough structure imposed to keep the discussion focused and moving along. Another reason the therapist must exercise leadership skills is to deal with the group process issues, such as the arguments and resistance, which are an inevitable part of every group's therapy process.

But there is an apparent tension between this role and the collaborative model, since in collaborative therapy power is shared. There are several strategies which we use to preserve the collaborative spirit while allowing the therapist to function as leader. For one thing, the therapist can allow parents a role in determining the agenda for each session.

THERAPIST: Before we start, I would like us to set today's agenda. We will do this at the beginning of each session. I will have a major topic for each week and then you can add topics you want to be sure we cover. The idea is to make sure that we cover what seems important to each of us. So today's first major topic is effective play skills with children and how we can foster children's self-esteem and promote their positive behaviors. What topics would anyone like to add?

Our sessions always begin with parents and the therapist together setting the agenda and goals for the session, debriefing the assignment for the previous week, evaluating progress, and discussing how things are currently going at home. The therapist's job then is to connect parents' input—their questions, concerns, reactions to the assignments, and experiences at home— into the overall framework and new topics for that particular session. The trick is keeping a good balance between the parents' individual needs and the group's needs for leadership. The sessions always conclude with assigning the tasks to be completed before the next session. The following are some other strategies which we find helpful in leading the sessions.

Setting Limits

One of the most important aspects of the therapist's leadership role is to prevent the group process from becoming disrupted. The therapist must impose sufficient structure to facilitate the group process. We have found it necessary to establish some rules to keep things running smoothly—for example, only one person may talk at a time. If someone breaks this rule we simply say, "One person at a time, please." Sometimes there is a parent in a group who is critical and verbally aggressive toward either their spouse or another parent in the group. In such instances we intervene quickly to stop the bullying pattern; otherwise, the other parent will withdraw. For example, the therapist may say in a supportive but firm manner, "I need to interrupt you right there." The therapist then explains why s/he is cutting off the speaker. For groups that are very verbal and that tend to digress or get sidetracked, it can be helpful to select a parent participant to act as co-leader at the beginning of each session. The job of this co-leader is to be a timekeeper, to help identify parents who are sidetracking the discussion, and keep the group focused on the main topics for the session. If a different participant is invited to act as co-leader for each session, the task of monitoring the group discussion becomes everyone's responsibility and there is collaborative leadership.

In addition to keeping the group discussions orderly, the therapist enforces the time schedule. Meetings have a tendency to start later and later unless a definite starting time is established. Meetings should begin on time even if only two people are present. Similarly, the therapist needs to end the meetings on time. This may be difficult when groups are in the middle of an enthusiastic discussion; however, this is actually a good time to end a meeting, since everyone will leave feeling stimulated and excited about their involvement in the program.

Pacing the Group

Another important aspect of leading a group is pacing. Some parents pick up the concepts easily, while others need more time. The therapist must pace the group so that everyone understands the concepts and is ready to move on to the next component. This may mean that some group members become impatient, ready to move on. However, the skilled therapist will take advantage of the parents in the group who seem to have a good grasp of a particular concept by soliciting their help in explaining things to other members. For example, the therapist might ask one member of the group to summarize for the group the previous week's discussions, or ask another to come up with an application of a particular concept. These strategies emphasize the collaborative process. Throughout each session the therapist's leadership skills will involve paraphrasing and summarizing parents' viewpoints. This process helps uncover misunderstandings; it also helps parents review the material. Further, it demonstrates that the therapist is listening to their points of view.

Dealing with Resistance

Resistance is a necessary part of the therapy process and the therapist needs to be prepared for it. In fact, Patterson's (1985) research indicates that resistance will reach a considerable peak midway through the treatment process. Resistance may occur in a variety of ways such as failure to do homework, arriving late for group sessions, blaming the leader, blaming the child or life circumstances, negatively evaluating the sessions, or challenging the material presented.

Resistance may occur for many reasons, some having to do with the therapy change process (as Patterson's research suggests). For example, the resistance may be part of the parent's efforts to maintain self-efficacy and self-control in the face of family dynamics which are changing too quickly—in effect, the parent is "putting on the brakes." Perhaps the parent fails adequately to understand the concept which the therapist has explained. Perhaps the parent is resisting because he/she feels his/her stressful life circumstances make it difficult to find the time to do the assignments. Or perhaps parents have unrealistic expectations for behavioral change and are not prepared for the long hard work involved. The resistance may pertain more directly to some quality of the therapist. For example, the parent may not feel understood by the therapist—s/he may perceive the therapist as patronizing or think the therapist is presenting "pat" answers and solutions without really understanding his/her situation. On the other hand, resistance may stem from external factors. For example, perhaps the parent has had a previous learning experience which has given him/her a different explanatory model. Or perhaps the parent feels the child's behavior should change first, before any change in parental behavior.

Whatever the reason, the first task for the therapist is to put aside any notion that the parent's resistance is either a sign of failure on the part of the therapist, or a sign that the parent is noncompliant or unmotivated—a "difficult person." Instead, the therapist needs to recognize the resistance as an important marker in the therapy process—a developmental step for the parent.

MOTHER: I feel I just can't absorb it all and I'm getting behind at home. I just can't do all this play stuff, there isn't any time.

FATHER: Yeah, I go out of this group charged up, but when I get home I lose it. I don't start thinking about applying all this stuff until right before our group is to meet again.

When the therapist knows the parent is resisting a basic concept or doing something that is counterproductive to the goals of the therapy program, should the therapist confront and challenge the parent regarding this, or just let it go in the interest of fostering collaboration and offering support? The therapist may be worried that confrontation will jeopardize the goals of collaboration. Some therapists may be tempted to avoid conflicts with parents. Yet this failure to address the issue really constitutes a kind of collusion with parents in regard to their parenting practices. Consequently, how this resistance is handled by the therapist is crucial to the therapeutic relationship.

Once the resistance is identified, it should not be directly confronted, for this is likely to increase the parent's defensiveness (Birchler, 1988). Furthermore, it devalues the parent in front of the other group members. In fact, in one of the few studies to do a microanalytic analysis of therapist–client interactions, Patterson and Forgatch (1985) found that resistance met by direct confrontation or teaching on the part of the therapist actually increased parents' noncompliance. It is our contention that instead of confronting the issue raised by the resistant parent, the therapist needs to confront the resistance itself—gently, by asking about it in a nondefensive and nonconfrontational manner. In other words, the therapist needs to collaborate with the parent in understanding the resistance.

FIRST MOTHER: I just don't have the time to play—there always seems to be so much to do.

THERAPIST: What seems to get in the way of doing the play assignment?

FIRST MOTHER: I'm just so stressed out about everything in my life.

THERAPIST: So am I right in understanding that doing the play assignment is pretty stressful?

FIRST MOTHER: Yeah, well, he's just so abusive to me—he's so violent. It's hard to keep the play positive.

THERAPIST: Yeah, it's pretty hard to want to praise and play with a defiant child who has made your life so miserable. That seems like a logical reason for feeling resistance to doing the assignment.

FIRST FATHER: For me it's not so much that the child is stressful, but it's me that's so stressed out!

SECOND MOTHER: I find it hard because my older daughter keeps complaining she wants the play time too. So now I've got one more person making demands on me for time.

SECOND FATHER: Well, in our case we've got twins and each child had a major tantrum when I played with other child and then tantrumed again when I ended the play.

THERAPIST: You probably wonder if it's worth it! You can see from just this play exercise how families will resist change. Well, you know [to second father] one good sign in your situation is the fact the children didn't want the play with you to end. That's an important signal that the play was very reinforcing to them. Clearly time with you is really important to them!

THIRD FATHER: Well, you know in my situation I didn't want to do the play assignment. I felt stressed out and the kids were really on my nerves but I made myself do it. And do you know, it really helped. I was so surprised that I was actually calmer afterwards!

THERAPIST: That's great. Many of you will find the same thing happens to you after a while. But how did you get yourself mobilized to do the play when you really didn't want to?

THIRD FATHER: I just told myself I had nothing to lose by trying it once.

THERAPIST: Good for you! Well, for those of you who didn't do the play this week let's put our heads together and brainstorm about some ways it might be possible to try it next week. . . .

Other questions the therapist might ask to explore parents' resistance to the home assignments are, "What thoughts come to mind when you think about this assignment?" "What makes it hard to do?" "Does this seem relevant to your life?" "How could we make this more helpful?" "Can anyone in the group think of a way that might help her try the assignment?"

A common area of resistance is parents' reluctance to use Time Out as an alternative to spanking.

FATHER: Well, all this Time Out stuff is well and good, but in the final analysis I think spanking is what you really need to do. Especially when something bad happens, like a broken window.

THERAPIST: So you really see spanking as the final "big gun"?

FATHER: I do. You know, I was spanked by my father and it didn't do me any psychological harm.

THERAPIST: Tell me how spanking works for you and when you would be most likely to use it.

In a collaborative relationship the therapist deals with resistance by starting from the premise of respect for the legitimacy of the client's views—in this case, respecting the parent's preference for spanking as legitimate. She would then explore the viewpoint with nonjudgmental questions such as, "Tell me how spanking works for you? How often do you use it? How do you feel afterwards? How does your child feel about it? How does it affect your relationship? Do you ever feel you lose control when you spank? What do you see as its advantages? Are there any disadvantages? How did it affect your relationship with your parent when you were spanked as a child?" Similar questions might then be asked about the alternative approach, Time Out. "Let's look at an alternative approach. What are the difficulties with Time Out? What don't you like about it? What are its disadvantages? Are there any advantages?" Notice that the questions are in the form of "What do you mean?" or "How do you feel?" or "What do you think?" rather than "Why?" or "Why not?" These questions serve to clarify the parents' feelings, thoughts, and experiences surrounding the resistance and to facilitate problem-solving and collaboration.

In a parent group this kind of discussion between the therapist and a resistant parent would quickly draw everyone into the debate, whereas a judgmental or authoritarian response from a therapist would tend to result in group members becoming silent. When resistance to a concept occurs, we find it helpful to organize the discussion by listing the advantages and disadvantages, short-term and long-term consequences for the child and for the parent on a blackboard. At the end of this discussion, the therapist summarizes the ideas that have been generated, clarifies misperceptions, and adds his/her own interpretations if they have not already been covered. This process of collaborative problem-solving in the group serves to move people away from "absolutist" positions (i.e., seeing the situation in terms of right and wrong) and opens people up to new ideas which they may not have considered previously, thus reducing resistance. On the other hand, a noncollaborative approach where the therapist directly confronts the parents' ideas creates a boxing match where the therapist and parent each have to defend their own position in order to protect their integrity.

Once the reasons for the resistance are understood by both the parents and the therapist and problem-solving has occurred, the therapist is then ready to invite the parent to consider a short experimental period.

THERAPIST: I understand your viewpoint regarding Time Out and that you think children should be spanked for misbehaving. At the same time, Timmy seems to have been having more and more problems with being aggressive with his peers and at school and I know you are eager to help him with this problem. I'd like to suggest that we do an experiment. I'd like you to give it a try and act as if it will work. I'd like you to try doing Time Out for a month and keep records, and then at the end of a month let's evaluate how it looks. You see, if it doesn't work, you can always go back to the way you have been doing things and won't have lost anything. What do you think about that?

In the example above, the therapist does not attack the resistance by confronting it directly or repeating the rationale for why s/he thinks Time Out is right (and why the parent is wrong to use spanking). Rather, the therapist is engaged in a process of gentle persuasion. Although she does not confront the resistance directly, she confronts the difference of opinion with open, honest communication. This process of exploring the reasons for the resistance, followed by the exercise of looking at the advantages and disadvantages of spanking versus Time Out, is a kind of values clarification and problem-solving exercise which helps clarify feelings and experiences surrounding the issue. This strategy serves to join people rather than alienate them. It is more likely than direct confrontation to result in a gradual change in parents' perceptions and behaviors, especially if conducted in the context of a supportive relationship.

We have also used Gottman and Leiblum's (1974) "force field analysis" as a method of approaching resistance. In this context, force field analysis is a problem-solving approach which assumes that things become "stuck" when there is an equilibrium between the forces facilitating change and those that are opposing and restraining. When dealing with resistance to change, the therapist can get the parent group to:

(1) List facilitative or helping forces for change (e.g., a new untried tactic, a renewal of confidence and determination to succeed);

(2) List restraining or hindering forces for change (e.g., exhaustion, no breaks from the children to get out of the house);

(3) List alternative intervention strategies for:

    (a) strengthening existing facilitative forces (e.g., encouraging a mother to be more consistent by getting her to reward herself with something special when she is successful);

    (b) adding new facilitative forces (e.g., an offer by a member of the group to babysit so as to give a mother a break; convincing a previously reluctant father to involve himself in the program);

    (c) weakening or removing restraining forces (e.g., debating away a member's inhibitions about being firm and decisive with her child);

(4) List the advantages and disadvantages of each intervention.

Reframing is also a helpful strategy when responding to resistance. Once the therapist has collaborated to understand the reason for the resistance, then s/he can then reframe the treatment objectives in such a way that parents can cooperate and carry out the experiment. For example, one parent said she could not put the child in a Time Out room because she felt it would create bad feelings about the child's room and, more importantly, the child would feel abandoned. Further exploration by the therapist uncovered the fact that this parent had been locked for hours in her bedroom by her own parents! As a result of this discussion, the therapist and parent set up a Time Out strategy based on a chair in the corner of the living room rather than the bedroom. Over future sessions, the therapist reframed the situation to help the parent understand that short Time Outs with the parent in control help children to feel more secure in their relationships with their parents, and that children whose behavior is not controlled by their parents may actually come to feel psychologically abandoned. By joining with the parent and then reframing the situation so that the parent perceived the objective as promoting security (rather than abandonment), the therapist enabled the parent to accept the strategy for herself and her child. This is the essence of collaborative therapy.

THERAPIST ROLE No. 6: PROPHESIZING

Children's behavior improves slowly; regression in their misbehavior is inevitable, despite parents' hard work. When some families encounter these setbacks, they react with disbelief, depression, and anger. They may even decide to drop out of the program at this point. As a "prophesizer," the therapist can help prepare families for future relapses not only in their children's behavior, but also in their own behavior. The therapist's role as prophesizer also includes predicting resistance to change as well as forecasting improvement.

Anticipating Problems and Setbacks

One helpful strategy the therapist may use to prevent disillusionment for parents is to predict setbacks in children's behavior, anticipating potential problems and regression and discussing these with parents before they occur. The therapist can engage in a hypothetical problem-solving discussion of how parents might handle particular problems should they occur. For example, the therapist could prepare families for the negative behavior that is likely to occur when children encounter changed circumstances such as a prolonged illness, or a return from a week's visit with relatives or the other parent, or the arrival of stepsiblings who come to stay for summer vacation. After an episode of particularly difficult behavior

PROPHESIZING SETBACKS

in public, the therapist could collaborate with parents to prepare a plan for dealing with the behavior more successfully next time. Similarly, the therapist could help parents develop a strategy for having a more successful visit with their in-laws. By mentally rehearsing how they will handle the worst possible scenario, parents' anxiety is reduced because they feel prepared to cope effectively with a conflict situation. Moreover, when the "worst" does not happen, they are pleased with themselves and their progress.

The therapist also needs to prepare parents for the fact that there will be inevitable relapses in their own parenting behavior after the program has ended. The therapist should reassure parents that relapses are normal parts of the learning process. Relapses should be construed as a "signal" that some strategy needs to be implemented; parents can be encouraged to see them as an opportunity to practice or review. It is a good idea to rehearse what they might do when a relapse occurs. For example, they might call a group member, contact the therapist, practice program exercises again, review strategies and videotapes, arrange for time away to "refuel," or focus on positive alternatives. Here is an example of how the therapist might start preparing parents for relapses by reframing the usual interpretation.

THERAPIST: Expect and be prepared for relapses. They are part of your own and your child's learning process. The child needs to relapse and test the security of his environment every now and again to see if the rules still hold. Then once he knows his base is secure, he can tackle a new challenge. You know, it's a bit like the old adage: "two steps forward, one step back."

Predicting Parent Resistance to Change

It helps to predict in advance that parents will resist some strategies and assignments and to offer some reasons for this opposition. Otherwise, if the difficulty of making behavioral change is not acknowledged by the therapist, the parent may feel s/he is incapable of change. Some parents may even become angry at the therapist for asking them to do assignments that are so hard for them to do and "not part of their personality make-up." These feelings will lead to increased resistance. When parents are prepared in advance, they need not be surprised or anxious when these feelings occur; they can perceive these reactions as a necessary part of the behavioral change process.

THERAPIST: Be prepared to feel awkward when you do this kind of play. Be prepared for yourself to resist wanting to do it because it does feel awkward. And be prepared for your child not to like it at first. Whenever someone learns a new behavior, there is a natural tendency for family members to resist this new behavior and to revert back to the status quo. In fact, some family members might actually try to pressure you to return to the old way of doing things.

OR

You will probably feel awkward praising at first, especially if you haven't done much of this in the past. You may even feel your praise sounds phoney. So don't wait for yourself to feel warmth towards your child in order to praise. Just get the words out, even if they are kind of flat. The feelings and genuinness will come later. The more you practice, the more natural it will become.

OR

Lots of parents don't like Time Out at first. Compared to spanking it's more time-consuming, it is harder to keep the self-control you need (especially if you want "revenge" with your child), and it feels awkward. But with practice it will become automatic and your child will learn exactly what to do. You will feel good because you are teaching your child a nonviolent approach to dealing with conflict.

OR

We all find it difficult to change; indeed it can be painful. We get used to the figurative "goggles" or "specs" through which we look at the world in general, and our child in particular. To have to put on a different set of goggles can be quite confusing at first. We feel comfortable with what's familiar; so the new perspective is strange and rather scary. But that feeling soon wears off.

In addition, it is important also to tell parents to call in if they are having difficulties with any of the assignments, thereby indicating your willingness to listen to their resistance.

Another strategy to use when discussing resistance to change is to help parents understand that change is not without cost. Here it can be helpful to ask the parents to list the pros and cons of adopting a certain approach. For example, here is how we would list out the advantages and disadvantages of yelling and screaming.

THERAPIST: You find it difficult to give up the anger and resentment you feel all the time for your youngster's misdemeanors. Let's try to see why it is so hard. We'll make two columns headed "advantages" and "disadvantages" of letting go of anger.

PARENT: Advantages—I'd feel better; I'd be less tense; I'd be more rational. Disadvantages—It would look as if his behavior was unimportant to me; I'd lose self-respect; People may think I don't care in my rearing of children.

THERAPIST: You can see that there are some good reasons, to your mind, to not give up your anger. So change is costly. What you need to think through are the relative costs of changing as opposed to not changing.

Predicting Positive Change and Success

The therapist should build parents' expectations for positive change in behavior if they do persist with the assignments and implement the program. It is important for the therapist to express confidence and optimism in the parents' ability to successfully carry out the behavior required to produce positive changes in the child's behaviors. According to Bandura (1977), all psychological procedures are mediated through a system of beliefs about the level of skill required to bring about an outcome and the likely end result of a course of action. Efficacy expectations are thought to be the most important component. Successful treatment will depend on the ability of the therapist to strengthen the parents' expectations of personal efficacy ("I am able to do it").

PROPHESIZING SUCCESS

THERAPIST: We have found that after parents do the daily play sessions for several weeks and increase their praise statements, their children's behavior improves substantially. We have also found that when parents give their children attention for positive behaviors, they actually have more time for themselves in the long run, because their children stop behaving inappropriately to get their attention.

OR

We've worked with a large number of families now and, although we don't have perfect success, we've found at least two-thirds of parents are able to make impressive changes in their children's behaviors.

It is also important to predict that other family members can benefit from the program, even if they do not attend the sessions. For indeed, research (Patterson, 1982) has suggested that all members of the aggressive child's family are victims; they all experience the pain of the family interactions. If nonparticipating members of the family are not helped by the participating member to see some possibility of pay-off for themselves, they may actively sabotage the participating members' efforts to change. The therapist should therefore work with the participating members to see how the program can be extended in a nonintrusive way to other family members. For example, the therapist can predict that the siblings who previously have been "good" children may regress in an effort to gain attention and to compete for play sessions or a sticker chart which has been started with the target child. This reaction should be presented as a positive outcome for all the children, although more demanding for the parent. Predictions should also be made about the nonparticipating fathers who may initially be suspicious of the program. However, if mothers continue to praise and use Time Out competently, they will soon find fathers following suit.

The role of therapist as prophesizer is consistent with a collaborative model because the therapist brings his/her expertise and knowledge of possible family reactions to bear on the parents' unique situations and experiences—the single parent who is coparenting, the family with several children of differing ages, the mother with a noninvolved father, or the parent with backgrounds of alcohol or spouse abuse—and the parents bring their ideas and insights to bear on planning how to deal with those possible reactions. It should be obvious that the therapist can prophesize effectively only if s/he has collaborated with the parents to understand their situation. Moreover, by anticipating problems beyond the immediate child problems, the concept of "working together" is enriched.

THE SCRIPT FOR PARENTS: LEARNING TO COPE MORE EFFECTIVELY

The therapeutic process that we have been describing is one in which the therapist collaborates with parents in multiple roles in order to help the parents gradually gain the knowledge, control, and competence they need to cope effectively with the stresses of having a conduct-disordered child, including managing their child's behavior. To put it differently, the "script" for the parents involves learning more effective coping strategies and parenting skills so that ultimately child behavior problems are reduced and social competence is strengthened. Several themes are constant throughout the therapy process as part of this coping model "script" for parents.

Theme No. 1: Parents Learning to Problem-solve

By now it should be clear that problem-solving and collaboration between the therapist and parent go hand in hand throughout the sessions. Often we find parents have come to us initially with the belief that there is a single cause for the child's misbehaviors and consequently a single solution for the problem. The goal is for parents to come to realize by the end of the program that there is no single magical solution or recipe for parenting. Rather, parents become confident in their own ability to think sequentially and to analyze parent–child interactions, to search for external causes of misbehavior (as opposed to attributing it to the child's "bad" nature) and to generate a rich smorgasbord of possible solutions. They acquire the problem-solving strategies necessary to evaluate possible solutions in terms of their desirability and relevance, to commit themselves to trying them out, and to evaluate whether or not a particular solution is working. In essence, by the end of the therapy the parents have become their own therapists.

Theme No. 2: Parents "Coming to Terms"

The therapist gradually helps parents come to terms with the realistic facts concerning their child's temperament. They must learn to manage the anger and grief related to the loss of their hoped-for "ideal" child and learn to accept their child's difficulties and extra needs for committed parenting. Because many of these children's problems are to some degree chronic—characterized by unpredictable relapses, constant vulnerability to changes in routine, and the emergence of new problems whenever the child faces new settings or schedules—parents must be helped to face the fact that they must invest a great deal of time and energy in the hard work of anticipating, monitoring, and problem-solving for many years to come.

The therapist can prepare parents for this partly by helping them focus on long-term rather than short-term goals. For example, one common mistake is for parents to go for short-term pay-offs (i.e., giving into a child's tantrum to stop unpleasant behaviors) at the expense of long-term consequences (child learns to have tantrums to get what s/he wants). Parents need to be reminded of their long-term goals. For example, the therapist may point out that, in the short term, spanking or yelling may serve to stop the child's misbehavior, but in the long term may teach a child to hit or yell when frustrated, thereby fostering more aggression. Our therapists emphasize that the strategies taught in our program such as play, praise, and problem-solving must be repeated hundreds of times to be effective.

THERAPIST: Your child needs to have hundreds of chances to try to learn from his mistakes. Learning more appropriate social skills is just like when she was a baby and was learning how to walk. Do you remember how often she tried to get up and fell down or how long she held on to something before she could take off on her own? Well, this is just the same. It takes lots of small steps and experiments for a child to learn appropriate social skills. And just as you must constantly support the baby who is stumbling (so that she does not injure herself), so must you support the child who is developing her social skills.

Moreover, the therapist may even depict the environment provided by parents for these children as a sort of "prosthetic environment" of parent reinforcement, attention, discipline, and monitoring for a chronic problem. And, as with the child with diabetes, if parents withdraw the treatment, the child is likely to relapse. Words such as "repeated learning trials," and "opportunities to make mistakes" and "developmental struggles" help prepare parents for this long-term coping process. As one of our parents so aptly put it, "You mean there is no magic moondust?"

Theme No. 3: Parents Gaining Empathy for the Child

Besides helping parents come to terms with the hard work of parenting, it is also important to help them understand, empathize with, and accept their child's unique personality. It is especially hard for parents of "difficult" and demanding children to remain patient, to be constantly "on guard" for monitoring, and to limit set consistently. Parents can do this more easily and can be more supportive if the therapist has helped them to understand that some of the child's oppositional behaviors are really needs for independence or needs to test the security of their environment. Information about typical developmental struggles can help build not only patience, but empathy. Parents can also learn to reduce some of their unnecessary commands and criticisms if they have been helped to understand that children need the opportunity to learn from their own mistakes. Empathy for the child will foster a warm relationship, involving increased tolerance of mistakes and more appropriate discipline.

Theme No. 4: Parents aren't Perfect

Coping effectively implies coming to accept and understand not only their child's strengths and difficulties, but also their own imperfections as parents. The therapist helps parents learn to stop belittling and berating themselves for their angry or frustrated reactions and depressive or anxious thoughts. They come to understand that these reactions to their child are normal.

Theme No. 5: Parents "Refueling" to Ensure Maintenance

Along with parents becoming more confident and knowledgeable in their parenting skills and their ability to cope with the child's problems, parents need to recognize the importance of "refueling" themselves as individuals and couples. The therapist can assist this by asking parents such questions as, "How are you going to keep going when the program is finished?" "How do you keep yourself reinforced for the work of parenting?" The therapist can encourage the parent support groups to continue meeting after the formal program has ended, and can suggest that parents babysit for each other so they can get time away from their children. Monthly "booster shots" for the groups with the therapist can also be scheduled routinely so that there is a structure of ongoing support.

Theme No. 6: Parents Feeling Empowered

As we discussed earlier in this chapter, one of our primary goals in therapy is to help parents feel empowered so that they feel confident about themselves, their parenting skills, and their ability to cope with the new situations in which they and their children will find themselves over the course of time at home or at school. Empowerment is the antithesis of dependence on the therapist. It emcompasses competence, but it is more, namely, the *conviction* of one's own competence, a sense of security about one's own abilities and capacities. A collaborative therapist empowers clients not only through building skills, but through continual validation of the client.

We empower parents using a three-pronged approach: first, by giving them the knowledge base concerning children's developmental needs, behavior management principles, and individual or temperamental differences and how these affect social relationships; second, by helping them learn the important skills involved in communication building, social relationships, problem-solving, tactical thinking, and enhancing their children's academic skills; third, by accepting and respecting their values and beliefs and trying to understand how these impact their family life, rules, and relationships. The specific content and processes we use have been described earlier and are outlined in Table 4.1.

EPILOGUE: SUPPORT FOR THE THERAPIST

The therapist's conscious use of a variety of roles such as collaborator, empowerer, supporter, teacher, interpreter, leader, and prophesizer helps to change parents' behaviors and attitudes, to alter their attributions about past and present behaviors, and most importantly to increase their perceived self-efficacy and their range of effective coping skills. In this sense, the therapist's role with parents is a model for the kind of relationship we are encouraging parents to develop with their children—in both cases, a nonauthoritarian, nonpaternalistic relationship.

Just as parents get tired of the hard work of parenting, the therapist may tire of the hard work of filling these roles. The implementation of these roles with a group of parents, especially in the face of parent confrontations and resistance, can at times be a formidable task. Collaboration requires a considerable degree of clinical skill—more so than other models, such as that of adviser, listener, or analyst (Table 4.2). It is important that the therapist also has a support system in which s/he can analyze a difficult situation or group problem with colleagues and plan the most effective treatment strategy. By discussing a parent's situation with other therapists, it is possible to brainstorm and problem-solve on how to reframe it, interpret it, or explain it in a different way so it makes sense to the parent, as well as to decide which role the therapist should assume in this situation. The added support and objectivity of colleagues can help the therapist immensely, sustaining enthusiasm and the will to persist in the face of highly resistant families.

Table 4.1 Sources of increased self-empowerment

	CONTENT	PROCESS
KNOWLEDGE		
Child development	Developmental norms and tasks	Discussion
Behavior management	Behavioral (learning) principles	Books/pamphlets to read
Individual and temperamental differences	Child management (disciplinary strategies)	Modeling (videotape, live role play, role reversal, rehearsal)
	Relationships (feelings)	Metaphors/analogies
	Self-awareness (self-talk, schema, attributions)	Homework tasks
	Interactions (awareness of contingencies, communications)	Networking
	Resources (support, sources of assistance)	Developmental counseling
	Appropriate expectations	Videotape viewing and discussion
	Parent involvement with children	Self-observation/recording at home
		Discussing records of parents' own data
		Teaching, persuading
SKILLS		
Communication	Self-restraint/anger management	Self-reinforcement
Problem-solving (including problem analysis)	Self-talk (depressive thoughts)	Group and therapist reinforcement
Tactical thinking (use of techniques/methods)	Attend–ignore	Self-observations of interactions at home
Building social relationships	Play–praise–encourage	Rehearsal
Enhancing children's academic skills	Contracts	Participant modeling
	Consistent consequences	Homework tasks and practice

continued

Table 4.1 (*continued*)

CONTENT	PROCESS
Sanction effectively (Time Out, loss of privileges, natural consequences)	Video modeling and feedback
Monitoring	Self-disclosure
Social/relationship skills	Therapist use of humor/optimism
Problem-solving skills	Relaxation training
Fostering good learning habits	Stress management
Self-assertion/confidence	Self-instruction
Empathy for child's perspective	Visual cues at home
Ways to give and get support	
Treatment/life goals	Discussion/debate
Objectives (targeted child behaviors)	Sharing
Ideologies	Listening
Rules	Respecting/accepting
Roles	Negotiating
Relationships	Demystifying
Emotional barriers	Explaining/interpreting
Attributions	Reframing
Prejudices	Resolving conflict
Past history	Clarifying
	Supporting
	Adapting

VALUES
Strategic thinking (working out goals, philosophy of child rearing, beliefs)

Based on Herbert, 1988.

Table 4.2 Checklist for evaluating the collaborative process
Please evaluate the parent group leader's sessions based on the following criteria:

	Doing Well	Could be Improved	Not Observed	Comments
I. LEADER GROUP PROCESS SKILLS				
Builds rapport with each member of group				
Encourages everyone to participate				
Models open-ended questions to facilitate discussion				
Reinforces parents' ideas and fosters parents' self-learning				
Encourages parents to problem-solve when possible				
Fosters idea that parent will learn from each others' experiences				
Helps parents learn how to support and reinforce each other				
Views every member of group as equally important and valued				
Identifies each family's strengths				
Creates a feeling of safety among group members				
Creates an atmosphere where parents feel they are decision-makers and discussion and debate are paramount.				
II. LEADER LEADERSHIP SKILLS				
Establishes ground rules for group				
Started and ended meetings on time				
Explained agenda for each session				

continued

Table 4.2 (continued)

	Doing Well	Could be Improved	Not Observed	Comments
Emphasizes the importance of homework				
Reviews homework from previous session				
Summarizes and restates important points				
Focuses group on key points presented				
Imposes sufficient structure to facilitate group process				
Prevents sidetracking by participants				
Knows when to be flexible and allow a digression for an important issue and knows how to tie it into session's content				
Anticipates potential difficulties				
Predicts behaviors and feelings				
Encourages generalization of concepts to different settings and situations				
Encourages parents to work for long-term goals as opposed to "quick fix"				
Helps group focus on positive				
Balances group discussion on affective and cognitive domain				
Predicts relapses				
Reviews handouts and homework for next week				
Evaluates session				

III. LEADER RELATIONSHIP BUILDING SKILLS

Uses humor and fosters optimism

Normalizes problems when appropriate

Validates and supports parents' feelings (reflective statements)

Shares personal experiences when appropriate

Fosters a partnership or collaborative model (as opposed to an "expert" model)

Fosters a coping model as opposed to a mastery model of learning

Reframes experiences from the child's viewpoint and modifies parents' negative attributions

Strategically confronts, challenges and teaches parents when necessary

Identifies and discusses resistance

Maintains leadership of group

Advocates for parents

IV. LEADER KNOWLEDGE

Demonstrates knowledge of content covered at session

Explains rationale for principles covered in clear, convincing manner

continued

Table 4.2 (continued)

	Doing Well	Could be Improved	Not Observed	Comments
Prepares materials in advance of session and is "prepared" for group				
Integrates parents' ideas and problems with important content and child development principles				
Uses appropriate analogies and metaphors to explain theories or concepts				
V. LEADER METHODS				
Uses videotape examples efficiently and strategically to trigger group discussion				
Uses role play and rehearsal to reinforce learning				
Reviews homework and gives feedback				
Uses modeling by self or other group members when appropriate				
VI. PARENTS' RESPONSES				
Parents appear comfortable and involved in session				
Parents complete homework, ask questions and are active participants				
Parents complete positive evaluations of sessions				

Reproduced from Webster-Stratton & Herbert (1993) by permission.

In sum, it is important for the therapist also to view him/herself in a coping model—capable of making mistakes with parents, learning from the mistakes, being realistic about treatment goals, not expecting magical solutions, and feeling refueled by each family's gradual successes. From the therapist's point of view, one important advantage of the collaborative group therapy model is that it creates a feeling of support for the therapist because of the joint ownership of solutions and outcomes. Besides reducing the dependency of families on the therapist, collaboration is reinforcing for the therapist in that it is gratifying to see parents coping independently. Lastly, the collaborative process constantly provides new learning for the therapist, keeping us challenged, stimulated, and growing in our professional lives.

REFERENCES

Alexander, J.F., Barton, C., Schiavo, R.S. & Parsons, B.V. (1976). Systems-behavioral intervention with families of delinquents: Therapist characteristics, family behavior, and outcome. *Journal of Consulting and Clinical Psychology*, **44**, 656–664.

Backeland, F. & Lundwall, L. (1975). Dropping out of treatment: A critical review. *Psychological Bulletin*, **82**, 738–783.

Bandura, A. (1977). Self-efficacy: Towards a unifying theory of behavioural change? *Psychological Review*, **84**, 191–215.

Bandura, A. (1982). Self-efficacy mechanisms in human agency. *American Psychologist*, **37**, 122–147.

Bandura, A. (1989). Regulation of cognitive processes through perceived self-efficacy. *Developmental Psychology*, **25**, 729–735.

Beck, A.T., Rush, A.J., Shaw, B.F. & Emery, G. (1979). *Cognitive therapy of depression*. New York: Guilford.

Behrens, M.L. (1954). Child rearing and the character structure of the mother. *Child Development*, **25**, 225–238.

Birchler, G. (1988). Handling resistance to change. In I. Falloon (Ed.), *Handbook of behavioral family therapy* (pp. 128–155). New York: Guilford.

Brammer, L.M. (1988). *The helping relationship: Process and skills* (4th ed.). Englewood Cliffs, NJ: Prentice-Hall.

Brown, G.W. & Harris, T. (1978). *Social origins of depression*. London: Tavistock.

Dumas, J.E. & Wahler, R.G. (1983). Predictors of treatment outcome in parent training: Mother insularity and socioeconomic disadvantage. *Behavioral Assessment*, **5**, 301–313.

Dweck, C.S. (1975). The role of expectations and attributions in the alleviation of learned helplessness. *Journal of Personality and Social Psychology*, **31**, 674–685.

Eisler, R.M., Hersen, M. & Agras, W.S. (1973). Effects of videotape and instructional feedback on nonverbal marital interactions: An analogue study. *Behavior Therapy*, **4**, 5510–5558.

Gottman, J.M. & Leiblum, S.R. (1974). *How to do psychotherapy; and how to evaluate it: A manual for beginners*. New York: Holt, Rinehart, and Winston.

Herbert, M. (1978). *Conduct disorders of childhood and adolescence: A social learning perspective*. Chichester, UK: Wiley.

Herbert, M. (1980). Socialization for problem resistance. In P. Feldman & J. Orford (Eds.), *Psychological problems: The social context*. Chichester, UK: Wiley.

Herbert, M. (1988). *Working with children and their families*. Leicester, UK: British Psychological Society.

Janis, I. L. & Mann, L. (1977). *Decision making: A psychological analysis of conflict, choice, and commitment*. New York: Free Press.

Lynch, M.A. & Roberts, J. (1977). Predicting child abuse: Signs of bonding failure in the maternity hospital. *British Medical Journal*, **278**, 624–636.

McMahon, R.J. & Forehand, R. (1984). Parent training for the noncompliant child: Treatment outcome, generalization, and adjunctive therapy procedures. In R.F. Dangel & R.A. Polster (Eds.), *Parent training: Foundations of research and practice* (pp. 298–328). New York: Guilford.

Meichenbaum, D. & Turk, D. (1987). *Facilitating treatment adherence: A practitioner's guidebook*. New York: Plenum Press.

Patterson, G. (1982). *Coercive family process*. Eugene, OR: Castalia.

Patterson, G. (1985). Beyond technology: The next stage in developing an empirical base for training. In L.L.'Abate (Ed.), *The handbook of family psychology and therapy* (Vol. 2, pp. 1344–1379). Homewood, IL: The Dorsey Press.

Patterson, G.R. & Forgatch, M. (1985). Therapist behavior as a determinant for client noncompliance: A paradox for the behavior modifier. *Journal of Consulting and Clinical Psychology*, **53**, 846–851.

Patterson, G.R. & Chamberlain, P. (1988). Treatment process: A problem at three levels. In L.C. Wynne (Ed.), *The state of art in family therapy research: Controversies and recommendations* (pp. 189–223). New York: Family Process Press.

Rogers, C.R. (1951). *Client-centered therapy*. Boston, MA: Houghton-Mifflin.

Seligman, M.E.P. (1975). *Helplessness*. San Francisco, CA: Freeman.

Spitzer, A., Webster-Stratton, C. & Hollinsworth, T. (1991). Coping with conduct-problem children: Parents gaining knowledge and control. *Journal of Clinical Child Psychology*, **20**, 413–427.

Stuart, R.B. (1980), *Helping couples change: A social learning approach to marital therapy*. New York: Guilford Press.

Truax, C.F. & Carkhuff, H.R. (1967). *Toward effective counseling and psychotherapy*. Chicago, IL: Aldine.

Twentyman, C.T. & McFall, R.M. (1975). Behavioral training of social skills in shy males. *Journal of Consulting and Clinical Psychology*, **43**, 384–395.

Valman, H.B. (1980). The first year of life: mother-infant bonding. *British Medical Journal*, **280**, 308–310.

Wahler, R. (1980). The insular mother: Her problems in parent–child treatment. *Journal of Applied Behavior Analysis*, **13**, 207–219.

Webster-Stratton, C. (1984). A randomized trial of two parent training programs for families with conduct disordered children. *Journal of Consulting and Clinical Psychology*, **52**(4), 666–678.

Webster-Stratton, C. (1985). The effects of father involvement in parent training for conduct problem children. *Child Psychology and Psychiatry*, **26**, 801–810.

Webster-Stratton, C. (1990a). Long-term follow-up of families with young conduct problem children: from preschool to grade school. *Journal of Clinical Child Psychology*, **19**(2), 144–149.

Webster-Stratton, C. (1990b). Enhancing the effectiveness of self-administered videotape parent training for families with conduct-problem children. *Journal of Abnormal Child Psychology*, **18**, 479–492.

Webster-Stratton, C., Kolpacoff, M. & Hollinsworth, T. (1988). Self-administered videotape therapy for families with conduct-problem children: Comparison with two cost-effective treatments and a control group. *Journal of Consulting and Clinical Psychology*, **56**(4), 558–566.

Webster-Stratton, C., Kolpacoff, M. & Hollinsworth, T. (1989). The long-term effectiveness and clinical significance of three cost-effective training programs for families with conduct problem children. *Journal of Consulting and Clinical Psychology*, **57**(4), 550–553.

Webster-Stratton, C. & Herbert, M. (1993). What really happens in parent training? *Behavior Modification*, **17**, 407–456.

5 HELPING PARENTS UNDERSTAND BEHAVIORAL METHODS AND PRINCIPLES

THIS CHAPTER provides a brief guide to our rationale for selecting particular methods in working with families of children with conduct disorders. The overall principles determining the choice of therapeutic methods are the following: reducing antisocial behavior, alleviating personal distress, enhancing individual and social skills and (as a result) the quality of family life. Such benefits should endure beyond the immediacies of the treatment process. The techniques chosen should always be used within an overall planned program of management.

When using behavioral treatments with children, there are several ethical imperatives to be taken into account, and fully discussed with parents. The UK Royal College of Psychiatrists Working Party's *Guidelines to good practice* (1987), addresses these, some of which are paraphrased below.

■ Children may be limited in their understanding of a treatment or its implications, and consequently unable to give full consent. If so, it is essential that a behavioral treatment is applied in such a way as to take the special needs of children into account, particularly those arising from their dependency.

■ In evaluating the acceptability of a behavioral method or goal, the current social and professional consensus, taken in conjunction with the legitimately held values and beliefs of the patient, should be considered in relation to the seriousness of the disturbance and its repercussions to the patient and to society. The majority of behavioral treatments and procedures are ethically unexceptionable, but some may give rise to problems and anxieties. If the only effective method available involves distress or risk, it should be discussed with a clinical ethical committee.

■ When determining the goals of therapy, it is essential to consider the presenting problems as objectively as possible. Parents sometimes ask for treatment to make their child conform with family values, which may be at odds with those of society as a whole. Similar requests are sometimes made when a child fails to conform to a regime at a children's home or school. A judgment must be made about the reasonableness of such a request.

The proposed method of treatment should be explained to parents in detail—orally and through written explanatory information. This is important not only for ethical reasons, but for therapeutic reasons, since the parents are in a very real sense collaborating with the therapist in the treatment of the child's behavior problems. The parents' application of behavioral methods depends, for their effectiveness, on a clear explanation by the therapist of *what* is involved, and *why* it is thought likely to work (i.e., the rationale). Among the concepts to get across to parents are the crucial learning principles and their role in the development of behavior— normal *and* abnormal.

One way a therapist can introduce these ideas is as follows:

THERAPIST: Many of the problems of childhood are due not only to the child learning inappropriate (that is to say, undesirable) behaviors, but the consequence of the child's failure to learn appropriate (in other words, acceptable or socially desirable) behaviors. Many behavior problems in children (especially in the early years) are associated with inadequate skills of self-control. The word "learning" is the key idea here; indeed, it is the key to helping you and your child. There are one or two simple laws which you should find useful if you apply them to your child's—and, indeed, your own—actions.

After all, children have to be taught how to behave normally, that is to say, in a socially and morally acceptable manner. To do anything well demands good training; two persons are involved: a learner and a teacher. Fortunately, it is not necessary for children to discover their way around their world entirely by trial and error. We can save a lot of time, and circumvent some distressing mistakes, if we prove to be—as parents—wise guides and mentors. To this end we need first to know the basic principles and methods of learning, as aids to teaching children and bringing about change when necessary.

Our concentration on giving explanations to parents has its parallel in giving reasons to children when teaching them about life. Explanations— so-called "inductive methods" of teaching—help children internalize "lessons" about life. Similarly, providing parents with explanations in the form of general principles of learning and behavior gives them the ability to generalize our advice and/or their problem-solving to new behavior problems that may arise or to different problems presented by siblings of the target child. Another reason for providing a rationale for parents is to give them a knowledge base that empowers them by giving them a sense of competence. So where do we begin?

The differential use of attention (including praise) and ignoring is widely advocated as the first step in behavioral interventions within families and school settings. It is particularly pertinent if the child is not receiving enough positive reinforcement (e.g., attention) and/or is receiving it at inappropriate times. Forehand and McMahon (1981) propose an "attention rule": a child will work for attention from others, especially parents. If the child is not receiving positive attention, s/he will work to receive negative attention. Of course, there are some children who are not very responsive—indeed, appear counterreactive—to what adults think of as positive reinforcement in general and positive attention in particular.

The centrality of this issue makes the explanation of positive reinforcement the first of our learning principles to "get across" to parents of children with conduct and other behavioral disorders. Another reason is our desire to emphasize the "positives" in the child, building on his/her strengths and "good points." So we begin with the acquisition of prosocial behaviors and skills.

ACQUIRING/STRENGTHENING BEHAVIOR

Principle 1: Positive Reinforcement

This method of intervention, based on operant conditioning, attempts to influence or control the outcome of certain prosocial behaviors through the use of positive reinforcers, i.e., pleasurable consequences. Voluntary actions ("operants") that are followed by favorable outcomes for the individual are likely to be repeated. Correspondingly, antisocial behaviors can often be reduced by ensuring that they are not reinforced.

A therapist using operant methods can analyze a family system and find out through observation, discussion, or the use of video, how the various members reinforce undesired behavior in the target child and each other and intentionally or unintentionally ignore or punish desired behavior. With this knowledge of how the family system operates, it then becomes possible to make beneficial alterations in these distressed systems and subsystems by helping the family systematically rearrange the consequences of behavior so that all (or certain deprived) members receive social reinforcement for desired behaviors—or simply for being there, in other words, for "belonging."

It is useful to begin with an explanation of positive reinforcement:

THERAPIST: Children are "turned on" and "turned off" by different things. If the consequences of a behavior are rewarding (that is, favorable) to a child, that behavior is likely to increase in strength. For example, it may become more frequent! Put another way: If Pat does something, and as a result of his action something pleasant happens to him, then he is more likely to do the same thing in similar circumstances in the future. When psychologists refer to this pleasant outcome as the *positive reinforcement* of behavior, they have in mind several kinds of reinforcers: *tangible* rewards (e.g., sweets, treats, pocket money); *social* rewards (e.g., attention, a smile, a pat on the back, a word of encouragement); and *self-reinforcers* (e.g., the ones that come from within and which are nontangible: self-praise, self-approval, a sense of pleasure, or achievement). For instance, if you say, "Pat, that was nice of you to let Sally have a turn on your bike—I am very pleased with you," Pat is more likely to lend his bicycle again. (Note: We are dealing in probabilities, not certainties.)

Certain questions are crucial to think through with parents. They are presented below, along with a discussion of the treatment strategies they might generate.

Question No. 1: THERAPIST: Are you making good behavior worthwhile?

Some parents remember to reward ("reinforce") desirable behavior as below (these examples might be printed on cards):

Antecedents	*Behavior*	*Consequences*
Marjorie was asked to put away her toys.	She did so.	Her mum gave her a big hug and said thank you.

THERAPIST: Because of the social reward given by her mother, Marjorie is likely to tidy up her toys when asked again. Can you give some examples of actions you would particularly wish to encourage, strengthen, or increase in frequency, in your child? In order to improve or increase your child's performance of certain actions, you could think about how to arrange matters so that a reinforcing event (it might be an activity your child enjoys) follows the correct performance of the desired behavior. You might indicate your intentions by saying, for example, "When you have put your school clothes away, then you can go out to play." This is the useful "when–then" rule (sometimes referred to as the first/then rule).

Behavioral research shows that in order to have the most effect, reinforcers such as treats, favored activities, praise, and encouragement should follow as closely as possible upon the child's performance of the particular desired behavior. Thus the parent who is sensitively monitoring his/her child picks up on prosocial behaviors that need encouraging with favorable comment, and not only on extraordinary feats or achievements. They are also in a position to "nip misdemeanors in the bud" (almost at the intention-forming stage), a particular mark of effective parenting.

Question No. 2: THERAPIST: Are you making good behavior unworthwhile?

Some parents forget to reward ("reinforce") desirable behaviors as below:

Antecedents	Behavior	Consequences
Toby was to share his new bicycle with his brother at certain times (as a condition of getting it).	Toby was reluctant, but kept to the bargain.	His brother never showed appreciation; the parents made no comment, as if they had not noticed.

THERAPIST: Toby is likely to renege on his bargain. Do you, perhaps for what seem like good reasons (you are so busy), fail to notice when your child is being helpful, cooperative, and kind? You don't have to make long speeches or give tangible rewards (unless you promise them for outstanding achievements). Signs of pleasure on your part, a word of praise, will work wonders.

Question No. 3: Therapist: Are you making bad behavior worthwhile?

Some parents persistently overlook or ignore their children's undesirable actions, inadvertently allowing them to be reinforced by circumstances:

Antecedents	Behavior	Consequences
James asked his brother, Dennis, for a turn on his new bike.	Dennis told James to "go to hell" and pushed him away.	Nil! Mother made no comments. Dennis rode off without a word of criticism or encouragement to share.

THERAPIST: It won't be surprising if Dennis doesn't share his things next time around. He has been successful in getting his brother to withdraw his request and has won! Do you fail sometimes to notice your child's unacceptable actions? [*We return to this sort of question later in the chapter.*]

Principle 2: Negative Reinforcement

To get a child to behave in certain (desirable) way, and conversely, to stop undesirable behavior, the removal of an aversive stimulus is made contingent upon a required behavior; this procedure is known as negative reinforcement. Like the providing of a positive stimulus, the removal of a negative stimulus tends to increase the required behavior. Thus the mother says: "If you don't say 'please' when you ask for something, I'll turn off the TV." If the rate of saying "please" on appropriate occasions increases, turning off the television (that is to say the avoidance of it) has acted as a negative reinforcer.

The advantage of explaining the principle of negative reinforcement, apart from its centrality in coercive interactions, is the opportunity it gives the therapist to distinguish between punishment and negative reinforcement, and to go on from there to a discussion of the role of punishment in discipline—something most parents expect and want to discuss. The initial description might go as follows:

THERAPIST: Behaving in a manner that *avoids* an unpleasant outcome leads to the reinforcement of behavior, thus making it more likely to recur in similar circumstances. If your child does something you do not like, such as losing her temper too easily, your goal might be to *increase* her ability to think first and hold her temper. You might decide that the penalty is to dock some of her pocket money or use Time Out. We'll discuss this issue together. By penalizing her consistently for failing to do so, you are providing what is called negative reinforcement for her efforts to "keep her cool." For instance, if you say, "Donna, if you do not think first, but lash out at your sister, I will deduct half of your pocket money," then her resolve to think first and desist from hitting out will be strengthened. You may not have to apply the penalty if she believes your threat because of your record of keeping your word.

Although positive and negative reinforcement are distinct procedures, both serve to maintain, strengthen, or increase the likelihood that a behavior will be omitted. Positive and negative reinforcement procedures take four basic forms, which can be categorized as training methods: reward training, privation training, escape training, and avoidance training.

- Reward training: If you do the desirable thing, I will give you a reward.

- Privation training: If you don't do the desirable thing, I will withdraw the reward.

- Escape training: If you do the desirable thing, I will withdraw the penalty.

- Avoidance training: If you don't do the desirable thing, I will present a penalty.

Principle 3: Differential Attention (the Praise–Ignore Formula)

The discussion of positive and negative reinforcers leads naturally to a discussion of attention as a form of reinforcement:

THERAPIST: There is another aspect to reinforcement. Many behavior problems are attention-seeking strategies. The child learns that certain kinds of behavior appear to attract parental attention, and in consequence, these forms of behavior become part of their habitual pattern of behaving—what we call their "repertoire." Because parents are often unaware of what is going on, they unwittingly but frequently reinforce in the child the very behaviors that they most wish to discourage. For example, they may reward children with attention every time they misbehave, and ignore them when they are cooperating.

PARENT: But I'm not rewarding her; I'm always having to nag and scold her.

THERAPIST: The fact that this attention is angry or disapproving may be unimportant—unimportant in the sense of that actress who said, "I'd rather have bad publicity rather than no publicity at all." The point is that the child is succeeding in distracting you from whatever you were doing, say talking to someone or dealing with one of the other children. She wants to be center-stage. Fortunately, there is a way to remedy this situation.

That parents *can* provide meaningful, positive attention to the child in a consistent manner, while ignoring inappropriate actions, is a prerequisite for parent training. This principle needs to be explicitly presented to them. For the *"praise–ignore" formula* to work, certain conditions are essential (Birnbrauer, 1985): (1) parental attention must be capable of reinforcing the child's behavior; (2) the parent is capable of giving attention of the right kind at the right times; (3) attention, and not other consequences, is maintaining the inappropriate behavior; (4) ignoring is aversive or nonreinforcing; (5) nonreinforcement alone is an effective means of eliminating unwanted behavior; (6) continuation of the unwanted behavior will not be harmful to the child or others; (7) parental reactions are controlled by child appropriate and inappropriate behavior with some consistency—that is to say, the parents have reasonably consistent expectations from day to day and the child is able to learn the definitions of what is appropriate and inappropriate from changes in contingencies.

The therapist might explain this principle as follows:

THERAPIST: Here you have to do a balancing act. You need to combine attention (praise and approval) and what you might think of as "judicious" ignoring.

PARENT: How can you ignore bad behavior? Surely you're encouraging it and setting a bad example.

THERAPIST: Let me try to explain this method. All those things I mentioned—attention, praise, and approval—are what we call "stimuli." Meaningful stimuli are vital because they direct our behavior. Or to put this another way, it is crucial for the individual's survival that she *learn* to respond appropriately to stimuli. For instance, we can rely on most car drivers to respond to the stimulus of a red traffic light by stopping. If we could not, chaos would ensue. Children have to learn a complicated set of "stop," "caution", and "go" signals—something I'll come back to. In the course of time they come to rely and thrive on parental attention. As children grow older and are more self-reliant, we are not always as attentive to their "signals"—the stimuli of what they say and do and need—as we might be. And that can lead to problems. They might resort to disruptive behavior to gain our attention. If we want to change children's behavior, we must first change the way in which we ourselves have tended to react to this behavior in the past. To take our example of attention-seeking, we need to think about a new slogan. "Catch the child engaged in good behavior rather than always in bad behavior." This means that if we have been rewarding "bad" behavior with attention (angry or otherwise) and ignoring, for the most part, "good" behavior, then we must reverse our reactions and start ignoring the bad behavior as much as is feasible and reward the good. This sounds simple enough, but of course it raises all kinds of questions and potential complications. We need to try to deal with these by thinking through together a rather fuller explanation of what is happening in your particular situations.

In working with some families, the praise–ignore approach does not always live up to expectations. For loving parents do not simply praise and attend to their children; they also give opportunities for outings, hugs, and cuddles, provide comfort and interesting exchanges, listen and converse. These wider expressions of parental attention and approval are absent or contingently impaired in some families. If an assessment fails to reveal any meaningful relationship between parental approval and parental giving (taking other forms) then it may not be appropriate to recommend the praise–ignore formula. The therapist's focus might rather be upon strengthening the reinforcement value of parental attention through increasing pleasant events within these families by contracts and token systems. The "when–then" or "first–then" rule—"First you do your homework and then you may go out and play"—should be extended, according to Birnbrauer (1985), to the following formula: "First you do your homework, *then I will be pleased* and you can go out and play."

Where families are characterized by coercive exchanges and seriously deteriorated relationships, positive attention will be difficult for the parents to provide. Some parents will have to learn to do so for the first time; praise will not come easily to many of them. Role-play and modeling are invaluable here (Herbert, 1987a). If the mother is distressed, anxious about finances and other matters, socially isolated, and oppressed by other demands of running the household and strained relationships with her husband/partner, then her attention and energy may simply be in short supply. Such factors can contribute to the failure of therapeutic programs.

Ignoring, too, is not as easy as it sounds. Parents may need specific help in thinking through how and when to do it. An example is given below.

Emma was 9 years old, the only child of rather anxious and overprotective parents. They were very concerned at her difficult behavior during mealtimes when, although perfectly able to feed herself, she would refuse to eat unless fed, would throw food and utensils on the floor, and often refuse food entirely. Assessment revealed that at school lunches the child showed none of these behaviors. Nor were they displayed at home when she ate informally in front of the television in the evening. Her problem behavior was specific to family lunch at weekends and holidays, the only occasions when the whole family sat down together at the table. It appeared that this setting was providing Emma with an audience to which she gladly reacted.

In order to combat this, her parents were instructed to ignore any "naughty" behavior and only to speak to Emma when she was eating properly. They were not to feed her or coax her, and any food refused was to be removed without comment. Between meals, snacks were forbidden. The dining-room table was rearranged so that Emma's parents were not looking directly at her. In order to help them ignore her, which they found very difficult at first, they were told to talk to each other, and thus take their minds off Emma. Within three weekends Emma was eating normally and has continued to do so. Her parents also used behavioral principles in encouraging self-help skills and have themselves become less overprotective.

In conducting a treatment program in which parents are asked to praise and encourage their children, it is crucial that these responses should be *realistic*; if praise is used indiscriminately or "promiscuously," it is devalued. Praise and encouragement should also be *consistent* if they are to be of maximum value. It is of no value to praise a particular action one day and to praise its opposite the next, or to praise children for something one day and punish them for it the next. Such inconsistency leads to confusion, or worse. There are cases in which the only consistency children can expect from their parents is when they are behaving badly. Thus, paradoxically, they gain a sense of security only from misbehavior.

It is seldom good enough simply to tell parents, in a didactic manner, about these issues. It is not simply that the principles are too theoretical, too abstract, but parents cannot always "see" them applying to themselves or cannot see how to change what they do. Rehearsal and practice are necessary.

Principle 4: Shaping

The principle of shaping is that although children may not produce the specific desired behavior, from time to time they will nevertheless produce behavior that approximates it, or that at least resembles it more closely than does their normal behavior.

THERAPIST: It may be that although your child never seems to get on with his sister, there are nevertheless occasions when he is less provocative than usual. Shaping is particularly important here, with Archie being praised and encouraged for actions which approximate, albeit initially only minimally, the desired thoughtfulness. So you need to separate clearly in your own mind your child's desirable behavior from what is undesirable. Thus, for example, if Archie is waiting quietly for a turn from his sister for the computer game, this in itself is desirable, irrespective of whether it is the precise cooperation and friendship you are looking for. In practical terms, what this means is that you smile at your child and make a pleasant remark when he is being marginally nice and patient, while ignoring him when he is being what you call "thoughtless." At first he may be taken somewhat aback. He will hardly be used to being greeted with praise and a smile for being minimally thoughtful to his sister. But after the first few occasions, this welcoming approval may well be found to be much more pleasant, and therefore more reinforcing, than disapproving attention, and certainly much more fun than being ignored. So the more thoughtful, friendlier actions will become more frequent, perhaps even routine.

PARENT: How often and how long do I go on doing all this? Shouldn't the child know what's right without all this rigmarole?

THERAPIST: Children have to learn what is right. It can be an effort. Like us, they
enjoy incentives for hard work. To answer your first question: Once a particular
piece of desirable behavior has become firmly established, it is no longer necessary
to seek to reinforce it each time it happens. Indeed, to do so can become counterproductive in that the child becomes blasé about the attention and praise so that
it no longer carries particular value. Reinforcement from time to time becomes
sufficient, in particular when this reinforcement is offered primarily for
particularly good examples of the behavior concerned.

Principle 5: Clear Limit-Setting

Parents are often concerned about the issue of rules or expectations—what
limits to set on their children. For example:

PARENT: This issue of the rules is what I find so difficult. I don't know what I
should emphasize, what is important.

THERAPIST: Don't devise a long list of rules for the sake of having rules: Make sure
they serve the purpose of enhancing your child's safety, well-being and steady (not
hurried) progress towards maturity. You might ask yourself:

- Are the rules necessary?
- Are they simple?
- Are they fair?
- Does my child understand them?
- Does s/he know what will happen if the rules are broken?
- Do I (and my partner) apply the rules fairly?

Shall we work through these questions for your children? ...

It may help, with an older child, to write or type out the house rules (the "standing
orders") and post them up in the kitchen or elsewhere. Parents usually have some
"general rules" for day-to-day convenience and safety. This requires a reasonable
ratio of obedient to disobedient responses to parental requests, instructions, and
commands. You are probably doing well with toddlers if you achieve a success
rate of between 50–70%.

PARENT: I've read somewhere that you shouldn't impose your own personality on
the child.

THERAPIST: If we accept that there are excellent reasons for requiring that young
children show obedience to their parents—how else do they learn about life?—this
does not mean that parents should ask just anything, or too much, of their
children. Nor that they should be carbon copies of their parents. Some requests
or demands are reasonable and fair, indeed essential for their safety and progress

in life; but others certainly might not be so because they fail to take into account the children's right to their needs and point of view, or because they are inappropriate to their level of development. To ask a child to get dressed by herself is a reasonable requirement of a seven-year-old, but not of a two-year-old. In making demands of a child, you need to ensure that the request is appropriate to his/her age and ability, and that you are not expecting too much. Perhaps you would like us to think this through together.

PARENT: Yes, I'd like that. The trouble is that my partner and I can't agree on discipline. Does it really matter?

THERAPIST: It does. And this is one of the reasons we'd like him to join our discussions. If parents cannot agree on the more important matters of discipline, their child will soon spot the differences in outlook and drive a coach and horses through their family harmony. If the father is trying to instill good table manners while the mother is arguing, "What does it matter so long as she eats?" or the mother is trying to set up a sensible bedtime routine while the father says, "Another half hour won't hurt," mealtimes and bedtimes will soon turn into problem areas. Children soon learn the motto "Divide and conquer."

ANOTHER PARENT: My trouble is that I'm on my own and I don't always have the energy to insist on what I want her to do.

THERAPIST: Many mothers tell us about this dilemma. You have to make a decision about a short-term investment of energy for long-term advantage. Your daughter plays off that side of you that is exhausted and wishes to take the "line of least resistance" against that part that wishes to make a stand on an important matter of principle. If you can be firm and consistent for a week or two, you'll find that your child will come to believe that you really mean what you say and will be more obedient. It's a costly, but profitable investment of your time and resolve.

There is a case for advising parents that children should be encouraged to think about the reasons for rules so that they have standards for judging their own behavior and learn to reason things out for themselves. This training is particularly effective where explanations are given in terms of a few well-defined principles. When explanations and reasons center on a few clearly defined principles, they seem to enhance moral awareness and resistance to temptation. Helping parents (in poorly communicating families) to organize family meetings, even "chairing" them in the early stages, is a good way of ensuring that these matters are addressed (Herbert, 1992).

Parents need principles and practical techniques for encouraging and maintaining not only compliance, but also other prosocial behaviors. In relation to this point it is important for the therapist to advocate on behalf of children and check on what is being asked of them, and on what has or has not been taught them. Children can hardly be blamed for not doing what they do not know, are not capable of, or rightly see to be unreasonable. The following questions are pertinent:

■ Are the expectations of the child (rules, requirements) reasonable?

■ Does s/he know *what* to do?

■ Does s/he know *how* to do it?

■ Does s/he know *when* to do it?

Of course, children may have been taught, and know, the socially appropriate behavior or skill and when to produce it, but still not perform it. So there are four more questions:

■ How can I get him/her to do what I want him/her to do?

■ Now that s/he does it, how can I encourage him/her to continue doing it?

■ How can I get him/her to stop doing what I don't want him/her to do?

■ Now that s/he has stopped doing it, how can I encourage him/her to continue to desist from doing it?

Principle 6: Observational Learning (Modeling)

There is another important form of learning which it is important to convey to parents: observational learning or, less technically, imitation.

THERAPIST: Children learn much of their social behavior (and many other complex actions) by imitating others. They model themselves on their observations of the significant people in their environment, copying what they do and say. This form of learning, which is based on cognitive (intellectual) processes rather than by means of reinforcement training, is called "observational learning."

Very young children are restricted to instantaneous imitation, whereas delayed modeling of complex behavior requires symbolic abilities that emerge in the second year of life. The key question for parents to put to themselves is the following: *Is my motto "Do as I say, not as I do"*?

THERAPIST: The child's ability to imitate also has its negative side. It plays an important role in learning undesirable behavior. We often forget that children don't only do what we say but also what we do. You might list the behaviors you complain about in your child in one column and in a column next to it, list which members of the family do the same, or similar, things.

To teach a parent or a child new patterns of behavior, the therapist can give him/her the opportunity to observe a person performing the desired actions. Social workers, clinicians, and others in the helping professions, but most particularly parents or admired peers, are very important as models in shaping behavior. Modeling can be used effectively in at least three situations:

■ To acquire new or alternative patterns of behavior which the client has never manifested before (e.g., social skills, self-control);

■ To increase or decrease responses already in the client's repertoire (e.g., the disinhibition of a shy client's withdrawal from social interactions);

■ To reduce learned fears (e.g., avoidance of gym) or the suppression of impulsive antisocial behavior which gets in the way of social relationships.

Three variations of modeling—filmed modeling, live modeling, and participant modeling—tend to be used in clinical practice. Treatment implications are illustrated in Chapter 4.

Principle 7: Natural Consequences

A natural consequence is simply the consequence that would naturally ensue from the child's actions in the absence of intervention by the parent. If parents ensure (within limits of safety) that the child is allowed to experience the consequences of his/her own actions, this becomes an effective means of modifying behavior. If a child is rough with a possession and, for example, breaks it, s/he is more likely to learn to be careful if s/he has to do without it. If parents always replace the toy, s/he is likely to continue to be destructive.

Unfortunately from the point of view of the parents' and the child's best interests, children are frequently not allowed to experience the natural consequences of their misbehavior. Instead, the parent intervenes to "protect" their offspring from reality or to protect their own (mistaken) self-interest. The potentially educative (though punishing) consequences are circumvented by a kind parent; the result, however, of this kindness is that the implications (outcomes) of the situation often do not become apparent to the child and s/he goes on to repeat the same misbehavior over and over again. A good deal of discussion and debate with parents (particularly overprotective ones) is required here. The issue is to what extent (particularly with toddlers and teenagers) parents should intervene ("interfere"?) to protect the child from the inevitable risks of life. To what extent is the child allowed to learn from experience, i.e., to "learn the hard way"?

Principle 8: Self-management

In order to engender or strengthen self-control, techniques have been developed (e.g., Kendall & Braswell, 1982) to change the parent's or child's instructions to him/herself. Anger control training involves first raising the parent's consciousness of the circumstances in which s/he gets angry. It then moves through a series of stages: first the therapist models the performance of a task, making appropriate and positive self-statements (e.g., "Think first, act afterwards"; "It's not worth losing my temper"; "I'll count to 10 and stay calm"); the parent then practices the same statements, gradually moving to whispered, and eventually silent, self-instruction. Parents are encouraged to use self-statements so that they can observe, evaluate, and reinforce appropriate overt behaviors in themselves.

A variation in modifying self-statements is the self-talk analysis and training applied to the depressed or helpless-feeling individual. Such a person often makes self-statements that are exaggerated ("I can't cope any more ... I'm in a terrible mess ... There's no hope ... Oh, what am I to do?" "No one loves me ... there's no hope!") or illogical in the sense that they suggest a need to be all-competent, to show no weakness, to be acknowledged and loved *all* the time, to be forever right, or to be forever in the wrong. The therapist attempts, in conversation with the parent, to expose the faulty reasoning underlying the self-talk and to provide arguments and statements that counter and defuse the distressing situation.

Principle 9: Interpersonal Problem-solving Skills

These skills are learned from experiences in the family and in any other situations where the child interacts with others, so that the child must confront interpersonal difficulties and the need to cope with them. How well the developing child learns (and later the adult expresses) these skills depends upon the extent to which the child's family manifests these abilities, as well as the degree to which parents communicate in ways that encourage the exercise of such thinking in the child.

Interpersonal cognitive problem-solving skills training includes:

- *Problem-sensitivity training*, which is designed to help parents be aware of the range of problems which arise out of social interactions and to develop a sensitivity to the kinds of social situations out of which interpersonal difficulties may arise. It also involves encouraging the parent to examine relationships with others in the here and now.

- *Alternative solution thinking*, which involves helping the client to develop the ability to generate a wider variety of potential solutions to problems. Brainstorming is the creative art of generating the greatest number of ideas in the shortest possible time. It is ideally suited to group participation as well as individual application.

Other components of a problem-solving skills-training program include:

- *Means–ends thinking*, which is the ability to articulate, step-by-step, the means necessary to carry out the solution to an interpersonal problem. The skill encompasses the ability to recognize obstacles and to analyze the social consequences deriving from these solutions.

- *Consequential thinking*, which means being aware of the consequences of social acts as they affect oneself and others; it includes the ability to generate alternative consequences to potential solutions before acting.

- *Causal thinking*, which refers to the person's appreciation of social and personal motivation; it involves the realization that how one felt and acted may have been influenced by (and, in turn, may have influenced) how others felt and acted.

A collaborative vehicle for teaching these components of problem-solving is the use of role-play. It encourages parents to address problems directly and to see things from the child's point of view.

THERAPIST: If you understand *your* reactions to your child (teenager) you may better understand *his/her* reactions to you, and thus arrive at solutions which are workable for both of you. Let us role-play that situation you described as a "total mystery." First let me play the part of your child. You script it for me. Now let's go through it ... exactly as it happened.

[*Later*]
THERAPIST: Now let's reverse roles. I'll be you; you play the part of your child ...

[*Afterwards*]
How did it feel? Did being the child show you anything new, give you any insights? Let me tell you how I felt. How could we "script" it/play it differently? Would it end differently? Would you feel better about it?

Another method is as follows:

THERAPIST: Let us think about some scenarios that set the stage for confrontations or confusion. We need to ask why they are provocative or self-defeating and what better ways there might be to deal with the situation.

The following list gives some typical examples.

(1) The provocation: "I wouldn't have behaved like that when I was your age."
(2) The command in the form of a question: "Do you want to get dressed now? Won't you put away your toys for Mummy?" (No choice really intended.)
(3) The command to go to bed in the middle of an exciting TV program/unfinished game.
(4) The "unending" shop at the supermarket (i.e., no plan/game/incentive to keep the young child occupied.)
(5) The negative response (injunction) to the child's apology/act of reparation ("I should think so; it was naughty; don't do it again".)
(6) Endless criticism: telling the child everything s/he is doing is wrong.
(7) Shouting; talking sarcastically; losing control; overreacting.
(8) Stereotyping: "You teenagers are all the same."

REDUCING/ELIMINATING BEHAVIOR

There are several ways in which parents unwittingly contribute to the development and maintenance of problem behavior. A discussion of these may generate ideas for ways of reducing undesirable behaviors and interactions. The therapist can generate two central questions as a means of focusing this discussion.

Question No. 1: THERAPIST: Are you making undesirable behavior worthwhile?

Some parents unwittingly make undesirable behavior worthwhile, as in the following examples:

Antecedents	*Behavior*	*Consequences*
David was told to leave the TV off.	He kept turning it on.	It was eventually left on—to give people a bit of peace.

THERAPIST: In this instance the child's unacceptable action was rewarded—by getting his own way. In other words, the child received positive reinforcement for behaving in an undesirable manner, which made it even more likely to occur again. Can you think of any examples where, unwittingly, you may be providing your child with a "pay-off" for behaving badly?

Question No. 2: THERAPIST: Are you making undesirable behavior costly?

Some parents make undesirable behavior unworthwhile:

Antecedents	*Behavior*	*Consequences*
(a) Johnnie wanted to go to the park; Dad said there wasn't time before tea.	Johnnie kicked and shouted, lay on the floor and screamed, and began to play.	Dad ignored his tantrum; eventually Johnnie calmed down.
(b) Anna was having breakfast.	She kept getting down from her place.	Mum, after one warning, took away her breakfast and Anna had to go hungry.

Just as behavior that is reinforced tends to recur, so behavior that is not reinforced (example (a)) or punished (example (b)) tends to be discontinued. It is important to reassure parents that by "rewards" we are not referring to expensive, tangible things, and that by "punishments" we are not denoting things that are physical, harsh, or painful. We are trying to help children to see that certain behaviors produce desirable consequences (e.g., praise, approval, esteem, treats, privileges) in social living, while other forms of behavior do not. Many of the most important rewards consist of relatively common things (personal attention, warm smiles, friendly gestures, social acceptance, encouragement, the good opinion of others), while many of the most effective punishments consist simply of the absence or withholding of such things. Parents tend to forget that when they give children a frown of disapproval for some inappropriate action, they are punishing them by signaling to them the withdrawal of their approval.

It goes without saying that if children love, trust, and respect their parents—in other words, *identify* with them—their desire to please them (by and large) makes parents' rewards and sanctions very powerful. "Affection is a premium fuel for learning" is a useful axiom for all parents, especially parents of conduct-disordered children.

Principle 10: Time Out from Positive Reinforcement

In Chapter 1 it was noted that parents of conduct-disordered children tend to be ineffectual in applying sanctions to their offspring's aggressive, antisocial behaviors. Time Out has been shown to be an effective disciplinary method when taught to parents (Herbert, 1987a,b; 1989). The procedure is intended to reduce the frequency of an undesirable behavior by ensuring that it is followed by a reduction in the opportunity to acquire reinforcement, or rewards. In practice we can choose from three forms of Time Out:

- *Activity Time Out* where the child is simply barred from joining in an enjoyable activity but still allowed to observe it—for example, having misbehaved s/he is made to sit out of a game.

- *Room Time Out* where s/he is removed from an enjoyable activity, not allowed to observe this, but not totally isolated—for example, having misbehaved, standing at the far end of the sitting room or a classroom.

- *Seclusion Time Out* where s/he is socially isolated in a situation away from the reinforcing contingencies.

Time Out may last from three to five minutes. In practice, "activity" or "room" Time Out should always be preferred before any form of "seclusion" Time Out. The child is warned *in advance* about those of her/his behaviors that are considered inappropriate and the consequences that will follow from them. It is helpful to discuss with parents *in advance* the range of issues that may arise from the use of Time Out (see Chapter

7). Here we shall consider how they are encouraged to think about the nature of limits or boundaries to which Time Out might be applied:

THERAPIST: You could think of your child's behavior as falling into three color codes: green, amber, and red.

Green is the "go ahead" code for the type of behavior you want from your children, the actions you always remember to praise and encourage. If you use the green code consistently, the behavior should be well established by the time they go to school.

Amber is for "caution" behavior, which you don't encourage but tolerate because your child is still learning and making mistakes: something like hurling her toys across the room in a moment of fury. Any sort of stress such as moving house, illness, or upset in the family may cause the child to take a temporary step backwards in behavior. Be understanding if s/he suddenly starts wetting the bed or crying for attention following a bad dream in the night.

Red is definite "stop" (No! No!) behavior which needs to be curbed as soon as possible. Obviously anything which can be dangerous for him/her or for others, has a red code: running into the road, climbing the railway fence, attacking the toddler next door with his teeth.

The priorities for older children and teenagers will of course be different.

Time Out is not, however, a method without complications. If it is to be used effectively, it requires painstaking explanations for the child and parents, preemptive warnings for the parent of what can go wrong, and a prompt "trouble-shooting" response to the difficulties, if they do arise (see Herbert, 1987a; Webster-Stratton, 1992; also Chapter 7).

To take one example, Time Out is quite likely to lead to tantrums or rebellious behavior such as crying, screaming, and physical assaults. With older, physically resistive children, the method may simply not be feasible. When the behavior to be eliminated is an extraordinarily compelling one that all but *demands* attention (reinforcement) from those present, or when Time Out is difficult to administer because the child is strong and protesting, an equivalent of Time Out may be instituted by removing the sources of reinforcement from him/her. So if the parent is a major source of reinforcement, s/he could remove her/himself, together with a magazine, to the bathroom when the child's temper tantrums erupt, coming out only when all is quiet.

Time Out is a particularly potent aid to behavioral change and improvement in fiercely oppositional children (e.g., Day & Roberts, 1983) and is particularly valuable in cases of child abuse where noncompliance is a major complaint by parents. It allows parent and child an opportunity to "cool down" and it tends to have face-validity for those parents (during the early stages of a program) who demonstrate a punitive ideology of child-rearing and who find it difficult to engage in the positive aspects (so vital) of finding opportunities to encourage and praise their offspring. Sadly, the perceived punitive quality of Time Out gives it credibility for parents who have not yet moved on in treatment from an authoritarian view of discipline (and power-assertive practices) to more benign attributions as to why their children behave in the way they do. For the therapist, there is an important ethical issue in getting parents to counterbalance Time Out with positive attention (play, praise, additional contact), but it is more than an ethical issue: it is also good practice, for the best behavioral outcomes are obtained when a parent uses both praise and Time Out (see Hobbs & Forehand, 1975).

Principle 11: Response–Cost

The use of Response–Cost procedures involves a penalty being invoked for failure to complete a desired response. This may involve the forfeiture of rewards currently available—as for example, when failure to complete homework results in the loss of television privileges. It is a feature of the collaborative approach that with this, as with other methods, we ask parents to help us problem-solve—that is, to come up with appropriate costs and rewards. In the following case, a hyperactive boy, Matthew, was extremely disruptive and noisy. He made life miserable for his older brothers and sisters while they read or watched television by constantly interrupting them—making loud humming and wailing noises and also banging things. The Response–Cost method was explained to the parents in the following way: "To stop your child from acting in an unacceptable way, you need to arrange for him to bring to an end this *moderately* (but significantly) unpleasant situation immediately by changing the behavior in the desired direction." The parents worked out the following scenario for Matthew.

A bottle of marbles representing his weekly pocket money plus a bonus was placed on the mantelpiece. Each instance of misbehavior "cost" a marble (the equivalent of a specific sum of money). In a good week, Matthew could increase his pocket money quite substantially; in a bad week it could be reduced to zero. Of course, the "cost" of transgressions was highly visible to the boy. As always, sanctions were to be balanced by rewards, since punishment alone tells children what not to do, not what they are expected to do. An extension of the range of rewards for therapeutic interventions is enshrined in the Premack principle, where a preferred behavior is made contingent on correctly performing a non-preferred behavior. This principle, when worked out by the parents, required Matthew to play quietly for set periods, timed with a kitchen timer, and if he did this successfully, he was rewarded by stickers. These stickers could then be exchanged for treats. For example, he could play with his sister's computer game for 15 minutes, something he had always wanted to do and which was therefore a great incentive.

Principle 12: Contracts

It may sound distinctly odd (if not demeaning) to parents to consider negotiating a written agreement with a child or using business-style contracts to resolve family conflicts. Surely these are the domain of lawyers or salesmen—far too cold and commercial to apply to human relationships? But it is precisely because a contract is such a detached, objective way of dealing with emotional issues that sitting down as a family to draft an agreement can be effective (Herbert, 1987b). It is not only the content of the contract that is important; the *process* of arriving at the agreed terms can be therapeutic.

In coercive families, as we have seen, the cues or messages are frequently negative ones, the "sound and fury" of criticism, nagging, crying, shouting, and hitting out being the norm. Communication between members may not be so much aversive as impoverished or practically nonexistent. Where family systems include behavior control by the use of verbal and/or physical pain, they are likely to produce children who exhibit frequent ("high rate") aggressive actions (Patterson, 1982). Coercive interactions, maintained by negative reinforcement, are most likely to operate in closed social systems where the child must learn to cope with aversive stimuli such as incessant criticism.

This is where contracts come in. They can be used to "open" closed systems somewhat. Certainly, one way of increasing positively reinforcing communications while reducing punitive interactions is by sitting down to work out a contract with members of the family. The discussion, negotiation, and compromise in such therapist-led situations introduces the family to an important means of resolving interpersonal conflicts and tensions and to enhanced communication, which they may have experienced only rarely. Moving families on from aversive to friendlier interactions by means of contracting takes a good deal of skill and patience, and success is by no means guaranteed (see Herbert, 1992).

An illustration of contracting

The Grant family cautiously agreed to try to draw up a contract. At first their difficulties seemed insurmountable. Nearly all of them expressed unhappiness or discontent, particularly with Anne, a rebellious, aggressive

15-year-old who was threatening to leave home. Her mother, Avril, felt trapped, tired, and depressed, hemmed in by the defiance of Anne and the demands of a fretful, strong-willed toddler. Ten-year-old John was beginning to refuse to go to school. Avril was arguing incessantly with her husband James. He was preoccupied with his health and the possibility of being laid off work and, in her view, had opted out of responsibility for disciplining the children. In his opinion he got little attention from his wife. Statements that passed for communication were often punitive messages. "You're always undermining me," Avril accused James when he tried to respond to an earlier complaint she had made ("You always opt out at the first hint of difficulty") and reprimanded the children. There was a notable absence of affectionate words. Only the grandmother seemed above it all, but in private she confided that the atmosphere of endless bickering and recriminations made her feel sad and insecure.

Contract sessions were organized in the Grants' own home. The grand-mother proved vital as an impartial "chair" of the family discussions. The contracts that the Grants finally drew up took five sessions which were, after the initial slanging match, reasonably amicable. Having accepted some ground rules suggested by the therapist and rigorously enforced by the grandmother, the Grants appreciated, so they said, a structure that allowed a degree of communication they had been missing for years. At first old resentments tumbled out, but these statements seemed to have less power than when they had been either shouted out (without the chance of any discussion) or bottled up until they were like festering wounds. The parents, for instance, found that their fears of what Anne was up to at night were often unfounded or even ludicrous. Anne herself found that when she voiced her grievances quietly and calmly, rather than screaming at them, her family paid attention to what she was actually saying.

The following guidelines were followed in planning the contract:

- Keep the discussion positive. Recriminations are unavoidable, but the volume should be kept down and negative complaints turned into positive suggestions.

- Be very specific in spelling out desired actions.

- Pay attention to the details of privileges and conditions for both parties. They should (a) be important, not trivial, and (b) make sense to the person involved.

- Encourage positive and specific actions if the parent wishes her/his child or partner to desist from certain activities.

- Choose changes the clients want to bring about that can easily be monitored. If one cannot see whether an obligation has been met, one cannot readily grant a privilege.

- Make clear to all concerned the penalties for breaking the contract.

- Keep a diary of progress. It is helpful, during the contract discussion period, if family members write down five specific things they would like to see changed.

- The contract drawn up must embody the principles of mutual caring. Unless it does, it is likely to fail.

Besides Anne's behavior, there were many other family issues to be addressed, not least the marital tensions. Eventually the Grant family decided that they needed two contracts, one between James and Avril, the other between Anne and her parents. Specific rewards, such as praise, pocket money, and sympathy, were built in (see Anne's contract below).

CONTRACT BETWEEN JAMES AND AVRIL GRANT AND THEIR DAUGHTER, ANNE

Anne will endeavor to:

(1) Let her parents know about her movements when she goes out at night; she will tell them where she is, with whom, and let them know what time she will be home.
(2) Be less moody; she won't sulk when reprimanded or thwarted.
(3) Be more ready to say she's sorry; she will apologize when she's been in the wrong.
(4) Show more concern about her school work, i.e., do at least half an hour's homework at night.
(5) Stop being so rude and aggressive to her father, i.e., swearing and walking out when he gives her advice.

Anne would like *her parents* to:

(1) Stop criticizing her friends.
(2) Admit when they are in the wrong and be ready to apologize.

(3) Give her more pocket money (a sum agreed) and review the amount every six months in the light of rising expenses and changes in her commitments.

All agree:

(1) That the terms of the Contract will not be changed except by mutual discussion and agreement.
(2) That disputes will be settled by the witness (grandmother), whom all agree to be objective and fair-minded.
(3) That successful execution of the Contract for a month will be rewarded by a family treat (first month: an outing to a favorite restaurant).
(4) That failure to carry out individual terms of the Contract will result in a fine on each occasion: an amount of X for Anne; and Y for Mr. and Mrs. Grant, respectively. The money is to go in a penalty box kept by the grandmother; the proceeds will go to charity.

Signed ....

Success did not come overnight for any of them, but a slow, steady improvement did take place. By periodically taking out the Contract and referring yet again to the agreed terms, the family kept on track and maintained progress.

CASE ILLUSTRATION OF PARENT–THERAPIST DIALOGUE

In Chapter 3 an example was given of a parent struggling with an oppositional, defiant child. Assisted by the therapist, she defined one of her goals as follows:

PARENT: I expect him to obey me when I make a reasonable request or command, so that if (say) I ask him to put his things away, he does so without endless arguments or fits of temper.

The fragment of a therapeutic program that ensues illustrates the explanation, and practical difficulties, of applying behavioral methods.

THERAPIST: There are two general principles involved in putting right the unsatisfactory situation we have gradually disentangled and thus clarified. In retraining your child you will need first to *weaken* the undesirable actions and at the same time to *strengthen* a desirable action that is incompatible (i.e., competes) with the undesirable one. Your child tantrums too easily, so you will attempt to weaken tantruming while (at the same time) you strengthen a competing behavior such as "cooperative with mother."

PARENT: How do I go about that? It sounds OK in theory, but in practice . . . I just don't know! I get most embarrassed by his behavior when I take him shopping. My particular "disaster area" is the checkout part of the supermarket. People in the queue see him tantruming if I don't let him keep the chocolates and things he puts in my trolley.

THERAPIST: Try to think of a responsibility you can give him, one you can praise. Is there an alternative action—one that cannot be performed at the same time as the "problem" behavior?

PARENT: [after several ideas have been put forward and debated]: I suppose, while I'm going around the shop, I could have a game, asking him to spot things I need . . . and keep a score. The trouble is worst when we finish shopping. Certainly he cannot help me pack my box at the supermarket at the far side of the checkout and put sweets and chocolates into my basket, which (as I said) is what he usually does when at the other end. Maybe he can't help me and tantrum at the same time.

THERAPIST: If he goes through the checkout counter without grabbing things or putting on a tantrum, you could also praise his behavior ("You're a big boy, behaving so well"). Give him a reward when he gets home (a symbolic one—a sticker on his chart) and a tangible one (a biscuit) as you leave the shop. Repeat your reasons for this acknowledgment. Gradually you should be able to phase out the tangible reinforcers when tantrums are no longer a major part of his actions.

PARENT: I'll certainly try that. But what about his awful tantrums at home and his incessant whining demands?

THERAPIST: You could try ignoring tantrums. Let's discuss the use of ignoring. As soon as the misbehavior begins, turn away or walk away from your child; say nothing and try not to show any expression at all; resist getting into any debate, argument, or discussion with your child while he is misbehaving; if you think he deserves an explanation for whatever is upsetting him then say to him, "When you have calmed down we will talk about it."

PARENT: Trying to ignore Wayne is like trying to ignore a hurricane! He will follow me around kicking up a fuss, pulling at me, even hitting me.

THERAPIST: Shall we plan now what we are going to do if that happens? We could try Time Out. You could tell Wayne that when he has a temper tantrum, he will have to spend three minutes on his own. If he ceases his temper tantrum, take him out of Time Out after three minutes; if he continues, give him another three minutes, and so on. Use a kitchen timer. Explain *once* why you are going to use it; give *one* warning only of the imminence of Time Out each time he begins a tantrum. But having begun Time Out, use it on *every* occasion that he tantrums—unless he desists.

PARENT: What if he argues; and knowing him, he's bound to?

THERAPIST: Do not scold or dispute on the way to or during Time Out. Be matter-of-fact and very firm.

PARENT: Where shall I put him?

THERAPIST: Never use a frightening place for Time Out! But do use a place that is unrewarding (unstimulating) like a hallway or the end of the same room you're in, in a chair or on his own. The main thing is to be consistent and persistent. Then you should get results.

PARENT: What if it doesn't seem to work?

THERAPIST: Do persevere! Some behaviors change only slowly. If you take the line of least resistance, "giving in" on the odd occasion ("just this once") you won't be back to square one; it will be square minus one! You will actually make things worse for yourself.

PARENT: You said it was important to observe his actions carefully during the program.

THERAPIST: Yes. Check out whether you are getting anywhere. Monitor your progress and his. Go on counting the tantrums, recording them on the form I've given you. If you go on keeping a record you can observe the changes taking place gradually, day-by-day. Do not be discouraged if things get worse before they get better. If you remove the old reinforcers the child may well work harder (escalate the screaming, say) to get them back.

Helping Parents Understand the Context and Specificity of Problematic Behavior

The specificity of problem behavior often causes parents concern and puzzlement.

PARENT: Why is my child so well-behaved at school and so awful with me at home? It is so embarrassing that other people see or get a better side of my child than I do.

THERAPIST: I can understand how you feel. If it is any comfort, many parents say the same thing. If you think about and watch your child's behavior in different places and in different situations, you may notice that she behaves in a disobedient way, or has a tantrum, on some occasions but not others; that is, some situations seem to act as cues to her to behave in a particular way. Children (like adults) tend to tailor their behavior to the particular places and the different persons in which, and with whom, they find themselves. In the case of children this chameleon capacity often leads to misunderstandings between home and school—each blaming the other, when (often) they are difficult in the one setting but not the other for quite different reasons. Children tend to look around them, consider the rules, the firmness of the adult, how other children behave, and what is expected of them. Then they adapt their behavior according to the "benefits" and "costs" of the particular situation—what you might call the "pay-offs."

PARENT: What does this mean in practical terms for me and my child?

THERAPIST: It means that you have to take into account your child's behavior, the consequences of that behavior, and the context in which that behavior occurs. By studying these three things you are able to understand much more clearly what is actually happening when misbehavior occurs, and what strategies should be used. Let's try to solve this one together by looking at her actions in different settings and circumstances. For starters, you say she is better behaved when she has you to herself compared with when your other children are present, or when you have visitors. What other patterns are there?

SUMMARY

In this chapter we have described some of the behavioral methods available to the therapist and the discussion and dialogue that accompanies them. Twelve principles of learning which lead to practical strategies for parents to apply to their children have been described. The emphasis has not been solely on what the therapist tells the parent but why and how they might apply the methods. In other words, the collaborative approach has been highlighted—the process of partnership in thinking through as well as applying behavioral strategies to the management of children's problems. Another emphasis is on the constructive side of looking for children's strengths and virtues and building on them. This means putting a particular focus on acquiring new behaviors and skills, not only on the reduction or elimination of unwanted behavior. Throughout, the idea of empowering parents towards self-help rather than creating therapeutic dependency is given priority.

REFERENCES

Birnbrauer, J.S. (1985). When social reinforcement fails. Unpublished paper.
Day, D.E. & Roberts, M.W. (1983). An analysis of the physical punishment component of a parent training program. *Journal of Abnormal Child Psychology*, **11**, 141–152.
Forehand, R.L. & McMahon, R.J. (1981). *Helping the noncompliant child: A clinician's guide to parent training.* New York: Guilford.
Herbert, M. (1987a). *Behavioural treatment of children with problems: A practice manual.* London: Academic Press.
Herbert, M. (1987b). *Conduct disorders of childhood and adolescence: A social learning perspective* (revised edn.). Chichester, UK: Wiley.
Herbert, M. (1989). *Discipline: A positive guide for parents.* Oxford: Basil Blackwell.
Herbert, M. (1992). *Working with children and the Children Act.* Leicester, UK: BPS Books.
Herbert, M. (1994). Behavioural methods. In M. Rutter et al. (Eds.), *Child and adolescent psychiatry.* Oxford: Blackwell.
Hobbs, S.A. & Forehand, R. (1975). Effects of differential release from time-out on children's deviant behavior. *Journal of Behavior Therapy and Experimental Psychiatry*, **6**, 256–269.
Kendall, P.C. & Braswell, L. (1982). On cognitive-behavioral assessment: model, method and madness. In C.D. Spielberger & J.N. Butcher (Eds.) *Handbook of research methods in clinical psychology.* New York: Wiley.
Patterson, G. (1982). *Coercive family process.* Eugene, OR: Castalia.
Royal College of Psychiatrists (1987). *Guidelines to Good Practice.* London: Royal College of Psychiatrists Publications.
Webster-Stratton, C. (1992). *The incredible years: A trouble-shooting guide for parents of children aged 3–8.* Toronto, Canada: Umbrella Press.

PARENTS UNDERGOING THERAPY: AN EXPERIENCE OF GAINING KNOWLEDGE AND CONTROL*

6

ALTHOUGH THE the various types of family behavioral therapy programs referred to in Chapter 1 have received much attention in the literature, most if not all of this has been devoted to documenting their effectiveness. We know little about these programs from the *parents*' point of view. To put it a little differently, while the end-product of parent training has been well researched, the process has not; we know little about the actual process of change brought about by such programs. What happens when parents' behavior, attitudes, and practices are challenged and modified by a parent-training program? What emotional, social, and cognitive changes accompany changes in parenting practices? What difficulties do parents undergo as they work with the concepts presented in the program? How do these changes affect the family system—that is, what kinds of impact does the program have on different family members and on their relationships and interactions?

This chapter attempts to shed some light on this unstudied area by presenting the results of a qualitative research study by Webster-Stratton and Spitzer of a group of parents who participated in the Parenting Clinic videotape modeling parent-training program. We wanted to understand the process parents go through as they learn to cope more effectively with stresses related to their conduct-problem children's behavior. Since we had videotaped all our intake and therapy sessions as well as our consultation sessions, we had at hand a window into the experience of these parents, providing data on the therapeutic process. Through qualitative analysis, we examined how the parents experienced therapy, how they reacted to the videotape parenting program, what their questions and unique needs were while participating in the program, and what they felt was missing from the program. The scope of the data allowed us to describe the process of cognitive, social, and behavioral changes that parents underwent from the initial intake interview to the point where the program ended, approximately one year later.

* This chapter is derived, by permission, from Spitzer, Webster-Stratton & Hollinsworth (1991).

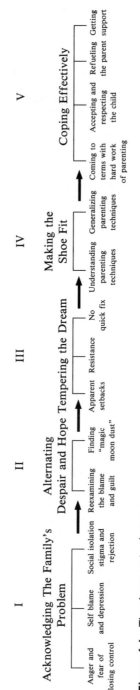

Figure 6.1 The therapeutic change process

During the initial two- to three-hour intake interviews, parents described their children's multiple problems and their efforts to handle them. In these interviews, they initially expressed feelings of despair, anger, shame, fear, and helplessness concerning their interactions with their children. Once they were involved in training, their attitude seemed to oscillate constantly between despair and irrational hope. As they gradually came to realize that their child's problems were chronic, and as their anger, guilt, and resistance gradually decreased, most families were able to change their expectations and settle for a less-than-total recovery of the family and the child. This stage was followed by one in which the parents worked at "fine tuning" or tailoring the program to their own particular needs.

The data suggest that the process of learning to cope more effectively as the parent of a conduct-disordered child comprises five phases: acknowledging the family's problem, alternating despair and hope, "tempering the dream," "making the shoe fit," and coping effectively (see Figure 6.1).

PHASE 1: ACKNOWLEDGING THE FAMILY'S PROBLEM

It is not easy for parents to admit that they have a child with behavior problems, a child who is different from other children. This difficult admission was the first phase in the process of change in parents' attitudes toward and interactions with their children. A major consequence of this admission—and perhaps the reason behind its difficulty—was that parents had to face their own conflicting attitudes and feelings concerning their child's problems. Three categories of acknowledging the problem were identified in the data: anger, and fear of losing control, self-blame and depression, and isolation.

Anger and Fear of Losing Control

During the intake appointments and initial therapy sessions, many parents talked about long months during which they waited for their child to get older, in the expectation that things would become easier for them. When things did *not* improve with time—when, instead, their child became increasingly defiant and noncompliant, a terror at home and at school—they began to realize that their child was different from most other children.

MOTHER: I remember waiting for him to turn three in June, and just waiting for this magical thing to happen. It never did. It's been very, very difficult from the very beginning. We're on pins and needles. [*Intake interview*]

As they felt a growing sense of inadequacy about how to handle these misbehaviors, their frustration with the child mounted. Parents talked about how their frustration and anger at their children escalated as they tried to discipline their children without success.

FATHER: My wife's been at work and comes home and asks, "How'd things go tonight?" I say, "Do the words 'living hell' mean anything to you?" That's our sort of little joke. I'm labeling the kids in my mind as never doing what I say and I'm very angry at them. [*Intake interview*]

MOTHER: I say to myself, "I'm not going to put up with this shit anymore." And I feel outraged, and it helps because I'm more willing to be the tough guy—but it leaves me a lot angrier. [*Intake interview*]

Along with the angry thoughts and feelings about their child, parents also expressed their sense of being victimized by their children. This sense of being a victim further inflamed their anger. Throughout the program, parents would frequently ask, "Why me?"

MOTHER: I feel persecuted by the children, especially at night when I first get home from work. Why do they do this to me? I've been fighting the freeways and my job, and now the kids. [*Session 8*]

MOTHER: Why is my child so different from others? I feel I'm really in the minority, because of all the mothers I've talked to, and they have never been hit by their child. I can't imagine—I mean it's absolutely unimaginable not to be slapped or kicked by your child. Other mothers have never experienced this. I'm a very nonaggressive person. I can't tolerate loud, aggressive people and I just don't associate with them—and I'm living with one! [*Intake interview*]

During therapy, parents began to reveal their angry feelings and were then able to discuss their fear of losing control of these feelings when trying to discipline their child.

FATHER: It's intense—I think I've been able to control it and I start thinking I've got to control myself. You know, I can't! It's like something's boiling inside of me and it's pretty emotional, pretty scary. [*Session 6*]

MOTHER: I've never done it, but I've thought of it when I get really, really mad. I've thought of running and throwing him out the window. But that's just what my head thinks, I've never done that. [*Session 13*]

Self-blame and Depression

The parents' anger and loss of control caused them to blame themselves and to feel depressed about these feelings and about their interactions with their children. They tended to evaluate their parenting skills as poor and to see themselves as a causal factor in their child's problems.

MOTHER: I'm stuck here—it will never get any better, this child is going to be a delinquent, I know it. I'm going crazy and I need help. [*Intake interview*]

MOTHER: Maybe I should just give up because I'm going down in a sinking ship. [*Intake interview*]

MOTHER: I tell myself it is more than I can cope with, you're a no-good mother, everything's out of control. [*Intake interview*]

MOTHER: Sometimes it's just a real small thing that sets him off. And all I can do is either hold him or spank him. And if I spank him hard enough he will stop. I don't like pounding on him but don't know what else to do. But at the same time I feel like I'm a child abuser or something when I do this. Because sometimes I have blown it completely and really spanked him hard.

Social Isolation, Stigma and Rejection

Another common theme identified throughout various stages of the program was parents' sense of being stigmatized and isolated from other parents of children of similar ages.

MOTHER: I was telling a friend who has daughters about my son and she said, "What, your son hits you? My daughters never hit me." I mean, other parents look at me like I just walked off another planet. So I feel very isolated. I feel like no one is like me—no one has my situation. [*Intake interview*]

Parents felt a lack of connection with and support from parents of "normal" children.

The next excerpt is taken verbatim from one of the parent groups talking about what they think would happen if they told their friends what their children are really like.

FIRST FATHER: You can't tell your friends how you feel about your child—you can't say, "My son is a bastard."

FIRST MOTHER: There's always the fear that if you share with somebody what your child is like, somebody will assume it's your fault, and think you screwed up as a parent.

SECOND MOTHER: Or they'll reject you and say, "God, I don't want to hear about this!"

THIRD MOTHER: They may say, "Gosh, my child never does that"—which is such a put down!

SECOND FATHER: Here's another one I've heard. "Oh well, we all have problems." That's like saying, "Well, I'm sorry you're having problems, but it doesn't matter to me."

FIRST FATHER: Yeah, it's the indifference that gets to me.

THIRD MOTHER: Well, that sort of comment implies you're supposed to keep a stiff upper lip.

THIRD FATHER: I didn't know it was this dangerous to have a child. I didn't know I had blanks when I went into this war.

FOURTH FATHER: Well, you know it's hard for me to ask for support sometimes because I might feel like I'm imposing.

FOURTH MOTHER: One thing I know is that if I tell someone about my problem—you know, talk about how bad my child is—I don't want them to think badly of her, so I'd rather not tell them.

Parents of conduct-problem children felt isolated from other parents, not only because they felt they had not been effective in producing a "normal child," but because they thought that if they were honest about their difficulties, they would experience rejection or indifference. Or, worse yet, they feared reprisals in terms of the impact this information could have on others' perceptions of and interactions with themselves or their child.

In addition to feeling isolated from friends and other parents, these parents also experienced rejection from teachers. During intake appointments, many of the parents reported that they had been asked by teachers to remove their child from preschools or day care centers. Some families had been asked to leave half a dozen daycare centers by the time their child was five years old.

MOTHER: At two years of age he was terrorizing the other children at preschool and we were asked to leave the school with no notice. There I was, scrounging around to find something else and it's kind of been like that ever since. After the cooperative daycare we tried a private preschool. I remember getting a phone call on my answering machine and holding my breath wondering whether the teacher was going to tell me to take him out . . . I would take him to preschool and I would come back after three hours and just the expression on the teacher's face—it was this horrified, painful expression. Then you would hear the reports of how your son had to have two people release him from a choke hold on another child or how he was pouring water on someone's head. [*Intake interview*]

MOTHER: I would hear all these horrible, horrible reports from the teachers who would say he's going to be in the office every other day when he's in kindergarten. The teacher is telling me now about what my child will be like two years from now and all the problems I'm going to have with him. [*Intake inverview*]

MOTHER: He's three years old and he's always on probation. The teacher just greeted me with one of those really painful expressions I'm so familiar with: "Your son did this." They told me not to bring him back. I was just so embarrassed. [*Intake interview*]

PHASE 2: ALTERNATING DESPAIR AND HOPE

Reexamining the Blame and Guilt

As parents participated in the parent-training program and learned new parenting strategies such as play skills, effective reinforcement, and non-violent discipline approaches, their regret and guilt about their earlier lack of parenting knowledge and about their previous use of punitive approaches, and—unfortunately, a new source of guilt—their failure to use these new approaches more consistently with their children were recurring themes.

MOTHER: These sessions have helped me feel a whole lot better about having more control about what's going on. I guess my biggest problem is that I feel guilty when I am not doing the right things and when I am going back to my other habits. I know we're not handling those (behavior problems) right, especially when he starts piling a lot of them at once, I tend to lose it completely and just scream hysterically at him, and spank him, which I don't want to be doing. [*Session 6*]

The anger and guilt arise from a tendency to attribute blame. Parents were initially preoccupied with identifying who should be blamed for the child's problems. While some parents externalized the child's problems and blamed the child's personality, an absent parent, teachers, or society in general, other parents internalized the child's problems and attributed them to their own personal inadequacies or poor parenting skills. As parents participated in treatment and viewed the videotape examples of other parents interacting in different ways with children of different temperaments, they began to reexamine the nature of blame and to understand how children with difficult temperaments required different degrees of parental supervision and different parenting skills in order to be successfully socialized. With this new awareness, parents were then able to focus more constructively on which parenting techniques would work best to bring out their child's prosocial behaviors and personality strengths, as well as strategies to decrease his/her aggression and non-compliance. Thus, the focus of the parents' attitudes gradually shifted from assigning blame for their child's problem to attempting to understand and manage it.

Finding "Magic Moon Dust"

While parents initially expressed guilt over their failure to control their child's misbehaviors, they also expressed feelings of excitement and even exhilaration about improving their interactions with their children as they began to learn new parenting strategies.

MOTHER: He wouldn't go to bed quietly, and the sticker chart took care of that just like that [*snapped fingers*]. The first day that I used the sticker chart and I started positively reinforcing him, his behavior changed so fast I could not believe it. I also felt the changes in myself and felt great about it. [*Session 4*]

FATHER: I have this weird feeling that after three weeks in this class, my son is instantly better. Through bad habits and exhaustion I was using too much power. So I backed off and we don't have the power struggles any more. [*Session 3*]

For most parents, after completing the first four programs on play, learning, praise, and tangible rewards, they experienced a major shift in their perception of their children's behaviors. They began to appreciate and notice their child's positive behaviors and deemphasize the negative.

MOTHER: By keeping track of praises I was able to be aware of all the positive things he does. It is so easy to get bent up and think, "He can't do anything right." All of a sudden you start listening to yourself saying, "You did a nice job there. Thank you!" Once I started to be specific in my praises, I noticed how many areas he is really trying to do right. You start thinking, "He's capable. He's probably been doing this a lot longer than I was willing to listen or give him credit for." [*Session 6*]

FATHER: Once it got into a more positive cycle and I had more patience because I wasn't getting all this negative stuff all the time, I found myself willing to put up with some shenanigans, not let him get away with it but also not go through the roof because I wasn't at the end of my rope after a day of many positives. [*Session 6*]

These new parenting techniques were perceived by parents initially as "magic moon dust" that could cure all their child's problems. Often parents experienced some immediate relief as their children made initial improvements, leading them to believe that their children's problems would be easily solved. Sometimes they seemed to feel that these changes in their children's behavior would alleviate other family problems. Thus, parents anticipated a "total cure." In this phase, parents did not consider the possibility that their child's behavior might regress or that improvement might cease at some point. Moreover, parents did not comprehend the long-term commitment and the sheer amount of work that would be necessary to maintain these initial improvements.

PHASE 3: TEMPERING THE DREAM

We called the third phase in the process of parents learning to cope with their children's conduct problems "tempering the dream." In this phase, parents faced the fact that there are no magical solutions and realized that they would need to adjust their hopes and expectations. Three categories were identified in the data as part of tempering the dream: "apparent setbacks," resistance, and "no quick fix."

Apparent Setbacks

Soon after the parents started to apply what they were learning in the program, unexpected changes started to take place—changes in the family dynamics, the target child, and the parents themselves. Some of these changes were in conflict with the parents' expectations for the program, resulting in anxiety and anger in some cases. Three common themes characterized these apparent setbacks: role reversal within the sibling relationships, conflicting parenting, and child's regression in spite of parents' hard work.

Role reversal was evident when parents reported that as the target child's behavior improved, the behavior of the sibling (mostly the younger child) became more deviant.

MOTHER: Our younger child, who has always been the one that's hard to get ready for bed, is cooperative lately. Boom! He's the first one ready because he knows if there's extra time, I'll play Lego with him. Now the older child, who has always been easy to get into bed, is dragging his feet. Try dragging a chunky eight-year-old up the stairs to bed. [*Session 8*]

The parents noticed that as they were practicing the strategies taught in the program with the target child, the other children in the family were demanding the same or more attention, thus taxing the already depleted resources and energy of these parents.

Conflicting parenting occurred when one partner participated actively in the program while the other parent either did not participate, was critical of the program, or was invested in maintaining the status quo. These differences in level of participation led not only to debate as to the best way to handle the child's misbehavior, but also to conflicts and blame related to the marriage. Thus, at this stage, the program seemed to some parents to result in marital stress. Conflicting parenting also operated in the case of some single parents where there was a former spouse, a boyfriend, or a grandparent who was involved in raising the child but was not participating in the program.

MOTHER: Now, what's happening is he goes to his father's house for one or two nights a week and his father doesn't reinforce him at all. And I tried to explain to him the sticker charts are not to be used as punishment, and he just sort of says, "Yeah, yeah, yeah, I know this stuff." [*Session 8*]

Regression, the third type of setback, occurred when the child's behavior seemed to regress in spite of the parents' hard work. In their anticipation regarding the ideal effects of the program on the child's behavior, parents made no allowances for limited progress or regression in the children's behavior. Therefore, when parents encountered regressions, their reaction was one of disbelief, depression, and even anger.

MOTHER: In the last two weeks, we've had a 75–85% regression. Complete—well, almost complete—reversal to where she was before this class began. I'm not certain why. I was really sick; maybe that had something to do with it. All of a sudden, out of the blue, she's had some real bad episodes and last week it was every day. It's like we've never been in this class. And the time before that—up through Christmas—was wonderful. I mean both of us had to hold her down to get her dressed on Saturday, amidst screaming and kicking and spanking. [*Session 9*]

MOTHER: I had some really good weeks, and was real impressed with Jessica and how she responded to everything, and then she had a couple of bad moments. It was a big surprise to me. Because I had gotten so used to her good behavior, and then she surprised me. [*Session 8*]

MOTHER: It's like with the Time Outs, my daughter with bedtime, she's gotten real great as far as going to bed. Then all of a sudden she'll regress and we'll kind of forget about Time Out. And you think this problem is all gone and it's not coming back—and it comes back! [*Session 13*]

MOTHER: I really feel that I give a lot. I see myself giving a lot of praise, a lot of attention, a lot of the right things. I know a lot of the times that I'm doing the right things, but then I get *so* burned out. I feel like I'm doing *so* much that I know is good and I'm not getting enough back. Sometimes I get so burned out and totally worn out. I'm tired of doing all these right things. I'm just tired of parenting. [*Session 9*]

These emotions arose from a perceived lack of congruence between the parents' hard work at implementing the program's strategies and the child's failure to improve—so much work, so little progress. In some cases, as shown in the next example, the parents felt the children actively resisted their efforts to change the family dynamics.

MOTHER: This morning I told him, "Well, you just did a really great job on your homework, I'm just real pleased, you just got it done, and like now you don't have to run." And he goes, "Yeah, yeah, right mom, yeah, yeah, right." And I'm getting mad. Almost a sarcastic feedback, like well, I've heard it several times in the past couple of weeks. It's almost like he's hip to the fact that I am praising him, it's like he doesn't buy it. [*Session 6*]

FATHER: I feel like no matter what I do it backfires, and I'm not finding anything good to do here, and you feel punished for your efforts and ask, "Why me?" [*Session 16*]

Resistance

In general, parents did not have realistic expectations concerning the demands the program would impose on them and on their family life. They expressed anger and resistance as they experienced setbacks and changing family dynamics. They expressed resistance when they discovered that favorable changes in their child's behavior could be brought about and maintained only to the extent that they were committed to implementing the program; to some, this commitment meant an excessive investment of time and energy. Although most parents accepted the philosophy and rationale of the program, during this phase many exhibited resistance to parts of the program, especially those parts which required extra work or were time-consuming. Frequently this resistance was manifested in parents' failure to complete the weekly homework assignment. When asked about the homework, parents would give excuses such as a lack of time to play with their child or to buy stickers, forgetting what the assignment was, too much stress at home and at work, procrastination, and difficulty in being motivated.

Sometimes parents resisted homework assignments involving interactions with their children because they perceived their children as controlling or nonreinforcing; it was as if the parent did not want to do anything that would cede further control to the child. In cases where the child was verbally abusive of the parent, parents were even less inclined to spend time with their child. There was no reinforcement for doing so.

MOTHER: I feel like I am being held hostage some of the times by the kids, with some of the things we've tried. When I was doing the play time with the kids, I began to feel abused in that I would always be the bad guy, and Laars would always be doing something to the bad guy. He loves this time, but he orders me around. He is using words, "Do what I tell you," "I am going to decide what we are gonna do today." "I hate you. You are stupid, Mommy, you are not nice." ... So far the videos said let the child lead the way, and he does not seem to want to do much more than have this real negative interaction. What it does to me is make me not want to do this play time. For me there is no reward. The more I realize the right things to do, the more the wrong things loom huge to me. And I'm feeling really discouraged by that. [*Session 5*]

MOTHER: I find it so hard to find five minutes to play with my daughter where I'm not saying, "Put the knife down. Put the hammer down. Don't kill your sister. Don't kill the cat."

Another area of parent resistance for some parents was substituting Time Out for spanking. Many parents questioned the rationale and effectiveness of Time Out, finding it to be time-consuming and minimizing their control. These parents would argue that spanking and yelling, in contrast to Time Out, were expedient as well as immediately effective; spanking and yelling gave them a feeling of maintaining control.

FATHER: You gain respect out of fear, in many ways. I think all this stuff is good and all that garbage but ... I don't buy all this stuff. There comes a time when you can't say, "Oh that's great. You threw the ball and broke the window—that's nice." There comes a time when you get hold of that kid and you take it out on him. What I'm basically saying is at first once the kid has gone so far, you can threaten him with the moon falling in and he couldn't care less. What I'm saying is at first if you let him know if he gets out of control then it's not going to be Time Out or anything else—it's spanking time and that's it! As far as I'm concerned, you can try Time Out and all this good stuff, but there comes a time when this is it—no Time Outs, nothing but the belt! [*Session 8*]

FATHER: There have been times when spankings have really made a difference for him and I know it's perverse, but it almost seems to make him feel like he needed something to get him in control. It's kind of like the movies with somebody screaming and carrying on and somebody slaps them in the face and they feel instant relief. I know it sounds bizarre, but it works. [*Session 8*]

Another example of resistance is parents who perceived the parenting techniques as "manipulative" and devious.

FATHER: You say to your child, "You were bad so what we're going to do is set up a system. Then when you're good a little bit, we'll give you a reward." It seems like it sets kids up to be bad, so by being good they get something. [*Session 6*]

No Quick Fix

The combined effect of the setbacks and resistance was apparent in a deterioration of the "total cure" myth and a dissipation of the "magic moon dust" phase. Parents gradually came to understand that they could not correct the flaw in their child and that there was no quick fix or cure for their child's problems or for their family as a whole.

MOTHER: I think we've seen them improve but it'll vary. If things are going bad, they generally go bad all day. There are some days when nothing works and I can't say a single positive thing. But there are other days, and more of them when the kids are doing better. You can kind of tell when you wake him up. I'll go wake him up, I'll rub his back a little bit, if he wakes up, rolls over, and hugs me, I know it's a good morning. And if he says, "Leave me alone," it's going to be tough. [*Session 13*]

Parents realized that although their child's behavior did improve, as did their overall parent–child interaction, the child's temperament and associated problems were long-term. The chronic nature of the problems would continue to exact a heavy toll from parents, requiring them to monitor the child continuously. This change in parental perceptions of the duration of the child's problems was necessary in order for them to make a long-term commitment to the implementation of the program.

FATHER: I've had a couple of horrible weeks. I feel like I have to be "on" all the time. I think I have to be telling myself to just try and mellow out, and it's difficult. [*Session 8*]

PHASE 4: "MAKING THE SHOE FIT"

In this fourth phase of learning to cope more effectively with their children's problems, parents became preoccupied with "making the shoe fit"—that is, tailoring the concepts shown in the standardized videotape examples to their own family situations and parenting style. This phase was a critical determinant of parents' degree of success in implementing the program. Data indicated that failure to tailor the program resulted in diminished success because of parents' inappropriate expectations, either for themselves or for their children. Two categories of "making the shoe fit" were identified in the data: understanding parenting techniques and generalizing parenting techniques.

Understanding Parenting Techniques

The analysis indicated that, in general, parents acquired a good understanding of the rationale for the parenting principles and techniques presented in the videotapes. However, some difficulties were apparent concerning their understanding of how to implement specific approaches in a realistic and age-appropriate manner.

For example, the tangible reward program, although highly accepted by most parents, posed difficulties for some in terms of the monetary cost of the rewards. Some parents tended to set up unrealistic reinforcement menus involving expensive items that they could not afford; when the child earned the agreed-upon number of points, they could not follow through. Thus they inadvertently sabotaged their program. In addition, some parents tended to rely exclusively on material items in their reinforcement menus, ignoring nontangible inexpensive reinforcements such as activity time with parents or special privileges.

Reinforcement menus were developed by some parents with inappropriate expectations and without concern for the child's developmental status or the frequency and type of misbehavior. More specifically, parents demonstrated difficulties around the appropriate timing of the rewards (i.e., how long the child should wait before getting the reward), choosing the type of behaviors to put on the list, and weighing the cost for each behavior (e.g., 2 points = sharing, 5 points = extra reading time, 25 points = visit to the zoo).

Of even greater concern to some of these parents of conduct-problem children was the fact that some children began to use the reward system as a tool in their power struggle with their parents; as a result, parents felt the tangible reward system actually decreased their control. Children refused to do anything without a reward, or took control of the reward system by getting access to the stickers.

MOTHER: What I am finding is that he is keeping on top of it (star chart). It's like he says, "Well, Mom, I can't even earn a sticker, there is nothing to pick up." He did go a long way, but this is very expensive. I was trying to give so many stickers per dollar value, I don't want him to have to wait so long that he loses interest. I was paying $50.00 a week. [*Session 6*]

Another parenting technique that posed difficulties for many of these parents was reducing the number of commands. Difficulties arose around two parental behaviors: stopping chain commands and giving the child adequate opportunity to comply to a command. Having come to expect their child's noncompliance, parents had compensated with frequent repetitions of their commands—chain commands. They found it difficult to stop this reflex habit.

FATHER: I am the kind of a person that is very directive. I direct my son in almost everything he does, and so I am having a hard time dropping down the number of commands. [*Session 7*]

Issues of parents having unrealistic expectations—failing to consider the child's developmental status or type of misbehavior—also arose in regard to implementation of Time Out. For example, some parents had a hard time finding an appropriate place to do Time Out in their home or used this as an excuse to avoid using Time Out with their children. Others over-used Time Out, using it for child misbehaviors which should have been ignored or for behaviors which were actually age-appropriate. Sometimes it was difficult for parents to know which parent strategy (Command, Time Out, Ignore, Consequences, Distraction) should be used in response to a particular misbehavior or in a new situation.

Generalizing Parenting Techniques

Data indicated that some parents, in the process of "making the shoe fit," had difficulties generalizing the particular parenting techniques shown in the videotape scenarios to other children, other problems, and other settings. They did not readily see how a given parenting strategy could be used with different behaviors across different age groups. For example, without help from the therapist, some parents could not take the concept of the Ignore technique, which is demonstrated on the videotape in relation to tantrums, and generalize its use to a response to whining and swearing.

Parents also expressed difficulties understanding how to use the techniques in different settings. They commonly struggled with the use of Time Out and Ignore in public settings, and with more than one child.

MOTHER: He usually is just fine, but it's the minute that you get him into a store. Like yesterday at the store, he was going up to people, poking his hand and stopping them from moving, or grabbing them, like grabbing women's skirts from behind. And the hard thing in the store is, you can't take him out and put him in the car for Time Out. [*Session 10*]

The data suggested that parents had difficulties generalizing the techniques when they were dealing with content areas not directly shown in the video-tape scenarios. Interestingly, they had less difficulty when their training involved group discussions. Presumably, the parent group sharing and problem-solving provided a rich array of examples of parents applying the concepts in different situations, which helped enhance parents' ability to generalize the concepts, i.e., to learn the skills.

PHASE 5: COPING EFFECTIVELY

In the last phase of the process, parents began to exhibit effective coping strategies. Parents who reached this phase could laugh at their own vulner-abilities, express empathy for their children's problems, and understand their children's developmental needs. In this phase, parents expressed the foreknowledge that they would survive their children's and their own relapses. They became experts at responding to their children's special needs, which allowed them to act as their children's advocates in the larger community. As they discovered that they could cope successfully with the daily hassles of having a conduct-problem child, they gained confidence in themselves and in their ability to cope with future problems. Four categories of coping effectively were identified in the data: coming to

PROMOTING PARENTS' PROBLEM-SOLVING AND
EFFECTIVE COPING STRATEGIES

terms with the hard work, accepting and respecting the child, self-refueling, and feeling supported.

Coming to Terms with the Hard Work of Parenting

Parents came to realize that they had "high maintenance," temperamentally difficult children. They came to terms with the reality that their children's problems were chronic, characterized by the unpredictable relapses, constant vulnerabilities to changes in routine, and the emergence of new behavior problems whenever the children entered new settings such as school or new schedules. They faced the fact that these problems require parents to invest an exorbitant amount of time and energy for many years into the hard work of constantly anticipating, monitoring, and problem-solving. During this phase, parents were able to manage their anger and grief related to their hoped-for "ideal" child, to accept their child's difficulties, to appreciate their strengths, and to invest themselves in committed parenting.

MOTHER: I'm continually watching at home: How can we avoid these problems? How can we avoid the activating event? How can I derail something before it explodes? Okay now, cool it down. They're getting excited. Let's break it up. [*Session 15*]

FATHER: He still has these fits, but they are further apart and less severe—not as violent as they used to be. He relapses, but they're still not like they used to be. [*Session 15*]

Accepting and Respecting the Child

In this phase, parents indicated empathy, acceptance, and understanding of their child's particular temperament and sensitivity to the child's developmental struggles. They accepted their child's needs for independence and for the opportunity to learn from her/his own mistakes. They also understood the importance of their patience and support in the developmental process of the child.

MOTHER: In the last three weeks I've noticed a synthesis of all the sessions we've had, and me basically changing the way I interact with Hannah in a dramatic way—spontaneously. Now when I interact with her I tend to look at her eyes and I realize I can't remember my parents ever doing that. I'm giving her more space and time—more room to make mistakes, screw up, and make messes. I'm trying to give her more independence, when she wants to do something let her do it, rather than saying you're going to spill the milk all over the floor. It's fine if she spills the milk, she'll learn what happens and we've actually been getting on really well. [*Session 20*]

MOTHER: Elsie was all upset about cleaning her room and was furious that she couldn't fold these short-sleeved shirts. She was crying and hitting the floor. My first thought was to be critical or sarcastic but, you know, then I sat down and looked at her and said, "You must feel frustrated when you can't fold them." She screamed louder and said she'd like me to teach her how to fold the shirt. I said okay, and she folded the rest of them. You know when she gets into that mood, she can go on for an hour, but it seemed by sitting down and asking her how I could help and showing I understood her feelings, it ended up being better. [*Session 16*]

Part of gaining this empathy for the child was parents being able to see beyond their own frustration and anger, to understand the feelings and perspective of the child.

FATHER: You know, something we haven't talked about specifically in this parenting class, although it is in everything you've talked about, is respecting children and their space in the world. You know, they should be treated as equal human beings—it doesn't mean you don't set limits and all that stuff but it means you know that they're human beings and as deserving of respect as you are. [*Session 20*]

Coping effectively means that parents come not only to accept and understand their child's temperament and difficulties, but also to accept their own imperfections as parents. They no longer belittled and berated themselves for their angry thoughts, but saw the emotional responses as normal ones and understood their need to keep personal self-control. In the next example, the father is able to stop his angry response, to see his daughter's viewpoint and then to recognize her capacity to help him cope.

FATHER: I went into the bathroom to get Sara to finish brushing her teeth and there was a puddle of water on the floor and a roll of wet toilet paper and I was angry and ready to lose it and said, "This is it!" as I threw the toilet paper. You know what she said? "Dad, don't talk to me like that. You know you can scare me." Normally she would have cried, but now I think she was thinking of my point of view. I said, "You're right, and I'm sorry. I'm real tired and it's wet in here." I felt saved by her. [*Session 20*]

Self-refueling

Along with becoming more knowledgeable and confident in their parenting skills and in their ability to cope with the child's problems, coping parents also indicated the importance of caring for themselves as individuals and couples. As the blame, guilt, fear, and anger subsided and the child's behavior improved, the parents were able to get babysitters so that they could spend time away from the children. Parents expressed the view that taking time for themselves and being with their partners was a "refueling" process which allowed them to gain a more positive perspective and to maintain the energy they needed to cope with their child's problems.

MOTHER: If I'm grading my kids for controlling their aggression and for compliance and good behavior, I need to ask myself, "How many times do I lose it?" "How am I doing in keeping my temper and my anger, and how well am I doing in rerouting my thinking when I'm short-circuiting?" I need to keep track of that and reward myself. Hey, it's okay to get an ice-cream cone or treat yourself to a babysitter for an hour or buy a new blouse. Hey, it dawned on me that my behavior needs to be measured too, since that's what we're really all discussing, how we can change to effect change in our children. Well, I even mentioned that to the kids and David was really cute, and said, "Well, Mom, we

EMPOWERING PARENTS

can move our sticker charts over on the refrigerator and make room for you too."
[*Session 13*]

Gradually parents also experienced some refueling through their children. As their efforts began to pay off, parents started to talk about how their children were actually reinforcing them.

MOTHER: I started in the mornings: instead of yelling at them to wake up because I had to go to work and rushing around, I wake them both up by giving them a back rub and then I wake them up real gently and they just love it. Now they come up to me and say, "Mom, we need positive strokes." About two weeks ago they came up when I was sitting and started rubbing my arm and said, "You need positive strokes, Mom." So they are reciprocating now, which I thought was real interesting. [*Session 14*]

Getting Support

During this phase, parents no longer felt isolated and stigmatized because of their parenting or their child's problems, but rather were actively engaged in seeking support. The parents indicated that the parent group provided a safe place where they could be honest and vulnerable about their difficulties. Often to their surprise, they found that the other parents all had had similar experiences and emotional responses. Thus the parent group provided a tremendous sense of connection with other parents.

FATHER: Out of all the thousands of people that you meet from day to day and you have dealings with, I feel very fortunate to have this class and this group of people that has really enlightened and enriched my life. And, ah, it's going to make me a better person from knowing everyone here. [*Session 14*]

FATHER: Even when this program is finished, I will always think about this group in spirit. [*Session 24*]

MOTHER: Well, this class has really made such a huge difference in my life, you know to the point of, I would say, making it or breaking it. I don't know where the boys and I were headed. I was at the point of saying, "I can't deal with them" and telling my ex-husband, "You can have them." The class and the sharing—I'm just so thankful. [*Session 12*]

MOTHER: This group's all sharing—and it's people that aren't judging me, that are taking risks and saying, "Ellen, have you tried this? or considered you are off track?" You know, we're all putting a lot into this and my feeling is the more we as individuals put into it, the more we get out of it. It's the turning point—every class has been building stronger and stronger. I know we're going to make it—I'm going to make it—the boys are going to make it. The three of us are going to live happily ever after—we're going to have our problems. [*Session 18*]

SUMMARY: THE THERAPEUTIC CHANGE PROCESS

The process experienced by the parents who were enrolled in this videotape parent training program was one of gradually gaining knowledge, control, and competence to cope effectively with the stresses resulting from having a conduct-problem child. Initially, parents had to acknowledge that their child had behavior problems which they did not know how to handle. They expressed feelings of anger, fear of loss of control, guilt, and self-blame at not being able to interact more effectively with their child. Once they began to implement the principles and strategies presented in the program, they moved from despair into the second phase characterized by feelings of enormous relief and the belief that the program would provide an easy solution for their child's and family's problems. Parents were engaged in emotional regulation coping strategies and, especially, positive reappraisal

(Folkman et al., 1986). They perceived the problem to be less severe than they had thought, and believed they understood how to cope easily with it.

The third phase, involving limited improvement or regression in the child's problems, conflicting family dynamics, resistance, and a realization of the substantial amount of work needed for long-term improvement, served as cues from the environment that parents needed to reconstruct their view of reality. As Folkman and Lazarus (1988) have indicated, "The extent to which cognitive coping strategies work depends in part on how much distortion of reality is involved, and whether or not the cognitive construction is likely to be challenged by the environment." These continuous environmental challenges tempered the parents' unrealistic expectations for the program and allowed them to refocus their energies on acquiring the new parenting strategies.

As parents moved into the fourth phase, they worked hard at adapting the techniques taught in the program to their own situations and needs. Their coping strategies involved the problem-solving techniques of gathering more information and planning what they needed to do (Folkman & Lazarus, 1988). Although they experienced difficulties applying some of the parenting strategies, parents were able to gain knowledge and control by using the problem-solving techniques.

In the last phase, parents expressed empathy with their child and acceptance of their child's problems. They affirmed their ongoing commitment to maintaining progress. While they still reverted to earlier phases and experienced some relapses and feelings of anger and self-blame from time to time, they had learned to expect these as normal reactions and as clues to the need for helping their child learn how to handle a problem. Once parents gained confidence in their knowledge and felt a sense of competence, they were able to cope more effectively by learning to utilize a support system and to "refuel" themselves. With greater personal resources and a sound support system, they reappraised the difficulties involved in having a conduct-problem child. This time, however, their positive reappraisal was the result not of unrealistic expectations, but of their own effective coping skills as parents and their recognition of conduct-problem children's long-term, ongoing needs for a social environment that acknowledges their ability to behave appropriately.

THREE-YEAR FOLLOW-UP: MOVING BEYOND THE INTERVENTION— "THE WORK CONTINUES"

Recently we have begun a study that will be a qualitative analysis of the long-term impact of our parenting interventions at the Parenting Clinic. Our initial selection of subjects for interview is limited to mothers who are articulate, who demonstrated a good comprehension of the parenting principles while they were in the program, and who represented both single-parent and dual-parent family structure. We wanted to understand through qualitative interviews what had occurred within their family dynamics in the years following their 20-week parenting programs, whether they continued to use the skills they had learned, how they coped with child relapses, and generally how they perceived their experience in the Parenting Clinic. Our preliminary data suggest that families continue to work through a series of overlapping themes: "cutting loose", moving forward and building new support networks, becoming competent strategists, and learning self-acceptance. We do not see these phases as sequential but rather intertwined processes which parents were constantly developing.

THEME: CHANGED RELATIONSHIPS

"Cutting Loose"

In our follow-up interviews, parents talked about their fears regarding the ending of the program.

MOTHER: My immediate feeling was being cut loose. I felt very vulnerable. It was scary because it had been so wonderful to be with the other parents. Because that was the first time I had ever been around parents that had kids like mine . . . That was so reinforcing. I remember feeling terribly vulnerable when I left and being afraid that I wouldn't be able to continue . . . I wouldn't remember what to do. I was nervous. Over time I realized I had incorporated a lot of the basic stuff.

As they looked back on their experience in the parenting program, these mothers talked about their experience as a kind of crossroads or watershed—a time when they moved from feeling helpless and incompetent to realizing that there were choices and alternative approaches to coping more effectively with their child's problems. Parents feared that once the program was over they would not be able to maintain their efforts or would not know what to do when a new behavior problem came up. Their feelings of vulnerability returned. They felt worried about relapses and uncertain of their own skills. The ending of the parenting groups represented a loss of support—not just from the therapists who provided assistance in trouble-shooting behavior problems but also from the other parents.

MOTHER: I look back on my experience with the Parenting Clinic as a crossroads. I have told people, "I shudder to think where we would be now without having gone through that." I felt such a profound sense of failure as a parent. I didn't know what to do. I was going to let him go and live with his Dad forever. I couldn't handle it.

MOTHER: My life is more stressed now because of working full time and the stepkids moving in. But the way I feel about parenting is that I know what to do whereas before I'd be so frustrated and discouraged and think nothing would ever change.

Having learned new skills and behavioral principles, they began to feel optimistic and competent with their parenting approaches, especially as they saw improvements in their children's behavior problems.

MOTHER: I was afraid we couldn't maintain the changes without the support of the group and having to go in and report each week. I felt a sense of loss of the group because we had developed really good relationships and I knew that I would miss those people.

Parents who had not seen as dramatic behavior changes in their children as in others were worried that things would not continue to improve without the help of the sessions.

MOTHER: It took a long time for the principles in the program to really have an effect ... The first year afterwards, things were still very hard—to travel, to go somewhere else, the level of aggression was still very high for her. It takes a long time to get results—like three years. Now you can see the results.

Moving Forward: Building Networks and Finding Support

All of the parents we interviewed talked about the importance of their parent group and the tremendous support which the group gave them. Just knowing that other parents had children who were also challenging and difficult to manage helped to "normalize" their problems, to take away the stigma and reduce the isolation. Over the subsequent years, these memories of the other families in their group who also had difficult children provided a kind of mental relationship which helped them to survive the tough moments of self-doubt.

Because of this positive experience in a supportive group, all the parents we interviewed had attempted to set up or get involved in other parent support groups in subsequent years. Several parents had become involved in CHAD, an organization for parents of attention deficit disorder children; others had joined school parent organizations; another had started her own parent support group in her community; another joined the adoptive parents support group; another had joined a Parents' Corps of Little League; and several others continued to meet with parents from their group and to call them for support. In general, parents seemed to find the most support from other parents who openly acknowledged the difficulties of parenting and were nonjudgmental.

MOTHER: I've hooked up with other parents that have children like mine and it's been incredibly helpful. One friend of mine has kids just like mine and we have our club, "The Dark Side of Erma Bombeck" because you have to have humor in this. We have one rule that you can call any time. She and I have really gotten ourselves through this. And she's the one I talk to most often. But some other parents who have adopted kids, I talk to them too.

MOTHER: My husband talks about missing the group. More than me because I keep in touch with more people that give me feedback. But now that we are going to ADD group, that's nice for my husband.

In addition many parents had kept up their connections with the therapists by periodically checking in about a concern. Sometimes this was only once or twice a year. Nevertheless, knowing that the Parenting Clinic's support was available appeared to be an important mental link for most families.

MOTHER: I keep in touch with the therapist at the Clinic by phone, so I'm not really feeling the loss. That's been positive. I feel like there's continuity and I still see it as a resource. I've stayed close to the people in the class.

MOTHER: When I've been frustrated and not able to solve problems I call up the Parenting Clinic and I felt like there's this forever, underlying support there.

Almost all the families requested follow-up sessions or a refresher course. They saw these as a helpful way to trouble-shoot new issues as the children grew older.

MOTHER: I think for these type of kids and bumbling parents trying to deal with this it would be nice to have follow-ups or refresher classes. I think we hit the same issues as the children get older, only at an upgraded level.

Dealing with Isolation and Stigma

One of the most painful aspects of these parents' accounts of the subsequent years was the rejection and lack of understanding and blame that they felt from other parents, parents of well-behaved children. All had experienced the pain of other parents refusing to let their children play with their children. All still felt judged by other parents—even though their children were doing much better at home and at school.

MOTHER: Our neighbors won't let their kids play with my children because they think we're horrible people. One thing for me that has been particularly hard is the messages I've gotten from other parents at school, much more than neighbors and stuff. I mean the neighbors come over to my house and realize I'm an okay person, that I'm not one of those dysfunctional single mothers. But at school those parents really don't want their children playing with my children.

MOTHER: The hardest thing for me is the judgment of other people. I grew up being well liked and now all these people are passing judgment on me as a bad person because of my kids' behavior.

Even worse, these parents continued to experience isolation and a lack of understanding from their extended family members. These feelings of being judged and misunderstood by their family and their embarrassment about their children's behaviors often resulted in the families avoiding contact with other family members.

MOTHER: The messages I get today are that I am a bad parent because of the way my kids act. And I know deep down I'm not. But when you get these messages, I get them from my family, my extended family! I have given up going to family reunions because my kids are always the ones in trouble and it's not worth it. It's too hard.

However, their anger about their family's lack of support seemed to have lessened as they realized it was a lack of understanding. They had moved beyond their anger, having learned not to position themselves in vulnerable situations and to look for their support elsewhere.

MOTHER: I don't take my children to the office the way other parents do—it's too hard for me, but I still feel incredibly better about my parenting now.

MOTHER: I get no support from my family with this issue. They just don't get it. It's like if you haven't had cancer you don't know what it's really like. I'm convinced some of my closest friends think it's my fault—they could do better. I've wanted to say so many times, "you walk in my shoes and then make a judgment." I think the big thing is having friends who have kids like mine.

THEME: STRIVING TO MAINTAIN POSITIVE RELATIONSHIPS WITH THEIR CHILDREN

Taking it Moment by Moment

All of the parents told stories of the successes and improvements that had been made in their children's social skills over the subsequent years. They felt proud and confident of their own and their children's accomplishments. This newly found pride has, it appears, two sources. First, these parents had learned to look for and celebrate the positive moments with their children.

MOTHER: I have learned with these kids to take each day moment by moment. I used to look at the day as a 24-hour unit—now I celebrate the wonderful moments with him when they come. And we have more wonderful moments all the time.

MOTHER: Someone gave me a journal, but I hate to write because I do so much of it at work. Instead I record the neat things that happen with my children and there are times I'll go and read it. For example, times when my kids are really insightful or funny or when they do something I feel good about, I record it. I've been doing that for three years now and it's wonderful.

They noted the contrast between this perspective on their children and their perspective before treatment.

MOTHER: I think what can happen is you could be so overwhelmed with the intensity of the difficult times that you don't see the good times. I know that was happening when I went to the Parenting Clinic.

A second—and more complex—source of their pride in their children's successes arose from their own recently developed sensitivity to their children's temperament and emotional state. The interviews reflected parents who had learned to read the cues in a situation and to decide what the optimal approach would be. It was as if the parents had become sensitive barometers to their children's reactions and knew how to adapt to the weather.

MOTHER: I don't make as many plans. I sort of wait and see how the day is going.

MOTHER: We really try to look at the right time for doing something. He's supposed to read to me every night but I can sense if it's not going to be successful and he needs to be doing something else. At one time I might have forced him— but now my motto is "seize the moment."

Becoming a Strategist: See the Big Picture

Related to their new ability to adapt to their child's state-of-the-moment, these parents seemed not only to understand the principles behind behavior management and how to use the skills with their children, but had become "expert strategists."

MOTHER: In the beginning we didn't have the skills. And that isn't to say we aren't intelligent. We are both highly educated, hard-working people, it's just that we didn't have the skills and now we know how to use them.

MOTHER: It's the ability to first analyze, then internalize some of those parenting coping skills that makes life easier.

MOTHER: We're more skilled which helps a lot. I think skills with high-maintenance kids are worth their weight in gold because it's still tough with skills. I can pull out things such as charts and I know ways of distancing the battle. Things are better in that respect.

They were able to anticipate potential problems with their children and to head them off with preventive approaches; they had parental radar constantly on the alert. As one parent put it, they are "constantly viligant" in order to help the children stay out of trouble. They had learned how to structure each day so as to maximize their children's potential for success.

This did not mean they let their children do whatever they wanted— quite the contrary, most parents found that they needed to structure their children's time, to establish clear expectations of what was required of them and clear descriptions of the consequences for not complying. Attending to their children's need for behavioral guidance required steadfastness and rigor.

MOTHER: He is such a volatile kid, I have found that I have to be incredibly structured. Everything is: "If you do this, then you can do this." You know,

"When you follow the rules this week, then on Friday you get to rent a tape" which is a big reward for him. It's constant, "When you get your shoes on in the morning then you can watch TV." It works. For example, to get him into bed at night I had to develop a set of structured steps and now he's incorporated them so it's not an issue.

MOTHER: I have to be constantly vigilant, keep ahead of him because he acts before he thinks.

Like the planner or strategist, parents seemed to have a wide-angle view—to be cognizant of their long-range goals and to choose the most effective parenting in accordance with not only the desired behavior but also the larger goal. This ability to be a strategist requires that parents see the big picture as well as be attuned to the moment-by-moment inter-actions. As one parent put it, she now had a blueprint for decision-making which helped her feel in control, on track.

MOTHER: I try to take more time for him now. My housekeeping suffers because I'm a single parent and I can't do everything. But in the big picture you know the messy house doesn't matter that much.

MOTHER: I can head off probably 80% of the problems with the parenting tech-niques I learned. I have a set of principles now that I work from—a blueprint.

Coping with Relapses

All of the parents talked about times when their children had relapses in their behaviors. Typically they felt a sense of panic and fear that all their prior efforts had been useless. Yet they described a variety of ways of coping with these relapses.

MOTHER: I remember this time my son got into this horrible cycle—worse than before we went to the Parenting Clinic. I was afraid all the gains we had made were lost—we were in a negative cycle and I was panicked. I was resentful because I had done so much for him like taking him to miniature golf and McDonalds and then when we got home he went crazy because there was something he didn't like. He was very destructive—throwing things everywhere because he couldn't get what he wanted. But then I realized he can only focus on the feeling of the moment. Later I also realized he had been good all day—that it was only one night.

In this example the parent deals with her reaction to her son's relapse by reflecting on his temperament—that is, that he is an impulsive child who cannot focus on the earlier feelings and positive events that his mother had provided. Once she reminds herself that her child can only deal with the feeling of the moment—here, his anger—she is able to diffuse some of her feelings of anger towards him for his ingratitude. Second, she places the event in context—she is objective about the situation and realizes that for most of the day his behavior has been good. Many of the parents talked about their conscious cognitive work at deemphasizing the negative moments with their children and focusing on the positive times.

Parents also coped with relapses by reframing them as normal or natural. By understanding that relapses were natural and to be expected, they were better able to prepare themselves to deal with them as well as to decrease their panic and fear. They also reframed the way they perceived these regressions by treating them as "learning experiences."

MOTHER: I remember that learning is a process of making mistakes and a little kid doesn't know everything you do as an adult—sometimes this is so obvious but when you live every day with a little character that's running around it is easy to forget.

Yet another coping strategy was reframing the relapses as challenges which, given their new-found sense of competence as parents, they felt prepared to meet.

MOTHER: The challenges keep changing and with different kids, but now I know ways to attack each one as it comes up. I don't think any more when old things come up again, "God! we failed", or "I thought we had taken care of that, it didn't work." I don't look at it that way, rather it's just going to be challenges all the way and we'll just keep applying what we have learned.

They felt confident that they had the skills to do what was necessary to help teach their child some new social behavior.

MOTHER: Now when he relapses I just assume there will be a way to problem-solve it. And I have ideas instead of going around finding books everywhere. Like I'll go to the teacher and say, "Okay, we need to work out a plan" and I feel like it's manageable.

Some parents turned to the Parenting Clinic for support when they had relapses with their children. Paradoxically, this strengthened or revived their sense of competence, for they perceived it as a resource they knew how to utilize—one of their skills or strategies for coping.

MOTHER: His behavior went downhill really fast when we separated. So I went to the Parenting Clinic as it felt like a place to go for resources and support and it's really worked. I've had to eat all my words about my fears—I guess we have more skills and my child has more skills now.

Other parents talked about how they had attempted to slow down the pace of life for themselves and build in restful times so that they are "refueled" and ready for the relapses when they happen.

MOTHER: I've been divorced for six years now and I used to think I had to be doing all these social things when I didn't have the kids. Now at least one night a week I come home, read the paper, do laundry, and rest—I try to use that time so that when my kids are with me I have the energy for them and can give them attention. I wouldn't be able to give them the attention they need if I didn't take time for myself. So that's one means of support for me.

Advocating for your Child

Other parents recognized the importance not only of keeping up their own parenting skills at home to help their child but also the necessity of being involved in what happens to their child at school.

MOTHER: There is no doubt that my being active in PTFA helped our kid and you don't have to be working in the classroom, but if you're working outside the home it does behoove you to find a way to be active in school activities so that they recognize you're going to be there. I call up if he gets a demerit slip and his story isn't consistent with the writing on the slip. I call up and find out the teacher's perspective and I write a note. One time I wrote a note to the principal that resulted in a meeting of the recess teachers. That in the long run supports my son and other kids. You need to know what is happening in school.

Sometimes parents talked about the relapses in themselves and how they were able to get themselves back on the program.

MOTHER: My husband and I used to fight over how to handle our daughter. In the group we agreed on how to handle her behavior. I had to learn to stop interrupting and correcting my husband even if I disagreed. Well, yesterday I didn't support him and he was really upset with me. So this goes deeper than parenting, more about loyalty and remembering to be supportive to the other.

THEME: PARENTS' ACCEPTANCE OF SELF AND THE CHILD

Maintaining and Building Self-Esteem

One aspect of these interviews three years after treatment that was markedly different from our earlier interviews while the parents were still in the program was the parents' emphasis on conscious efforts to maintain and build their self-esteem. Because of the mothers' feelings of blame and stigma from family, neighborhood, and school which we described above, they had to work hard at reaffirming their own worth.

MOTHER: My friend and I who have children who are more challenging, we laugh at other parents who think they're such good parents when they're in fact the ones who have really easy kids. I think it's one of the biggest challenges when you have this kind of child, to feel okay as a parent because you do not get those messages from other people. That's just the reality.

For these mothers, a key factor in maintaining a strong sense of self was distancing—literal and figurative—from their child with conduct disorders.

MOTHER: I'm not a natural mother—so I needed help to learn the skills and it still is a lot of work. Getting some space and time for myself helps immensely. Talking to friends and getting away from the children helps me regroup.

MOTHER: I think he needs other adults in his life besides me. I think he needs time away as much as I need time away.

This theme is distinct from the "refueling" discussed earlier. Whereas the purpose of refueling was to be able to give more to the child, here the emphasis is on time apart as a means of maintaining and strengthening the mothers' sense of identity. These mothers recognized the importance of having a strong sense of self apart from being a mother in order to function well as a parent.

MOTHER: I have to create my own reward system. I realized I have to establish an identity other than parenthood. I mean, I very much identify myself as a single parent but I take great pride in my work. I go off with other women when I don't have the kids.

MOTHER: I still feel ownership and get embarrassed by him. That's one place I'd like to work at. I need a little more separateness . . . Even though I know it isn't true, I still feel that if I was a better parent he would be better. I know that isn't true but my gut still says it is, so I wish I could have a little bit more gut distance from him so I could feel a little happier myself. If I got that distance I'd deal with him better and it would all work better, but I haven't been able to make that jump yet.

This literal and figurative distancing—a form of establishing boundaries— allowed these mothers to depersonalize their child's behavior problems and to put them in a wider developmental context.

MOTHER: When he misbehaves I am able to keep it in the context of a learning experience for him, a need for me to be consistent and to think. I ask myself, "What does this really mean? Is this something I should just let ride? How significant is it?" I don't blame myself now.

Grieving, Accepting, and Changing Standards

Three years after treatment, while these children's behavior problems had improved (they were within normal range according to teacher and parent reports) on standardized measures, they were still very much a challenge to manage.

MOTHER: He used to be out of control all the time, almost daily with him, well now it happens maybe twice a year, or three times. Other people would come in and say he was totally outrageous, but I don't consider it totally outrageous. I have a different standard of what outrageous is than if I had my nieces and nephews as children.

MOTHER: He's still volatile. He can escalate from zero to a hundred in the snap of a finger and be that way for hours. He will throw furniture and take the room apart and totally wipe me out. Because I came from a mellow, laid-back family— and he's got a different temperament. He cannot wait one minute for dinner or anything.

Parents seemed to realize and accept that the road ahead with their children was not going to be easy and they would be required to work hard at helping their children be successful.

They still talked about what they had thought their parenting experiences would be like in comparison with the reality. As had been true in our earlier interviews, there was a sense of parents grieving over the hoped-for child, the harmonious home life, the easy road.

MOTHER: You know, you grow up thinking you are going to be a certain type of parent—and I had wonderful parents. Well, you know, I've had to learn that in our family we're not going to sit around the table and have wonderful discussions—they cannot sit still for more than five minutes.

MOTHER: Parenting is work. I wish it would be more fun and less work.

MOTHER: I still put a lot of time into parenting and probably a lot more than I have the energy for or a lot more than most people, but now I'm enjoying it a lot more, that's the difference. But it takes a lot of time.

But balancing this note of loss was a strong theme of acceptance—acceptance of their children's needs and temperament, acceptance of the hard work of parenting—along with self-respect and, at times, celebration of self for having made the necessary accommodations.

MOTHER: I think I have had to do a lot of grieving about these children not being the kids I thought I would have. But I feel a bit better about me as a parent today. I don't feel great because, you know, this culture measures parenting in terms of how your child behaves and my kids do not get high scores in that area ... but it's so much better now.

MOTHER: I have the handles I need to help him, but I think we're going to have a hard life along the road. I don't see it ever being easy. I don't think he is going to have an easy life. He just doesn't have the temperament to have an easy life. Yes, I wished for that and I still wish for that, and I wish there was a cure but I don't think there is. It is better now than it was.

MOTHER: This indicates how far I've come. Last summer another woman and myself took eight kids camping and five of them were on Ritalin. That was so empowering for me. First of all, as women to be able to go camping ... second, that we were taking eight kids and five of them challenging kids and we did great. So I guess that's a real measure that I'm feeling a lot better about being a parent.

SUMMARY

What have we learned? These follow-up interviews indicate that generally parents are coping well, are maintaining their parenting skills, and are feeling optimistic and in control of the situation. This is in contrast to our interviews three years earlier which were full of blame, loss of control, and helplessness. Parents no longer felt "under siege" by their children; they had taken charge. Nonetheless, the interviews indicated that parents were having to devote a great deal of mental, physical, and emotional energy

PROMOTING PARENT SELF-EMPOWERMENT

providing an optimal environment for their temperamentally difficult children and in maintaining their self-esteem. This work was largely being done without the support of extended family, parents of other children in their children's classrooms, or their teachers. The challenges certainly continue—for them and for the therapeutic community. Short-term efforts are insufficient: as therapists we need to find ways to support these families in their efforts on behalf of their children. We need to educate society at large in order to reduce the stigmatization and isolation that these families face in their day-to-day encounters.

MOTHER: I hope that one day we can start operating from automatic and it doesn't take so much time and effort. I know parenting is always going to take a lot of effort but I wish it didn't have to be such focus. But I have an idea for what to do—that's probably a real important thing.

REFERENCES AND FURTHER READING

Boggs, S.R., Eyberg, S. & Reynolds, L.A. (1990). Concurrent validity of the Eyberg Child Behavior Inventory. *Journal of Clinical Child Psychology*, **19**, 75–78.

Cunningham, C.E., Davis, J.R., Bremner, R., Dunn, K.W. & Rzasa, T. (1993). Coping modeling problem solving versus mastery modeling: effects on adherence, in-session process, and skill acquisition in a residential parent-training program. *Journal of Consulting and Clinical Psychology*, **6**, 871–877.

Eyberg, S. & Ross, A. (1978). Assessment of child behavior problems: The validation of a new inventory. *Journal of Clinical Psychology*, **16**, 113–116.

Folkman, S. & Lazarus, R.S. (1988). Coping as a mediator of emotion. *Journal of Personality and Social Psychology*, **54**(3), 466–475.

Folkman, S., Lazarus, R.S., Dunkel-Schetter, C., DeLongis, A. & Gruen, R.J. (1986). Dynamics of stressful encounter: Cognitive appraisal, coping, and encounter outcomes. *Journal of Personality and Social Psychology*, **50**, 992–1003.

Forehand, R.L. & McMahon, R.J. (1981). *Helping the noncompliant child: A clinician's guide to parent training*. New York: Guilford.

Glaser, B. (1978). *Advances in the methodology of grounded theory: Theoretical sensitivity*. Mill Valley, CA: The Sociological Press.

Glaser, B. & Strauss, A (1967). *The discovery of grounded theory: Strategies for qualitative research*. New York: Aldine.

Hollingshead, A.B. & Redlich, F.C. (1958). *Social class and mental illness*. New York: Wiley.

Kazdin, A.E. (1985). *Treatment of antisocial behavior in children and adolescents*. Homewood, IL: Dorsey Press.

Loeber, R. (1985). Patterns and development of antisocial child behavior. In G.J. Whitehurst (Ed.), *Annals of child development* (Vol. 2) (pp. 77–116). New York: JAI Press.

Loeber, R. & Dishion, T.J. (1983). Early predictors of male adolescent delinquency: A review. *Psychological Bulletin*, **94**, 68–99.

Patterson, G. (1974). Interventions for boys with conduct problems: Multiple setting treatments and criteria. *Journal of Consulting and Clinical Psychology*, **42**(47), 471–481.

Patterson, G.R. & Chamberlain, P. (in press) A functional analysis of resistance. In H. Arkowitz (Ed.), *Why don't people change? New perspectives on resistance and noncompliance*. New York: Guilford Press.

Patterson, G.R. & Stouthamer-Loeber, M. (1984). The correlation of family management practices and delinquency. *Child Development*, **55**, 1299–1307.

Reid, J., Taplin, P. & Loeber, R. (1981). A social interactional approach to the treatment of abusive families. In R. Stewart (Ed.), *Violent behavior: Social learning approaches to prediction, management and treatment*. New York: Brunner/Mazel.

Robins, L.N. (1981). Epidemiological approaches to natural history research: Antisocial disorders in children. *Journal of the American Academy of Child Psychiatry*, **20**, 566–580.

Seidel, J.V., Kjolseth, R. & Seymour, E. (1988). *The Ethnograph*. Littleton, CO: Qualis Research Associates.

Spitzer, A., Webster-Stratton, C. & Hollinsworth, T. (1991). Coping with conduct-problem children: parents gaining knowledge and control. *Journal of Clinical Child Psychology*, **20**, 413–427.

Strauss, A.L. (1988). *Qualitative analysis for social scientists*. Cambridge: Cambridge University Press.

Webster-Stratton, C. (1981). Modification of mothers' behaviors and attitudes through a videotape modeling group discussion program. *Behavior Therapy*, **12**, 634–642.

Webster-Stratton, C. (1984). Comparing two parent training models for conduct disordered children. *Journal of Consulting and Clinical Psychology*, **52**, 666–678.

Webster-Stratton, C., Hollinsworth, T. & Kolpacoff, M. (1989). The long-term effectiveness and clinical significance of three cost-effective training programs for families with conduct-problem children. *Journal of Consulting and Clinical Psychology*, **57**(4), 550–553.
Webster-Stratton, C., Kolpacoff, M. & Hollinsworth, T. (1988). Self-administered videotape therapy for families with conduct-problem children: Comparison with two cost-effective treatments and a control group. *Journal of Consulting and Clinical Psychology*, **56**(4), 558–566.

PARENT INTERVENTION CONTENT: TYPICAL QUESTIONS

IN THIS chapter, we present a number of questions and objections which parents frequently raise when we are discussing the various content areas. In raising these issues and offering some explanations we might use in our groups, our intention is to help therapists prepare for the nature of parent discussions. If parents do not raise these questions, out of reluctance or for some other reason, we suggest that the therapist raise these issues him/herself in order to foster problem-solving and discussion.

This chapter, then, serves as an overview of the major content areas covered in our parenting programs. We do not discuss the specific content in detail, as this information has been presented at length in several other texts (e.g., Barkley, 1987; Forehand & McMahon, 1981; Herbert, 1987; Patterson et al., 1975; Webster-Stratton, 1992a,b). Rather, for each major content area we first give a brief rationale and the key points, as we feel it is essential that parents understand the rationale for each component of the program, followed by a discussion of parents' typical questions and objections to the content of our training programs.

PLAY SKILLS

Regular parent–child play times help build warm relationships between family members, creating a "bank" of positive feelings and experiences that can be drawn upon in times of conflict. Through play, parents can help their children learn to solve problems, test out ideas, and explore their imaginations. Moreover, play is a time when parents can respond to their children in ways that promote children's feelings of self-worth and competence. Play with parents not only helps children feel deeply loved, thereby fostering a secure base for their ongoing emotional development, but also, just as importantly, promotes parents' feelings of attachment and warmth towards their child.

This is particularly important for parents of conduct-problem children who, as we discussed earlier, may be feeling resentful, critical, angry, distant, and hopeless about their relationships with their children. Typically there is negativity on both sides: these parents feel negative towards their children out of anger over their children's misbehavior, the children in turn are negative towards their parents. Consequently, it is not uncommon to find that parents of such children are not playing with them and are "keeping their distance." Therefore the first step in breaking this negative cycle of behaviors and feelings is to infuse some positive times into the relationship, through play. For parents of highly aggressive children, playtimes could be the first pleasurable times they have had with their children in months or even years.

Good playtime between parents and children not only fosters warmth in the relationship, but also helps children develop the vocabulary they need for communicating their thoughts and feelings. It also helps them learn the social skills of turn-taking and fosters their ability to understand the feelings and perspectives of others. In fact, studies have shown that children tend to be more creative, to have increased self-confidence, and to have fewer behavior problems if their parents engage in regular playtimes with them and, when doing so, give them their supportive attention. Unfortunately, the fact is that many parents of conduct-problem children do not want to play with their children because of the stress associated with their interactions; and when they do, they do so with divided attention or in ways that undermine or interfere with their children's play. Along with the negativity mentioned above, the reason may be that they simply do not know how to engage in supportive play.

Therefore we begin our parent intervention program by asking parents to play with their children for at least 10 minutes every day and by offering them some pointers on ways to play successfully with their children. We discuss the most common pitfalls parents encounter when playing with their children and advise them how to avoid those pitfalls. The following are the major points we highlight:

- Follow the child's lead.

- Pace at the child's level.

- Don't expect too much—give the child time to think and explore.

- Avoid too much competition with children, especially where the adult always wins.

- Praise and encourage the child's ideas and creativity; don't criticize.

- Engage in role play and make-believe with the child.

■ Be an attentive and appreciative audience.

■ Use descriptive comments instead of asking questions.

■ Curb the desire to give too much help; encourage the child's problem-solving.

■ Reward quiet playtimes with parental attention.

■ Laugh and have fun.

Typical Questions and Concerns About Play with Children

Questions from parents fall into different categories. Typically, some parents will question the importance of playing with their children, either out of defensiveness or genuine curiosity. Others will grant the importance of playing with their children, but will raise questions about our recommended approach—either questioning the approach based on its divergence from their assumptions about parent–child play or asking for further direction based on having tried the approach and encountered problems. Some will raise objections reflecting a fear of exacerbating the child's behavior problems. And therapists must always expect to hear some objections reflecting hostility or resistance. We offer the following as a representative sample.

Shouldn't we be talking about discipline?

I don't get it ! I came here for help with my child's behavior problems and we're talking about play. What does this have to do with helping my child improve his behavior? Besides, my child has been so impossible that, to tell you the truth, I don't feel like playing with him. Not only that, he doesn't seem to want to play with me either!

When we talk about play we are also, in a roundabout way, discussing a discipline approach. For discipline is defined as "training that develops self-control and efficacy." Play is a highly effective and positive way to foster children's competence, independence, and feelings of self-confidence. The approach to play that we have discussed provides children with opportunities for legitimate control and power in their social interactions.

By giving attention to children's appropriate play, parents are reinforcing their positive social behaviors.

The basic principle behind the development of many common behavior problems is that children will work for attention from others, especially parents, whether it is positive attention (praise and reward) or negative attention (criticism and punishment). If children fail to get positive attention for appropriate behavior, then they will work to gain negative attention by misbehaving. If parents actively participate in play, thereby giving their children positive attention, children will have less need to resort to negative behavior to force parents to respond to them. In fact, many parents have told us that when they tried giving their child a regular half-hour dose of play each day, their children were better behaved and the parents found more personal time for themselves.

As for the issue of not wanting to play with a difficult child, or the child not wanting to play with his/her parent: True, it is hard for parents to take the time to play positively with their children if they are angry at them for breaking a window or depressed about how they are making family life miserable. Children will detect these feelings and accordingly may not want to play with their parents. This is a negative stalemate situation. Yet it is a mistake for the parent to wait for the child to break the negative cycle. Someone has to end the negative interactions, and it is not likely to be the child. Therefore, the parent needs to watch for moments of positive interaction and capitalize on these by engaging the child in some play. As these playtimes become frequent and more positive, children will look forward to them—as will parents.

But playing with my child is a waste of time

> Let's get real. Sure, my child behaves better if I play with him, but I can't be expected to just sit around and play all day! I've got a lot of other things to do! Isn't play with friends just as good?

Parents—especially parents of oppositional and highly aggressive children —may find it difficult to see the value in taking precious time out of their busy and stressful lives for something as seemingly frivolous as play. As their therapists, we need to be realistic in our expectations. At our clinic, we generally ask parents to do a minimum of 10 minutes of playtime with their child each day. We encourage them to see this time as an investment in their child's future, not unlike regularly putting a deposit in the bank. If they build up their child's psychological "bank account" through regular playtime, they will experience behavioral "pay-offs": in other words, as their child becomes secure in the knowledge that he will have regular time with his parents and that time with him is valued, he will have less need to devise inappropriate ways of getting their attention. Parents may be persuaded to invest that time if it is pointed out to them some extra attention now may buy some additional personal time later.

As for the issue of peer play versus parent play, both types of interactions are important for children's social development. Young children engage in parallel play with each other where each child is playing independently. As they grow older, normal children become both more cooperative *and* more competitive with each other during playtimes. Resolving these conflicts and learning to help, to share, and to enjoy each other's successes are important aspects of play with peers. However, conduct-problem children have more difficulties with peer play. They are more impulsive, more aggressive, less cooperative, and generally not much fun—thus, they are more likely to experience peer rejection. For this reason, parent play with conduct-problem children is particularly important, for the benefits of peer play are quite different from the benefits of play with parents. During playtimes parents are focusing on their children; they can help them learn to solve problems, to wait and take turns, to share and cooperate, to explore their imaginations, and to communicate their feelings. Moreover, when a parent gives positive attention to his/her child's play, that child's sense of self-worth is increased. These benefits are unlikely to occur in peer play for normal children, and certainly not for conduct-problem children.

But play with children is boring!

Play with my child is so boring—she keeps doing the same things over and over again. Should I structure her play to make it more stimulating?

When young children are playing, they tend to repeat the same activity over and over again. How often have you seen a toddler repeatedly fill and empty a box? How often have you groaned inwardly when asked to read the same story yet again? Certainly, repetitive play soon bores most parents. It is tempting for parents to quicken the pace by introducing some new idea or a more sophisticated way of using a toy.

Therapists should caution parents that this temptation arises from the parent's need, not the child's. It is the parent who feels a need for more stimulation. Children need to rehearse and practice an activity over and over in order to master it and to feel confident about their abilities. If they are shortchanged in this repetition, if they are pushed into a new activity, they may feel frustrated and give up playing with their parents because they feel incompetent at their former activity and/or the new activity. They feel unable to meet their parents' expectations or the challenge of the task. The end result is decreased self-esteem and a lack of confidence.

Parents need to be sure they pace the play according to their child's tempo. Encourage parents to allow plenty of time for their children to practice an activity and to use their imagination. Caution parents not to push a child simply because they are bored. They should wait to change the play until the child decides to do something different. Remind them that children move much more slowly from one idea to another than adults. Pacing slowly will help encourage the child to concentrate on one activity for an extended period of time—an especially important skill to learn for the impulsive child with a poor attention span.

But don't children need structure in their play?

> I always thought that you should use playtimes to teach your children things like colors, shapes, rules, and so forth. How will children learn if you don't structure their play and correct their mistakes?

Some parents believe it is important to structure their child's play by turning it into a lesson: how to build the castle the right way, how to make the perfect valentine, how to complete a puzzle correctly. Possibly they believe that in this way they are effective teachers and are making play a worthwhile activity. But this emphasis on the "right" or "best" way to do something produces a string of commands, instructions, and corrections from the parent that usually make the experience unrewarding for both the child and the adult.

Consider, for instance, what happens when Lisa and her mother settle down to play with Lisa's new doll house. Mom says, "First let's put the fridge and stove in the kitchen." Lisa suggests a place for the kitchen, and her mother responds, "Okay, and now all these other kitchen things must go over there too." She then goes on to say, "And the living-room furniture must go here." As Lisa begins to put some of the furniture in the living room, her mother shows her where to put the bathroom items. Soon Lisa will either start refusing to comply to all these arbitrary rules out of a need to establish her own individuality or she will stop playing, sit back, and watch her mother organize everything in the correct rooms. By now, Lisa's mother is doing all the playing. She has given Lisa little opportunity for thinking about how to organize the furnishings, whether conventionally or creatively. Further, she has missed the opportunity to learn about her daughter—to discover what Lisa might have wanted to do with the doll house. Had she waited, she might have found that Lisa's play was highly imaginative, with beds placed outside for "camping" or living-room furniture in every room.

The first step to effective play with children is for parents to recognize the importance of following the child's lead—letting children explore their own ideas and imagination, rather than parents imposing their own structure by giving commands, rules, or instructions. We suggest to parents that they do not try to teach their children anything in play. Instead, they should try to imitate their children's actions and do what the child requests. It can be especially hard for the parent of a conduct-disordered child to let go of control during play, for fear that the child will become disruptive. We explain to parents that by accepting and going along with their children's rules and ideas, they are actually modeling compliance for their children—that is, in fact teaching their children how to be more compliant. Parents will soon discover that when they sit back and give their children a chance to exercise their imagination, their children become more involved and interested in playing, as well as more creative and cooperative. This approach not only fosters the development of the child's ability to play and think independently, but also to be more compliant outside the play situation.

What if children want parents to structure their play?

> Usually he insists on my leading the play or else he doesn't seem to know what to do. What can I do?

When children's play with their parents has typically involved the parents structuring their children's play, telling them what to do and how to do it, it may be difficult and somewhat frustrating for the children when the parents begin to take a less directive approach. The child is used to playing according to his/her parents' rules; suddenly s/he is expected to come up with his/her own ideas for play. This new-found freedom may leave a child feeling insecure, unsure what to do, and anxious about making mistakes. Most likely, the child will try to get the parent to respond as usual by asking, "Dad, you show me how" or "Mom, I can't do it—I need your help to do it" or "Mom, I don't know what to do." If this is the case, the parent may want initially to comply and offer the child some assistance, but gradually withdraw the level of parent control while reinforcing the child's independent activities and creativity. With time and with parents' support and reinforcement, the child will become confident of his/her decisions and ability to play independently.

Should parents play anything the child wants?

All my child plays with is Ninja Turtles. I hate Ninja Turtles!

In following the child's lead, there are times when the parent will be asked to play something that s/he objects to. A good rule of thumb is that if the child's suggested play activity makes the parent uncomfortable then it is probably a good idea to play something else, for the child will pick up easily on the parents' discomfort or inability to enjoy the playtime. In the Ninja Turtle example above the parent might say matter-of-factly, "I would like to play something other than Ninja Turtles—do you have some ideas?" If the child cannot think of anything else, the parent might suggest several things that the child usually likes to do, such as "How about that Lego model you were working on?" or "How about that new puzzle you got for your birthday?" It would be important in this instance not to engage in a power struggle or argument with the child about Ninja Turtles; rather the parent should try to divert and distract the child to something else. It may even be necessary if the child is persistent for the parent to start independently playing with something else as if it was a very enjoyable activity. Soon the child will want to get involved and the parent can gradually be less directive.

What if children want to engage in aggressive play— should parents follow their lead?

My child only wants to wrestle with me or run around shooting guns. Will this make him more aggressive?

Certainly aggressive toys bring out children's aggressive behaviors—but even if parents do not allow their children to have guns or Ninja toys, frequently children will act them out in their fantasy play. Whether parents actively promote aggressive behaviors by giving children aggressive toys or merely play along with an aggressive fantasy, they are reinforcing aggressive play. Instead parents should minimize the amount of attention and reinforcement that children get for aggressive behavior through their use of differential attention. If the child tends to be highly aggressive in play, the parent will want to praise nonaggressive play behaviors such as talking quietly, being gentle, helping, and walking slowly. Then when the child begins to yell or shoot or be aggressive with a toy, the parent can withdraw her attention (ignore the behavior) but give back her attention as soon as the child stops the aggressive behavior.

Wrestling is another matter. Many fathers especially enjoy wrestling with their children—particularly sons. This is usually a good time for both the children and parents and does not need to be omitted out of fear of encouraging aggression. However, parents of conduct-problem children need to exercise caution, for their children may become so "wired" with wrestling that they risk hurting themselves or others. Parents will need to monitor this and de-escalate wrestling play before it gets out of control.

Isn't descriptive commenting just psychological jargon?

Descriptive commenting seems pretty weird to me, it feels artificial and phoney. Even my child asks me to stop talking so funny. I don't really understand why I should do this. When I ask my child questions, I feel I know what he has learned. I don't see how descriptive commenting is more helpful than question-asking in helping my child learn.

Descriptive commenting, a running commentary on children's activities, often sounds like a sports announcer's play-by-play description of a game. Because for most people it is a novel way of communicating, parents often feel uncomfortable and artificial when they first try interacting with their child in this way. But this is merely the awkwardness we feel whenever we attempt something unfamiliar. Remember learning to drive a car or play the piano? The discomfort will diminish as parents practice in a variety of situations. And if parents are persistent in learning to do descriptive commenting, they will find that their children come to love this kind of attention.

Many children will notice that their parents are talking to them differently. Some who have difficulty accepting change may ask their parents to "stop talking so weird." Parents should not be deterred by this negative response—it is to be expected! Whenever any family member behaves differently, the rest of the family will initially resist the change in an effort to revert back to what is familiar and safe. However, with time this form of communication will not only become the status quo in parent–child interactions but will be imitated by the children in their communication with siblings and friends.

Descriptive commenting is also more effective than question-asking in teaching children vocabulary and actively encouraging their language development. For instance, a parent might say, "You're putting the car in the garage. Now it's getting gas," and so forth. Soon parents will find that their children are spontaneously imitating their parents' commenting. Parents can then praise their learning efforts and they will feel excited about their accomplishments. Occasionally parents have a tendency to ask a string of questions while playing: "What animal is that?" "How many spots does it have?" "What shape is that?" "Where does it go?" Through such questions, parents usually intend to help their children learn. But all too often it has the reverse effect, causing them to become defensive, to retreat into silence, and to be reluctant to talk freely.

In fact, question-asking, especially when parents know the answer, is really a type of command since it requires children to perform. Queries that ask children to define what they are doing or making are in a special category: they often occur before the child has even thought about the final product or had a chance to explore his/her ideas. Through the question, the parent puts the emphasis on the product rather than the process of play. Descriptive commenting, on the other hand, is a nonthreatening way of communicating with children without demanding performance.

Don't children need to learn how to lose?

> I get into such battles with him when we play board games—don't I need to teach him how to lose? I really feel I need to teach my child how to follow the rules so that he doesn't run into problems thinking he can change the rules whenever he wants with others.

Most parents occasionally find themselves in a power struggle with their children over who won a game, what the rules are, etc. To some extent this is inevitable, but many parents unwittingly set up a competitive relationship with their children. When playing board games, for instance, they may feel it is necessary to teach their children to play by the rules and to be good losers. Or they may simply do their part of an activity or game so well that their children cannot help feeling incompetent. Consider a mother and son who are playing with building blocks. For a few minutes Billy is happily absorbed in getting the first wall of his house to stay up. When it finally does, he looks to Mom for approval only to find that she has a whole house finished. Besides feeling less competent, Billy also feels he is somehow involved in a competition with his mother—one, moreover, that he is not equipped to win. At this point, Billy may give up playing or may resort to other ways of getting control of the situation, such as having a tantrum or knocking down the house his mother built.

Young children do not really understand the rules and sequences of board and card games. Not until they are seven or eight do they begin to show signs of true cooperative interaction, and even then, their understanding of rules may be somewhat vague. Nonetheless, they can enjoy playing at a game with adults as long as excessive competition and a concern with rules are avoided. If children come up with different rules for a game that allow them to win, this should be permitted. Parents need not worry about their children not learning to lose; many other aspects of their lives will teach them that. If parents, when playing with their children, cooperate with their rules and model acceptance, then children are more likely to go along with parents' rules in other situations. Finally, we suggest to parents of conduct-problem children that they initially avoid competitive games with their children, and instead play unstructured activities. When their playtimes are going well they might want to try some board games, as long as they can avoid power struggles—for the key point is for the parents and children to be having fun together.

How should I end the play session?

My child doesn't want to stop the play! Every time we end, it's a real hassle with screams and protests—so much so that I don't even want to start the play for fear of the ending.

Understandably, sometimes parents are reluctant to play with their children because they fear that there will be a big fuss when they want to stop. The solution is for parents to prepare a child for the end of a play session. Five minutes before the end of a play period a parent could say, "In a few minutes it will be time for me to stop playing with you." It is important for parents to ignore any protests or arguments, and to do their best to distract their child by focusing on something else. When five minutes have passed the parent may simply state, "Now it's time for me to stop playing. I enjoyed this time with you." The parent should walk away and ignore any pleading.

Once children learn that they cannot manipulate parents into playing longer, the protests will subside. And when they realize that there is a regular play period with a parent every day, they will have less need to protest, knowing that there will be another opportunity to play with a parent the next day. Remember, a child who protests following the end of playtime is also saying that s/he had such fun that s/he does not want to stop!

Isn't this unfair to my other children?

I'm a single parent with several children. I try to play with one child, and my other children act up for attention.

Children in a family watch to see who is getting attention for what. If children notice that one sibling is getting special daily playtimes with a parent, it is inevitable that they will want the same treatment. If at all feasible, the parent should have separate playtimes with each child. This fosters children's sense of uniqueness and individuality in their relationships with their parents. If this is not feasible due to the number of children and lack of a partner to help, it is still possible to use these play strategies while playing with several children at once. During the play sessions the parent must go back and forth between the children, giving attention and praise to each child individually.

Couldn't a lack of parental control and structure in play contribute to increased child misbehavior?

> I'm afraid that if I let my child take the lead in play I will be reinforcing his obnoxious, bossy behavior. He'll say, 'Don't put that there!' or he'll grab something out of my hand and say, 'Give me that!' He's always told me what to do so I don't see how this will help him be more compliant—quite the opposite!

Some parents are worried that if they follow their children's lead in play, they will be encouraging them to be bossy and manipulative. The truth is that children are not made bossy by such an approach. In fact, the opposite is true: Parents who decrease their own bossiness in play interactions, going along with their children's ideas, are modeling compliance and acceptance of others' requests and ideas. This parental support for children's ideas not only increases children's self-esteem and confidence but is likely to be imitated by children—that is, the children whose parents demonstrate a sharing and respectful attitude are more likely to be compliant and accepting of their parents' requests in other situations, as well as with their peers.

Couldn't imaginative play result in crazy behavior?

> I see my child talking to make-believe friends and making up all kinds of things that aren't true. Isn't that a sign of emotional disturbance? Isn't it a form of lying?

Some adults are reluctant to engage in imaginative play: to crawl on the floor making train noises or to act out fairy tales. They feel silly and embarrassed. Fathers in particular seem to feel uncomfortable playing house or dress up games with their children. We have been told by some parents that they consider make-believe to be a sign of emotional disturbance. This is far from the truth. When children engage in make-believe play, they are learning to manipulate representations of things rather than the concrete objects themselves. Most healthy youngsters are doing this by the age of three, and some as early as 18 months. Imaginary companions are common among four-year-olds. Play that involves fantasy steadily increases into middle childhood (about age eight) and then begins to disappear.

It is important for parents to encourage this kind of play because it helps children to develop a variety of cognitive, emotional, and social skills. Parents should be encouraged to allow boxes and chairs to become houses and palaces, and doll figures to turn into relatives, friends, or favorite cartoon characters. Fantasy helps children to think symbolically and gives them a better idea of what is real and what is not. Role-play helps them to experience the feelings of someone else, which helps them to understand and be sensitive to the emotions of others.

TEACHING PARENTS ABOUT PRAISE

Parents of conduct-problem children often find it hard to praise their children. Perhaps believing that children should behave appropriately without adult intervention or that praise should be reserved for exceptionally good behavior or outstanding performance, many parents would never think of praising their children for playing quietly or for doing their chores without complaining. While some parents believe they should not have to praise their children for everyday behaviors, many others simply do not know how or when to give praise and encouragement. Perhaps they themselves received little praise from their own parents when they were young; unaccustomed to hearing praise, the words may seem awkward and artificial. Or perhaps they are so stressed that they cannot see praiseworthy child behaviors when they do occur.

Consequently, we teach parents to look for positive behaviors and to praise them. Here are the major points we emphasize:

■ Make praise contingent on behavior.

■ Praise immediately.

■ Give labeled and specific praise.

■ Give positive praise, without qualifiers or sarcasm.

THINK ABOUT USING MEGAPHONES
WHEN YOU PRAISE YOUR CHILD

- Praise with smiles, eye contact, and enthusiasm as well as with words.

- Give pats, hugs, and kisses along with verbal praise.

- Catch the child whenever s/he is being good—don't save praise for perfect behavior.

- Use praise consistently whenever you see the positive behavior you want to encourage.

- Praise in front of other people.

- Don't worry about spoiling children with praise.

- Increase praise for difficult children.

- Model self-praise.

Sometimes parents will say that their child is so deviant that they can find nothing to praise. Many times these are depressed parents who cannot see the prosocial behaviors in their child. If this is the case the parent can watch videotapes of parent–child interactions and be helped to identify the positive behaviors to be reinforced. Regardless of whether the reinforcer is attention, a hug, a smile, or verbal praise, the task of teaching a child a new behavior is long and difficult, and often very slow. It involves trying to reinforce the positive behavior every time it occurs. If there are two adults in the family, they should discuss which behavior they want to improve and how they will try to reinforce that behavior. With both participating, things should go more quickly. In addition, adults can double the impact of praise by praising children in front of other adults and by modeling self-praise.

Many parents who do not praise their children do not praise themselves, either. If they listened to their internal self-talk, they would find that they are rarely or never saying things like, "You're doing a good job of disciplining Johnny," or "You handled that conflict calmly and rationally," or "You've been very patient in this situation." Instead, they are quick to criticize themselves for every flaw or mistake. They must learn to speak to themselves in positive statements and to create positive experiences for themselves as incentives or rewards. They will then be more likely to do the same for their children.

Typical Questions and Concerns About Praise

Don't children know *how to behave?*

My child should know how to behave. Surely I don't need to praise her for everyday things like doing chores or sharing toys.

Rules or statements about expected behavior are not sufficient for motivating behavior. The only way a child learns to engage in a particular behavior is by having that behavior reinforced. If it is acknowledged and reinforced by the parent, it is more likely to occur again. If it is ignored, it is less likely to be repeated. A rule or statement of expectations without reinforcement when those expectations are met will be without long-term effect. Consequently, expecting a child to behave well without rewards or praise is unrealistic. No good behavior should be taken for granted or it will soon disappear.

Doesn't praise spoil children?

Isn't there a danger of spoiling my child with praise? Won't she learn to cooperate only for the sake of some external reward or adult approval?

If there are any examples of children who have developed behavior problems as a result of receiving too much praise, we have not heard of them. Children are not spoiled by praise, nor does praise train them to work only for external approval or rewards. In fact, the opposite is true: children who are motivated only for external approval and attention tend to be those who have received little praise or reinforcement from adults. As a result, their self-esteem is so low that they are always seeking others' approval, or they demand a reward before complying with requests. On the other hand, children who are frequently praised by their parents develop increased self-esteem. This positive self-esteem eventually makes them less dependent on approval from adults and external rewards; they are more able to provide themselves with positive reinforcement.

Children who receive positive messages about themselves from their parents are also more likely to praise others. This can have far-reaching effects. The principle that operates here is "you get what you give." Research indicates that children who give many positive statements to others are popular in school and receive many positive statements from others in return, which in turn bolsters their self-esteem. So remember: children imitate what they see and hear. If they receive frequent positive messages from their parents, they are more likely to internalize this form of thinking and use it in positive "self-talk" to motivate themselves and in positive communication with the people around them. Of course, the opposite is also true. If parents are negative and critical, their children will imitate this behavior as well in their "self-talk" and in their communication with others.

Isn't there a difference between encouragement and praise?

I make a point of encouraging my child. Isn't that enough?

Some parents believe that they should encourage their children but not praise them. Often these are the same parents who worry about spoiling or ending up with children who work only for external rewards. They make supportive comments, but try to avoid any statements that sound like praise. Out of concern that their encouragement might really be praise, they continually edit what they say. This creates an unnecessary complication, since children are not likely to notice the difference. Parents should not worry about the form of their positive statements but simply give encouragement/praise whenever they notice a positive behavior.

Shouldn't praise be saved for really outstanding achievements?

I prefer to save my praise for something that's really worth praising—an A in math, a perfectly made bed, or a really good drawing. Doesn't this help a child reach for the top?

The problem with this attitude is that no one—child or adult—achieves perfection without much imperfection. A goal is attained by completing many steps along the way, and the process involves attempts and failures as well as achievements. A parent's focus should be on the process of drawing, trying to make the bed or attempting the math problems. Otherwise, the opportunity to praise may never come! Children of parents who reserve their praise for perfection usually give up trying before they have attained it. If parents can focus on the fact that their child is trying to make the bed or do the dishes, they will be gradually shaping her/his behavior in the desired direction. In other words, praise should reward the effort to achieve, not just the achievement.

In addition to praising children's attempts at doing something positive, parents should also praise their children's everyday mundane positive behaviors such as: talking with a quiet voice, going to bed when asked, complying to a request, saying "please," sharing a toy with a friend, and so forth. Parents should not hoard praises or save them for outstanding achievements, lest these positive everyday behaviors will disappear. No positive behavior should be taken for granted!

Avoid combining praise with commands, criticisms, or put-downs

I tease my kids quite a bit when they do something well—is there a problem with this?

Some people give praise and, without realizing it, undermine it by being sarcastic or combining it with a punisher. This is one of the most disruptive things a parent can do in the reinforcement process. Sometimes parents mix praise with teasing. More commonly, seeing children do something they have not done before seems to tempt parents to give a sarcastic or critical remark about the new behavior. For example, a father may say to his children, "Tony and Angie, you both came to the table the first time I asked you. That's great. But next time how about washing your face and hands first?" Or a mother may say, "Lee, I'm glad you're trying to make your bed, but you are doing it all wrong. Look how bumpy it is—start with the sheets first, then straighten them, then put the pillow on. ..."

In these examples, the parents may feel they have praised their children's efforts but they have undermined their praise by adding commands and criticisms. Perhaps they think that giving praise allows them to "slip in" some criticism or instructions. In any event, the children will tend to hear the parents' comments as criticisms, not praise—that is, they will hear that they failed to do a good enough job. They may react with discouragement and stop trying in the future. It is important that when parents give a child praise, it should be clear and unequivocal, without reminders of prior failures or observations about a less-than-perfect performance or commands regarding future performance.

Can praise be used with children who consistently misbehave?

> My child has been consistently naughty. She is nothing but trouble. I can't start to praise her until she changes her ways.

When parents feel this way about their children, we have a stalemate situation. For example, Sam is constantly irritated by the fact that his eight-year-old son Steve is defiant and uses smart talk whenever he asks him to do something. Moreover, his teachers have reported their concern about Steve's inattentiveness, aggressive behaviors with his peer group, and poor reading skills. As a result, Sam is never in a mood to notice that Steve regularly sets the table and completes his chores. If this were pointed out to him, Sam would likely say "So what?" because he has become totally focused on Steve as a disobedient and "difficult" child. With attitudes like these, a parent is unlikely to praise or reward the child, and it is unlikely that the child is going to be able to initiate a behavior change. To end the stalemate, someone has to stop the negative interactions, and it is up to the parents. Praise is the best tool at their disposal.

Even a child who misbehaves 90% of the time is doing some things right. That 10% of his/her behavior which is positive or appropriate provides an opportunity for using praise to build the child's self-esteem and to break the negative cycle. Parents have to learn to spot the positive things their children are doing and to praise them for their efforts. Then children will likely repeat and expand these positive behaviors.

In other words, parents need to realize that only if adults take the responsibility for changing first—for ending the stalemate—is there the likelihood of positive changes in the relationship. This same principle is true of any relationship—with spouses, older children, or working colleagues. If one becomes obstinate and refuses to make a positive change in one's own behavior, the status quo is maintained and the relationship is unlikely to improve.

What if praise feels unnatural and phoney?

It's not that I have any real objection to praising my child, it just isn't something that comes naturally to me and so I don't do it.
If I make a conscious effort to praise him, I just end up feeling phoney.

Praise may seem phoney when it is first used—any new behavior feels awkward in the beginning. This is a natural reaction and is to be expected. But the more parents use praise, the more natural it will feel.

Very often parents who find praise unnatural are people who were never praised as children and who never praise themselves. Far from praising themselves, they are often very self-critical about their mistakes, conflicts, and difficulties. Although they may tell their children about problems they have, they rarely mention their successes, aspects of themselves they feel good about, or things they feel good about having done. These parents do not model self-praise. Yet it is important for children to see their parents modeling self-praise statements. A mother might say aloud to herself, "I did a good job on my assignment at work," or "That was a tough situation but I think we handled it well," or "That casserole I made tonight tasted good." By modeling self-praise for our children, we teach them how to internalize positive self-talk.

Isn't praise manipulative?

Isn't it rather manipulative to use praise to bring about a particular behavior in my child?

The word manipulative implies that a parent is contriving secretly to bring about some desired behavior against the child's wishes. In fact, the purpose of praise is to enhance and increase positive behavior with the child's knowledge. Praise (and rewards) which is clearly described brings out the best behavior in children because they know what is expected of them.

What if a parent forgets to praise?

Sometimes I forget to praise and do it later—is there a problem with this?

Sometimes praise is given hours or even days after the positive behavior has occurred. For instance, a mother may mention that she appreciated her daughter cleaning up the kitchen or putting out the garbage a week after it happened. Unfortunately, praise loses its reinforcing value over time. Furthermore, when it comes long after the behavior, it tends to sound more artificial.

While delayed praise is better than no praise at all, the most effective praise is that which is given within five seconds of the positive behavior. This means that if a parent is trying to encourage a new behavior, she should watch for every occasion when the child attempts the behavior. Parents should praise children as soon as they begin to perform the desired behavior, rather than waiting for the clothes to be put on perfectly or the toys to all be put away before praising. The praise should be frequent and consistent in the beginning, and then gradually it can be replaced by more intermittent praise.

What about when the praise seems to disrupt the play?

When I go in and tell him he is playing well with his sister, they stop playing. I feel I should have just left them alone—they were doing so well.

While we recommend that parents play daily with their children and use praise during those play sessions, there are other times when children are playing by themselves that parents may want to praise as well. However, going into a room to praise children for their quiet, cooperative play may have the unwanted consequence of disrupting the play. Sometimes the children will stop playing and ask the parent to stay and play. When parents first start going in to praise their children, they can expect this reaction. The parents' behavior may be new for the child, and parents' positive enthusiasm can make children want to spend more time playing with their parents. Nonetheless, as children get used to parents peeking in their rooms to notice how they are playing, it will become less disruptive and the children will know their parents feel good about their cooperative play. You might ask, "Why praise children when they are playing quietly? If observing them and commenting is disruptive, why not leave them alone?" However, if children's independent and cooperative play goes unnoticed by parents, it will gradually decrease and be replaced by arguments and fights—which will be guaranteed to receive parent's attention!

What about when a child rejects praise?

Whenever I try to praise my child, he throws it back in my face. He never seems to believe what I say. It's almost as if he doesn't want me to praise him.

Temperamentally difficult and aggressive children can be hard to praise. Their behavior often makes parents angry and undermines their desire to be positive. To make matters more difficult, these children may reject praise when it is given to them. It seems that such children internalize a negative self-concept because of the constant criticisms they have experienced from parents and teachers as well as the rejection and ridicule from their peer group. When parents present them with an alternative, positive view of themselves, the children find this image difficult to accept, preferring to cling to their familiar negative self-image.

While "difficult" children are hard to praise and reward, they need it even more than other children. Their parents must constantly look for positive behaviors that they can reinforce until the children begin to internalize some positive self-concepts. At that point they will no longer have a need to reject praise in order to maintain their poor self-image. However, this is easier said than done. It can be incredibly difficult for parents to continue to be positive with a difficult child who rejects their praise and their efforts to break a stalemate. The therapist will need to support such parents while they go through this difficult phase.

TANGIBLE REWARD PROGRAMS

We have found that for some oppositional and conduct-disordered children, parental praise is initially not enough reinforcement to turn around a difficult problem behavior. However, a tangible reward can be used by parents to provide the added incentive necessary for a child to achieve a particular goal. A tangible reward is something concrete: a special treat, additional privileges, a toy, or a favorite activity. Tangible rewards can be used to encourage such positive behaviors in children as toilet training, playing cooperatively with siblings, learning how to get dressed, getting ready for school on time, completing homework, cleaning up the playroom, and so on. When using tangible rewards to motivate children to learn something new, the therapist needs to stress the importance of parents continuing to provide social rewards (i.e., attention and praise) as well. The impact is much greater when both types of rewards are combined; each serves a different purpose. Social rewards should be used to reinforce the small efforts children make to master a new skill or behavior. Tangible rewards are usually used to reinforce the achievement of a specific goal. Once children learn a new behavior, tangible rewards can eventually be phased out and parental praise will maintain the existing behavior.

In general, there are two ways of using tangible rewards. The first is for the parent to surprise the child with a reward whenever s/he behaves in some desired way, such as sharing or sitting still in the car. This approach works if the child already exhibits the appropriate behavior fairly regularly and the parent wishes to increase the frequency with which it occurs. The second approach is for the parent to plan in advance with the child (or explain to the child in advance) the reward which will follow from a certain behavior—as in a contract. This type of program is recommended when parents wish to increase an infrequent behavior. For example, a parent might set up a sticker chart for two children who fight frequently. She could start by telling both children that they will receive a sticker for every half hour in which they are sharing and playing quietly. Then she could discuss with them some special thing they would like to work for, such as having a friend overnight, reading an extra story at bedtime, going to the park with Dad, choosing their favorite cereal at the grocery store, going to a movie, picking something from a surprise grab bag, and so forth. It is a good idea to make the treat list fairly long with small, inexpensive items as well as bigger items. This list can be altered as children come up with new suggestions. Preschool children between the ages of three and four may be rewarded by the special sticker or token itself without needing a back-up reinforcer. Youngsters aged four to six should be able to trade in stickers for something each day if they like. Children of seven and eight can wait a few days before getting a reward.

It is important for parents to remember that tangible reward programs will be effective only if parents:

- Define the desired behavior clearly.

- Choose effective rewards (i.e., rewards that the child will find sufficiently reinforcing).

- Set consistent limits concerning which behaviors will receive rewards.

- Make the program simple and fun.

- Make the steps small.

- Monitor the charts carefully.

■ Follow through with the rewards immediately.

■ Avoid mixing rewards with punishment.

■ Gradually replace rewards with social approval.

■ Revise the program as the behaviors and rewards change.

While reward programs may seem simple, there are, in fact, many pitfalls to be avoided if they are to be effective. The therapist will need to spend time reviewing charts and trouble-shooting issues that arise as parents begin these programs.

Typical Questions and Concerns About Tangible Rewards

Aren't you bribing children?

When you give stickers or points or prizes, aren't you bribing children?

What is the difference between a bribe and a reward? A bribe is an attempt to produce the desired behavior; a reward is reinforcement for the desired behavior. Consider a father in a bank who says to his screaming child, "Eliza, you can have this chocolate bar, but stop screaming." Or a father whose child has been getting out of bed at night who says, "Sunjay, I'll give you this snack if you go back to bed afterwards." In these examples, the chocolate bar and the snack are bribes because they are given before the desired behavior has occurred. They are not contingent on the behavior, regardless of what the parent intended. In fact, bribes reinforce inappropriate behavior, since the "reward" (that is, the bribe) followed the inappropriate behavior. Ironically, parents are teaching their children that if they behave badly, they will be rewarded.

Rewards are given for positive behaviors after they have occurred. It is helpful for parents to remember the "first–then" principle. That is, *first* the child must behave appropriately or comply, *then* s/he gets the reward. In the bank example, Eliza's father could have said before going to the bank, "Eliza, if you stay by my side quietly in the bank, I will give you a chocolate bar when we are finished." Sunjay's father could have said, "If you stay in your bed all night without getting up, you can earn a special treat tomorrow after school." The parent gives the reward only after seeing the desired behavior.

Won't children become dependent on tangible rewards?

I worry that my children may become dependent on such rewards to motivate them—and life doesn't always reward work with success in work. What happens when I want to get them off the reward system?

Parents often worry about using tangible rewards—or too many tangible rewards. They are concerned that instead of developing internal controls, their children will learn to behave correctly only for a "pay-off." This is a legitimate concern and it could possibly happen in two kinds of situations. The first involves the parent who is "sticker dependent," giving stickers or points for desirable behavior, but never providing social approval (attention and praise). In essence, this parent is teaching the child to perform for pay-offs rather than for the pleasure both parent and child feel about the accomplishments. The use of tangible rewards should be seen as a temporary measure to help children learn new behaviors. They must be accompanied by social rewards.

The second situation arises when the parent does not plan to phase out the tangible rewards and maintain the behaviors with social approval. In other words, the children are not given the message that the parent expects them to eventually be able to behave on their own without tangible rewards. For example, a parent might say to a child who has been earning stickers for making his bed in the morning, "You have been earning stickers every day for making your bed and that's great—now let's make the program even more fun. In order to get a sticker you have to make your bed and get your own breakfast each morning." Once parents have taught the new behaviors, they can gradually phase out the tangible rewards and maintain them with social reinforcers. For instance, a parent might say, "Now that you are going pee in the toilet almost all the time, and earning lots of stickers, let's make the game more fun. Now you have to have dry pants for two days before earning a sticker." Once the child is successful on a regular basis for two days, the interval can be extended to four days, and so forth, until stickers are no longer necessary. At that point, her mother may want to use stickers to help her with a different behavior. She could say, "You remember how well you did learning to go pee with the sticker game we played? Well, let's help you learn to get dressed in the mornings using stickers." Thus, reward programs can be phased out and begun again for different behaviors.

An important aspect of a reward program is the message that accompanies the reward. Parents must communicate clearly that not only do they approve of their child's success, they also recognize that the child's effort— not the pay-off, *per se*—is responsible for the success. In this way, parents help strengthen the child's internal motivation and sense of competence.

Rewards which bankrupt parents or are earned too easily

I can't afford these programs, I don't have the money to buy rewards.

Believe it or not, we have seen reward programs that almost bankrupted their planners. All children will want to include expensive items such as a bicycle or a trip to Disneyland on their reward menu. Some parents may give in and place such items on the list, either because they think their children will never earn enough points to get them or because they feel guilty and would like to be able to give them these things. Still others include expensive items because they have trouble setting limits with their children.

Even if parental motives are good, inclusion of unrealistic rewards is destructive to the program. All too often children do earn the required number of stickers or points. Parents then find themselves in the awkward position of either being unable to afford the reward, or of giving their children the reward but resenting it. In this case, children receive a mixed message about their parents' pleasure in the achievement of the goal. This defeats the purpose of a reward program and undermines the parents' credibility for future efforts to promote positive behaviors. Even when families can afford more expensive rewards, exclusive use of these teaches children to learn to expect big rewards for their successes. The emphasis is placed on the magnitude of the reward, rather than on the satisfaction and pride felt by both parent and child at the child's success.

Generally it is a good idea to set a limit on the expense of any one item on a list, such as two dollars or less, depending on what the family can afford. Children can be told this at the beginning. Although they will ask for expensive items and test the rules around this, in general inexpensive (or nonmaterial) things are more powerful reinforcers. Young children often like to earn time with parents, such as extra story time, or a trip to the park. Small food items such as raisins or candy, or the right to choose their favorite cereal or dessert can also be appealing. Older children like to earn money and special privileges such as extra television, having a friend overnight, using the telephone, and so forth.

Tangible reward programs don't work with my child

My child is uninterested in tangible reward programs—I've made up charts for her before and she acts uninterested in the program. Aren't some children just not motivated by such things?

It is a rare child who is uninterested in rewards. Chances are that it is some other aspect of the program that is not working—most likely the behavioral expectations. Programs sometimes fail because too many negative behaviors are tackled at once; too many behavioral goals have been set. We have seen highly motivated parents start reward programs that included compliance to parental requests, not teasing siblings and peers, going to bed without an argument, and getting dressed on time in the mornings. Such programs are too complex. The pressure to succeed in many different areas of life may be so overwhelming that children give up before starting. Rather than "not motivated," the child may be too discouraged.

Another drawback in specifying a number of behaviors is that it requires constant monitoring by the parents. To take just the first goal in our example, compliance to parental requests, for a parent to monitor compliance and noncompliance throughout a day will require a tremendous amount of effort, since these situations occur so frequently. Remember, if parents cannot realistically monitor their child's behavior and follow through with consequences, the best-designed program is bound to fail.

There are three main things to consider when deciding how many behaviors to help children learn at one time: the frequency with which each behavior occurs; the child's developmental stage; and the parent's ability to carry out the program. With regard to frequency, remember that behaviors such as noncompliance, whining, teasing, or arguing may occur often and therefore will require much parental supervision. Realistically, parents will not be able to focus on more than one such behavior at a time. On the other hand, behaviors such as dressing, brushing teeth, or wearing a seat belt in the car occur relatively infrequently and three or four of these could be included on a chart at the same time.

The second important point to consider is the developmental stage of the child. Young children require easily understandable programs that focus on one or two simple behaviors at a time. Learning to be compliant to parental requests or staying in bed at night are major developmental tasks for a young child. Each will require many repeated learning trials over time and much patience on the part of the parents. However, for older children (school-age and adolescent), tangible reward programs can become more complex because they can understand and remember them better. In addition, the problem behaviors at this stage usually occur less frequently and are easier to monitor. For a school-age child, therefore, it would not be unrealistic to establish a program that included points for completing various chores by a well-defined time, finishing homework without a reminder, and being dressed and ready for school in the mornings.

Evaluation of how much monitoring parents can realistically expect of themselves is the third factor in deciding which child behaviors to focus on. Even if a parent has no outside job, that parent is unlikely to be able to monitor child compliance throughout the day if she has more than one child at home. Therefore, she may want to choose a period of the day when she can focus on problem behaviors. For instance, she might decide to monitor a child's behavior for two hours when the baby naps, or in the morning when the older child is in school. On the other hand, a mother who is rushed to get ready for work in the morning and exhausted by evening may only have the energy to monitor problem behaviors every morning for half an hour. The therapist must make every effort to be sure that parents are setting up programs that are realistic for them—so that there is every chance for parents to be successful in their first efforts at behavior change.

Another possible reason that programs fail is that they focus exclusively on negative behaviors. Parents may clearly identify a negative behavior they want to eliminate, such as fighting. Their program outlines the rewards that their children will receive for going an hour without fighting. So far, so good; but the program has not gone far enough. While it tells children clearly what they should not do, it neither describes nor rewards the appropriate replacement behavior. Thus, in this example, inappropriate behavior is receiving more parental attention than appropriate behavior, and consequently behavior is likely to worsen.

It is important to help parents identify the positive behaviors that they want to replace the negative behaviors and to include them in the tangible reward program. Children should be rewarded for sharing and playing quietly together, as well as for going 60 minutes without getting into an argument with brothers and sisters. It is critical that the positive behaviors be spelled out at least as clearly as the behaviors that are to be eliminated.

Unrealistic goals

I offered my child a new bike if he got an A in math, but that was totally unsuccessful.

One reason many reward programs fail is that parents set their behavioral expectations so high, with correspondingly difficult conditions for earning the reward, that their children feel that earning a reward is impossible and give up trying—or do not even try in the first place. A good reward program incorporates the small steps involved in achieving the goal. First, ask parents to observe how often the misbehaviors occur over several days. This baseline will be the key to establishing the right steps for their child.

For example, for the parent who is trying to motivate her child who has difficulty in math, it will be necessary to provide praise and reinforcement for each small step toward the desired goal of an "A". That means giving the child points for doing daily homework exercises correctly or for a good score on the week's math test, or even for individual problems done correctly. With this approach, the child has a good chance of becoming more confident of his/her math ability and eventually being successful. Remember, the idea is to make progress by small steps towards the desired goal.

Saving tangible rewards for special achievements

> I save big rewards for something really special—like getting all his math questions right. The problem is he hasn't earned anything yet.

Some parents save tangible rewards for their children's special achievements such as getting As on a report card, cleaning up the entire house, or being quiet during a two-day car trip. These are instances of setting too high a goal or making the steps too big. Not only do the parents wait too long to give the rewards, but they reserve rewards for perfection. As mentioned above, if parents expect perfection in order to reward their child, it is unlikely that s/he will ever earn a reward. This gives their children the message that everyday behaviors and everyday efforts do not really count.

Help parents think about giving small, frequent rewards. For example, parents who want a quieter car trip might prepare a surprise bag (crayons, books, puzzles, games) to be opened every 80 to 100 miles if their children have been quiet and there have been no fights. Such rewards can help satisfy the children's need for stimulation during a long car ride. Certainly parents can plan rewards for special achievements, but they should also use them for smaller steps along the way, such as doing math homework, putting away toys, sharing, sleeping all night, and going to the bathroom. Only by rewarding the smaller steps can the larger goals of good grades, consistent compliance, or good relationships with friends be accomplished.

Rewards seem to cause more misbehavior

> This reward system has caused a lot more problems in my house—now he demands rewards to do something or comes to me arguing to me that he has earned a sticker. And when his sister earned a prize for her sticker chart, he ripped his chart off the wall and threw a giant fit.

It is not unusual for parents of conduct-disordered children to develop power struggles with their children around their sticker charts because of their difficulties with limit setting. If rewards are resulting in more misbehavior, the parent has lost control of their reward program. Something is undermining the reinforcing effect of the reward.

There are several ways parents can lose control of their reward program. The first is by rewarding "almost" performance—that is, giving rewards to children when they have not actually done the required behavior or earned the required number of points. This usually happens because children argue for them, claiming that they have done everything required. Unfortunately, it undermines the rules of the contract as well as parents' authority. It is also likely to result in the children escalating their begging and debating with parents over the attainment of points. Instead of a behavior problem being solved, a new one—excessive arguing—is created. A second difficulty occurs if parents leave the stickers and/or rewards around the house so the children have access to them. Why work for the reward if you can get your hands on it directly? Lack of follow-through can be a third problem. This happens when the children have followed the program but parents fail to notice the positive behaviors or forget to give them the stickers. When rewards do not follow promptly on the heels of the behavior, their reinforcing value is minimal. (The same is true when parents are inconsistent about rewarding desired behavior.)

Tangible reward programs require a lot of work on the part of parents in order to be effective! Parents must consistently monitor their children's behavior in order to determine whether they have earned stickers or points. Parents should give stickers to children who *claim* they performed a specified behavior (such as sharing) only if the parents have observed the behavior or know with certainty that it was done. If parents and children are working on high-frequency problems such as noncompliance to requests, no teasing, or whining for 15 minutes, then a great deal of vigilance will be required. Rewards are most effective if they are given immediately after the desired behavior is performed. Also, in order for these programs to work, parents must hold firm on their expectations. All children will test the limits and try to see if they can get rewards for less work. That is natural, but it means that parents must be prepared for this testing, stay committed to the plan or "contract" and ignore any arguments or pleading when their children have not earned enough points. Finally, parents need to control access to the rewards. Prizes and stickers should be hidden and the awarding of points and stickers determined by parents, not their children.

Handling disappointment

> Some days my child hasn't been able to earn anything and he gets very upset, so
> sometimes I just give him a point so he will feel better. Is that a problem?

What happens when parents put a lot of effort into setting up a reward program but their children fail to earn points? The parent may be tempted to respond to the child with criticism or lectures on trying harder. Unfortunately, not only does this give children a discouraging message about their ability (which could become a self-fulfilling prophesy), but the negative attention and ensuing power struggle could inadvertently reinforce misbehavior or noncompliance with the program. In other words, the child would get more pay-off for not doing the program than for doing it.

If a child fails to earn points or stickers, it is best for the parent to say calmly, "You didn't get one this time, but I'm sure you'll earn some next time." Parents can predict their positive expectations for the future. However, if the child continues to have difficulties earning points, parents should make sure that they have not made the steps too big or unrealistic.

Using loss of rewards as a punishment for children

> If my child is bad I take away his points—the only problem is now he has minus
> points.

> Well, I give green tokens for good behaviors and red tokens for bad behaviors.

Some parents create tangible reward programs and then mix in punishment. For instance, a child may receive stickers for sharing and have them taken away for fighting. The stickers then take on negative rather than positive associations. This approach can be even more problematic if the child is left with a negative balance. If the most that a child can hope for from good behavior is to get out of "debt," all positive incentive for good behavior is gone. The natural outcome is for the child to become discouraged and abandon all efforts to change.

It is important for parents to keep their reward program separate from their discipline program. They should not remove earned points or rewards as punishment, because this will defeat the purpose of the program, which is to give attention to appropriate behaviors. The parent who gives green tokens for good behavior and red for bad is giving attention and reinforcement to both good and bad behaviors. Instead, the idea is for the positive behaviors to have a positive response and the negative behaviors to be ignored or disciplined with logical consequences. If parents want to use privilege removal as a discipline technique, they should keep off the reward menu any privileges they foresee withdrawing (e.g., TV time, use of bicycle).

LIMIT-SETTING

Once we have taught parents of conduct-problem children the importance of using play, praise, and rewards for promoting more appropriate behaviors in their children, then the therapist can help parents learn how to decrease inappropriate behavior through effective limit-setting. Indeed, research indicates that families who have few clearly communicated standards or rules are more likely to have children who misbehave.

However, while clear limit-setting is essential in helping children behave more appropriately, it is also important to remember that all children will test their parents' rules and standards. Research shows that normal children fail to comply with their parents' requests about one-third of the time. Young children will argue, scream, or throw temper tantrums when a toy is taken away or a desired activity prohibited. School-age children, too, will argue or protest when barred from something they want. This is normal behavior, and a healthy expression of a child's need for independence and autonomy. What makes the oppositional defiant or conduct-disordered child different from the normal child is that s/he is refusing to comply with a parent's requests about two-thirds of the time— that is, the parent is engaged in a power struggle with his/her child over getting him/her to do something the majority of the time. This high rate of noncompliance makes it very difficult for parents to socialize their children adequately.

Why Do Children Resist Parents' Requests?

As we have said, children test parents' rules not only in order to express their individuality, but also to see whether their parents are going to be consistent. It is only by breaking a rule that children can determine whether it is actually a rule or just a one-time command. Only consistent consequences for misbehavior on the part of parents will teach children that good behavior is expected. If parents' rules have been inconsistent in the past, if they have not enforced their rules or have enforced them inconsistently, then children's protests and noncompliance will escalate.

Such children have learned from experience that if they protest long enough and hard enough, they can get their parents to back down.

The therapist needs to help parents expect and be prepared for this testing. When such protests happen, parents should be helped to understand that these are not personal attacks, but learning experiences, ways that their children can explore the limits of their environment and learn which behaviors are appropriate and which are inappropriate. Therapists can help parents recognize the importance of consistency by explaining that consistent limit-setting and predictable responses from parents help give children a sense of stability and security. They can be assured that children who feel a sense of security regarding the limits of their environment have less need constantly to test it. Of course, the therapist needs to be sensitive to the fact that negative life stressors, such as marital discord, single parenting, poverty, unemployment, depression, and lack of support may make it difficult for parents to be consistent. However, strengthening parents' sense of competence regarding the way they limit-set and respond to children's protests can help buffer the disruptive effects of these stressors on parenting skills. The following are the major points we highlight:

- Make commands short and to the point.

- Give one command at a time.

- Use commands that clearly specify the desired behavior.

- Be realistic in your expectations and use age-appropriate commands.

- Don't use "stop" commands.

- Use "do" commands.

- Make commands polite.

- Don't give unnecessary commands.

- Don't threaten children.

- Use "when–then" commands.

- Give children options whenever possible.

- Give children ample opportunity to comply.

- Praise compliance or provide consequences for noncompliance.

- Give warnings and helpful reminders.

- Support your partner's commands.

- Strike a balance between parental and child control.

- Encourage problem-solving with children.

Typical Questions and Concerns About Limit-setting

Should the parent always be in charge?

> Isn't it better for children to be free to do their own problem-solving and learn from their mistakes rather than to impose a lot of rules and limits on children? Won't this approach help children to develop their own internal controls—and won't adult-imposed limits create children who rely on adults to come up with the limits?

Sometimes parents perceive limit-setting as an interference with children's right to self-determination or their need to learn to work out problems for

KEEP YOUR RADAR ANTENNAE TURNED ON AT ALL TIMES

themselves. But to take a concrete example, if two children are fighting over a book and the parent does not step in to set limits on the fighting, the arguing will probably continue and result in continued arguing and the more aggressive child getting the book. Therefore the aggressive child will be reinforced for his inappropriate behavior—after all, he got what he wanted—and the other child will be reinforced for giving in because the fighting ceased when he backed down. In situations like this one, the parental role is to set clear limits, to protect children from hurting each other and from being hurt. Especially in the case of seat belts, hitting, not taking bicycles out onto the street, for instance, it should be obvious that parents need to exert firm control over their children. But also in areas such as television watching, parents need to be in charge. Limits should be stated as absolutes and in a positive, polite, and firm manner.

There are other situations, of course, where parents can give control entirely over to their children. Why not allow children to have control over decisions such as what clothes to wear, whether or not to eat all the food on their plates, what stories to read before bed? Allowing children to be "in charge" of these decisions helps them develop a sense of autonomy and allows them to learn from experiencing the consequences of their own choices. Under yet other circumstances, parents can share control with their children by involving them in problem-solving. Here the parents' role is to help children understand different perspectives and to encourage them to come up with alternative solutions. While this problem-solving approach will be a slow process, and becomes effective only when they are older, introducing negotiation and discussion with children as young as four or five can provide excellent early training. For instance, there are times when parents can involve their children in the decision regarding a rule. Consider two preschool children who are fighting because they both want to play with the bubbles and there is only one bubble blower. Their father might respond by giving a command: "First, Doug, you will use it. Then, Susie, it will be your turn." But an alternative approach—one that involves sharing control—would be for the father to involve both children in deciding how to handle the problem. He might say, "There is only one bubble blower and two of you. What should we do? Do you have any ideas?" If Doug and Susie come up with some solutions, then Dad can reinforce their problem-solving ability. By avoiding the authoritarian approach, he can encourage his children to find their own solutions to a problem and help them learn to think through different solutions.

Can a parent do too much limit-setting?

I feel that I am limit-setting—or rather yelling and telling the kids what not to do—all day long. My problem is not in failing to limit-set—could I be doing too much limit-setting?

Few parents are aware of the actual number of commands they give their children. Would it surprise you to hear that the average parent gives 17 commands in half an hour? And in families where children have conduct problems, the number rises to an average of 40 commands in half an hour! Moreover, research has shown that the children of parents who give an excessive number of commands develop more behavior problems. Frequent commands, then, do not improve a child's behavior. For one thing, if parents are giving 20 to 40 commands in half an hour, it is impossible for them to follow through with each command. The result is that confusing messages are given to children about the importance of commands: sometimes the commands are important and need to be followed, and other times they are dropped by the parents. How is the child to know which are the important commands to follow? Another reason frequent commands are not helpful is that usually the rapid commands are being given at the time when the child is being oppositional and noncompliant. This parental attention (in the form of repeated commands) actually reinforces the child's noncompliance. Therefore, it is essential for parents to evaluate both the number and type of commands they give their children and to reduce them until they are giving only necessary commands, commands they are willing to follow through on with consequences for noncompliance.

Some parents tend to give a command when the child is already engaged in the action or to repeat a command even when the child has begun complying. For example, the parent tells the child to get her shoes on when she is already in the process of putting on her shoes. This tends to sound like criticism to the child; it implies that she is not complying when in fact she is complying. Thus it undermines her efforts to be compliant. Other parents give commands about issues that are not actually important to them. They might say, "Color that frog green," "Wear your blue shirt," or "Finish your dessert." Does the parent really care about these issues? If the issue is not an important one, then children should be allowed to decide such matters for themselves rather than become involved in a battle of wills with their parents. The key idea here is that parents should reserve their commands for the important issues.

Before giving a command, parents should think about whether the issue is really an important one, and whether they are willing to follow through with the consequences if their child does not comply. One exercise that can be helpful is to write down the important rules for their family. Parents will probably find that they have between five and ten that are "unbreakable." These should be posted on the fridge or in some other place where all the family can see them. In this way, everyone, including babysitters, will know what the rules are. Such a list might include:

- Seat belts must be worn in the car at all times.

- Hitting is not allowed.

- Throwing is not allowed indoors.

- TV must be off until 7 o'clock.

- Food must stay in the kitchen.

Once the therapist has helped parents clarify the important rules, parents will find not only that they become more precise when stating the rules and the commands that enforce the rules, but also that they are able to reduce the number of other, unnecessary commands. Thus with fewer and more precise commands, they will find it easier to follow through with consequences for the child. The result is that their children will learn that parental commands are important and that compliance is expected.

Isn't it better to "disguise" or "soften" commands?

> My child is more compliant when I disguise my commands. If I give an order, he rears back. So I say, "Oh my goodness, your coat is on the floor." Sometimes I get him to do what I want by demanding the opposite, for example, "You're not going to put away the toys."

While some parents of conduct-problem children are authoritarian and have too many rules and commands, others avoid establishing any rules at all. They feel guilty when they tell their children to do something that their children might object to. Parental guilt can occur for many reasons: guilt because of divorce or a distressed marriage, guilt because the parent works full time and has precious little time with the child, guilt because the child has a chronic disease or developmental delay, guilt because the child was adopted or had a parent that died and so forth. In these cases, guilt over the particular family problem can make the parent somewhat overprotective and wanting to prevent the child from experiencing any further pain or distress. So in order to ease their guilt, these parents disguise their commands with vague and indirect language. Some typical examples of vague or nonspecific commands are, "Watch out," "Be careful," "Be nice," "Be good," "Knock it off," and "Just a minute." These statements can be confusing to a child, because they do not specify the expected behavior. Indirect commands are phrased in such ways as, "Don't you think you should ..." or "It would be nice if you ..." or "Why don't we ... ?" or "How about ... ?" This form of command can confuse a child because it is unclear whether the behavior is optional or expected.

Another type of "disguised" command is the one that a parent states as a descriptive comment. For instance, Delia says to her daughter, "Oh Denise, you're spilling your milk." Or Derek's father looks out the window and says, "Derek, your bike is still in the yard!" In addition to lacking clarity, these statements contain an implied criticism. Not only is it difficult to get a child to comply with statements, as opposed to direct commands ("Hold the glass with both hands" "Put your bike away"), but the critical aspect of such statements is likely to breed resentment.

Still another type of "softened" command is the "Let's" command: "Let's wash the toy dishes," "Let's get ready for bed." This kind of command can be confusing for young children if their parents have no intention of becoming involved. For instance, a mother who has been playing with her two sons in the kitchen now wants them to put away the toys. She says, "Let's put the toys away." Unless she is willing to help them, they probably will not cooperate and she will become cross with them; but the fault lies with her command, which does not clearly convey her expectations. It is important for parents to be specific about the behavior they want from their child when they give a command. If Kim asks her mother to play with her, instead of the mother saying "Just a minute," she might say, "Wait five minutes, then I'll play with you." Instead of telling Robbie to "Be careful" when he is spilling juice, the parent might say, "Use both hands to pour the juice into your glass." Instead of "Let's put the toys away," the parent should say, "It's time for you to put the toys away."

Paradoxical commands such as, "Don't eat those peas" (when the parent in fact wants the child to eat the peas), may work in the short run because they provide some humor and cajoling. However, such mixed message commands have the potential of backfiring. Since in this instance, children are actually noncomplying to the parents' stated request, the parent is actually teaching the child to noncomply and to do what the parent is asking them not to do. There may be situations in the future where the parent truly *does not* want the child to do something and the child does not believe him/her. (This is the parental version of the "Boy Who Cried Wolf" situation.)

"Chain" commands and "repeat" commands

> I have to ask my child at least 10 times to get him to go to bed or to get dressed in the mornings. I feel like such a nag but he doesn't seem to hear me when I make requests.

Sometimes parents string commands together in a chain, without giving their child time to comply with the first command before going on to the next. For young children, this can result in information overload. For example, Eva tells her four-year-old, "It's time for bed. I want you to put your markers away, pick up your papers, go upstairs and get your pajamas on, and then brush your teeth." A series of commands such as this is difficult for children to remember, especially active children with a short attention span. Most can retain only one or two things at a time. Another problem with rapid commands is that the parent is not able to praise the child for complying with any of the individual commands, so that the child is not reinforced. Eventually, this results in more noncompliant behavior, partly because the child simply cannot comply with everything, partly because there is no reinforcement for compliance.

A related type of communication problem involves the parent repeating the same command over and over again as if the child has not heard it. Many parents repeat the same order four or five times, and their children quickly learn that there is no real need to comply until the fifth time. Moreover, chain commands reinforce noncompliant behavior by the amount of attention conveyed by the constant repetition. Instead of repeating commands as if they expect their child to ignore them, parents should state the command once, pronouncing it slowly and then waiting to see whether the child will comply. If it helps parents to wait, they might want to count silently as they watch to see how their child will respond. This will help parents resist the impulse to nag—or curb their habit of nagging. Then, if the child complies, they can praise the response and if not, they can enforce a consequence.

Aren't angry commands and threats useful at times?

> It's not until I get really angry or threaten to take away something that my child will finally do what I want.

If parents are angry when they give a command, they often inject criticism, a putdown, or other negative comment. Sometimes these are included with a command as a way of venting frustration because the child has not done something that the parent has asked him to do many times before. Billy's

Dad might say, "Billy, why won't you sit still for once in your life!" Or he might tell Billy to sit still in a sarcastic tone of voice, "Can't you do any better than that? What a baby!" Or, "I'm sick of this mess—you're a slob—clean this up."

Parents need to avoid criticizing their children when they give a command. Negative commands cause children to feel incompetent and discounted. They react by becoming defensive and less inclined to comply. Children's feeling about themselves as worthwhile people should be considered at least as important as obedience. Commands should be stated positively, politely, and with respect. Otherwise, the child may choose not to comply as a way of retaliating for a parent's criticism and as a way of defending their own self-worth.

"Stop" commands and prohibitions versus positive commands and permissions

Why should commands always be stated positively? Isn't it better to give a clear message about the misbehavior?

Another type of negative command is a "stop" command. A stop command is a type of negative statement that tells a child what not to do. "Stop shouting," "Don't do that," "Quit it," "Shut up," "Cut it out," and "Enough of that" are all stop commands. Not only are these critical of the child, but they focus on the misbehavior instead of telling the child how to behave correctly.

Sports psychologists have found that if the coach tells the pitcher, "Don't throw a fast ball," a fast ball is just what the pitcher is likeliest to throw—not out of orneriness, but simply because that is what the coach's words have made him visualize. It is worth making every effort, therefore, for parents to give positive commands that specify the behavior they want from their child. Instead of saying, "Stop yelling," or "Stop splashing," the parent should say, "Please speak quietly," or "Keep the water inside the tub." Whenever a child does something the parent does not like, the parent should try to think of what alternative behavior s/he wants and then phrase the command to focus on that positive behavior.

A related issue is that of prohibitions versus permission. Many times parents' commands prohibit their children from doing something they want to do, such as playing with friends or watching more television. In such instances parents tell their children what they cannot do, but forget to tell them what they can do instead. When children feel rigidly restricted and prohibited from fun activities, they may react with protests and non-compliance. Commands that prohibit a child from doing something should include permission or suggestions for alternative activities. A parent might say, "You may not watch TV now, but you can play with this puzzle with me," or "You can't play with Daddy's tools, but you can build a fort in the basement." Giving an alternative to the prohibited behavior can help reduce power struggles because, instead of staying with the issue under dispute, the parent is turning the child's attention towards another activity, one which the child is free to engage in.

Decreasing resistance through warnings

> My child hates being interrupted when she is working on something—how can I deal with her resistance to limit-setting?

Sometimes children react adversely to parental commands when they are given abruptly, without any warning. Picture this scene: Jenny is totally absorbed in building a castle with her blocks. Suddenly her father walks into the room and tells her to go to bed. What happens next? Probably much protest and resistance from an unhappy Jenny.

Whenever feasible, it is helpful to give a reminder or warning prior to a command, in order to prepare for the transition. If Jenny's Dad had noticed that she was engrossed in playing with her blocks and said, "In two more minutes, it will be time to put your blocks away," Jenny would probably not have made a fuss. There are many ways to give warnings. For young children who do not understand the concept of time, a timer can be helpful. Then parents can say, "When the timer goes off, it will be time to put these blocks away." For older children, parents can refer to a clock.

Children's requests and preferences should be considered, as well. For instance, if an eight-year-old is busy reading a book, the parent might ask, "How many more pages are there before the end of your chapter?" If the child replies, "One more page," the parent could say, "Okay, when you finish that page, I want you to set the table." When parents are responsive to their children's wishes and give them some lead time, they are more likely to obtain compliance.

How important is consistency?

> How important is it to be consistent with limit-setting? I mean, if you say bedtime is 8 p.m., how harmful is it to then let a child stay up until 9 p.m. one night?

Effective limit-setting does not require parents to be authoritarian or to enforce the rules rigidly regardless of circumstances. Rather, the emphasis is on parents thinking carefully before giving a command to be sure that it is necessary and that they are prepared to follow through with the consequences. When thinking about commands, it is important to strike a balance between a child's choices and adult rules. Once a parent has decided a command or household rule is important, then s/he should be consistent in following through with its enforcement. If parents are consistent with their commands, then children will learn to accept them and their initial protests will subside. On the other hand, if parents are inconsistent about the importance of their rules and fail to follow through with commands, children will learn to protest and test them more and more often.

Consistency is a virtue, but not when it becomes an inflexible policy. For instance, if the parent's household rule is an 8 p.m. bedtime, and one night the parent's usually reserved child finally opens up five minutes before bedtime, a competent parent will realize this is a good time to make an exception to the rule and let the child stay up later to talk. Inconsistency, in this case, is justified by the parent's sensitivity to the unique needs of the child at that moment. On the other hand, if the parent found that delaying bedtime with conversations was becoming a pattern every night, then the parent would need to reenforce the rule regarding bedtime. Because of the initial inconsistency about the importance of an 8 p.m. bedtime hour, the child would undoubtedly protest loudly the first few nights—but with a consistent response would eventually settle down to the routine. However, if parents are aware that they are being inconsistent or making an exception to the usual rule, it can help to explain this to the children so that they are prepared ahead of time for things to resume to normal on subsequent days. Such an approach can help minimize some of the costs of inconsistency.

TEACHING PARENTS ABOUT IGNORE SKILLS

Oppositional and conduct-disordered children use high rates of irritating behaviors such as whining, teasing, arguing, swearing, and tantrums. These inappropriate behaviors are usually not dangerous to the children or other people but usually lead to peer rejection and isolation, which further decrease the self-esteem of these children. If parents are able to ignore these misbehaviors systematically, they can often be eliminated.

The therapist will find that ignoring is one of the most difficult approaches for parents to use. Many parents will argue that ignoring is not discipline. Thus, the therapist needs to help parents understand why this approach works and what the principle is behind its effectiveness. The rationale for ignoring is straightforward. Children's behavior is maintained by the attention it receives. Even negative parental attention such as nagging, yelling, and scolding can be rewarding to children. Parents who ignore their children when they behave inappropriately give no payoff for continuing misbehavior. If the ignoring is consistently maintained, children will eventually stop what they are doing, and as they receive approval and attention for appropriate behaviors, they will learn that it is more beneficial to behave appropriately than inappropriately.

While ignoring is highly effective with this class of behaviors, it is also probably the hardest technique for parents to carry out. The following are the key points we emphasize:

- Avoid eye contact and discussion while ignoring.

- Physically move away from the child but stay in the room if possible.

- Be subtle when ignoring.

- Be consistent.

- Combine distractions for the child with ignoring.

- Return attention to the child as soon as misbehavior stops.

- Limit the number of behaviors to ignore.

- Give attention to the child's positive behaviors.

Typical Questions and Concerns About Using the Ignore Approach

Isn't ignoring children's misbehavior unrealistic and irresponsible?

> I just can't see ignoring a child when he or she is smart-talking—being defiant and disrespectful. Why let a child verbally abuse you? These behaviors need discipline!

Frequently parents of behavior-problem children do not feel that ignoring is sufficient discipline. However, ignoring *is* an effective discipline approach because it maintains a positive parent–child relationship based on respect rather than fear. Ignoring teaches children that there is no payoff (such as parental attention in the form of gaze reactions or inter-actions, including power struggles) for inappropriate behaviors. When parents do not visibly react to these misbehaviors, their children lose their motive for continuing to use them. And when children come to realize that swearing and talking back do not get a reaction from their parents, whereas asking nicely does consistently result in approval and positive attention, they will begin to substitute positive behaviors for their negative ones. Moreover, when a parent ignores swearing or screaming instead of yelling at or criticizing the child, the parent is showing the child that s/he can maintain self-control in the face of conflict and anger—an effective model.

How long should you ignore?

I can do the ignoring approach for only so long—then I explode and yell at him.

Sometimes well-intentioned parents start to ignore misbehavior such as tantrums or arguments without being prepared for their child's response. For most children, when ignored, will initially react with an increase in negative behaviors. They are attempting to see if they can get their parents to back down. For instance, five-year-old Megan wants to go outside. She argues with her mother about this for several minutes. Finally her mother tells her she may not go outside and proceeds to ignore any protests. Megan escalates her demands to see if she can get what she wants. This goes on for 10 more minutes until her mother, exasperated and worn down by the arguments, says, "All right, go outside!" By giving in for the short-term benefit of making life more peaceful, the mother has created a long-term problem: Megan has learned that if she argues long and hard enough, she will get what she wants. Thus, her inappropriate behavior has been reinforced.

Remember to warn parents that when they first start ignoring a mis-behavior, it will usually get worse. If they are going to use this approach, which is powerfully effective, they must be prepared to wait out this period if the behavior is to improve. If they give in, their children will learn that persisting in the misbehavior is an effective way to get what they want.

Choosing to ignore misbehavior does not mean that there is nothing positive a parent can do to improve the situation. In fact, failure to provide distractions or suggestions for alternative, more appropriate behavior can lock parents and children into a power struggle and cause the children to prolong the misbehaviors. Consider this scenario: Tony asks his father to buy him a toy while they are out shopping. His father refuses and Tony starts yelling and screaming. His father effectively ignores this by walking away, and in a couple of minutes the screaming subsides. At this point, Tony's father might try to distract him with a new activity or something else to think about. Instead, he just waits for Tony to come and join him. Tony, feeling ignored, begins to scream again in an attempt to gain his father's attention.

Sometimes parents can use distraction to reduce their children's negative reaction to being ignored. Distractions are particularly useful with two- and three-year-olds, but they also work with older children. Once Tony stopped screaming, his father could have told him that when he saved up enough money from his allowance, he could buy the toy he wanted. The principle is to ignore the child's misbehavior in response to being told he cannot have something, and then distract him as soon as he starts behaving more appropriately. Of course, if the child misbehaves again in response to the distraction, the parent will need to resume ignoring.

What if you can't ignore the misbehavior?

> I can't ignore foul language. He verbally abuses me, and I don't think it's right to let him do that to me. It fills me with such rage that after ignoring it a couple of times I just lose it and yell at him.

Sometimes parents try to ignore a misbehavior that really bothers them. Then as the misbehavior escalates, they suddenly feel they cannot stand another minute of it and they explode with anger. There are several problems here. First, these parents wait until they are boiling with anger and about to lose control. Second, they give the child no warning. Third, this approach does not teach children anything except an explosive response to frustration.

Parents may not even be aware of the mounting anger that certain of their children's inappropriate behaviors trigger in them until they explode. The therapist can help parents learn to monitor their reactions to particular misbehaviors. Then, if parents find that swearing or whining (or any other behavior) triggers a strong emotional response, they may decide that it is not possible to ignore this behavior for very long. If this is the case, then the therapist should suggest the "Three Strikes and You're Out" Rule: parents tell their children that interrupting (or swearing) three times will result in a Time Out. The first time a child interrupts, the parent might say, "That was your first interruption." Then "That was the second interruption," and finally "That was your third interruption. Go to Time Out." This approach warns the child that the behavior is inappropriate and alerts the parent to his/her mounting annoyance level. With this approach, the parent is clear about exactly what type of behavior will result in Time Out and models an effective, calm, and rational approach to a problem behavior.

What if I am ignoring my child but others are not?

I tried ignoring his tantrums, but all the other children in the classroom laugh at him and at home my husband refuses to ignore such misbehavior—so what good does it do for me to ignore?

This is an important point. If the child's misbehavior is being reinforced or given attention by other children or adults in the room, then the parent's ignoring is probably going to be ineffective. In such a case, the parent needs to remove the child to another place where the child can be ignored effectively (as in a Time Out). Otherwise, another strategy should be used, such as telling the child s/he will lose a privilege or have to do a chore. Meanwhile, the parent should be sure to minimize the amount of attention the child is getting. Parents may also want to consider informing relatives, babysitters, neighbors, teachers, etc. ahead of time of the strategy and the targeted misbehaviors. If parents can get the cooperation of relatives and teachers to ignore some of these annoying behaviors, while reinforcing those positive behaviors that are opposite to the ones they are ignoring, then they will be likely to get quicker results.

How can you ignore a child who clings onto you?

I find that when I ignore his tantrums and yelling, he gets worse and starts to pull on my body and follow me around screaming. Sometimes he even ends up breaking something. It drives me crazy and I explode.

Sometimes it is reasonable for parents to ignore their child's misbehavior by walking out of the room. This can be an effective technique if the child is clinging and physically demanding attention from the parent. However, the difficulty with leaving the room is that the parent will not be able to pay attention to and reinforce appropriate child behavior when it occurs. When ignoring a clinging child, it may help for the parent physically to move away—to stand up and walk to another part of the room. This way the parent can monitor their child's behavior and reinforce her/him as soon as s/he stops misbehaving. If the child follows the parent, holding to his/her legs or arms, it may then be necessary to leave the room. One advantage to leaving the room for a few minutes is that it gives the parent time to calm down, to take a deep breath, and to regain perspective and focus on what is essential. However, the parent should return as soon as possible, in order to be able to reinforce appropriate behaviors when they occur.

Threatening the ultimate ignore?

> Okay, well, if ignoring works then I decided to use the ultimate ignore. He wouldn't get dressed and I asked him a hundred times so I finally said, "If you don't get your shoes on I will leave without you." Well, he wasn't ready so I got in the car and drove down the street. When I came back he was dressed and standing crying on the street—so it worked.

Parents who take ignoring to an extreme and threaten to leave their children—or, as in this case, actually do leave—believe that the fear caused by their leaving will mobilize the children into being more compliant. While such threats may get Ryan out through the door, they have several long-term disadvantages. In order to continue to be effective, all threats need to be backed up with the threatened consequence. Once a child realizes the parent is only pretending to leave, s/he will respond with similar threats: "Go ahead and leave me. See if I care!" The parent is then left in a powerless position because the child has called his/her bluff. Not to leave is to fail to follow through. Yet leaving is really no option, since a young child is not safe alone at home. The emotional hazard is also great, as threats to abandon children make them feel insecure and lead to poor self-esteem. Furthermore, parents are providing a powerful model, namely, avoiding conflict by running away from it. The child may begin threatening to run away or may leave home to test the power of this tactic for getting what s/he wants.

Parents should be cautioned never to threaten to leave or abandon their children, no matter how great the temptation. There are more effective strategies for inducing compliance. If parents can muster the self-control to ignore the behavior that makes them feel so angry, their child will begin to behave more appropriately, and the parent's frustration will decrease. If parents cannot use ignoring, they may need to try another discipline technique such as Time Out, chores, or loss of privileges. While these strategies will take more of parents' time in the short run, unlike leaving they teach children that the parent–child relationship is secure, regardless of conflict. These strategies are far preferable because they are based on respect, rather than on fear of abandonment.

TEACHING PARENTS ABOUT EFFECTIVE "TIME OUT" SKILLS

In the initial weeks of intervention, the therapists' main focus is to teach the parents the importance of providing the problem child with ongoing and regular communication and expression of parental love, support, and understanding. This provides the foundation for the child's ongoing emotional and social development. Next, the therapists teach parents how to provide clear limits and consequences for their children's misbehavior. Many parents have tried spanking, lecturing, criticism, and expressions of disapproval when their children are aggressive and noncompliant. However, research has shown that these are ineffective methods of discipline and usually parents of aggressive children find themselves spiraling into more and more spanking and yelling in order to get their children to respond. In fact, nagging, criticizing, hitting, shouting, or even reasoning with children while they misbehave are forms of parental attention and therefore actually reinforce the particular misbehavior; they result in children learning to nag, criticize, hit, shout, or argue in response to their parents.

We teach parents to use Time Out for high-intensity problems, such as fighting, defiance, hitting, and destructive behavior. The therapist can explain to parents that Time Out is actually an extreme form of parental ignoring in which children are removed for a brief period from all sources of positive reinforcement, especially adult attention. Here are the key points we emphasize:

- Monitor anger in order to avoid exploding suddenly; give warnings.

- Don't threaten Time Out unless prepared to follow through.

- Give five-minutes Time Out with two-minutes silence at the end.

- Ignore child while in Time Out.

- Be prepared for testing.

- Hold children responsible for messes in Time Out.

- Support a partner's use of Time Out.

- Carefully limit the number of behaviors for which Time Out is used.

- Don't rely exclusively on Time Out—combine with other techniques, such as ignoring, logical consequences, and problem-solving.

- Expect repeated learning trials.

- Use nonviolent approaches such as loss of privileges as back-up to Time Out.

- Use personal Time Out to relax and refuel energy.

- Be polite.

- Build up "bank account" with praise, love, and support.

Parents are often quite resistant to using this method, principally because Time Out has several short-term disadvantages. First, it is inconvenient: it requires advance planning and a special place to conduct the Time Out. Second, it is time-consuming and requires that parents keep themselves under control for a long period of time. Third, it is frustrating for parents because the child's misbehaviors may get worse before they get better, since children typically scream, bang on the walls, or break something during Time Out. Some parents resist Time Out because they do not think it results in enough remorse and pain from children, which they think are necessary for punishment to work effectively (some children even indicate they like Time Out!). Still other parents resist Time Out because they feel it represents rejection of the child. Conversely, many prefer spanking as the ultimate punishment because it is efficient and immediate, and most likely will stop the inappropriate behavior in the short term. The therapist's job will be to help parents understand how Time Out has more long-term advantages and is worth the extra effort in the short run.

Typical Questions and Concerns About Time Out

Isn't spanking preferable to Time Out?

I think spanking is better than Time Out because it works to get my child to obey; it's quick and lets the child know I am in control. After all, I was spanked as a child and I turned out okay.

Spanking is commonly used by parents because it is quick and usually stops the misbehavior in the short term. The problem with spanking is that it has long-term disadvantages. The first is that when a parent spanks a child, s/he models an aggressive response to misbehavior; children who are spanked frequently learn to resort to aggressive responses when they are frustrated. Even worse, when parents spank, they are often out of control or feel out of control. Besides being a frightening experience for their children, this loss of control creates feelings of guilt in the parents once they calm down. They may then respond by overcompensating with gifts (sometimes causing a child to endure spankings for the sake of the rewards) or by avoiding any use of discipline in the future. Another difficulty with spanking is that it tends to "wipe the slate clean" for children, leaving them with no ongoing sense of remorse for misbehavior. Frequently, the result is children who are compliant and conforming in the parents' presence but who are likely to behave inappropriately elsewhere. Yet another result of spanking is that children learn to hide or lie about problems in order to avoid being hit. In fact, the more hurtful the discipline—whether it be degrading criticisms or physical punishment—the more devious and resistant children become.

The task for the therapist is to teach parents an ethical approach to discipline that simultaneously lets children know which behaviors are inappropriate, gives children the positive expectation that they will be able to do better next time, and conveys that they are deeply loved. Methods such as ignoring, logical consequences, loss of privileges, problem-solving, and Time Out are effective discipline approaches that meet these criteria. Besides its ethical advantages, Time Out offers several practical advantages over spanking. It models a nonviolent response to conflict, stops the conflict and frustration, provides a cooling-off period for both children and parents and maintains a respectful, trusting relationship in which children feel they can be honest with their parents about their problems and mistakes. Unlike spanking, Time Out also forces children to reflect and fosters the development of an internal sense of responsibility or conscience.

One of the ways we deal with parents' resistance is by means of a values clarification exercise. We have the parent group list the short-term advantages of spanking versus Time Out. Next we list and discuss the long-term advantages of spanking versus Time Out. Through this process parents come to realize that spanking has short-term advantages for the parent (not the child) and long-term disadvantages for both. On the other hand, Time Out has short-term disadvantages for the parent and long-term advantages for both. Parents' understanding that they are working towards a long-term solution rather than a short-term "quick fix" helps create a willingness to try alternative approaches.

Isn't Time Out psychologically harmful?

I disagree with Time Out—it is harmful to children because parents are withdrawing their love, which is devastating for children.

Some parents avoid using Time Out because they want their relationships with their children, including discipline, to be democratic and equal. They believe that parents should never impose their authority or exercise their power over their children, and that reasoning with youngsters about their problems is preferable to putting them in Time Out. They may feel that Time Out is disrespectful to children and even a form of rejection, because it represents withdrawal of love.

First of all, it is important not to equate Time Out with a general style of child-rearing. Some parents are autocratic and expect complete obedience from their children. Such people may use Time Out to crush children's independence, creativity, problem-solving, and questioning of values. For example, they may use Time Out frequently throughout the day and for minor offences. Such parents might say in a critical tone of voice, "What is wrong with you? You never remember to pick up your things—You are driving me crazy! Go to Time Out." This approach does not help children to believe in themselves and inspires hostility from the child. Other parents are democratic; they solicit children's input and explain why certain behaviors are appropriate or inappropriate. These parents may use Time Out, not as punishment, but to teach children that there are consequences for misbehaving and that it is necessary to calm down before handling a conflict situation. For example, such a parent would say to the child who has just hit his brother, "I can see you are angry about your brother using your toy, but hitting is not okay in our family; you need to use your words. Please go to Time Out for five minutes." Remind parents that democratic child-rearing does not mean unlimited freedom with no rules, but rather freedom within limits. These limits have to be set and imposed, and within most families they usually include not hurting people or destroying things and cooperating in a respectful way with each other.

Secondly, Time Out should not be perceived as a substitute for reasoning with children and teaching them. It is only one tool to be used briefly when a child's anger or frustration level is high. Later, when things calm down and the child is behaving appropriately, parents can model, teach, and talk about other more appropriate problem-solving behaviors. Time Out is only one type of discipline strategy, and discipline strategies (including Time Out, logical consequences, loss of privileges, and ignoring) are only one aspect of managing behavior. Parents must capitalize on the many opportunities to teach their children appropriate behaviors—praising, encouraging, and building self-esteem whenever their children do something positive. Moreover, the parents' ability to model effective communication, conflict resolution, problem-solving, positive self-talk, playfulness, and empathy for another's feelings is integral to children's social and moral development. In a sense, what parents do is build up their family "bank account" with deposits of love, support, and understanding. Every now and again it will be necessary for a parent to temporarily make a "withdrawal" from the bank account and use Time Out. Therefore, it is important to keep the account constantly growing.

Isn't Time Out ineffective for some types of children?

> I've tried this Time Out stuff and it doesn't work—he just gets angrier and more destructive and misbehavior occurs again the next day. When he's in Time Out he has broken shelves and thrown things against the walls, which leaves holes in the wall. I don't think this is right.

Be sure to prepare parents for the possibility that when they first start using Time Out, the inappropriate behavior may get worse before it gets better. In fact, when some children are put in a Time Out room, they react violently by throwing things, breaking things, even hammering holes in the door. Some parents react by opening the door and spanking the child. Others refuse to use Time Out again for fear of getting the same response.

The therapist should explain that it is not uncommon for children to react strongly to Time Out, especially in the beginning. After all, if they can yell long and hard enough they may be able to get what they want—and if this has worked in the past to get a parent to back down, they will try long and hard enough until they are convinced that no matter what they do, such misbehavior results in no pay-off. On the other hand, they will discover that calming down quietly gets them out of Time Out sooner.

The therapist can help parents plan for possible difficulties with Time Out. If the child damages things in a room during a Time Out, parents can respond in several ways. First, the original command (if this is a Time Out for noncompliance) must be repeated. For example, if the child was in Time Out for not putting his bike away, then s/he will first have to put it away. Afterwards, s/he should be asked to clean up the Time Out room. If s/he has broken something, then s/he should be held responsible for paying for it out of his/her allowance or have some privilege removed for that day. If messes in Time Out are a frequent problem, then the parent may need to find a bare room (as bare as possible) or hallway which will be less interesting or reinforcing because it will provide a minimum of opportunities for making messes or breaking things.

Isn't Time Out too noisy to be used?

> I don't see how I could do Time Out: I live in an apartment with thin walls and
> if I put my son in Time Out he would scream violently so much that my
> neighbors would complain—they might even refer me to Child Protective
> Services. Already they complained to the landlord about the noise my son makes
> while he is playing.

A child yelling, screaming, swearing, and banging on the door during Time
Out can be an exhausting experience for parents. It is difficult to listen to
children misbehaving without feeling anxious, depressed, or angry, and
wondering "Will she ever stop this?" or "What did I do wrong?" or "It
can't be good for him to get so upset." It is also disconcerting for
neighbors to listen to a child screaming in an apartment when they do not
know what the parent is doing to evoke such a reaction. Their criticism of
parents is often based on their own fear that something abusive might be
happening to the child. Thus not only the child's reactions but also the
fear of complaints from neighbours can make it hard for parents to
continue Time Out for the full five minutes. After a noisy Time Out,
parents may suffer a "hangover" from trying to use Time Out and may
decide not to use it in the future. If this happens, the child has "won": s/he
has been successful in getting the parents to back down.

It is important to explain to parents that Time Out will be difficult at
times because all children will test the limits of discipline. This means that
if parents use Time Out for hitting, their children will hit again several
times in order to determine whether Time Out will follow predictably and
consistently. If they do not experience a consistent response from their
parents, children will continue to use hitting as a method of handling
conflict. The therapist needs to help the parent problem-solve how to
remain consistent, how to cope with the stress of enforcing a noisy Time
Out, and how to handle complaints from others who witness or overhear
the Time Out. Some possible strategies for the parents to cope with Time
Out reactions are to try distractions such as calling a supportive friend,
turning up the volume of the TV, listening to some calming music on
headphones, or doing some deep-breathing exercises. Parents can be
urged to try to plan their first attempts at Time Out during times when
neighbors are at work, so that they will not be overheard. Parents can also
explain the program to their neighbors so that neighbors understand
what the parent is doing and why this approach is being used. Neighbors
can be told that within several weeks there will be less and less use of
Time Out and that the overall noise level will be considerably reduced
if initially the child is forced to stay in Time Out until s/he is able to be
quiet.

Where can I do Time Out?

I don't see how I can do Time Out because I have no space. I live in a small trailer which has one bedroom, a bathroom, and a living room. It's packed with things. There is no place to do Time Out.

The therapist needs to help parents carefully consider where they will have Time Out for their children. Preferably it should be in a dull, boring room that has been made safe for a child to be alone in. Some families who have little space will need to use a bedroom for Time Out. This works for some children, but may not for others. The problem with the bedroom is that it usually contains items the child finds interesting. (The same can be true of any room.) Thus the lack of the parents' attention will be partially compensated for by the interesting features of the room—and the Time Out will lose its effect.

There is also the issue of safety—both of the child and of property. Some children cannot be safely left alone in the bathroom. For the highly aggressive child, any breakable items will need to be removed. If this is impossible (i.e., if the child is liable to damage a door or furniture) some other place must be found, such as a hallway. For some young children between the ages of four and eight, a Time Out chair can be used. This chair should be placed in an empty corner of a room or hall, away from all family activities and the television. However, if parents use a chair, they will also need to have a room as a back-up in case their child refuses to stay on the chair.

How long should I do Time Out?

He deliberately threw a rock and broke a neighbor's window. I was so mad I sent him to his room for a day-long Time Out. I don't think five minutes is long enough for something as bad as breaking a window—that misbehavior needs a more serious consequence.

A general rule of thumb is three minutes for three-year-olds, four minutes for four-year-olds and five minutes for children aged five and older. Time Outs longer than *five* minutes are not more effective. However, children should not be let out of Time Out until there has been two minutes of quiet, signaling that they have calmed down. This means that when you first use Time Out it may last longer (30 to 40 minutes) if children continue to scream. Once they learn that screaming does not get them out and that being quiet does, the Time Out will usually be short (five minutes or so).

The main idea is to make it as brief as possible and then immediately to give them an opportunity to try again and be successful.

It is easy for parents to believe that Time Out is more effective if they make it longer—especially if their children have done something really bad like breaking a window or stealing. Some parents add time on whenever their children yell or misbehave in the Time Out room. This is especially problematic if parents are also yelling through the door, "That is one more minute for that scream," since this attention will actually increase the misbehavior. Overly long Time Outs tend to breed resentment in children, and the isolation keeps them from making new efforts to behave appropriately, thereby learning and experiencing success.

Some parents have just the opposite problem. They use Time Out for a minute and then let their children out when they bang on the door, cry, or promise to behave. Unfortunately, letting children out when they are still misbehaving reinforces that particular inappropriate behavior. The message communicated is, "If you kick (or cry or promise) hard enough, I'll let you out."

The most effective Time Out need only be five minutes, provided there has been two minutes of quiet at the end. Adding time on for misbehaving does not make it more effective or eliminate the problems and, in fact, may do just the opposite. Remember, with children, there is no need for the punishment to fit the crime. Time Out is not meant to be like a jail sentence for adults. Its purpose is to provide a cooling-off period and a clear, unrewarding consequence for misbehavior. The objective is for parents to get their children out of Time Out either in five minutes or as soon as they are quiet, so as to give them another chance to be successful.

What should you say to the child while he is in Time Out?

> When a child misbehaves, what should you tell the child about Time Out? I usually remind him several times while he is in Time Out that he needs to be quiet before he can come out—sometimes this makes him scream longer, but I'm not sure he remembers what he needs to do.

Some parents inadvertently give attention to their children while they are in Time Out. For instance, Timmy yells in the Time Out room, and Timmy's Dad responds to each yell with "You must be quiet before you can come out." Other parents respond to their children each time they ask, "How many more minutes?" Still others go in and out of the Time Out room, either to check on their children or to return them when they come out. All these actions defeat the purpose of Time Out and are very reinforcing for children.

There should be no communication with children when they are in Time Out. No matter how many times a parent explains to a child that s/he must be quiet to get out of Time Out, the child will not really understand the rules of Time Out until s/he has experienced them. For example, once children have experienced no response from their parents for yelling profanities, but have experienced that their quiet behavior gets them out of Time Out, they will begin to really understand the concept. If a parent is likely to feel compelled to enter a Time Out room for fear that his daughter will break something, any items she could break should be removed from the room or a new location found. If a child keeps coming out of the room, it may be necessary to put a lock on the door for a short while until she learns that she cannot come out until she is quiet. If the parent uses a Time Out chair and the child manages to attract the attention of the dog, siblings, or other adults, it may be necessary to move the chair to a duller location, away from the rest of the family.

Once Time Out is over, shouldn't you remind him of why he was put there?

> I always discuss the problem with him again after Time Out is over—I want to be sure he understands why he went into Time Out in the first place. I don't want him to be making the same mistake again.

Sometimes parents feel they have to remind their children why they had to go to Time Out—"You were put in Time Out because you hit. Remember not to hit. It makes me really angry." This is rubbing the child's nose in the mistake and reviving the image of the child misbehaving. The reminder of past misbehavior becomes, for the child, a prediction of future misbehaviors. It is better to say, "Now let's try again. I know you can do it." Once Time Out is over, the parents should view this as a clean slate or a new learning trial—a chance to try again and be successful. They should predict success, not remind children or "lecture" them on what they did wrong.

What should you do if your child runs away?

> My child runs away when I ask him to go to Time Out—I end up chasing him and dragging him to Time Out. Sometimes I have to spank him to get him to go to Time Out. Then when I finally get him in Time Out, he won't stay there and keeps coming out.

When parents resort to spanking or physical restraint to get their children to go to or stay in Time Out, they may justify their use of these violent techniques by saying that they were used as a last resort after all else failed, or they may believe that since the spanking or restraint resulted in Time Out, their use was justified. The problem with this "the-end-justifies-the-means" analysis is that violent forms of discipline defeat the purposes of Time Out and focus only on the short-term goals of getting children to comply and maintaining control. Unfortunately, the short-term benefits are outweighed by the long-term disadvantages, as discussed above: increasing children's aggression and providing a model for violent approaches to conflict situations. Such situations are much better handled by combining Time Out with a loss of privileges. This technique models a nonviolent approach that maintains good relationships with children.

The therapist can suggest alternative strategies. First, if young children will not stay in the Time Out room, the parent may have to install a temporary lock. In most instances the parent will only need to use it once or twice before the child learns that s/he must stay in the room until s/he is quiet. If the children are five or six years old and they come out of Time Out, parents can try a different approach. After one warning ("If you don't go back into Time Out now, you'll have your bike locked up for 24 hours," "There'll be no bedtime story tonight," or "No soccer game after dinner"), if the child still refuses to go into Time Out, then the parent must enforce the loss of the privilege and the Time Out is dropped. Loss of privileges are not as effective with young preschool children because they cognitively have a difficult time seeing the connection between the misbehavior and the consequence enforced at a later time.

If the children are old enough to understand the concept of time and they refuse to go into Time Out in the first place, add an extra minute to Time Out—but only up to 10 minutes. At that point the parent should give one warning about a loss of a privilege: "If you don't go to Time Out now, you will not be allowed to watch television tonight." For younger children who refuse to go to Time Out, the parent can calmly but firmly take their hand and bring them to Time Out.

Time Out won't work if it's not painful to the child

> My child just goes to Time Out and doesn't cry or anything. He used to scream and yell when I sent him there, but now he shows no remorse or guilt or pain. So I don't think Time Out is working anymore because he doesn't show any discomfort.

Some parents believe that in order for Time Out to be an effective form of discipline it must result in a child expressing pain or remorse over the misbehavior. If this doesn't happen, they mistakenly think it is not working and stop using it. They may consider spanking more effective because it is more likely to result in tears and expressions of remorse. However, as we have seen, physical punishment, even when it eliminates undesirable behavior in the short run, tends to cause more problems because it teaches a violent approach to conflict and does not help children to learn how to problem-solve or cool down so that they can cope with a problem. Tears may satisfy a parent's need for "just deserts," but do not necessarily reflect effective discipline.

Time Out does not need to result in tantrums, crying, or expressions of guilt in order to be effective. In the beginning, young children may react violently when Time Out is used, but if it is used consistently and frequently, most will eventually take it without much anger. We have even found that some children put themselves in Time Out when they feel they are losing control. Thus, Time Out helps children learn self-control.

Parents should be warned that some children will tell them that Time Out does not bother them, but they should not be fooled by this approach. Their children may be only bluffing. Besides, Time Out can achieve its purpose even if the child is not bothered by it. Remember, the purpose of Time Out is not to get revenge or make children experience pain, but rather to stop the conflict and withdraw the reinforcing effects of negative attention for a misbehavior. It gives children a cooling off period and a chance to think about what they have done.

What about the child who refuses to come out of Time Out?

I put my child in Time Out for refusing to do her homework and she just stayed there—she wouldn't come out and eventually she fell asleep. What should I have done?

Time Out can result in at least two types of stand-offs instigated by children or by parents. The first involves those children who refuse to come out of Time Out once it is over. Some parents respond by letting their children stay in the Time Out room as long as they wish. This is inappropriate in the instance where Time Out is used as a consequence for noncompliance to a command. In such cases, parents are not following through with the original command; their children learn that they can get out of doing something by staying in the Time Out room.

If a child refuses to come out of Time Out to take out the garbage, the parent should close the door and add two minutes to the Time Out. This can be continued for up to 10 minutes and then a privilege can be withdrawn. If the child is in Time Out for hitting, the door can be opened and the parent can say, "Your time is up. You can come out now." It is all right in this instance if the child refuses to come out, because there is nothing that the parent has asked her to do. The parent can simply respond, "Come out whenever you are ready," and ignore any refusal.

Another type of stand-off happens when a parent refuses to talk to a child for an hour or even a whole day and, in a sense, carries out an extended Time Out. As mentioned earlier, this does not teach children how to deal with conflict in an appropriate fashion; rather, it teaches them to withdraw from conflict. Refusing to speak to children for long periods after misbehavior only escalates tension and anger. This refusal of attention is in effect an extended Time Out; as discussed above, overly long Time Outs breed resentment and, in this case, defeat communication. In this situation, the parent should think about what is bothering him or her, what behavior is expected and then state it clearly. For instance, "I'm angry that you broke my vase. You will have to clean up the mess now and pay for it out of your allowance. I'll help you pick up the pieces."

How do you do Time Out in public?

> The reason I like spanking is because it is portable. I can use that strategy at the grocery store or park when he misbehaves. I don't see how you could use Time Out in situations like that.

When children misbehave in public places such as restaurants, movie theaters, and grocery stores, parents are often reluctant to use their usual forms of discipline. Some worry about how other people will react if they use Time Out with their children in public. Others are afraid their children will escalate their misbehavior into a full-blown tantrum, so they avoid discipline. Still others do not see how Time Out can be used anywhere but at home, and resort instead to threats and spankings. As a result, many children have learned that grocery stores and restaurants are places they can get their own way because their parents will give in to avoid a scene.

Once parents have established Time Out as a consistent consequence for certain misbehaviors at home, it is important to impose the same consequence when these misbehaviors occur in public places as well. This may mean leaving the grocery store to do a modified five-minute Time Out in the car or next to a tree in a park. If there is no place for a Time Out, the parent can say, "If you don't stop yelling (or whining or whatever), then you'll have a Time Out when we get home." Once parents have followed through once or twice, their children will learn that the rules apply regardless of where they are, and they will stop testing and learn to behave more appropriately.

Can you use Time Out too much?

> It seems like I have him in Time Out most of the time he is home. Sometimes he is in there 20 times a day. Is there a problem with this?

Time Out is frequently used for all kinds of things, from whining, yelling, and screaming to throwing, hitting, and lying. Some parents report using it 20 to 30 times a day! This overuse deprives misbehaving children of opportunities to learn or demonstrate good behavior. It does not teach them any new and more appropriate ways to behave. While it keeps them out of parents' hair in the short run, in the long run it can cause bitterness and make children feel that they can do nothing right.

If any parents have become "Time Out junkies," the therapist needs to help them to focus on one or two misbehaviors that will result in Time Out. After three or four weeks, when these behaviors are eliminated, another one can be identified. More importantly, the therapist must help the parents ensure that they are spending more time supporting, teaching, and encouraging appropriate behaviors than focusing on negative ones. Sometimes parents are clear with their children about the consequences for misbehaving but do not provide attention and encouragement for appropriate behaviors. In other words, much emphasis is placed on what children should not do, and there is considerably less emphasis on what to do instead. Time Out will only work when parental attention and positive consequences for appropriate behaviors are frequent.

Won't Time Out turn my child in a compliant "little robot"?

> I don't want my child to be compliant all the time. I want her to be assertive, to question authority, and not to be a little robot. Isn't timing out for non-compliance going to make my child into a little marine recruit? For instance, I certainly want her to say "no" to strangers.

This question is related to the preceding question because it refers to the misuse or abuse of Time Out. Just as it is possible to use Time Out too much, it is also possible to abuse it by using it as the sole discipline technique. Rather, the therapist should help the parents determine which misbehaviors (e.g., hitting, destructive acts) would be appropriate for a

Time Out consequence, which misbehaviors will be handled through problem-solving, logical consequences, loss of privileges, and praising alternative positive responses.

However, this parent may be raising a larger question than the use of Time Out *per se*—that is, how much to discipline children's misbehavior or enforce compliance. As we discussed in the Limit-Setting section, the first task for parents is to decide what their important household rules are and to limit their rules and commands to the important issues which they are prepared to follow through on. Thus the parent allows the child to make his/her own choices when possible, fosters independence and self-assertion, but sets clear and consistent limits when children are breaking important rules or hurting others.

The other issue raised by this parent is one of whether forcing children to be compliant could lead them into potentially dangerous situations because they do not know how to say "no" to strangers or to people who ask them to do inappropriate things. The key point here seems to be for parents to teach their children how to respond to adults (or children) who are asking them to do something that is unsafe or dangerous—in this case, the child needs to learn how to be assertive.

Time Out doesn't work

I've tried Time Out and it doesn't work for my child.

Some parents claim that Time Out does not work for them. The reason may be any of those we have discussed, or it may simply be that they have tried it a few times and then given up. It is a mistake, however, to try Time Out four or five times and expect the problem behavior to be eliminated.

Time Out is not magic. Children need repeated learning trials. They need many opportunities to make mistakes and misbehave, and then to learn from the consequences of their misbehaviors. Just as it takes hundreds of trials for a baby to learn to walk, so it takes children hundreds of trials to learn appropriate social behaviors. The therapist's job is to remind parents that even when Time Out is used effectively, behavior changes slowly. Parents need support from therapists to be patient. Remind parents that it takes children at least 18 years to learn all the mature adult behaviors their parents would like to see them demonstrate.

What do you do when you know you are so angry you won't be able to do a Time Out?

Sometimes I feel so angry I just don't have the patience to do Time Out—I just want to hit him and make him suffer.

Parents overreact to their children's misbehaviors because they are exhausted, angry, or depressed about some other events in their life. A father who gets angry at his daughter may really be angry at his wife for ignoring his efforts with the children. Or a mother who has had an exhausting day at work and had a conflict with her secretarial staff may become cross with her children for making noise and not letting her relax. Depending on the mood and the energy level of the parent, the same behavior from a child can seem cute one day and obnoxious the next.

Even the kindest, best-intentioned parents get frustrated and angry with their children. No one is perfect. But the important task is for parents to recognize the "filters" they bring to their perceptions of their children at any particular time, and to learn to cope with their anger or frustration. Sometimes it is the parent who needs a Time Out. If a parent is depressed because of work problems, it may be a good idea to take a Time Out away from the children in order to relax and gain perspective. If a parent is angry with his/her spouse, s/he may need Time Out to problem-solve. In helping children become less aggressive and more able to problem-solve and handle conflict constructively, it is vital that parents use personal Time Out when they feel anger building, and to model ways to resolve conflict and ways to support one another.

TEACHING PARENTS ABOUT NATURAL AND LOGICAL CONSEQUENCES

One of the most important and difficult tasks for parents of oppositional and conduct-problem children is to help their children become more independent and responsible. The therapist can help parents learn to foster their children's decision-making, sense of responsibility, and ability to learn from mistakes through the use of natural and logical consequences. A natural consequence is whatever would result from a child's action or inaction in the absence of adult intervention. For instance, if Ryan slept in or refused to go to the school bus, the natural consequence would be that he would have to walk to school. If Caitlin did not want to wear her coat, then she would get cold. In these examples, the children learn from experiencing the direct consequences of their own decisions—thus they are not protected from the possibility of an undesirable outcome of their behavior by their parents' commands. A logical consequence, on the other hand, is designed by the parent. It is conceived of as "punishment to fit the crime." A logical consequence for a youngster who broke a neighbor's window would be to do chores in order to make up the cost of the replacement. A logical consequence for stealing would be to take the object back to the store, apologize to the store owner, and do an extra chore or lose a privilege. In other words, when parents use this technique, they hold children accountable for their mistakes—by helping them make up the error in some way.

In conflict to ignoring and Time Out, natural and logical consequences teach children to be more responsible. These strategies are most effective for recurring problems where parents are able to decide ahead of time how they will follow through in the event that the misbehavior recurs. For example, the parent who says, "If you aren't dressed for school by 8 a.m., you will have to go in your pajamas" or "If you spend all your allowance on candy, you'll have no money for that movie you want to rent" is informing the child ahead of time what will be the consequence if s/he continues the behavior. Then the child has a choice and is in effect responsible for the outcome. On the other hand, the parent who does not let the child know ahead of time is not necessarily helping the child see the connection between the behavior and the negative outcome.

These are the main points we emphasize concerning natural and logical consequences:

■ Make consequences immediate.

■ Make consequences age-appropriate.

■ Make consequences nonpunitive.

■ Use consequences that are short and to the point.

■ Involve the child whenever possible.

■ Be friendly and positive.

■ Give the child a choice of consequences ahead of time.

■ Be sure parents can live with the consequences they have set up.

■ Quickly offer new learning opportunities to be successful.

Typical Questions and Concerns About Natural and Logical Consequences

What kinds of misbehaviors would I use a natural or logical consequence for?

I get confused about when I should ignore a misbehavior or use Time Out or use logical consequences. How do I decide which approach is correct?

Natural and logical consequences are most effective for recurring problems where the parents can decide ahead of time with the child what will happen if the child continues the behavior. For example, a parent might warn a child, "If you can't keep the gum in your mouth, it will be taken away" or "If you don't eat at meals, there will be no food until the next meal" and so forth. This approach can help children to learn to make decisions, be responsible for their own behavior, and learn from their mistakes. Time Out is best reserved for more serious problems when the child is hurting someone or breaking something. For these aggressive acts, it is not appropriate to give the child a warning; a warning only conveys a message that they have another chance to be aggressive. Ignoring, on the other hand, can be used for minor annoying behaviors that are not hurting anyone, such as whining, messy eating, tantrums, and protests.

What kinds of consequences are developmentally appropriate for children?

I tried making my three 3-year-old child clean up his poopy pants as a way of discouraging him from messing in his pants—but that just made an incredible mess in the bathroom and I ended up yelling at him.

When I found my teenager smoking, I told her that if she got an asthma attack (which she gets) then she would have to earn the money to pay for her asthma medicine—was that logical?

I let my four-year-old child go to school in bare feet in the middle of winter as a way of teaching him to get his shoes on in the morning—isn't that a natural consequence?

When thinking through the use of logical and natural consequences as a means of reducing children's inappropriate behaviors, it is important to be sure that parents' expectations are appropriate for the child's age and abilities. Because of the cognitive skills involved, natural consequences will work better for school-age children than for preschoolers. For example, young children will not often see the connection between not eating dinner and being hungry two hours later. Consequences that young children do understand are "if—then" statements that have an immediate consequence, for instance, "If you don't keep your gum in your mouth, I will have to take it away." Or for a child who points scissors at someone, "If you can't use the scissors carefully, then I will remove them." In these examples, the logical consequence of not using something appropriately and/or safely is having it removed right away.

Most natural and logical consequences work best for children five years of age and older. They can be used with younger children, but parents must first evaluate carefully whether the children understand the relationship between the consequences and the behavior. For instance, if Alexandra is not ready to be toilet-trained but she is made to clean her underpants or change her bed, she is being unjustly punished; the consequence is inappropriate for her abilities. However, to deny dessert or snacks to a child who has refused to eat dinner is an appropriate consequence since the child learns that not eating dinner causes hunger. Whether it is appropriate to expect a teenager to pay for her asthma medicine when she chooses to smoke depends upon the cost of the medicine and her ability to earn that amount of money. Of course, natural consequences should not be used if children may be physically hurt by them. For example, a preschooler should not be allowed to experience the natural consequences of sticking a finger into an electrical outlet, touching the stove, running in the road, or going barefoot in freezing weather.

What about consequences that are neither natural nor logical?

When he swore at me, I washed his dirty mouth out with soap. He doesn't swear at me anymore! Wasn't that logical?

Occasionally parents come up with consequences that are not naturally or logically related to an activity. Consider the mother who washed her son's mouth out with soap because he swore at her. While she might argue that it is logical to clean out the mouth of a youngster who has been swearing, the "logic" is based only on a figure of speech (swearing = "dirty" talk). Her action is likely to make her son feel degraded and angry. Other parents create consequences that are too punitive: "Since you wet your bed last night, you can't have anything to drink after noon today" or "Because you didn't eat your dinner, you will have to eat it for breakfast" or "Since you hit me, I'm going to bite you." Children will feel resentful and may even retaliate against such consequences. They will be more likely to focus on the cruelty of their parents than on the consequences of their own behavior.

A calm, matter-of-fact, friendly attitude on the part of parents is essential for deciding upon and carrying out consequences. The natural consequence of not wearing a coat when it is cold outside is to become chilled. The logical consequence of not doing homework might be to miss a favorite television program. The natural consequence of not putting clothes in the hamper is that the clothes do not get washed. These consequences are not degrading, nor do they cause physical pain. Instead, they help children to learn to make choices and to be more responsible.

Are some consequences too remote to be effective?

> I let him watch TV instead of doing his homework so that he could experience poor grades on his spelling test. Indeed, he came home with many corrections—but he just seemed more helpless and I'm not sure the natural consequences approach worked.

The natural and logical consequences approach does not work when the consequences of misbehaviors are too remote in time. The natural consequences of not brushing teeth would be to have cavities and to have to submit to dental work. But this would never be effective as a motivator—the cavities would not show up for five to ten years! Similarly, overeating may have long-term consequences that are too distant to affect children's behavior in the short term. Permitting youngsters not to do homework and to watch television every night until the end-of-the-year report card shows they have failed is another consequence that is too delayed to have any influence on their daily study habits. Such long-term punishers may instead lead children to feel hopeless about their abilities.

For preschool and school-age children it is important that the consequences closely follow the inappropriate behavior. If Dan damages another child's toy, then the toy should be replaced as quickly as possible and he should have to help pay for it through chores or from his allowance. If Lisa does not put her clothes in the laundry hamper, they will not be clean when she wants to wear them. In this way, Lisa and Dan will learn from their inappropriate behavior and will probably behave more appropriately the next time. Of course, the preschool child may not be bothered by whether he has bowel movement in his pants or is wearing dirty clothes or goes outside without a coat. In these cases, the parent will need to decide whether the issue is important enough to limit-set or can be left up to the child.

Can some consequences be too punitive?

> I find that sometimes I feel really nasty when I use logical or natural consequences. For example, the other day I sent my children to school without breakfast because they weren't ready on time— I felt terrible sending a child to school without breakfast.

When attempting to carry out natural and logical consequences, some parents find it difficult to allow their children to experience the outcomes of their actions. They are so empathetic towards their children, or they feel so guilty for not coming to their aid, that they intervene before the consequence occurs. For instance, Carol tells her daughter Angie that the natural consequence of dawdling in the morning and not being ready for daycare on time will be to go in her pajamas. When the time comes to enforce this, she cannot bring herself to let Angie go in her pajamas and dresses her instead. Such overprotectiveness can handicap children by not allowing them to develop their own coping strategies, rendering them incapable of handling problems or mistakes.

When using consequences it is important for parents to think about the pros and cons of applying this technique to particular misbehaviors. Advise parents that they must be certain that they can live with the consequences and are not giving idle threats. In the example above, Carol should have first considered whether or not she would be willing to follow through and take Angie to daycare in her pajamas if she continued to dawdle. Failing to follow through with an agreed-upon consequence will dilute parents' authority and deprive their children of opportunities to learn from their mistakes.

Can some logical consequences be too long?

> My child kept forgetting to put his bike away and left it in the driveway, so I locked it up for a month. Do you think this was too long?

Sometimes parents come up with a consequence that lasts too long and constitutes undue punishment. Say that seven-year-old Ben rides his bicycle in the road after being told to stay on the driveway. The logical consequence would be for the parents to lock it up. Locking it up for a month, however, would be excessive; it would certainly make Ben feel resentful at the injustice. Moreover, he would be deprived of any new opportunities to handle his bicycle more responsibly. Although some people believe that the stronger (and longer) the punishment, the more effective it will be, the opposite is true—because a shorter punishment allows an earlier opportunity for behaving appropriately.

A more subtle consequence in Ben's case would have been to lock up his bike for 24 hours and then allow him the chance to ride it according to the rules. If four-year-old Kathy is using crayons and starts coloring on the kitchen table, a logical consequence to present her with might be, "If you can't keep the crayons on the paper, then I will have to take them away." If she continues to color on the table, then the crayons would have to be removed. However, they should be returned within half an hour to give her another opportunity to use them appropriately. The principle is to make the consequences immediate, short, to the point, and then quickly to offer the child another chance to try again and be successful.

Remind parents that the consequences approach, like any other parenting technique, takes time, planning, patience, and repetition. Most of all, it requires a calm, respectful attitude.

TEACHING PARENTS TO TEACH THEIR CHILDREN TO PROBLEM-SOLVE

How do young conduct-problem children typically react to their problems? By crying, hitting, swearing, running away, refusing, or tattling to their parents. These responses to problems usually do not lead to solutions; in fact, they create new problems. Of course, all children will exhibit these responses to conflict, but research has indicated that when presented with interpersonal problem situations, conduct-problem and rejected children find it difficult to consider alternative courses of action. They search for fewer clues or facts and generate fewer appropriate solutions to conflict situations. They produce a high percentage of aggressive and incompetent solutions than do cooperative children and have a more difficult time anticipating the consequences of their solutions. They act aggressively and impulsively without stopping to think of nonaggressive solutions. On the other hand, there is evidence from research that young children who employ a wide range of alternative and competent strategies on problem-solving tasks tend to play more constructively, are better liked, and are less aggressive. Therefore the purpose of this component of the program is for the therapist to teach parents how they can teach their children appropriate problem-solving skills.

The therapist should emphasize the importance of parental modeling as a way to teach children problem-solving skills. It is a rich learning experience for children to watch parents discussing problems with other adults, negotiating and resolving conflict, and evaluating the outcomes of their actions. While parents may not want their children to observe all their discussions, many daily interactions provide good opportunities for children to learn. For instance, children learn much of their behavior by observing how parents react to life's daily hassles. They learn from noticing how their parents say "no" to a friend's request. They watch with interest how Dad receives Mom's suggestion to wear something different. Is Mom sarcastic, angry, or matter-of-fact in her request? Does Dad pout, get angry, cooperate, or ask for more information? Watching parents decide which movie to see on Saturday night can teach much about compromise and negotiation. Parents can help further by thinking out loud their positive problem-solving strategies. For example, a parent might say, "How can I solve this? I need to stop and think first. What plan can I come up with to make this successful?" If parents themselves do not routinely problem-solve, then the therapist will need to teach them these skills first before teaching them how to help their children learn to problem-solve.

In addition to parents teaching their children problem-solving skills indirectly through modeling, the therapist also teaches parents the specific skills to teach their children when problem-solving. These steps include: helping the child to define the problem, acknowledging the child's feelings, helping the child generate solutions and think about the consequences of the possible solutions, deciding which solution to try, and reinforcing the process. We suggest that the parents begin to teach their children these skills by role playing or acting them out with puppets or books. We recommend that these discussions occur at neutral times, not in the heat of battle. Once parents have taught children the steps and the language to talk about problems, they can then begin to help them learn how to use the skills in the midst of real conflict.

Here are the main points we emphasize:

- Help children define the problem.

- Talk about feelings.

- Involve children in brainstorming possible solutions.

- Be positive and imaginative.

- Model creative solutions.

- Encourage children to think through the possible consequences of different solutions.

■ Remember that it is the process of learning how to think about conflict that is critical, rather than getting "correct" answers.

Typical Questions and Concerns About Problem-Solving

Shouldn't you tell children the correct solutions?

> I feel I need to tell my children how to solve the problem because they don't come up with the right answer on their own—in fact, some of their own solutions are really bad!

Many parents believe that telling their children how to solve a problem helps them learn to problem-solve. For example, two children may have trouble sharing a bicycle. The parent responds to the child who has grabbed the bicycle from the other child (who has refused to share the bike) by saying, "You should either play together or take turns. Grabbing is not nice. You can't go around grabbing things. Would you like that if he did it to you?" The problem with this approach is that the parents are telling the children what to do before they have found out what the problem is from their viewpoint. It is possible, after all, that the parent has misdiagnosed the problem. For example, in this case it was not entirely the fault of the child who grabbed the bicycle because the other child had used the bike for a long time and had refused to share it even when asked nicely. As the child continued to refuse to share, the other child escalated to grabbing. Moreover, the parent's approach in this example does not help the children to think about their problem and how to solve it. Rather than being encouraged to learn how to think, they are told what to think and the solution is imposed upon them.

It is more effective for parents to guide their children into thinking about what may have caused the problem in the first place, rather than to tell them the solution. Parents can invite their children to come up with possible solutions. If parents want to help them develop a habit of solving their own problems, children need to be asked to think for themselves. They should be urged to express their feelings about the situation, talk about ideas for solving the problem, and talk about what might happen if they carried out various solutions. The only time parents need to offer solutions is if their children need a few ideas to get them started.

Is there such a thing as too little guidance?

> Well, I just tell my children to work it out on their own. I think that's the only way children will learn to problem-solve. Don't you agree?

The opposite problem occurs when parents think they are helping their children resolve conflict by telling them to work it out for themselves. This might work if the children already have good problem-solving skills, but for most young children, this approach will not work. In a case where Max and Tyler are fighting over a book, nonintervention will probably result in continued arguing and Tyler, the more aggressive child, getting the book. Therefore, Tyler is reinforced for his inappropriate behavior, because he got what he wanted, and Max is reinforced for giving in, because the fighting ceased when he backed down.

The parents' role is to teach their children to work it out on their own by guiding them. Parents can encourage their children to talk aloud as they think and then can praise their ideas and attempts at solutions. In this way, the parents are reinforcing the development of a style of thinking that will help them to deal with all kinds of problems throughout their lives. Parents need to encourage their children first to come up with many possible solutions. Then they can help them to shift their focus to the possible consequences of each solution. The final step in problem-solving is to help children evaluate their possible solutions. For children aged three to eight, the second step—generating solutions—is the key skill to learn. While older children are more easily involved in anticipating consequences and evaluating them, youngsters need to be helped to generate possible solutions and to understand that some solutions are better than others.

Feelings don't have much to do with problem-solving, do they?

I don't talk much about feelings with my children. What value is there in this?

When some parents problem-solve, they avoid discussing feelings. They focus exclusively on the thinking style, the nature of the problem, the solution, and the consequences. They forget to ask their children how they feel about the problem or how the other person in the situation may have felt. Yet these are aspects of defining the problem. It is also important for parents to be aware of their own feelings. Hearing a daughter report that she has been sent home from Julie's house for hitting may provoke feelings in the parent such as anger, frustration, or even depression. A parent would need to gain control of these emotions before trying to help her child with her feelings about the situation.

Parents need to encourage their children to think about their own feelings in a problem situation or in response to a possible solution, and parents can help their children consider the other person's point of view in the situation. For instance, a parent might ask, "How do you think Julie felt when you did that? How did you feel when she did that?" Parents need to raise the question about how a child might discover what someone else feels or thinks. "How can you find out if she likes your idea? How can you tell if she is sad or happy?" This will help parents encourage their children to be more empathetic and, because they try to understand other people's feelings and viewpoints, will result in more willingness to problem-solve, compromise, and cooperate. When parents discuss children's feelings, it also helps children to realize that their feelings are important and that their parents empathize with them.

BROADENING THE FOCUS OF INTERVENTION

As we noted in Chapter 1, researchers have convincingly demonstrated that parental personal and interpersonal factors (depression, marital discord, etc.) and contextual factors (lack of support, increased environmental stressors, etc.) disrupt parenting behavior and contribute to parent training treatment relapses (e.g., Webster-Stratton, 1990a,b). As a result, more broadly based expansions of parent training have been developed to address more of these personal and interpersonal issues that affect family functioning. In our own work with families at the Parenting Clinic we have expanded the focus of the content of our interventions to include: *Personal Self-Control* strategies such as how to cope with anger, depression, and stress; *Effective Communication Skills* such as active listening, expressive speaking, and avoidance of destructive styles of communicating (e.g., blaming, mind-reading, criticizing, stonewalling, patronizing, commanding); *Problem-Solving Skills* such as using a structured format for handling interpersonal conflict with spouses, employers, extended family members, or children; and *Ways to Strengthen Social Support and Self-Care*. It is beyond the scope of this book to discuss the content details of each of these components; more information on these topics may be found in the parent trouble-shooting guide (Webster-Stratton, 1992a) and from our ADVANCE therapists' manual (Webster-Stratton, 1992c). In a recent study we reported that families who received this broader program of training in personal and interpersonal skills showed significant additional improvements in parents' communication skills, problem-solving skills, and consumer satisfaction, as well as children's increased knowledge of prosocial solutions (Webster-Stratton, in press). These data suggest that interventions such as these may strengthen the family's "protective factors," thereby mediating the effects of other, more intractable risk factors such as socioeconomic disadvantage and negative life stressors.

REFERENCES

Barkley, R.A. (1987). *Defiant children: A clinician's manual for parent training.* New York: Guilford.

Forehand, R.L. & McMahon, R.J. (1981). *Helping the noncompliant child: A clinician's guide to parent training.* New York: Guilford.

Herbert, M. (1987). *Behavioural treatment of children with problems: A practice manual.* London: Academic Press.

Patterson, G.R., Reid, J.B., Jones, R.R. & Conger, R.W. (1975). *A social learning approach to family intervention.* Eugene, OR: Castalia.

Webster-Stratton, C. (1990a). Long-term follow-up of families with young conduct problem children: From preschool to grade school. *Journal of Clinical Child Psychology,* **19**(2), 144–149.

Webster-Stratton, C. (1990b). Predictors of treatment outcome in parent training for families with conduct problem children. *Behavior Therapy,* **21**, 319–337.

Webster-Stratton, C. (1992a). *The incredible years: A trouble-shooting guide for parents of children aged 3–8.* Toronto, Canada: Umbrella Press.

Webster-Stratton, C. (1992b). *The Parents and Children Videotape Series: Programs 1–10.* Seth Enterprises, 1411 8th Avenue West, Seattle, WA 98119, USA.

Webster-Stratton, C. (1992c). The Parents and Children Videotape Series: Advance Programs 5–7. Seth Enterprises, 1411 8th Avenue West, Seattle, WA 98119, USA.

Webster-Stratton, C. (in press). Advancing videotape parent training: A companion study. *Journal of Consulting and Clinical Psychology.*

8 EPILOGUE: FUTURE DIRECTIONS

WHEN IT comes to behavior problems, nothing seems to have changed very much over the years. Take the following quotation:

> The children now love luxury. They have bad manners, contempt for authority; they show disrespect to their elders and love to chatter in places of exercise. They no longer rise when the elders enter the room. They contradict parents, chatter before company, gobble up dainties at the table, cross their legs and are tyrants over their teachers.

This could be a member of the present-day older generation bemoaning the lowering of standards among the youth of today. But, in fact, the complainant, writing in the fifth century BC, is Socrates. Or take the following quotation from an Egyptian priest, 6000 years ago: "Our earth is degenerate; children no longer obey their parents." In light of this longevity, can we, today, expect to put an end to children's behavior problems? Certainly not! Children always have, and always will, "misbehave." It is a natural, normal, and, in many senses, necessary aspect of growing up. Children rightfully resist unreasonable demands from parents. Even when those demands are reasonable, children have to test out limits and rules, and shape their identity by clashing against that of their parents.

But, of course, there are behavior problems and *behavior problems*. As in all things, moderation is a virtue and excess risky and even dangerous. The conduct problems that typify the population who are the subject of this book are extreme and risky behavior problems. These children exhibit persistent patterns of aggressive antisocial behavior and significant impairment in their everyday functioning at home or school. Their conduct is considered out of control and unmanageable, by their parents and their teachers. In the preschool years, typical "externalizing" behaviors include noncompliance, aggression, tantrums, and oppositional-defiant behaviors; in the school years, violations of classroom and adult authority such as disruptive behavior, truancy, and delinquent activities (e.g., vandalism, shoplifting). These "aggressive" children are at increased risk of being rejected by their peers and/or abused by their parents. Research has indicated that the emergence of "early onset" conduct problems in early childhood (in the form of high rates of oppositional, aggressive, and noncompliant behaviors) is related to health and behavioral problems in adolescence—drug abuse, depression, juvenile delinquency, and school drop out. Conduct disorders put children at risk, in terms of blighting their futures; they put parents at risk of abusing (even losing into care) their children; they put society at risk with the seeds of violence and delinquency they propagate for the future.

Indeed, child and adolescent conduct disorder is part of a broader picture of family violence. The widespread nature of extreme forms of aggression within the family was noted in the 1970s and has been substantiated ever since (e.g., Browne & Herbert, 1994). Clinical observations, empirical research, daily newspapers, and news bulletins have painfully described acts of violence between spouses and from adults towards their own children. These accounts have increased public awareness and forced us to recognize that violence within the family is a common phenomenon of modern society. In turn, this has dispelled the myth that the family home is a peaceful, nonviolent environment. In fact, "people are more likely to be killed, physically assaulted, hit, beaten up, slapped or spanked in their own homes by other family members than anywhere else, or by anyone else in our society" (Gelles & Cornell, 1990, p. 11).

The broader context of conduct disorders—problems of violence, criminality, child abuse, and sheer misery for countless children and their parents—can seem overwhelming. Yet we who work with conduct-disordered children and their families can take heart, for intervention during the early preschool years is clearly strategic. Successful early intervention can substitute prosocial behaviors and conflict resolution skills for children's aggressive behavior before this behavior results in peer rejections and well-entrenched negative reputation, both of which tend to perpetuate conduct disorders.

If conduct problems have proven so intractable in the past, it is largely because they were viewed as moral problems rather than behavioral problems. There is little doubt that Behavioral Parent Training is the treatment of choice for early-onset conduct disorder and for young children with oppositional-defiant disorder. Whereas conduct disorders have proved to be resistant to traditional psychotherapies, we have seen encouraging developments in recent years in the application of behavioral methods applied in group settings and in individual family casework. Reviews of these parent-training programs are highly promising (Kazdin, 1987). Moreover, in contrast to traditional parent-training intervention programs, which were costly and time-consuming, and rarely reached those most in need of services, the videotape-modeling parent-training programs, such as those developed by Webster-Stratton, are a relatively low-cost program of treatment which can be used for mass parent training in prevention and intervention (Webster-Stratton, Kolpacoff & Hollinsworth, 1988).

Nonetheless, despite the general overall success of a variety of parent training programs in producing *statistically significant* changes in parent and child behaviors, there is also evidence that some families do not respond to treatment and continue to have children with *clinically significant* behavior problems after treatment. Long-term follow-up studies suggest that 30–50% of treated parents and 25–50% of teachers report children to continue to have behavior problems in the deviant or clinical range (e.g., Webster-Stratton, 1990).

Researchers have convincingly demonstrated that parental personal factors such as depression, marital discord, lack of social support, and environmental stressors disrupt parenting behavior and contribute to parent training treatment relapses (e.g., Dumas, 1984). As a result, more broadly based expansions of family training have been developed to address these family interpersonal issues (e.g., marital communication, stress management). These broader-based interventions may help mediate the negative influences of these family stressors on parenting skills; those which have been completed have suggested promising results (e.g. Dadds & McHugh, 1992; Webster-Stratton, in press).

Another possible reason for the nonresponse to parent training intervention for some families, suggested by studies with older conduct-disordered children and adolescents, is that the intervention has come too late, after children's negative behavior patterns and negative reputations with peers and teachers have been established. Once established, these are difficult to reverse. Our own studies with younger conduct-problem children show more positive results. Early intervention—in the critical transitional period from preschool to school, when the parents are still the primary socialization influences in the child's development (as opposed to peers and teachers)—offers promise for preventing the trajectory from Oppositional Defiant Disorder to Conduct Disorder.

It could also be argued that, for some families, the lack of long-term effectiveness of parent training programs and the failure of child behavior improvements to generalize beyond the home to school and peer relationships may be attributable to the fact that, particularly for older children, the school environment, including peers and teachers, plays a role in the development and maintenance of conduct disorders. Perhaps an exclusive focus on the home environment and parenting skills is simply too limited to achieve long-term family and child benefits.

As previously noted in Chapter 1, poor academic performance is highly related to early conduct problems (Sturge, 1982; Reid, 1993) and may be another factor influencing the effects of family training. It is becoming clear that treatment needs to aim beyond within-family change, expanding to the child's broader social context of the school. Given the academic delays and failure to comply to school rules typical of conduct-disordered children, and given the influence of the school environment and teachers in particular on conduct disorders, it is surprising that training programs for parents of conduct-disordered children have not, in general, involved teachers in treatment. Typically, teachers are left struggling alone in the classroom with a difficult and noncompliant child who exhibits academic as well as behavior problems. Moreover, despite the documented links between underachievement, language delays, reading disabilities, and conduct disorders, there have been no attempts to increase the effectiveness of parent-training programs by adding an academic skills training component for parents. Parents need to know not only how to help their children with their behavior problems at home, but also with their social and academic difficulties (e.g., reading and writing) at school. In addition, parents need to know how to support the efforts of their children's teachers. We believe that if parents and teachers can help these children with their academic skills, there may be important secondary benefits on social behaviors.

There are still many problems to overcome. At least seven issues will continue to require investigation:

- The role of cognitive/attitudinal/demographic/cultural and child (biological) factors in moderating the effectiveness of training.

- Theory- versus technique-based programs.

- Features of conduct-problem parents and children that are predictive of training outcome.

- Treatment acceptability and consumer satisfaction.

- The added impact of child training and teacher training programs to parent intervention programs.

- The effect of long-term support groups of families of children with conduct disorders.

- The added impact of academic skills training programs to parent-training programs.

The role of cognitive influences, not only in child therapy but in the under-standing of parent's theories and attributions about children and their development (e.g. Goodnow, 1988), has assumed increasing and well-deserved significance in this field. Research into cognition and clinical practice utilizing the fruits of discoveries in this area should make for more effective behavioral-cognitive methods for the treatment of conduct disorders. Social learning theory, with cognitive concepts at its core, has already demonstrated its usefulness (Herbert, 1991). Research into developmental issues is another potentially fruitful means of increasing the clinician's success. Any increase in our knowledge of normal moral development, of moral and social reasoning, and of child-rearing influences on such development, will feed advantageously into our clinical work.

A vital issue in reaching a larger number of families is the dissemination of parent training skills. This can be most successfully accomplished through the collaboration of various professionals—psychologists, psychiatrists, teachers, nurses, social workers—who work with these families. And it is, in our opinion, within the collaborative model that there is particular scope for improving our service to, and success with, families of children with conduct disorders—collaboration, that is, with

SUPPORTING AND ADVOCATING FOR PARENTS

our clients. Even more than other therapeutic models such as that of analyst, collaboration requires a creative touch. Here we have the fascinating but difficult-to-define "mix" of art and science. There is a component that has been shown to be necessary (but not sufficient) in this kind of work; the therapist must be extraordinarily skilled in coping with the resistance to change that characterizes many of the families referred for treatment, for collaboration requires that they actively participate in treatment, not just passively assent to it. Ordinarily, this level of clinical skill requires several years of supervised clinical experience (see Hollin, Wilkie & Herbert, 1986, on training in Applied Social Learning Theory). The use of a collaborative style in putting across behavioral technology is a *craft*—an amalgam of creativity and applied science. And it is here that the excitement for much future research lies, in defining, describing, and applying the ingredients precisely. In order to be truly successful in impacting on this disorder, our interventions must involve a reduction in professional boundaries and a collaboration process that extends to *all* the pivotal partners in the lives of children—their parents, teachers, nurses, physicians, psychologists, school personnel such as school nurses and social workers, and, of course, the children themselves. The prospect of such a degree of collaboration is indeed exciting.

REFERENCES

Browne, K. & Herbert, M. (1994). *Family violence*. Chichester, UK: Wiley.

Dadds, M.R. & McHugh, T.A. (1992). Social support and treatment outcome in behavioral family therapy for child conduct problems. *Journal of Consulting and Clinical Psychology*, **60**, 252–259.

Dadds, M.R., Schwartz, S. & Sanders, M.R. (1987). Marital discord and child behavior problems: a description of family interactions during treatment. *Journal of Clinical Child Psychology*, **16**, 192–203.

Dumas, J.E. (1984). Interactional correlates of treatment outcome in behavioral parent training. *Journal of Consulting and Clinical Psychology*, **52**, 946–954.

Gelles, R.J. & Cornell, C.P. (1990). *Intimate violence in families*, (2nd edn.) Beverly Hills, CA: Sage.

Goodnow, J.J. (1988). Parents' ideas, actions and feelings: Models and methods for developmental and social psychology. *Child Development*, **59**, 286–320.

Herbert, M. (1991). *Clinical child psychology: Social learning, development and behaviour*. Chichester, UK: Wiley.

Hollin, D.R., Wilkie, J. & Herbert, M. (1986). Behavioural social work: Training and application. *Practice*, **1**, 297–304.

Kazdin, A.E. (1987). Treatment of antisocial behavior in children: Current status and future directions. *Psychological Bulletin*, **102**, 187–203.

Reid, J.B. (1993). Prevention of conduct disorder before and after school entry. Relating interventions to developmental findings. *Development and Psychopathology*, **5**, 241–261.

Sturge, C. (1982). Reading retardation and antisocial behavior in children. *Journal of Child Psychology and Psychiatry*, **23**, 21–23.

Webster-Stratton, C. (1990). Long-term follow-up of families with young conduct problem children: From preschool to grade school. *Journal of Clinical Child Psychology*, **19**(2), 144–149.

Webster-Stratton, C. (in press) Advancing videotape parent training: a comparison study. *Journal of Consulting and Clinical Psychology*.

Webster-Stratton, C., Kolpacoff, J. & Hollinsworth, T. (1988). Self-administered videotape therapy for families with conduct-problem children: Comparison with two cost-effective treatments and a control group. *Journal of Consulting and Clinical Psychology*, **56**, 558–566.

APPENDIX A:
ASSESSMENT AND
THE CONDUCT DISORDERS

THE CONTEXT of assessment of parent–child interactions and behaviors may vary from naturalistic observations to structured play situations in laboratory or clinical settings. In a review of assessment issues in child psychopathology, Achenbach (1978) concluded that the most accurate observations of children's behavior are related to the context in which they were made. Direct observations of peer, marital, and parent–child interactions, self-report and parent/teacher ratings are primary means of assessing family and individual attributes. Observational techniques have been developed for the assessment of individual children (e.g., Patterson, 1982) or parent–child interactions (e.g., Dowdney et al., 1984). Parents' and teachers' reports, based on either interviews or questionnaire responses, constitute another source of clinical and research information about children's behavior problems.

Bates and Bayles (1984) are of the opinion that parental reports of children's behavior consist of objective, subjective, and error components. They found support for an objective component through significant mother–father and parent–observer convergences in ratings of children's behavior. Moderately high interparental correlations are found in most studies in the literature. Maternal reports of children's behavioral dysfunction have been found to exhibit higher congruence with clinician's ratings in structured play sessions than paternal reports (Earls, 1980).

In a meta-analysis of 119 studies, Achenbach, McConaughty, and Howell (1987) examined the degree of consistency between different informants (parents, teachers, observers, peers, self) on ratings of children's behavioral and emotional adjustment. They found mean correlations of around 0.6 between similar informants (e.g., pairs of parents) and 0.28 between different types of informants (e.g., parent–teacher). There were generally higher levels of agreement for the younger group, and for undercontrolled rather than for overcontrolled problems.

Achenbach and his colleagues suggest that variations in assessment between different informants can be viewed as a function of different experiences with children, and that multiaxial assessments could account for situational variability in children's behavior.

The form of any assessment approach involves some important assumptions about behavioral attributes. Behaviorally orientated psychologists tend to view behaviors with, say, aggressive or anxiety attributes, as instances or samples of response classes rather than as outward and visible signs of internal or underlying dispositions. As Wiggins (1973) observes, the language of personality, to the extent that it is used by social behaviorists, is employed descriptively rather than inferentially. Conventional trait attributions are thought by critics to represent nothing more than giving two names to the same class of behavior. Thus, if a child is seen to hit another child, there is no reason to infer that the child who does the striking is not only aggressive but also has a "need for aggression." Behaviors with aggressive attributes would be classified in terms of their frequency, intensity, and duration. Diverse attributes would be considered to be members of the same response class if it could be shown that such attributes enter into the same functional relationships with antecedent, concurrent, and consequence stimulus conditions, rather than because they coexist or covary in a group of persons. Issues of stability and generality become empirical questions rather than assumptions. Given a change in stimulating conditions, particularly conditions of reinforcement, the frequency, intensity, or duration of the response class of interest should be predictable from a knowledge of the functional relationships between these attributes and the stimulus conditions which control them.

The Collaborative Approach to Assessment

Our approach to assessment, based as it is on cognitive behavioral ideas, depends on collaborative empiricism. This means checking with the person concerned and arriving at a common understanding. It means engaging the person in the explorative process that underlies assessment, discussing data from measures, their meaning and implications. The collaborative approach requires the therapist to be sensitive to the interpersonal style of the client, which means conducting the assessment in an atmosphere of "caring interest."

Measures

Below is a cross-section of instruments (and brief reviews of their assessment and purpose) which we have applied in our work with children with conduct disorders. Because none of these measures is free of some source of bias or judgment, the use of multiple assessment methods is essential to overcome the limitations of any one measure. Moreover, our clinical assessment involves much more than measures regarding the child's anti-social behaviors. We might include assessments of the marriage, peer inter-actions, parent psychopathology, environmental stressors, and general family functioning. Given the possible "ripple effects" which we discussed in Chapter 3, it is difficult to delimit the relevant measures to be a circumscribed set.

PARENT PERCEPTIONS OF CHILD ADJUSTMENT

Parents complete these forms evaluating their child's behavior before and after treatment and at follow-up assessments.

Child Behavior Checklist (CBCL)

The parent form of the CBCL (Achenbach & Edelbrock, 1983) consists of 20 social competence items and 118 behavior problems. Parents are asked to report the occurrence of these items generally over the previous six months. It has been shown to discriminate clinic-referred from non-referred children. The items constitute multiple behavior-problem scales derived separately for boys and girls in different age groups. The scales form two broad-band groupings in all sex/age groups: Externalizing Behavior (aggressive, antisocial, and undercontrolled) and Internalizing Behavior (fearful, inhibited, overcontrolled). The Social Competence score and the Externalizing, Internalizing, and Total Behavior Problem scores are of primary relevance to treatment. The CBCL has established norms; intraclass correlations were 0.98 for interparent agreement and 0.84 for test-retest reliability.

Eyberg Child Behavior Inventory (ECBI)

The ECBI (Robinson, Eyberg & Ross, 1980) is a 36-item behavioral inventory of child conduct problem behavior of 2–16-year-old children. The response format yields two scores: a total problem score, which indicates the total number of behavior problems parents are concerned about, and an intensity score which indicates the frequency with which conduct problems occur.

TEACHER PERCEPTIONS OF CHILD ADJUSTMENT

Teachers complete these forms before and after treatment and at follow-up.

Behar Preschool Questionnaire (PBQ)

The PBQ (Behar, 1977) includes 30 items, each rated on a 0–2 point scale, and is completed by teachers of children aged three to seven years. Test-retest reliabilities have ranged from 0.60 to 0.99. Factor analyses have yielded three subscales (Hostile-Aggressive, Anxious-Fearful, and Hyperactive-Distractable). In addition, there is a Total Behavior Problem Scale which reflects a summary score of all three subscales. Of these scales, the Total Behavior Problem Scale is of most importance because it samples a broad range of conduct problems.

Teacher Report Form of the CBCL (TRF)

The TRF (Edelbrock & Achenbach, 1984) is designed to obtain teachers' ratings of many of the same problems that parents rate on the CBCL. It omits CBCL items that teachers would not ordinarily be able to rate, but includes additional items ratable by teachers. The TRF consists of teachers' ratings of four general competence characteristics which give a total adaptive score, and 112 behavior problems which give a total problem score. The TRF has been shown to have good validity, reliability and stability. Test-retest reliability correlations have ranged from 0.90 (one week) to 0.74 (four months).

Teacher Rating Scale of PCSC

This is the teachers' independent judgment of the child's competence in the four domains covered on the children's PCSC: cognitive competence, physical competence, peer acceptance, and maternal acceptance. Three items per subscale are presented. Domain scores are calculated as the mean of these items. The internal consistency ranged from 0.70 to 0.80, and this measure has been shown to discriminate conduct problem children from normal children (Harter, 1982).

Teacher Child Adaptive Behavior Inventory (ABI)

The ABI (Cowan & Cowan, 1982) is an adaptation of a scale developed by E. Schaefer & W. Hunter. Factor analyses of the 91 items yielded four factors: antisocial behavior, academic competence, shyness, and somatic symptoms. Each factor comprises four or five items.

Teacher Assessment of Social Behavior

This measure (Cassidy & Asher, 1992) is designed for teachers to rate each child on four behavioral dimensions: prosocial, aggressive, shy/withdrawn, and disruptive. Each dimension is assessed using three items, for a total of 12 items. In order to minimize potential dependency in the ratings teachers provided for the different items, each item is presented on a different page. On each page a roster of all students' names appears underneath the item, with a five-point scale next to each name. The scale ranged from a "1" (very uncharacteristic) to a "5" (very characteristic). The authors conducted factor analyses providing evidence for the four factors and reported adequate internal reliability. Cronbach's alphas ranged from 0.62 to 0.91. Significant correlations were found between the teacher assessments and peer sociometric measures. Particularly good agreement occurred between teachers and peers in regard to the aggressive and prosocial dimensions.

CHILD PERCEPTION OF PERSONAL ADJUSTMENT AND COPING

The children are tested on this measure pretreatment and again six and 12 months later.

Perceived Competence Scale for Young Children (PCSC)

The pictorial scale of the PCSC for young children is a downward extension of the PCSC for older children (Harter, 1982). Versions are available for children at preschool and kindergarten and for first and second graders. Factor analyses for both age groups revealed two factors, General Competence (cognitive and physical) and Social Acceptance (peer and maternal). The pictorial scale is administered by showing the child a picture, reading a brief statement, and asking the child to pick the child in the picture who is most like him. The PCSC was chosen because it is the best measure of self-esteem and social competence available for young children with good validity and reliability ranging from 0.60 to 0.85 for subscales.

Child Social Problem-Solving Test-Revised (SPST-R)

The SPST-R developed by Rubin and Krasnor (1983) derives from the Spivak, Platt, and Shure (1976) Preschool Interpersonal Problem-Solving Test (ICPS). It is designed to assess both quantitative and qualitative dimensions of problem-solving. Each child is presented with pictures of a series of problem situations and is then asked what the story character could do or say to accomplish the desired goal. Two such responses are requested for each situation and then the child is asked what he/she might do in such a situation. The answers are then scored based on type of solutions offered (e.g., prosocial, antagonistic, authority, trade/bribe, and manipulative). Interrater reliability for the SPST-R has been reported at 85% by Rubin and Krasnor (1983).

The mechanism for scoring the child's verbal responses to the SPST-R pictures was coding according to Rubin's scoring protocol, which included 28 codes. We summarized the data into four summary scores based on our theoretical interest in differentiating appropriate social responses (e.g., trade, ask) from inappropriate social responses (e.g., trick, hit, force) to the social situations presented. In addition, we sought to use summary variables which could possibly theoretically link to our parent–child interaction variables. The four summary variables formed were as follows:

(1) *Total Agonistic* which includes inappropriate codes such as attack, damage, force, trick, bribe, or any nonnormative response given as a method to obtain the desired object.

(2) *Total Prosocial* which includes ask, saying "please," wait, share, or trade given as a method to obtain the desired object.

(3) *Positive Friendship* which includes prosocial attempts to make a friend such as invitations, introduction, compliments, and polite conversation.

(4) *Negative Friendship* which includes inappropriate attempts to make a friend such as conditional offers (I'll hit you if you don't . . .), threats, commands, impractical responses, or avoiding the person.

Child's Attributions

We use an attribution measure which is an adaptation of Dodge and Newman's (1981) interview measure. The measure consists of four different scenarios which are familiar to preschoolers but where the actor's intention is ambiguous. The child is presented with two different alternative explanations about what happened, one involving aggressive intent and one portraying the situation as an accident. The child is asked to choose between the two alternatives. The result is a total score ranging from 0 to 4 with 4 indicating the highest level of aggressive attribution.

Loneliness and Social Dissatisfaction Questionnaire (LSDQ)

The LSDQ (Asher & Wheeler, 1985; Asher, Hymel & Renshaw, 1984) is a 24-item verbal questionnaire wherein children are asked to respond to questions by answering "yes", "no", or "sometimes." The questionnaire has been shown in recent research (Cassidy & Asher, 1992) to be understood and reliably assessed in children aged five to seven years; they also reported that poorly accepted children were more lonely than other children and children with the most loneliness were more aggressive and disruptive than other children. The reliability coefficient for the scale was 0.79 for internal consistency. The answers give a single loneliness score for each child.

MOTHER OBSERVATIONS OF CHILD BEHAVIORS

Phone calls are made to mothers twice a week for four weeks prior to treatment and following treatment.

Parent Daily Report (PDR)

The PDR (Chamberlain & Reid, 1987) consists of a list of 19 negative and 19 prosocial behaviors commonly exhibited by children. Parents are asked to select those negative and positive behaviors that they perceive as major problems. During phone calls, the checklist is read to the mothers, who have been asked to observe and report on the occurrence or nonoccurrence of the "target" behaviors for the previous 24 hours. The interviewer also asks about the occurrence of spanking, Time Out, and low-rate events.

Previous studies have reported test-retest reliability of the PDR from 0.60 to 0.82. The PDR correlates significantly with concurrent home observation data collected by independent observers (Chamberlain & Reid, 1987). It is possible to derive a positive and negative score which has been shown at termination to function as the best predictor of status at follow-up (Patterson, Reid & Maerov, 1978.)

Mother Daily Discipline Interview (DDI)

The DDI (Spitzer, Webster-Stratton & Hollinsworth, 1991) consists of 60 categories of discipline responses. When the parent responds on the daily PDR that a particular behavior problem has occurred, then the Parent Discipline Interview begins by asking, "How did you handle this problem?" The parent's responses are written down verbatim and coded by two independent trained coders. The DDI has six summary scores: physical force, critical verbal force, limit setting, teaching, empathy, and guilt induction. One week test-retest reliability has ranged from 0.38 to 0.73. The DDI correlates significantly with laboratory observations of parent discipline behaviors with their children.

INDEPENDENT OBSERVATIONS OF MOTHER–CHILD AND FATHER–CHILD INTERACTIONS

Each mother–child and father–child dyad is videotaped for a total of 30 minutes. During the "free play" time parents are told: "Play with your child the way you would normally do at home." They are given a tic-tac-toe game and toy clown and later on these are taken away and puzzles and coloring books are brought in. Next, during the "child-directed play", they are asked: "Follow your child's lead in play for the next five minutes." Finally during the "parent-directed play" they are told: "Get your child to go along with your play this time."

Dyadic Parent–Child Interactive Coding System (DPICS)

The DPICS (Robinson & Eyberg, 1981) is a widely researched observation measure developed specifically for recording behaviors of behavior problem children and their parents. The DPICS, which consists of 29 behavior categories, is used to code both the home and videotaped laboratory parent–child interactions. From the behavior categories, three separate summary variables are formed for parent behaviors: Total Praise, Total Critical Statements, Total No Opportunity Commands (commands where child is given no opportunity to respond). For the target child there is one variable (sum of frequency of whine + cry + physical negative + noncompliance). In addition, a new nonverbal affect dimension developed by Webster-Stratton has been added to the system: Parent and Child Affect. Every five minutes coders pause and rate the parent or child affect on a scale ranging from unrestrained negative affect (5) to exuberant affect (1). These specific behaviors have been selected from the DPICS coding system in order to focus on parent and child behaviors which have been shown to discriminate clinic from nonclinic families.

A variety of reliability analyses, ranging from interobserver agreement among coders to generalizability analyses, have supported the measurement precision of the DPICS scores. In our work the product-moment correlations calculated between observers for each behavior variable have ranged from 0.73 (child noncompliance) to 0.98 (critical statements). The DPICS has favorably withstood psychometric investigations, showing that the behavioral measures are justified on content grounds, that outside reports of behavior coincide satisfactorily with the DPICS scores, and that expected behavioral changes following treatment are readily indicated by the DPICS scores (Robinson & Eyberg, 1981).

INDEPENDENT OBSERVATIONS OF PEER INTERACTIONS

Peer Problem-Solving-Interaction Communication–Affect Rating–Engagement Coding System (PPS-ICARE)

This coding system was developed by our staff as a derivative of Gottman's Rapid-MACRO and MICRO coding system for analyzing peer interactions (Gottman, 1983; Gottman & Katz, 1989). Our coding system includes 40 behavioral categories which are summarized to include six variables: Positive Communication, Negative Communication, Conflict Management, Friendship, Level of Play, and Rule Violation. In addition, the coders rate the child's affect on a scale ranging from "unrestrained negative affect" (1) to "positive affect" (5).

Laboratory procedures involve asking each child to come in with his/her best friend. The friend needs to be within two years of the target child's age and the same sex as the target child. There are three sets of instructions given to the children once they are in the playroom: (1) For the 15-minute Unstructured Play period, the children are told to have fun playing. They provided with a castle set, a large bean bag game of tic-tac-toe and a box of Lego. (2) For the Cooperative Play period, the children are asked to make the "best thing they can together." They are given an Etchasketch and a box of Lincoln logs. They are told that a picture will be taken of their joint project when they have finished. (3) For the Competitive Play period, the target child is taken out of the room to show his mother his picture. While this is occurring the friend is being shown a Sega Genesis computer game which only has one dial. The friend is shown how to play it and told he only has 10 more minutes to play. After the child is engaged in play the target child is shown back into the room. We have provided this structure to the play interactions in order to elicit the behaviors of interest.

FAMILY AND PERSONAL ADJUSTMENT

In order to assess the relationship between specific family factors and child behavioral adjustment and to determine the family's needs in addition to parent management skills the following widely used self-report measures are completed by both mothers and fathers.

Marital Adjustment Test (MAT)

Marital adjustment may be an important factor affecting child's psychological, behavioral, and physical health, i.e., parents who are supportive to each other and reinforce each other's parenting skills have children with fewer behavior problems. (Our experience is that about half of the families are experiencing marital conflict in conjunction with having a disruptive child.) The MAT (Locke & Wallace, 1959) is a widely used self-report measure of marital satisfaction completed by each spouse separately. It has good reliability, Cronbach's alpha 0.93–0.96, discriminates reliability between distressed and nondistressed couples, and significantly correlates with other marital scales.

Beck Depression Inventory (BDI)

A measure of depression is important because of evidence suggesting that maternal depression may be a major factor interfering with good parenting and the child's psychosocial adjustment (Griest, Wells & Forehand, 1979).

The BDI (Beck, 1972) consists of 21 items, each rated on a 0–3 point scale which gives a rapid assessment of the severity of depression as well as specific symptoms. It has been shown to correlate significantly with clinician's ratings of depression (Metcalfe & Goldman, 1965) and with objective behavioral measures of depression (Williams, Barlow & Agras, 1972). Split-half reliability is 0.86.

Brief Anger-Aggression Questionnaire (BAAQ)

The BAAQ (Maiuro, Vitaliano & Cohn, 1987) is a brief six-item measure developed for assessment of anger levels. Four studies with 401 men have indicated respectable internal consistency (alpha = 0.82), test-retest reliability ($r = 0.84$), construct validity, and criterion validity. The BAAQ is used to assess the parents' adjustment.

Family APGAR

The Family APGAR (Smilkstein, Ashwor & Montano, 1982) is a brief five-item questionnaire designed to assess a family member's satisfaction with five components of family function: adaptation, partnership, growth, affection, and resolve. Four studies with populations of college students, patients in a family medical clinic, and clients in a psychiatric program have shown the APGAR to have good internal consistency (alpha 0.80–0.86), test-retest reliability ($r = 0.83$), and validity.

Family Crisis-Oriented Personal Scales (F-COPES)

The F-COPES (McCubbin, 1987) consists of 30 coping items which assess family problem-solving attitudes and behaviors utilized in problematic situations. The scale has good internal consistency (alpha = 0.77), test reliability ($r = 0.71$), and validity (77).

OBSERVATIONS OF FAMILY PROBLEM-SOLVING

Couples were asked to engage in a 15-minute discussion of two self-identified problem areas. The length of time has been found to be adequate in Gottman's previous research which has varied discussions from 15 minutes to several hours (Gottman, 1979). These videotapes are transcribed verbatim and then each statement is coded according to PS-ICARE, which is described below.

Problem-Solving-Interaction Communication—Affect Rating—Engagement Coding System (PS-ICARE)

The PS-ICARE was developed by our staff to record problem-solving skills, communication strategies, affect dimensions, and marital engagement or disengagement. The problem-solving coding system included: (a) problem definition (agreement about problem), (b) solution generation, (c) evaluation, agreement, and planning about solutions, and (d) conflict process skills. In addition, coders rated couples' problem-solving on two dimensions, collaboration and engagement. The engagement scale ranged from "low engagement" (1) (stony face, indifferent) to "high engagement" (5) (head nods, leaning forward, responsive). The collaboration scale ranged from "low collaboration" (1) (abrasive, dismissive, stonewalling) to "high collaboration" (5) (cooperative, mutually reinforcing, joint ownership of problem). The communication and affect coding dimensions were a derivative of a global rapid marital coding system (RCISS) developed by Gottman (1983) and the detailed Specific Affect Coding System (SPAFF) by Gottman (1991). The communication system included 24 communication skills leading to two summary scores, one for positive communication (e.g., validate, compromise, praise, summarize, open-ended questions) and one for negative communication (e.g., deny, complain, ignore, coerce, moralize, blame).

EXTRAFAMILIAL STRESSORS

Life Experience Survey (LES)

Life stressors (e.g., unemployment, death of family members) may be an important predictor of a child's physical health and psychosocial adjustment. The LES is a 57-item measure that permits the respondent to assess positive and negative life experiences over the previous year. It has been found to have adequate test-retest reliability (six week, 0.56–0.88) (Sarason, Johnson & Seigel, 1978).

Parenting Stress Index (PSI)

The PSI (Abidin, 1990) contains 126 items, which are divided into two major domains reflecting stress in the parent–child relationship. The first domain represents parent characteristics and includes seven subscales: depression, attachment, restricted role, competence, isolation, spouse support, and health. The second domain represents child characteristics and consists of seven subscales: adaptability, acceptability, demandingness, mood, distractability, activity, and reinforcement. The PSI has been shown to have acceptable content, concurrent and construct validity, and test-retest reliabilities range from 0.71 to 0.82.

REFERENCES AND FURTHER READING

Abidin, R.R. (1990). *Parenting Stress Index: Manual*. 3rd edn., University of Virginia: Pediatric Psychology Press.

Achenbach, T.M. (1978). The Child Behavior Profile I. Boys aged 6–11. *Journal of Consulting and Clinical Psychology*, **46**, 478–488.

Achenbach, T.M. & Edelbrock, C.S. (1983). *Manual for the Child Behavior Checklist and Revised Child Behavior Profile*. Burlington, VT: University Associates in Psychiatry.

Achenbach, T.M., McConaughty, S.H. & Howell, C.T. (1987). Child/adolescent behavior and emotional problems: Implications of cross-informant correlations for situational specificity. *Psychological Bulletin*, **101**, 213–232.

Asher, S.R. & Wheeler, V.A. (1985). Children's loneliness: a comparison of rejected and neglected peer status. *Journal of Consulting and Clinical Psychology*, **53**, 500–505.

Asher, S.R., Hymel, S. & Renshaw, P.D. (1984). Loneliness in children. *Child Development*, **55**, 1456–1464.

Bates, J.E. & Bayles, K. (1984). Objective and subjective components in mothers' perceptions of their children from age 6 months to 3 years. *Merrill Palmer Quarterly*, **30**, 111–130.

Beck, A.T. (1972). *Depression: Causes and treatment*. Philadelphia, PA: University of Michigan Press.

Behar, L.B. (1977). The Preschool Behavior Questionnaire. *Journal of Abnormal Child Psychology*, **5**(3), 265–275.

Cassidy, J. & Asher, S.R. (1992). Loneliness and peer relations in young children. *Child Development*, **63**, 350–365.

Chamberlain, P. & Reid, J.B. (1987). Parent observation and report of child symptoms. *Behavioral Assessment*, **9**, 92–109.

Cowan, C.P. & Cowan, P.A. (1982). *When partners become parents: the big life change for couples*. New York: Basic Books.

Dodge, K.A. (1985). Attributional bias in aggressive children. In P.C. Kendall (Ed.), *Advances in cognitive-behavioral research and therapy* (Vol. 4) (pp. 73–110). Orlando, FL: Academic Press.

Dodge, K.A. & Newman, J.P. (1981). Biased decision-making processes in aggressive boys. *Journal of Abnormal Psychology*, **90**(4), 375–379.

Dowdney, L., Mrazek, D., Quinton, D. & Rutter, M. (1984). Observation of parent–child interaction with two- to three-year-olds. *Journal of Child Psychology and Psychiatry*, **25**, 379–407.

Earls, F. (1980). Prevalence of behavior problems in 3-year-old children: A cross-maternal replication. *Archives of General Psychiatry*, **37**, 1153–1157.

Edelbrock, C.S. & Archenbach, T.M. (1984). The teacher version of the child behavior profile: boys aged 6–11. *Journal of Consulting and Clinical Psychology*, **52**, 207–217.

Eyberg, S.M. (1992). Assessing therapy outcome with preschool children: progress and problems. *Journal of Clinical Child Psychology*, **21**, 306–311.

Freidrich, W. & Boriskin, J. (1976). The role of the child in abuse: Review of the literature. *American Journal of Orthopsychiatry*, **46**, 580–590.

Gottman, J.M. (1979). *Marital Interaction: Experimental Investigations*. New York: Academic Press.

Gottman, J.M. (1983). How children become friends. *Monographs of the Society for Research in Child Development*, **48**(2). Serial No. 201.

Gottman, J.M. (1991). The Specific Affect Coding System. University of Washington: Unpublished Manuscript.

Gottman, J.M. & Katz, L.F. (1989). Effects of marital discord on children's peer interactions and health. *Developmental Psychology*, **3**, 373–381.

Greist, D., Wells, K.C. & Forehand, R. (1979). An examination of predictors of maternal perceptions of maladjustment in clinic-referred children. *Journal of Abnormal Psychology*, **88**, 277–281.

Harter, S. (1982). The Perceived Competence Scale for children. *Child Development*, **53**, 87–97.

Harter, S. & Pike, R. (1984). The Pictorial Scale of Perceived Competence and Social Acceptance for young children. *Child Development*, **55**, 1969–1982.

Kazdin, A.E. (1985). *Treatment of antisocial behavior in children and adolescents*. Homewood, IL: Dorsey Press.

Locke, H.S. & Wallace, K.M. (1959). Short marital adjustment and prediction tests: Their reliability and validity. *Marriage and Family Living*, **21**, 251–255.

Loeber, R. (1985). Patterns and development of antisocial child behavior. In G.J. Whitehurst (Ed.), *Annals of child development* (Vol. 2) (pp. 77–116). New York: JAI Press.

Loeber, R. & Dishion, T.J. (1983). Early predictors of male adolescent delinquency: A review. *Psychological Bulletin*, **94**, 68–99.

Maiuro, R.D., Vitaliano, P.P. & Cohn, T.S. (1987). A brief measure for the assessment of anger and aggression. *Journal of Interpersonal Violence*, **2**, 166–178.

Margolin, G. & Jacobsen, N.S. (1981). Assessment of marital dysfunction. In M. Hersen & A.S. Bellack (Eds.), *Behavioral Assessment: A practical handbook* (2nd edn.) (pp. 389–426). London: Pergamon.

McCubbin, H. (1987). *Family assessment inventories for research and practice*. Family Stress, Coping and Health Project, University of Wisconsin-Madison.

McMahon, R.J. (1987). Some current issues in the behavioral assessment of conduct disordered children and their families. *Behavior Assessment*, **9**, 235–252.

Metcalfe, M. & Goldman, E. (1965). Validation of an inventory for measuring depression. *British Journal of Psychiatry*, **111**, 240–242.

Patterson, G.R. (1982). *Coercive family process*. Eugene, OR: Castalia.

Patterson, G., Reid, J. & Maerov, S. (1978). The observational system: Methodological issues and psychometric properties. In J. Reid (Ed.), *A social learning approach to family intervention*. Vol. 2: Observations in the home setting (pp. 11–19). Eugene, OR: Castalia.

Reid, J.B., Baldwin, D.V., Patterson, G.R. & Dishion, T.J. (1988). Observations in the assessment of childhood disorders, In M. Rutter, A.H. Tuma & I.S. Lann (Eds.), *Assessment and diagnosis in child psychopathology* (pp. 156–195). New York: Guildford.

Robins, L.N. (1981). Epidemiological approaches to natural history research: Antisocial disorders in children. *Journal of the American Academy of Child Psychiatry*, **20**, 566–680.

Robins, N.L. (1966). *Deviant children grown up*. Baltimore, MD: Williams & Wilkins.

Robinson, E.A. & Eyberg, S.M. (1981). The dyadic parent–child interaction coding system: standardization and validation. *Journal of Consulting and Clinical Psychology*, **49**, 245–250.

Robinson, E.A., Eyberg, S.M. & Ross, A.W. (1980). The standardization of an inventory of child conduct problem behaviors. *Journal of Clinical Child Psychology*, **9**, 22–28.

Rubin, K.H. & Krasnor, L.R. (1983). Social-cognitive and social behavioral perspectives on problem-solving. In M. Perlmuller (Ed.), *minnesota symposia on child psychology* (Vol. 18). Hillsdale, NJ: Lawrence Erlbaum.

Sarason, I.G., Johnson, J.H. & Seigel, J.M. (1978). Assessing the impact of life changes: Development of the Life Experiences Survey. *Journal of Consulting and Clinical Psychology*, **46**(6), 932–946.

Seligman, M. & Darling, R.B. (1989). *Ordinary families, special children*. New York: Guilford.

Shure, M.B. (1981). Social competence as a problem-solving skill. In S.S. Wine & M.D. Smye (Eds.), *Social competence* (pp. 158–185). New York: Guilford.

Smilkstein, G., Ashwork, C. & Montano, D. (1982). Validity and reliability of the Family APGAR as a test of family functioning. *Journal of Family Practice*, **15**, 303–311.

Spitzer, A., Webster-Stratton, C. & Hollinsworth, T. (1991). Coping with conduct-problem children: parents gaining knowledge and control. *Journal of Clinical Child Psychiatry*, **20**, 413–427.

Spivak, G., Platt, J.J. & Shure, M.B. (1976). *The problem-solving approach to adjustment*. San Francisco, CA: Jossey-Bass.

Webster-Stratton, C. (1982). Long term effects of a videotape modeling parent education program: Comparison of immediate and one year follow-up results. *Behavior Therapy*, **13**, 702–714.

Webster-Stratton, C. (1984). Comparing two parent training models for conduct disordered children. *Journal of Consulting and Clinical Psychology*, **52**, 666–678.

Webster-Stratton, C. (1985a). Mother perceptions and mother–child interactions: Comparison of a clinic-referred and a nonclinic group. *Journal of Clinical Child Psychology*, **14**, 334–339.

Webster-Stratton, C. (1985b). Predictors of treatment outcome in parent training for conduct disordered children. *Behavior Therapy*, **16**, 223–243.

Webster-Stratton, C. (1985c). The effects of father involvement in parent training for conduct problem children. *Child Psychology and Psychiatry*, **26**, 801–810.

Webster-Stratton, C. (1989). The relationship of marital support, conflict and divorce to parent perceptions, behaviors and childhood conduct problems. *Journal of Marriage and the Family*, **51**, 417–430.

Webster-Stratton, C. (1991). Stress: A potential disruptor of parent perceptions and family interactions. *Journal of Clinical Child Psychology*, **19**, 302–312.

Webster-Stratton, C. & Hammond, M. (1988). Maternal depression and its relationship to life stress, perceptions of child behavior problems, parenting behaviors, and child conduct problems. *Journal of Abnormal Child Psychology*, **16**(3), 299–315.

Webster-Stratton, C. & Spitzer, A. (May, 1990). *The relationship of parent discipline strategies to mother personal adjustment and stressors, reports of child conduct problems and observations of mother–child interactions.* Abstract published in Western Institute of Nursing, Vol. 23, entitled "Nursing Research transcending the 20th century".

Webster-Stratton, C., Kolpacoff, M. & Hollinsworth, T. (1988). Self-administered videotape therapy for families with conduct-problem children: Comparison with two cost-effective treatments and a control group. *Journal of Consulting and Clinical Psychology*, **56**(4), 558–566.

Weissberg, R.P. & Allen, J.P. (1985). Promoting children's social skills and adaptive interpersonal behavior. In L. Michelson & B. Edelstein (Eds.), *Handbook of prevention*. New York: Plenum Press.

Wiggins, J.S. (1973). *Personality and prediction: Principles of personality assessment.* Reading, MA: Addison-Wesley.

Williams, J.G., Barlow, D.H. & Agras, W.S. (1972). Behavioral measurement of severe depression. *Archives of General Psychiatry*, **27**, 330–333.

APPENDIX B: ABC CHART

Caregiver ABC Record Chart
[This form to be completed by the Caregiver]

Child's name: _____ Child's age: _____
Caregiver's name: _____ Date: _____
Week: _____

Time	Antecedent: what happened beforehand?	Behavior: my child's Belief: my feelings, attitudes, views at the time	Consequences: what happened next?	Distress rating 0–5 (see criteria below)

Rating criteria

0	1	2	3	4	5
↓					
NO	LOW				VERY
distress					HIGH

Level of distress felt
during the episode

Adapted from Herbert, M. (1990). *Childcare and the family: A resource pack*.
Published by The NFER-NELSON Publishing Company Ltd., Darville House, 2 Oxford
Road East, Windsor, Berkshire SL4 1DF, England.

INDEX

ABC model, 84–5
  diary keeping, 86–7
  record chart, 333
academic deficits, 16
acceptance (core condition), 115,
    216–17, 231–2
Activity Time Out, 187
adjustment, child, *see* children,
    adjustment
advocating, 117–18, 229
affection, learning and, 187
aggression
  against animals, 45
  against other children, 46
  against parents, 44–5
  against siblings, 45
  dismantling house, 46
  in play, 244–5
  sexual, 46
  see also anger
alternative-solution thinking, 184
analogies, use of, 135–8
anger
  in commands, 274–5
  control training, 29, 183
  parents', 67–8, 201–2
  see also aggression
animals, aggression against, 45
assessment of families, 73–100,
    317–29
  child's behavior, 78–89
  collaborative model, 75–6,
    318

conceptual problems, 76–7
early contact, 74–5
eliciting family views, 79
family adjustment, 326–8
family as system, 96–9
joining phase, 73–4
measures, 318–29
monitoring change, 99–100
'multiple-gating' approach, 99
organismic factors, 94
parental behavior, 89–95
process vs. content, 75–7
recording observations, 80–9
systemic thinking in, 77–8
theory in, 77–8
assignments, 128–9
  resistance to, 146
assumptions, unrealistic, 122–3
attention
  differential, 171, 175–8
  as reinforcement, 175–8
attention deficit/hyperactivity
    disorder (ADHD), diagnosis,
    10
'attention rule', 171
attention seeking, 240
attribution theory, 69
attributions, unhelpful, 121–3
avoidance training, 175

'bank account' analogy, 135–6
'battle choice' analogy, 137

Index compiled by A. C. Purton